Mo, Me, and America:
The Vanishing Rural Community

Randy Turk, PhD

© 2015 Randy Turk

All Rights Reserved.

No part of this publication may be reproduced, stored in a retrieval system, or transmitted, in any form or by any means, electronic, mechanical, photocopying, recording, or otherwise, without the written permission of the author.

First published by Dog Ear Publishing
4011 Vincennes Rd
Indianapolis, IN 46268
www.dogearpublishing.net

ISBN: 978-1-4575-4347-0

This book is printed on acid-free paper.

Printed in the United States of America

Disclaimer: All statements attributed to interview participants are the interpretation of the author with the intent of maximum accuracy.

To my parents, Fred and Ruth Turk,
and the people—past and present—
of Noble Township and Rush County, Indiana

Sherrill & Jim,

Nice meeting!
Hope you enjoy
the tour of Rural
America.

[signature]

Table of Contents

Preface vi

1   Self-Interview 1

Northwest

2   Kansas and Colorado 8
3   Wyoming 24
4   Southern Idaho 30
5   Oregon 48
6   Great Northwest and Family 61
7   Idaho Panhandle 66
8   Montana 74
9   Dakotas 89
10 Minnesota 100
11 Iowa 113

Missouri State Fair

12 State Fair 126

Middle States

13 Illinois 144
14 Michigan and Ohio 151
15 Back Home Again in Indiana 157
16 Kentucky 168
17 Tennessee 177
18 Arkansas 186

Southwest

19 Oklahoma 192
20 Texas 202
21 New Mexico 210
22 Arkansas Valley, Colorado 223
23 West Kansas 230

Lincoln Fly-in
24   Fly-in 242

Northeast
25   Pennsylvania, New York, and Vermont 250

Southeast
26   Virginias 266
27   Carolinas 293
28   Georgia and Alabama 310
29   Mississippi and Louisiana 330
30   The Trip Home and Reflections 343

Epilogue 346
Bibliography 349
Acknowledgemets 356

Preface

Mo, Me, and America is a story about people, community, and change, as seen through the eyes of those people and spoken in their voices. It also is a story about a boy, who is retirement age, and his dawg. Frequently, it is more about a dawg with a sense of independence and strong character. My goal in writing this book is to capture as much of the twentieth-century living history as is available from those who call it home.

The value of living history was created from stories told to me by my parents, grandparents, aunts, uncles, great aunts, great uncles, and a great-grandparent. They told me stories of Civil War Reconstruction days in Kentucky and about first family cars. My great uncle told me stories about his walk from Indiana to Washington state (and later Alberta, Canada) to begin a new life during the late 1800s. Learning history from those who lived it became captivating for me to explore beyond family and Indiana.

Long drives from visits in Eastern Indiana to my home in Wichita (and later, Lake of the Ozarks) gave me reason and time to reflect. I thought about contributions that my family members had made to the story of my rural America, my youth experiences. I had garage chats with one uncle; toolshed chats with another; hunting-and-fishing chats with a third; and grain-elevator chats with an aunt. I listened to stories about my mother's youth from an aunt who was very close to her in age. Shade-tree chats with grandparents. Parent-and-sister chats at the meal table. My dad and I had discussions over the tire of a tractor and while feeding hogs.

These conversations were not only a part of my heritage but also stories about rural America. There were stories about neighborhood wheat thrashing, community barn construction, and helping an ill neighbor harvest his crops. I realized that these family stories—our living history—would have been lost if they had not been told to my cousins and me.

Value of these stories during family reunions became obvious; siblings and cousins retold several stories about our parents, grandparents, aunts, uncles, and even a few about each other. After one of those reunions, my drive home had a completely different reflection from prior trips: I realized the value of my ancestors' stories. The fun of retelling these stories, the rejuvenation of our past, and the history of our family all enabled me to realize that stories portrayed a living history. If our family history is connected by stories, then history of rural America is linked by the stories of their residents.

Twentieth Century marked a period of significant change in farming and rural America. The year nineteen hundred saw nearly forty out of one hundred American workers employed on a farm. By the end of the century less than two out of one hundred were farm workers. Today, three out of four rural counties no longer depend on agriculture as their primary economic base. The rural America we know today is much different than the rural America when I was a kid, and much greater difference than my parents' childhood days.

A sense of urgency occurred when the last surviving member of our family's older generation passed away. Fading memories of life in rural America—when Main Street was crowded on Saturday nights, towns were full market areas, and gas stations repaired autos and trucks. The memory of movie theaters, sock hops, drive-in restaurants, and adults who believed they were responsible for every child in the neighborhood are vanishing with time.

The question became, who will travel and write the stories of the people? The more haunting question became, if not me, then who? An idea was born. Mo, my Golden Retriever, and I would travel and talk with the people.

Accomplishment of research and travel requires planning. Planning has never my forte, so it was brief. A Starcraft pop-up-tent trailer, pulled by my ten-year-old truck, would be our home on the road. Our travel path will be determined by a straight line on a Road Atlas from our starting to ending points. The parameters of intended travel will be twenty-five miles either side of the line. Clothing will include jean shorts, sandals, t-shirts, and a dirty, ragged baseball cap. Additional items include such amenities as two coolers, case of bottled water, dawg food and bones, and a tool kit. Our first effort of planning was accurate, as the only change during the four trips was clothing to match the weather and travel parameters.

Our story chronicles the over-sixty days spent seeking out people willing to tell their stories. Our four trips began with the journey northwest to Seattle. The second trip took us to seven states, spreading from Illinois to Ohio and Michigan to Arkansas. Our third journey southwest included six states that spanned from Oklahoma and as far west as New Mexico and north again to West Kansas. The final excursion led us northeast to Vermont and south to Georgia before terminating in the Mississippi Delta and Louisiana Cajun country. In addition to the four trips, I talked with people at the Missouri State Fair and the local Lincoln, Missouri Annual Grass Airfield Fly-in. The 15,000-mile journey encompassed thirty-two states and occurred over a sixteen-month period.

The stories of 105 people collected during eighty-four interviews combine to chronicle a period of our history that covers over ninety years. Ages of participants range from 17 to 104 years. The interviews are informal and assume the format of a "conversation with a purpose," as described by Dave Erlandson, one of my many mentors. The setting for each conversation is where we meet. Three exploratory statements of inquiry, posed at the beginning of our conversation, drive the discussion: "Please tell me about your town or community"; "Tell me what it is like to live here"; and "Tell me how it has changed."

Interviews most typically occur in restaurants during breakfast, with a few during lunch. Other interview locations include courthouse steps, Main Street benches, picnic tables under shade trees, places of business, pickup trucks, house porches, and museums. Each participant determines the location; it is, after all, his or her story.

Restaurants, especially during breakfast, are the most assured setting for people agreeing to participate in an interview. The most difficult setting to gain an interview (practically impossible, in fact) is a person we meet on the street. No matter how small the town, how friendly the people, and how hard I try, people are not comfortable talking to a stranger they meet on the street.

Mo becomes the attractor for gaining interviews with people there. She works her magic. People stop to pet and talk with her as we walk the streets of rural American towns. After what seems like an eternity, the person recognizes that a human is attached to the other end of the leash and in rare cases greets me with a "hello." The standard greeting is a question regarding Mo's name or breed or simply saying, "She is pretty." I feel like the third person in a two-person conversation—because I *am* the third person. But I accept my role as Mo's human (as opposed to Mo being my dawg) and humbly enter the conversation, which usually results in an interview.

Perhaps now is a good time for you to meet Mo. It really does not matter if the time is good, because she will wear me out with persistence anyway. It is easier to agree and look as if I am in control as opposed to disagreeing and appearing to lose control.

Mo

I introduce myself from my travel sanctuary, the backseat of the truck. I choose the backseat and am not relegated to a place of inferiority, "the backseat." It is all mine, and there are no misunderstandings about who is in control.

My name is Mo. I am a seventy-five-pound red female Golden Retriever.

My real name is Molly Dawg of Walden, but I am known as "Mo." Randy, my human, has told you how important I am in persuading people to talk with him. He, however, neglects to tell people a lot of things: like how my keen sense of direction helps us find our way when he (not *us*) is lost, which happens more frequently than he admits.

The trip is a fun experience, filled with people and places. I get to see beautiful new scenery, be considered a well-traveled dawg, impress more people with my beauty and personality, have quality time with my human, and be a goodwill ambassador. People treat me with kindness by giving me a pet, dawg bones, and foot-to-hand shakes, as well as a baby back rib so large it extends out both sides of my mouth. Life is good!

Now is an appropriate time to explain the reality of a human-and-dawg relationship. First, I am the dawg of the family, and Randy is the human. People often refer to him as my "dad." The reality is—and he tells people with my encouragement—that my true dad is really a good-looking Golden. I want to be clear that there is nothing wrong with being a human, but I am a Golden Retriever and proud of it.

The human-and-dawg relationship requires certain unwritten, unspoken rules. One guiding principle for a good relationship is that the dawg establishes control while making the human believe that he is in control. For example, we stand inside a house door until our human lets us outside. We then immediately turn around and look in through the door window until the human lets us back inside. Are we in control? Hiding our control requires skill, finesse, and plain old dawg smartness. The ongoing process, although difficult, is necessary for a harmonious relationship. It is one that must be led by the dawg; humans are not very astute at finesse. The concept of the dawg being in control establishes the basis for lifetime interactions between the human and dawg. It is all about relationships.

Thanks for taking time to read my thoughts. I will check in throughout the book to explain things that my human forgets or simply gets wrong. Someone must do it.

Randy

Mo is a people attractor. Her big brown eyes are a human magnet. As I conceive the trips, I do not consider Mo's value in attracting humans to participate in interviews. The second day on the road, however, while on Main Street in Smith Center, Kansas, her value becomes obvious when she attracts Billie for an interview.

Mo is a proud dawg. She does not lack assertiveness. She possesses the art of persistence. Sometimes it is easier for me to go with the flow as opposed to being *right*. I begin to realize her value in gaining interviews, whether on the street, in businesses, or other areas. She plays an important role in making this book successful.

A chronicle of the trip provides a daily account of our travels. "The story inside the story," as I term it, provides Mo's pointed critique of human behavior. It further addresses details of our daily travels, such as being lost, finding a campground, and being welcomed by people while we wander main streets, airfields, and businesses in unfamiliar towns. It explains how I stumble onto 105 gracious people who are willing to talk with a stranger clad in a raggedy, overworn cap, T-shirt, faded jean shorts, and sandals.

The *Epilogue* contains a fictitious story about a farmer, who returns to his farm 100 years after his death. That farmer's assessment of a century's worth of change leads him to contemplate how he can adapt to the positive aspects of that change while recapturing aspects that made his hometown, community, and rural America the great places he remembers.

The rural Americans with whom we visit during our thirty-two-state journey address the past and how things have changed during their lifetime. They speak clearly to intangibles: things I could not physically see but could sense and feel, such as community, friendliness, support, and affection for their neighbors. They exude what I believe to be the true basic values of rural America.

I admire and will be forever grateful to each of the 105 people. They brought history to life by telling their stories. Our time together exceeded knowledge and stories; it gave me a sense of human kindness and new friends. They made this book possible.

CHAPTER 1
======

Self-Interview

When I browse books at my favorite bookstore, I am continually confronted with questions like "Why did the author write this book?" or "How did her or his biases influence the writings?" It seems important, if I have these questions, that I provide the information for my own readers, answering the whys and uncertainties, especially considering that research consisting of naturalistic data, such as interviews and observations, can be slightly influenced by researcher background. It is important that the reader has the information to assess my biases, if any.

A self-interview seems to be an appropriate format. With notepad in hand, I ask myself the three defining questions. I talk and take notes: no small feat. I must exercise discipline to keep my mind from wandering and addressing non-relevant issues. Everything, even minute issues, seems important. The process gives me a greater appreciation for other peoples' willingness to share their time and stories, as well as for their ability to stay focused on pertinent topics. My mind meanders; notes reflect wandering thoughts. Eight pages and forty-five minutes later, the process ends with a sigh. As I read the black ink on the yellow pages, I realize that deeply archived feelings and issues have surfaced during my response. The final step of making sense of the notes and constructing them into the following story requires self-discipline.

I spent my first eighteen years living on farms in Rush County in eastern Indiana, with seventeen of those years spent in Noble Township. Three miles from our farm, the township center, New Salem, was the home of the school district and a small shopping area. Rushville, the county seat and larger shopping area, was located five miles in the opposite direction of New Salem. We traveled beyond the township boundaries, but most of our activities, family, and friends seemed to reside within the township boundaries.

Members of my extended family, whom I saw at least weekly, formed a close social circle. We also gathered with our extended families during holidays. Visiting and working with each other during the day were common occurrences. I worked with my grandparents, uncles, and cousins on our farms. My extended family was an integral aspect of my life.

Our farm lifestyle enabled me to spend a lot of time with immediate family. We ate two meals a day together. My dad and I worked together on a daily basis during the summer. We might be working in different areas of the farm, but we were striving toward the same goal: making a living from the soil. During fieldwork, I marked our daily progress with a red rag that I hung on the fence to identify our starting point. Ten hours on a tractor deserved knowledge of progress. My red-and-white dawg, Bird, rode on the tractor with me all day, except for varmint chasing time. She would be with me from dawn until dusk.

The opportunity as a teenager to work on a farm provided worthy lifelong skills. Learning entailed more than physical skills: it taught me to be creative in use of my time and see things that needed be done. Most of all, it embedded a mindset to accomplish the little tasks that led to achieving the greater mission. Organizing daily tasks allowed me to meet schedules on our farm, help a neighbor bale hay at 11 a.m., and make a 6 p.m. high school summer baseball game.

New Salem, the township center, was the home of our first- through twelfth-grade school. The school, which was synonymous with the school district, consisted of one 3-level building. My grandmother graduated tenth grade in 1899, the school's highest level. My mother and father, as well as their brothers, sisters, and most of my cousins, graduated from New Salem High School.

Six of my aunts and uncles and a grandparent lived within a three-mile circle. Extend that distance a few miles, and all my mother's family and much of my dad's family lived in that circle. Needless to say, I had all the supervision I needed during my childhood. All too often, I heard the statement, "I will call Ruth [my mother and second oldest in her family]." Of course, that statement meant an aunt or uncle had decided Mom needed to be informed of my behavior—or misbehavior, depending on the interpretation.

During my parents' school years, New Salem was a thriving town with a post office, bank, barbershop, stores, and grain elevator. The town had diminished considerably by *my* school years but still included a few stores, a grain elevator, and two full-service truck stops with restaurants to serve the numerous semi-trucks traveling on US Highway 52. The truck stops disappeared soon after Interstate 74 assumed US Highway 52's function as the primary route between Indianapolis and Cincinnati. New Salem's few remaining businesses quickly followed the demise of the truck stops.

Today, New Salem is no longer considered a town but has been classified as an "unincorporated housing area." The reclassification causes me concern for the future of my hometown. I recall my parents showing me small areas with deteriorating houses where once had been a town with a school. My fear is that my grandchildren will see and hear the same thing about New Salem, the town I loved and called home.

Little Flat Rock Christian Church and New Salem School further defined my community. Much of our social life thrived around these two entities, with involvement in youth groups and school activities such as Future Farmers of America, 4-H Club, and sports. School activities such as band, chorus, senior-class play, and sporting events brought people to the school. On eight winter Friday nights, the first floor of New Salem School would be packed with people attending the evening's activities. It seemed as if the whole township gathered at 5 p.m. for a fundraising dinner sponsored by a school or local organization. A little after 6:00, the migration would begin down the forty-foot hallway to the gymnasium for the junior varsity and varsity boys' basketball games. About 9:30, after the final buzzer, the crowd would make the reverse walk back to the cafeteria for coffee, dessert, and more conversation. Adults discussed the game, crops, or other worthy news, while students gathered in the gymnasium to enjoy a sock hop.

The loss of the high school about eight years after my graduation (and eventually, the loss of the entire school) entailed much more than losing an education center; it eliminated a social circle and a place and time where adults met and talked. More importantly, it eliminated a time when adults interacted with kids. Many of those conversations made me feel important and enhanced my self-worth. It might be a pat on the back, a compliment about the way I had played that night, or a question about my grades or dairy-show heifer. The list of adults who enhanced my self-worth is endless.

Although Noble Township was the focus of our community, we had friends throughout the county, plus Saturday night was the big family shopping night in Rushville. The downtown was full of people shopping and socializing. Parking spots were at a premium. My peers and I inherited the courthouse-sitting curb when we were about six years old. Even though curb-sitting was a big deal, it was short-lived. By the time I was nine years old, Saturday-night shopping had been moved to Saturday afternoon. This occurred with the advent of television. For our family, it coincided with a new post-World War II car, a Nash. A notable social event—family shopping—became an element of history.

High school ushered in a huge change in my life. I assumed more responsibility for my actions, education became more focused with higher-level science and math courses, dating and social life consumed more time, and sports escalated in importance. I began a transition to adulthood. The notable change made little sense, as I had the same teachers in the same classrooms as a junior high school student. My assembly hall student desk was located two rows closer to the west section, which was senior turf. I roamed over to see my sister and check out the area. For some reason I did not stay as long as I had planned. My seat was the front desk in the center-row, with the trophy case and huge Eagle, our mascot, just feet in front of me. My uncles and their peers had earned some of the many trophies. I respected and admired them, so I knew our basketball or baseball teams had to add to the collection: not just for them but for school spirit and community pride.

Four years passed quickly with academics, sports, and social life. On the second Wednesday of May 1960, I left the cornfield at 5 p.m. to prepare for my high school graduation. With thirty-seven of my peers, I entered the gym for the final time as a student—the same gym that had been my home away from home, the gym where I had spent hours practicing and playing basketball. We walked across the stage and shook hands with the principal—the same principal my mom, dad, aunts, and uncles had shaken hands with when they had received their diplomas.

After graduation, I only entered the gym two times before the school answered to the wrecking ball. We did leave a trophy.

Time passed quickly as I winged my way through life: married with two phenomenal children; a twenty-plus-year Air Force career as a fighter pilot; public school math teacher, coach, and principal; a master's degree, followed by a doctorate of philosophy degree; and fifteen years as a graduate-school professor in educational leadership at Wichita State University. My children have dedicated their professional lives to service. My son is a pastor of an inner-city church. My daughter, a university professor, tackles many social issues, mostly involving children. They and their families live 2,000 and 400 miles from my home, respectively.

The family aspect of my life has changed. I am a regular visitor to Rush County. My sister and I operate the family farm, which is identifiable by "the big red barn." Many neighbors claim that it is a community icon. Our primary focuses of soil preservation and building upkeep resonate from the family values we learned as kids. We recently completed a project to re-side and reroof the barn. It has not looked so good since we were teenagers; this is the point.

The farming community of Noble Township has changed. The farms are larger and fewer in numbers. The number of residents is fewer. The result has been the closing of many businesses. The Fifth Wheel, a restaurant where I ate the official Indiana State dinner of a breaded tenderloin sandwich, chocolate milkshake, and french fries, has been closed for several years. It was a rare experience at the Fifth Wheel for someone to not be talking basketball or farming.

The closing of the grain elevator, where my aunt Betty had once been the manager, marked an important community loss. In addition to being an agriculture business, it had also been a social center. Farmers would sit around a piece of plywood that lay atop a barrel to talk and play euchre, a card game. The farmers ranged in age from a teenager to seventy-plus years old. It was a treat for me me as a 13 to 18-year old teenager to listen and learn from adults. They made me feel as an equal. Bird, my dawg, would go with me to the elevator. She always accompanied me into the large office/waiting area. Aunt Betty would say as we entered, "Randall Turk, that dawg is not allowed in here." To which I would respond, "I know, Betty. Bird, go lay down where Betty cannot see you." I would play cards and talk with farmers. I learned a lot of dos and don'ts sitting around that old piece of plywood.

The overall environment of Rush County changed with the school closure and loss of population. Demise of township schools has taken a toll on community pride. The residents do not have an entity on which to focus their pride. There are no more Carthage Raiders, Arlington Wildcats, Milroy Cardinals, Manilla Owls, Mays Tigers, Morton Memorial Tigers, Raleigh Sir Walters, and New Salem Eagles. The New Salem Lion's Club has preserved a semblance of the Noble Township culture with their construction of a community center building. The Community Center is the site of the New Salem High School annual alumni banquet. The hall is filled with grey-haired graduates. Soon the last graduating class will hold its fifty-year anniversary.

Rushville has done well to withstand the loss of farms and population. They have offset some of the population loss and characteristics of the losses by attracting small manufacturing plants and other businesses. Main Street, however, is not the same. Several businesses have closed, many of which were mom-and-pop or family businesses. Corporate franchise stores, which provide a greater variety, have replaced the family store. But it is not the same.

I recall walking into the Stevens' Brothers clothing store during August each year to purchase three pair of Levis. One of the owners would start the conversation by stating, "Randy has grown. It looks like he will need a size larger this year." I would usually see Dave Knight, a local racecar driver and dime-store manager, when I visited his Ben Franklin Dime store. Someone at the Drug Store (a pharmacy) would help me choose a birthday card or an appropriate gift.

Entering Rushville via South Main Street marks the noticeable absence of Dutch's Drive-in. The empty lot says it all: "The 50s is part of history."

Rural America is full of New Salem and Rushville facsimiles. Rural towns and communities are filled with people like Sandy, Larry, Connie, Joe, George, Jerry, and Vincent, who remained and farmed, as well those like Harold and Kay, who remained but chose a different profession. They are my relatives, classmates, or friends. They are the living story of rural America.

I left Noble Township to attend college with the intent of earning a degree, serving my country for five years as an Air Force fighter pilot, and returning to central Indiana to teach school and operate a small farm. Upon graduation from Butler University, I entered Air Force pilot training as a second lieutenant. Flying became a passion, and I never quit. Following the Air Force, I taught math for four years in a public school system in the Seattle area, where my son and daughter graduated high school. I continued my career in education in Texas and at Wichita State University. I finally returned to rural America but not to a farm.

I still miss a farm with a few cattle and a couple of horses.

I often wonder why people who have a strong attachment to a place and a lifestyle leave. Then I question why they do not return. The leaving may be to explore, which I term the "Jim Bridger Syndrome" after the noted explorer of the early 1800s; it denotes a need to see what lies over the hill or perhaps reflects a sense of restlessness.

As a youth I lived in the same house for seventeen years. As an adult I have never lived more than seven years in a house. I did live fourteen years in Wichita, but in three different houses. After seven years, when things become routine, I feel the need to relocate. Maybe it is the challenge to rebuild—friends, a house—or just to roam. I do not have an answer. I do know one thing: It is always good to visit the people of Rush County. In Rush County, I feel at home.

Northwest

CHAPTER 2

Kansas and Colorado

July 7, 2010: The day I have waited for five years. Mo and I are packed and setting out on our first of hopefully many more trips to rediscover rural American by gaining stories from the people of small towns and communities. Of course Mo is ready; I have been packing for a few days, which tells her we are going on a long trip in the truck.

Pre-dawn and we are on the road. Our first stop will be Topeka, which is about a five-hour drive. I chose Topeka for the first leg of the trip because it is close to the dealer where I purchased my Starcraft trailer, and I need another lesson on trailer procedures.

As normal, we mostly choose the back roads, which I have traveled many times. Our route includes Missouri Highway 2, an east-west road across the west-central part of the state. Nearing the Missouri-Kansas state line, I pass a sign depicting the site of Morristown, which existed for only a few years during the 1860s. I have passed this town at least fifty times, always asking the same questions: What is the history of Morristown, and what led to its short life?

As always, I drive past. This time, however, is different. I accomplish one of my soon-to-be-famous trailer *turn-arounds* and go back to read the signs and walk the area where the thriving town once stood. The decision to turn around and go back to Morristown is monumental for me. It is a mindset of flexibility during travels, which hopefully will prevail during my journeys.

The brief written description tells me that Morristown was the site of a September 17, 1861, Civil War battle between the Kansas Militia and the people of this Missouri community. Approximately 200 fled and never returned to Morristown. The loss of several businesses, as well as the people led to the demise of the town.

A night in Topeka Kampground of America (KOA), a practice trailer set up and teardown, and Mo and I are traveling west on Interstate 70 for a short stop at the Starcraft dealership, where I purchased my camper. The quiet drive provides solitude to ponder the question of whether we should follow my itinerary and go to Smith Center or modify the plan and go to Marysville, Kansas, a pony express station during the early 1860s.

We arrive at the trailer dealership with no decision about our next stop. After a short lesson from John and Stephanie on camper operation, Mo and I continue our westward travel to Manhattan for the first of many fast-food tailgate lunches: a sandwich for me and a dog bone for Mo. As we leave the fast-food parking lot, a polite honk from a motorist behind us prompts me to make a fast decision about our afternoon. A left turn places us on the route to Marysville.

Marysville, the seat of Marshall County, has a population of approximately 3,500.

Marysville began in 1852, when Frank Marshall operated a ferry for westward travelers. He named the town "Marysville" after his wife, Mary, and named Marshall County for himself. Business flourished due to the ferry's location on the Oregon and Mormon Trails. In 1854 Frank Marshall received permission to open a post office. He became disenchanted with his new home and left for Colorado soon after his unsuccessful run for governor in 1857. The town grew and became famous after its founder left, gaining notoriety during 1860 and 1861 as the "Number 1 Home Station" from the eastern starting point of the pony express. Each rider would carry the mail 75 to 125 miles, changing horses every twelve to fifteen miles. At the home station, the rider would relinquish the mail to the next rider for his portion of the over-2,000-mile trip to Sacramento, California. The pony express, even though it operated for only nineteen months, linked the eastern and western United States during a crucial time of history: April 1960 to October 1961.

Mo's and my sixty-eight-mile drive up US Highway 77 takes us to Marysville and a large statue of a pony express rider. The statue, which is at least ten feet high and fifteen feet across, is a likeness of Jack Keetley, a local rider during 1860-61. A walk around the commemorative statue allows me to recognize the Pony Express Museum: hopefully the site of my first interview.

I walk the short distance to the museum, where I ask the attendant what will become a familiar question: "Whom do you suggest I interview that can tell me about your town?" She replies, "Brenda at the chamber of commerce office."

I approach the chamber office with some reservations. Actually, *fear and doubt* would be a better description. This is the first person I will ask for an interview. My anxieties include the idea that she might say, "You are doing *what*?", "How do I know you are who you say you are?", or maybe, "I don't have time." I feel like the entire research project depends on this interview, a feeling that will remain fairly continuous throughout the sixteen months of traveling and talking with rural Americans.

My fears are temporarily put to rest when Brenda extends a warm, friendly greeting and states that she would be happy to participate in an interview. She is a wealth of knowledge about the community, pony express, and history. Her responses to my questions reflect the story of Marysville.

Brenda begins her story by stating that Marysville was not always the quiet, peaceful town we are experiencing on that beautiful summer afternoon. She states:

> In the middle 1800s, the trail now known as US Highway 36, Broadway Street, and the Pony Express Highway, was the dividing line of two towns with opposite views about slavery. A small group of South Carolinians came in 1855 to settle a pro-slavery town. They named their town Palmetto, to commemorate their home-state tree. Today, a half block of original bricks remains where Palmetto once stood.

She pauses and emphasizes, "All brick roads downtown contain original bricks."

Brenda clearly states that history is a very important aspect of Marysville. Preservation of the pony express is an example of their historical prowess. Every year, Marysville participates in the reenactment of horseback riders traveling the route. The ride starts on alternating years in Marysville or Sacramento. "People meet the riders in Marysville every year, even if it is two o'clock in the morning. The 150th-year reunion was this year during the day. Marysville had a big festival with a BBQ and games."

The pony express began on April 3, 1860, and ceased operations on October 27, 1861, because a new system, the telegraph, was a more efficient means of communication. Letters would travel from St. Joe, Missouri to Sacramento, California—a distance of 1,840 miles—in ten days. The cost was five dollars for the first five ounces and five cents for each additional ounce. Brenda proudly boasts, "The pony express never lost one letter, and only one rider was killed." Brenda's enthusiasm about the pony express is indicative of her pride and passion of history, life today, and hopes for the tomorrows of Marysville and Marshall County.

As our discussion moves from the pony express to other historical events, I am amazed how a small town in eastern Kansas had such an impact on the settlement of the west. During the western migration of the 1800s, eight trails passed through Marysville, while eighteen traversed Marshall County. The group that was trapped and eventually froze to death at Donner Pass in the Rocky Mountains had a connection to Marshall County: The travel party had their trip delayed five days at Independence Crossing because of high water, and the five-day delay in Marshall County resulted in their late arrival at Donner Pass.

The people of Marysville have a vision for the future. The old theatre has been refurbished and shows movies. Marysville is known as the "Black Squirrel City," a species protected by a city ordinance. Showing community pride, Brenda states, "I cannot remember anyone receiving a ticket for hitting a black squirrel." She clarifies this statement as meaning it reflects the respect the people have for the law and for the rights of others, including protected animals. The county fair, which is in its 95th year, provides opportunities for 4-H projects and a community gathering.

Marysville is planning for the future. A community action group of five people developed and presented a plan to the city council. The city council used that plan as a springboard to improve Marysville. The council has funded many projects and participated in numerous 50-50 grants to improve the town. The town clearly shows the results of the team effort between the city council and the citizens.

At about 5:00 p.m., Mo and I leave Marysville and travel west on US Highway 36, the "Pony Express Highway." I am excited about the knowledge I have gained about Marysville, excited that I have successfully completed my first interview, and excited to believe that the research on rural America is possible. I can do this!

After driving about an hour, the euphoria quickly dwindles into anxiety. Where do we camp tonight? It is after six o'clock as Belleville appears on the horizon. I have been to Belleville several times and am almost certain of the absence of campgrounds. A couple of farmers' smile, shake their heads, and respond, "Not around here," when I ask if there is campground in Belleville.

Back in the truck heading west, I see a small sign that states "Campground," with an arrow pointing north. I wonder why those two farmers had not known about the campground. After driving nine miles north and five miles east, the direction from which I have traveled, a sign directs me to a barnyard. I now understand why the farmers were unaware of the campground. There are three camping spots, each with electricity and water hook-up. I sigh with big relief as I pull into one of the two remaining spots.

The only building, other than the campground restrooms, is a small farmhouse. An elderly couple eating dinner insists that I sit and talk with them as they eat. After learning that they are retired dairy farmers with children and grandchildren living in the area, I write a twelve-dollar check and settle in for the night. As I transcribe my conversation with Brenda, I reflect on the successful day: a camper set up without a glitch, listening to a great story about a historic rural town that is successfully moving into the future, and spending the night in a great place.

Tomorrow, our destination is Smith Center in Smith County, Kansas: the geographic center of the forty-eight contiguous states. Smith Center's 2010 population of 1,665 has reduced about 13% from 1,931 people in the year 2000.

With lights out and Mo sleeping on the couch, I wander off to sleep, thinking there will be many days ahead embraced with rich experiences and interesting stories of rural America.

The value of the Smith County area was displayed in 1853 (approximately twenty years prior to its organization), when seven Native American tribes engaged in a three-day battle to gain control of the land. The battle pitted the Pawnee, Delaware, and Omaha against their four adversarial tribes of Cheyenne, Comanche, Arapaho, and Apache. The Pawnee maintained control of their land when they and their two supporting nations won the battle.

Smith County was named in honor of a fallen Union soldier by the name of James Nelson Smith, who had been mortally wounded during the battle of Blue River near Kansas City.

Today, the productive land of Smith County supports the primary industries of farming and agriculture. Smith Center's population represents slightly less than half of the approximate 4,000 Smith County residents. The county was organized in 1872 with Smith Center being named the seat the same year.

The next morning, as Mo and I continue our westward journey on US 36, a wavy sea of yellow blankets accompanies us. The ripe wheat awaiting harvest by large combines sways in the gentle morning breeze. The picturesque scenery of wheat; tall, straight, green stalks of corn; green flattop fields of soybeans; and green pastures spotted with red or black cattle, signifies we are in rural American. The live view, scents, and breeze cannot be captured on canvas, in a photo, or with words. You have to be here. To me it is as lovely and majestic as shapely mountains, towering skyscrapers, and babbling streams. Perhaps some of the panorama takes me back to a fun time of life: the 1950s.

All too soon my dream ends with the termination of the sea of wheat and the windshield view of a convenience-store gas station. The store, located at the intersection of US Highways 36 and 281, marks the beginning of Smith Center, seat of Smith County. Highway 281 joins hands with Main Street as it passes north and south through Smith Center. Smith County marks the end of Kansas, as its northern boundary and the Nebraska-Kansas state line become synonymous. If you cross this line, Dorothy, you are no longer in Kansas.

After a left turn onto Main Street, I immediately have my spirits uplifted by another landmark of rural America: a coffee shop. It identifies itself by a sign stating "Second Cup Café and Pastries." It is a gathering place for local residents to discuss major issues such as weather, crop prices, and "our football team" (high school).

Smith Center High School has a reputation for having a successful football program. This fame was accented by winning seventy-nine consecutive games and five straight Kansas state championships during the past decade. The consecutive streak of wins and championships culminated with a defeat during their quest for a sixth straight state title. I chose Smith Center as one of my four planned stops on this journey to explore how a community supports excellence among its young athletes. I have a need to learn why the Smith Center High School football team was so successful. What caused such a strong commitment by youth and adults to achieve such success?

As soon as the truck and trailer find a resting spot, Mo and I immediately hit the street looking for someone to tell his or her story. We enter a small retail store and speak with the lady working behind the counter. After a short explanation of my research, she volunteers to sign a consent form: a requirement of all interviews. She asks me not to use her name. She explains that after high school graduation, she moved to a western area of America, where she worked until retirement. She then moved back to Smith Center. I ask, "Why did you move back?" She responds, "I don't know. I have several high school classmates living in the area."

After her statement, she appears to be uncomfortable with the interview process and states she does not want to continue. I thank her, and she thanks me for talking with her. She then busies herself with a task involving merchandise.

I am back on Main Street with the thought that my Wichita State University colleagues may have been correct: People are not going to tell me their stories. After leaving Mo to guard the truck, I walk a block north to Second Cup Café and Pastries with the hopes of a quick hamburger and time to heal my wounds.

Lunch turns out better than I expect. I choose a table toward the back. Meribeth, the waitress, perceives that I am having a less-than-great day and lifts my spirits with a cheerful greeting. I order and explain that I am seeking the story about Smith Center as a community and their football team. I then pose the big question: "Whom might I interview?"

What happens next is unexpected. Her body language shows exuberance prior to her statement of, "Me! Me. I can tell you."

I respond, "But you are working, and there are a lot of people waiting to be served."

"I can do both!"

The next forty-five minutes are unbelievable. Meribeth sits for anywhere from thirty seconds to a minute to tell her story, then jumps up and walks briskly to serve another customer, all the time looking over her shoulder and continuing her comments.

The owner soon appears from the kitchen to help serve the customers, and I fear the interview is doomed. Not true! She helps wait tables and shows her support and excitement by adding to the story. It becomes obvious that culture of Second Cup Café and Pastries includes a team effort with excitement about and dedication to their town.

I spend about an hour in Second Cup, listening to the stories and enjoying the enthusiasm and friendliness of the people, as most of the customers give me a welcome greeting. Meribeth, a high-energy meteorite, continues her pace and story with exuberance. As the lunch bunch departs for Friday afternoon business, she sits and concludes her story. Actually, she sits with brief interruptions, which entails burning energy by moving. I thank Meribeth and the owner, who prefers to remain in the background and allow her server to be the primary person. What an experience!

After I leave Second Cup and Pastries, I retrieve a sleeping Mo from the truck. As always, she is excited to walk down Main Street and greet people. She alternates between head-up tail waging and smelling new scents.

Mo

Oh boy, the smells are good! Walking by storefront windows, I cannot avoid seeing my reflection. I have to admit I am a good-looking Golden. I can tell my human is a bit concerned about talking with someone. He is not having a really good day. He also is not good at making new friends on the streets of small towns. Of course, he will you tell he is, but he is not. My forte is making friends, so I will give up smelling and become a friend-searching hound.

Here comes a man who is looking me in the eye. He recognizes my "coolness." Keep walking, get a little closer, now is the time. I smoothly drift to the left, and sure enough, here comes the big pet and "hello." I do a tail wag and the "Golden Hug," also known to humans as a "lean." Is he ever going to realize there is a human on the other end of the leash?

Eventually, my human says, "Hello." Our new friend greets my reticent human. They are soon sitting on a bench. And me? My work is done, so I lie down by my human's feet and catch a needed and well-deserved nap.

Randy

Thanks to Mo, I meet Billie, an eighty-one-years-young male and retired agriculture truck driver. Billie and I sit on a bench in front of a tire shop, which used to be a Chevrolet dealership. Our planned forty-five-minute interview lasts well over an hour and would have probably extended much longer had Billie not mentioned that his wife was at the beauty shop waiting for him to take her home.

Our conversation is as relaxed and slow-paced as Meribeth's interaction was energy-draining just to listen to. They are two dissimilar people with two differing stories that depict a similar message about Smith Center and its people.

I depart here from my plan to tell each person's story separately, and I combine Meribeth and Billie's stories as one. Their story themes complement each other as a single narrative about Smith Center. Meribeth is a middle-age female, and Billie is a Korean War veteran. Meribeth, who grew up in Smith Center and graduated from Smith Center High School in 1980, is a high-energy person, avid football fan, and a supporter of Smith Center High School and community. Billie, who spent his entire life in Smith County except for two years in the marines, grew up on a farm near Greenville and Athol, about eight miles west of Smith Center. "Athol no longer exists," Billie states. He graduated from Smith Center High School in 1947.

Meribeth and Billie's historical perspective differ because of their ages and the time period of their youth. Their stories depict a rich viewpoint of a community with a lot of heart.

Smith Center, like many small towns in rural America, is becoming smaller. Billie says, "Smith Center is about one-half what it used to be." He supports this statement by explaining that there used to be six filling stations downtown, while now there is only one, and it is out on the highway (US 36). He continues with yesteryear, stating, "All of the buildings downtown contained a business: no empty buildings. There was a grocery store, Simmons Furniture, and a light company. Now there is a day-care center and two eating joints downtown." Meribeth's perception—"One-third of the stores [downtown] are gone"—clearly states that the deterioration has been occurring for longer than her awareness.

The size of Smith Center High School has followed the same path as the downtown area. Meribeth claims, "When I graduated in 1980, there were sixty students per class. Now, in 2010, there are twenty-five to thirty students per class." The 50% decline further substantiates the loss of population. Billie believes that a significant reason for the decline in population is that farms are larger than when he was a child. He adds, "Farms have become a lot larger during the last fifteen to twenty years."

Billie pauses and continues, "A bright spot in the local economy is XL: a company that builds travel trailers. This business has made a positive impact on the economy. Pride in workmanship at XL is indicative of our community and the people." Meribeth makes the comment that the friendly people of Smith Center work hard and support their community. Meribeth's and Billie's stories display similarities about hard-working people, with a great sense of community, pride, and strong relationships among them.

The impact of lost population is personal as well as economic. Meribeth claims, "People move out. Mostly they go east. We lose good friends. It is hard to get people to move back because there are no jobs." Billie supports the population decline, saying, "Most people move out of Smith County due to lack of jobs. The population is getting older."

They both state that Smith Center, even with the loss of friends, is a great place to live. "Even though we have lost a lot of friends, the people are still the same. It is a peaceful place to raise kids. People of Smith Center hang out at each other's houses," claims Meribeth. Billie adds, "One thing about a small town: You know 90% of the people." Billie and Meribeth's comments are supported by several people saying "hi" to me: in the restaurant, while sitting on the bench, and during Mo and my walk down Main Street. I feel like a resident.

My expectation when I planned to stop at Smith Center was a story about football. Eight years before, I had worked on team-building with the staff of the Smith Center school district. It is obvious today that football is still a significant part of the school, but it does not override the motivation to excel as an academic institution that prepares good citizens. Meribeth tells me that building the football program starts in junior high school, with football summer camp and weight training. She believes, as Billie does, that the kids work hard to achieve success—in the classroom and on the field.

The concept of community becomes clearer when Billie makes a telling remark about the adults' efforts and success in improving the community by cooperation and work: "We put in a new track at the high school. We improved the airport by lengthening the runway and making it concrete, so larger airplanes can land. The community built a new high school in 1973." After some thought, Billie personalizes community with remarks about people supporting others during medical needs. "People help people each other. Our cancer treatment center is in Hastings, Nebraska: about ninety miles one-way. We take each other. Someone took me; now I am taking someone."

The kids, including football players, cheerleaders, and student fans are a microcosm of the Smith Center adult population. They have a strong work ethic, believe in community, have pride, and commitment to succeed. The young people of Smith Center emulate the attributes of their adult role models.

Billie's final story depicts him as a caring person. When Billie was in about fifth-grade he got a dog, which he named Pal. "Pal went everywhere I went. He even went to seventh and eighth grades with me. He would lie under my desk." Billie pauses then continues, "When I went to Korea Pal stopped eating. My parents coaxed him to eat by feeding him meat. The day I came home from Korea, Pal was laying at the end of the lane by the road waiting for me." Billie looks at me with wonderment and asks, "How did he know I was coming home?" I have no answer, except my thoughts that dawgs know more than we think.

I reach down and give Mo a pet, and with a tear in my eye, I stand and thank Billie. I say, "Please give my apologies to your wife for being late." He shakes my hand and thanks me for the opportunity to tell his story about Smith Center. Mo and I walk back to the truck in silence with a great appreciation for Meribeth and Billie's stories about a town with a lot of heart. The people in Smith Center are as beautiful as the wheat.

Soon we are on the road again with no planned destination other than some small town in northern Colorado. A quick check reveals that reaching Colorado by nightfall is not possible, so our plan becomes to travel for a couple of hours northwest and camp wherever. Before we leave Smith County, we pass Athol, the town Billie described from his childhood memories. Athol, with its north-south and east-west streets, sits idol along the highway, waiting for people to come and recapture its liveliness of yesterdays.

Immediately after passing Athol, we turn north on Kansas Highway 8, which becomes Nebraska Highway 10. After hugging and crossing the Republic River for several miles, we travel north and northwest on US Highways 136 and 6. The fields of tall, green corn and of course, yellow wheat provides a soothing, relaxing mood. The flat cropland, dotted intermittently with small towns, occupies my full attention. Suddenly I realize the sun is fast approaching the horizon. I begin to think, *Campground*. A little late, but nevertheless, I am back to reality. Once again, my thought process leaps to, *I need to upgrade my planning to include night destinations and campgrounds.* Magically, a sign states "McCook: 39 miles." A quick check of the map reveals a town large enough for a campground, which turns out to be a bad assumption. McCook does not have a campground.

McCook, located in Red Willow County of southwest Nebraska, originated in 1822. It is a town of about 7,500 residents. Population has remained fairly constant during the past ten years. Most of the businesses are located along US Highways 6 and 34, which run east and west. US Highway 83 traverses the town north and south. McCook, the largest town in the area, supports agriculture and other industry.

We enter town from the east, looking for a campground. About a half-hour later, after a thorough tour of the town and several questions to people on the streets and in businesses, the campground issue becomes real again. There are no campgrounds in McCook. Finally, someone tells me that Red Willow Reservation campground is about twenty-five miles north on US 83. Twenty minutes later, after seeing the backstreets of McCook and the high school three times, Mo and I find US 83 North.

The good news after driving thirty minutes is that we enter the small state park. The bad news is that the park is dotted with campers. Reality hits: There may not be a vacancy. Friday evening and beautiful weather entices people to state parks and other campgrounds. As I drive further into the camping area, I think how campground planning must become a higher priority. After two laps around the campground, I find a vacant spot. The camping spot is a long walk to the bathrooms and possesses a lack of shade trees, but it is the most beautiful sight in the campground.

As Mo and I walk around the campground, we see a group of retired people gathering with dishes of food. Approximately thirty men and women sit in a circle under a canopy and shade trees talking, laughing, and sharing good-smelling food. Later that night and the next morning, I am very fortunate to spend time with several people from the group. They live in rural Nebraska and have worked their entire lives as farmers or in a related agriculture business. Each person exhibits the character and values I remember from my youth. One retired farmer states that he is very happy I am doing the research and hopes I will be successful. He continues that he wishes he could travel like me. He says, "When you have been behind the plow for so long, it is hard to break loose and leave home for a long time."

Every person who has a dawg brings him or her to see Mo. Saturday morning as I am backing up the truck to hook onto the camper, I look in the mirror and see a man in Wranglers guiding me. After hook-up, I thank him. He dismisses his action as if it were something a person would normally do to help someone. I love rural America.

Mo and I receive many waves and wishes of "Good luck!" as we drive off for another venture into rural America. I think how fortunate I am this Saturday morning. I am very grateful for the new friends I made at Red Willow.

After a great breakfast at the Chief Restaurant and a friendly twenty-minute conversation with the manager, Mo and I continue our Saturday morning journey west on US 6. My plan is to visit a small town in northeastern Colorado. A quick review of the map reveals two familiar towns. Wray is the childhood home of a friend and colleague who now lives in Colorado Springs. His hometown was the site of our annual Thanksgiving weekend pheasant hunt, which featured Boomer, our 100-pound Golden Retriever. The other town, Holyoke, is the home of a student pilot whom I instructed while working at the United States Air Force Academy more years ago than I care to remember. Holyoke is more directly on our route, so Holyoke is our goal.

Holyoke, located in the northeast corner of Colorado, is the seat of Phillips County. The county was created by the state legislature in 1889 and named in honor of the Lincoln Land Company secretary. Phillips County has a population of about 4,500, while Holyoke has approximately 2,400 residents.

Back to reality as Mo and my drive on US Highway 6 finds us once again surrounded by a sea of gold wheat and tall, green corn. The two-lane road has few curves and fewer hills. The view of the high plains seems to go forever. I think I can clearly see the Rockies, which I cannot. It is just a "want-to-be illusion."

But I *can* clearly see—in my mind, at least—Dean, Mike, and my son, Greg, walking through harvested cornfields, pursuing the elusive pheasant. I see Boomer working his pattern to scare up the birds. The vision is a delusion from a great memory thirty years in the past: a memory I will cherish forever.

As I snap back to reality I have the vision of a windshield filled with the small town of Holyoke. We arrive in Holyoke a little after noon. Our initial stroll up and down Interocean Avenue, the primary business street and US Highway 385, clearly states that Holyoke businesses close at or before noon on Saturday. I comment to Mo, "This is going to be a bust. There is no one to talk with in Holyoke."

As we walk north on Interocean Avenue, I realize that one business is bustling: the grain elevator during wheat harvest. We immediately alter our route and quicken our pace. Being around a grain elevator during harvest season brings back a flood of memories. The smell of grain, the sound of the motors pumping grain into storage bins, and the excitement that time is of the essence all create an anxiety, making me increase my pace. A timely off-loading of wheat at the grain elevator is essential to continue harvesting in the field.

Mo

As I walk beside my human, I realize the grain elevator may be our only chance to make new friends. What I do not understand is why it took Randy so long to recognize that the grain elevator was the busiest place in Holyoke on Saturday afternoon. We meet several men scurrying around, unloading wheat from trucks into grain bins. They, however, all take a moment to pet me. Finally, one worker suggests we talk with the office manager. As we enter the office, the lady looks at me and says, "What a pretty dog." I already know that, but it is always nice to hear. She continues to pet me while she talks with the human element of our team. Another compliment: "Mo is really well-behaved dog." I know that also. After a Golden hug, she says to my human that she will call Steve, the general merchandise manager of the grain elevator, to see if he can come talk with Randy. A quick telephone conversation between Randy and Steve, and we are in the truck, heading out of town on a county road. Whoops! We miss the turn onto the road where Steve lives. Here comes another one of the famous middle-of-the-road turnarounds. This time we back into a farmer's driveway—sort of. We trace our path back on the road, turn right, and soon pull into a driveway in front of Steve's family home. I immediately see two Labs. One big bounce, and the Labs and I are off and running. I love my job!

Randy

Steve, who appears to be about forty-five years old, interrupts his planting of flowers for introductions and greetings. He invites me to sit on the porch, where we spend the next hour talking.

"Holyoke is a great place to live," Steve states before we have settled into our chairs. He continues by telling me that he grew up in Calhan, Colorado. My thoughts momentarily return to the late 1970s, when I would travel monthly about forty miles to Calhan to buy feed for my horses. The monthly trip was as much about hanging out in cowboy country as buying feed. I considered then—and today—the US Highway 24 corridor from Peyton to Limon as "cowboy country."

After I ask Steve to repeat his comments (because I have been living in the past), he continues by telling me that he attended and graduated from Kansas State University. He changed his major from bakery science to agriculture because, "I did not like the hours, plus I thought it would be easier to feed cattle than people."

Holyoke became home for Steve and his family in 1990, when he assumed the duties of grain merchandise manager. During that time, the population of the town fluctuated. In the 1990s, there was a population growth. Steve states, "It [the growth] was partially due to the new large hog-producing plant. The hog operation plant still exists but has deceased in size." He continues, "The farms have continued to become larger, thus reducing the number of farm families. An effect of less people and fewer farm families has been a reduction of kids participating in the local 4-H Club."

I pause giving Steve time to reflect. I see three retrievers romping and playing with a tennis ball and tug toy. Mo is having fun with her new playmates.

Grain farming is the largest industry in Holyoke and the surrounding communities. The grain elevator remains busy and is a large business in Holyoke. The grain elevator has increased its ability to handle grain. Steve states, "The grain elevator can handle six to seven million bushels of corn per day or one to one-and-a-half-million bushels of wheat. During the 1990s, each farm truck held 600–650 bushels. Now each truck hauls 1,050–1,100 bushels." The combines that harvest the grain are much larger today than a few years ago. Steve adds, "The bigger combines and trucks are indicative of the larger farms." Grain harvest season is a very busy time in Holyoke. "The grain elevator, to handle storing and shipping the grain during the approximate three-week harvest season, is open from 7:30 a.m. until 10 p.m. seven days a week. Extra employees are hired to handle the abundance of grain."

Holyoke is a traditional and progressive community. The traditional aspects include peoples' commitment to community and their neighbors. The priority for community improvement and enhancement of citizens' life demonstrates progressiveness. Steve states with a grin, "I told my kids if they did something wrong, tell me, because someone probably has told us before you get home." After a pause he continues, "The community rallies around families who have an emergency. Farmers harvest the crops of farmers with the misfortune. The farmers doing the helping will not take money for gas."

People of Holyoke want to handle, as a community, their emergencies and not receive help from the government. Steve believes that rural people take care of themselves. He further substantiates this belief by describing the volunteer fire department, emergency medical service, and the new hospital the community built in 2008. "We had great support from the community for this project [new hospital]. Mr. Higgenbottom, who was a banker, left a five- to six-million-dollar endowment to the town, with the stipulation that it be used to do good things for the community." The new hospital is an example of using the money wisely.

Steve concludes his interview by saying, "If someone ever tells you there is nothing to do in a small town, tell them, 'Baloney!' There is plenty to do. I am active in EMS [Emergency Medical System], a volunteer fireman, hospital board member, and youth coach. It may not be going to a pro game as a fan, but the things I do are fun." This statement summarizes Steve's view of his rural community. He believes that helping others and improving the community are joys in life.

The story of Holyoke, Colorado exemplifies that a community could maintain its solitude and traditional values while being progressive. Community improvement coalesces around doing small and greater things to enhance the life of its members.

Mo and I are on the road and once again have no plans for a place to spend the night. As the trip progresses west on US Highway 36 to Sterling, then north to Interstate 80, our goal for Saturday night becomes Cheyenne, Wyoming. Sundays are "no interview days," plus Cheyenne will give me an opportunity to see the "Cheyenne Days" rodeo arena.

KOA is our home for the night. Later that evening as we slowly drive past the quiet, dark rodeo grounds, I hear the announcer inside say, "The next saddle bronco contestant, Larry Mahan, will be atop Rowdy—a tough, bucking, twisting horse from the Beard ranch in Ellensburg, Washington. Larry is out of Texas, and Rowdy hails from the Frank and Charlotte Beard Ranch in Ellensburg, Washington." My thoughts return to the many rodeos I viewed from several stands, watching in awe the skills of the cowboys and cowgirls. My son, Greg, was one of those exciting cowboys for a few years, riding bareback broncos. His career was short but a valuable learning experience. The other cowboys, as well as Frank and Charlotte Beard, provided many learning opportunities during Greg's rodeo experience.

Later that evening, while sitting on a lawn chair at the campground listening to the late-night sounds of quiet, I reflect on the first four days of our journey. My thoughts turn to my apprehensions of finding people to tell me their stories. Every town has created concern of failure to acquire an interview. Mo has been helpful by attracting people. The people and their stories have been great. The small towns we have visited exhibit community spirit and commitment to progress. I am enjoying the people and their towns. I am having fun!

I am excited about traversing Wyoming and meeting people in the Rocky Mountains and along the Old Oregon Trail. Tomorrow will be another adventurous day. Next week will be exciting. Good Journey!

CHAPTER 3

Wyoming

Sunday morning, Mo and I are westbound for a ride on Interstate 80 to Rock Springs, Wyoming. Rock Springs has a campground; planning has improved. The countryside depicts acres and acres of grazing land, smattered with inactive oil wells. Sharp, jagged cliffs border the terrain. As we travel westward, my thoughts drift back 150 years, when settlers began their trek across this beautiful, rough landscape. I wonder about their thoughts. Then I try to imagine what the Native Americans, who had freely roamed these plains and mountains for centuries, thought about the wagon trains and people crossing or invading their domain. Miles pass as I am consumed with my historical thoughts. Fortunately, a wet, cold nose brings me out of my trance in time to stop for gasoline and a well-needed break . . . at least for Mo.

Fuel, drink, and a walk are followed by a reluctant dawg jumping into the truck. Our remaining drive presents a different landscape. The interstate takes us up the mountain until we reach the continental divide at Rawlings. Momentarily, it seems as if we are on top of the world. Then we are headed down the winding road toward Rock Springs: our planned destination for a well-deserved rest. Our trip along IS 80 is marked with a few trucks and fewer cars. The lonesome drive terminates at the KOA campground.

Early Monday morning we are off on side roads, searching for adventure. I am excited about traveling in the Rockies and meeting rural Americans of Wyoming and southern Idaho. Heading northwest on US Highway 30, I check the gas gauge and hunger meter. Much to my chagrin, they are both approaching empty. The plan is to have breakfast at a mom-and-pop diner and talk with some local folks before leaving the "Cowboy State." The near-empty fuel tank preempts the low-hunger tank. The prevailing question is: How could I pass so many gas stations in Rock Springs and not refuel?

Luckily, I spot a small town about a mile off the highway. The setting should be an indicator of what is to follow. I ignore the obvious and drive into town. After several laps around the four blocks of town and a couple of trailer turnarounds on dead-end streets, a man in a pickup truck stops alongside me. The driver leans out the window and asks if he can help me find something. I respond that I am looking for a restaurant and gas station—with the priority being a gas station. He chuckles and says, "Not in this town. Only pipeline workers live here. There are no businesses." In response to my sad story, he suggests I continue northwest about twenty-seven miles to Opal, Wyoming. He smiles and says, "Good luck!"

Mo
 Have you ever had questions that you *want* to ask, but do not, because the answer appears too obvious or perhaps insulting? I have several times, and one of those times is this morning. First and foremost: How can humans, who say they are the "higher species," do such dumb things? Two, we passed many gas stations in the town where we slept. Why did we not fill our gas tank? Third, why did we choose a town that obviously has no businesses from which to buy gas? Fourth, why do we drive down dead-end streets? These are just this morning's questions. I have more.
 Our twenty-seven-mile drive takes forever. There is stress in the front seat. No stress in the backseat. I am enjoying the scenery that is intermittently interrupted by statements about running out of gas. Talking and worrying about it is not going to help. Great, I see a town. The good news is our walk to buy gas will not be too long, if we run out now. Just as I am ready to sit down and relax, something flies out of the bed of a truck in front of us. My warning of a nose-poke to my human's arm and the infamous swerve are about a tie. We missed what seems to be a boot flying through the air. This is way too much excitement for a Monday morning. I am going to lie down and let Randy tell you about the boot.

Randy
 Nearing Opal, something bounces out of the bed of a pickup truck I am trailing—at a safe distance, of course. I make a quick swerve to miss a big rubber boot, thinking maybe I should cancel today. Instead, I flash my headlights to signal the driver. We stop for a short roadside meeting. I say, "A boot jumped out of the bed of your truck. The good news is no one was wearing it." He smiles and shakes his head in doubt, then says, "I think I have all my boots." He leans over the truck bed and starts counting. When the count stops at nine, he says, "Yep, I am missing a boot." He thanks me and drives back to retrieve his missing footwear while Mo and I head to the nearest gas station for fuel. The stop includes gasoline for the truck and coffee and a stale packaged pastry for me. A gulp of gas-station coffee and a bite of sugar-laden pastry stimulates my brain,

which allows my thought processes to function beyond walking with a gas can to fill a thirsty truck.

I have a mental log of the many questions I want to ask but never do. I add one more to the list: Why does someone have five pairs of boots in the bed of his truck? As you can tell, Mondays are tough for me, but not so tough that I forget the value of learning.

A fifteen-minute drive northwest on US 30 leads us to the two towns of Diamondville and Kemmerer, which are nestled in a beautiful basin of the Rocky Mountains in southwest Wyoming. Diamondville, named to represent the local rich coal, was the first of the two settlements. The towns, even though separated by about one mile, were founded almost thirty years apart. Diamondville, population about 700, was founded by Herman Church when he discovered coal around nearby Hams Fork Creek. Kemmerer, with approximately 2,500 residents, was founded about thirty years later. The early existence of both towns can be attributed to coal mining.

The early town of Diamondville was located near the top of a hill, where the early miners lived in shacks and dugouts constructed in the side of the hill. In 1898 the river was rerouted, and the town moved and platted in the valley where Diamondville stands today. In 1930, Diamondville Mine closed, ending the underground operation. Pittsburg and Midway Coal Company opened the current open-pit mine that remains operational. A drive around town reveals houses built in rows that give the appearance of a mining town.

A drive north leads me to a larger town with a distinguishable downtown area. Kemmerer, named for the financial backer Mahlon Kemmerer, is the county seat of Lincoln County. Patrick Quealy and his financial partner, Kemmerer, began a mining operation during the late 1800s. The Oregon Short Line Railroad connected with Union Pacific, providing needed transportation for coal and other new industries of cattle, sheep, and timber. The town began to grow and attract retail businesses, such as the 1902 opening of J.C. Penney's first "Golden Rule" store. Mr. Penney lived in the area for several years, overseeing his store. Today, the Penney's store in Kemmerer remains open for business.

Lincoln County was created in 1911, when it was developed from Uinta County, only to be divided in 1921 to add the two new counties of Sublette and Teton. Today, Lincoln County's L-shape runs 110 miles from north to south and fifty miles across at the base of the "L." Its current population is 18,567, with a recent growth of 2.5%. Paleontologists have analyzed rocks dating to the Great Lakes era (roughly 4,000 years ago). Shoshone Indians inhabited the area until European-Americans began to settle during the early 1820s. The southern part of the county, mostly desert, is rich in oil and natural gas, whereas the northern segment comprises high-country grazing land. The highest elevation is around 11,300 feet above sea level.

The downtown area and courthouse square emulate a basin of serenity. A walk around the town square and adjoining streets in Kemmerer verifies the peacefulness and tranquility. It seems as if the scenery and people are connected as one peaceful entity. It takes me only moments to join in their tranquility. One look at Mo and it seems that the tranquility has the same affect on Golden Retrieves, at least one. I am one thankful human for her calmness.

The people and atmosphere are so calm and quiet that I am uneasy about bothering anyone for an interview. The lady I finally work up the courage to ask about an interview is very polite and helpful. She states that she would be happy to spend the time for an interview, but suggests I go up the street to the museum and talk with Judy, a Lincoln County native who possesses a lot of knowledge about the area. Usually, the "but" in a sentence is followed by words meant to gain escape from the words "I would be glad to" that were uttered in the first-half of the sentence. I hope this situation is not a "usually."

Mo and I make the short trek up the street to the museum. Judy, who appears to be in her mid-thirties, is excited and anxious to tell the story of Kemmerer and the surrounding area. She begins, "I grew up on a ranch and was bussed about twelve miles to school. We also came to town to visit my grandparents." For someone like me, who has a bit of cowboy "want to be" in him, the smallest hint of cattle, horses, or rodeos leads to a conclusion of ranching being a significant industry. I immediately decide that this is going to be a good conversation.

Judy transfers our conversation to a historical perspective. "This area was a lake a million years ago. Anthropologists now come and dig. They must pay and can only dig in the stone quarry. They cannot dig on the butte." I pause to reflect on how our world has changed so much with the passage of time. This beautiful landscape of today was once a lake. Two questions run through my mind: How do things change, and what is our future?"

She snaps me back to reality by addressing a period of time that seems long ago. When placed into perspective, however, 100 years is rather recent:

> Kemmerer was incorporated in 1898; Diamondville was a town prior to Kemmerer, but it did not incorporate until 1901. Diamondville, a mining-company town, traces its history to the 1868 residency of Harrison

Church. It was a mining-company town; the residents were required to live in company houses and buy from company stores. Diamondville, of course, is no longer a mining-company town.

Two towns with very different origins and purpose today share the same basin and coexist with similar goals. She continues by explaining, "The three main industries include coal, [natural] gas, and oil. We get a lot of tourists during the summer."

Judy speaks about the demographics and ensuing implications of her community. She states what is becoming a common but sad fact: "Our town and classes [schools] are getting smaller. We must travel to Salt Lake City, about 125 miles, for major medical treatment." Then she mentions a common, positive element: "People follow high school sports, mostly football and basketball."

I ask her about the beauty of the museum and the statue on the town square. She explains that the museum is an old Latter-day Saints Church. Addressing the statue, she proudly states that it commemorates Edgar Herschler (1918–90). "Mr. Herschler, a Kemmerer native, served five terms in the Wyoming House of Representatives and was the only three-term governor of Wyoming [1975–87]."

Judy gives me a quick tour of the museum, which further reveals both the beauty of the majestic building and some historical artifacts that clearly speak to the heritage of the area. I thank Judy for sharing her time and her knowledge. As I make the short walk to the truck, I again ponder the concept of time. It allows majestic changes. The Diamondville and Kemmerer basin is a clear example: a landscape completely changed from ancient time until today. A shorter time of 100 years nurtured social and cultural change. Time is relevant to all things.

Mo and I retrieve the truck and camper and continue our northwest trek on US 30. Southeastern Idaho is our goal. As we travel, I think, *One highway, one broad goal, one turn. This should be an easy trip.*

We see the mountainous high country and grazing land of Lincoln County. Simplicity turns to complexity in a heartbeat, however, as a highway sign informs us that US Highway 30 splits into two routes. A quick grab of the map and review of my Garmin GPS clearly states that a decision looms on the horizon. Should we take US 30 and travel through the Bear Valley Wetlands or bear left and traverse Bear Lake? The important decision requires a stop along the road. The difference in mileage is inconsequential, so what *is* the dilemma?

Landscape and what we will miss with a chosen route? In reality, a flip of the coin would have been just as scientific as my thought process. I choose to prolong our time in Wyoming by following US 30 north via Bear Valley, as opposed to heading west for a drive along Bear Lake. The thirty-mile drive is scenic and provides me some Wyoming reflection time. The over-97,000 square miles of land presents a variety of landscapes and natural resources, as well as friendly, neighborly people—at least the ones I have met during my several visits. I was a visitor to Yellowstone during the expansive fires of 1988. The cities of Cody and Sheridan, and now Kemmerer, have a special aura for making me feel welcome.

A last look in my rearview mirror shows a small corner of the scenery that enticed early explorers like Jim Bridger and John Colter to discover Old Faithful and pave the way for you and me and eventual 1890 statehood. I bid farewell to Wyoming as I cross the state line and am greeted by a large sign stating "Welcome to Idaho."

Mo

Here we go again! My human is in a quandary (dawgs know big words) about something that is nothing. Both roads go to the same place; just choose one, and be quiet so I can sleep. I personally never worry about a route; I just do it. Hey, bunnies to the right! Let's go right! Sure enough, we head right on US 30. Glad I could make this decision. It was the easiest decision I have had all day, except for early this morning when I was confronted with: Should I sneak a drink of water out of Randy's cup? I am not telling the answer. There is no self-incrimination in my blood.

CHAPTER 4

Southern Idaho

A two-hour drive on US 30 leads us to Soda Springs, Idaho: a town settled on the Old Oregon Trail about 150 years ago. The picturesque town is nestled next to the Alexandria Reservoir in the Bear River Valley. Official town elevation is 5,760 feet. The town began in 1863 as Soda Springs Post. It was established in 1864 as the original seat of Oneida County. It served in that capacity until 1866, when the seat was moved to Malad City because of its growth and location on the stagecoach line. Soda Springs received its second chance to be a county seat in 1911, when Caribou was created as the last county in Idaho. Idaho became the forty-third state on July 3, 1890.

Modern day Soda Springs has maintained a population of approximately 3,000 since 1970.

One of Soda Spring's attractions is a continuous-flow geyser, which is known as the "Largest Man-Tamed Geyser." The geyser that only erupts with human control was discovered during a drilling process in 1937. Maximum height of the geyser is 100 to 150 feet. For me, however, the greatest attractions of Soda Springs are its natural beauty and friendly residents. The picturesque mountain peak at end of Main Street and location on the Old Oregon Trail define the aura of Soda Springs.

We arrive in Soda Springs around 3:30 in the afternoon. I immediately observe a quiet town, its well-maintained Main Street terminating at the base of a mountain peak. It is a beautiful scene that deserves several clicks of my camera. My walk up and down Main Street, and the surrounding areas reveal very few people. Mo takes a nap in the truck while I enter the courthouse, located on South Main Street. I have no idea why I choose the courthouse; it just seems the thing to do. I stop at the first office and ask whom I can talk with about this beautiful mountain town. The unanimous response is, "Preston! Preston!" I make the short trek down the hall to Preston's office. Preston, a native of Soda Springs and Caribou County, happily agrees to share his knowledge about this majestic area—as soon as he completes a small task. We agree that the courthouse lawn will be an appropriate setting. The beauties of Soda Springs remain forefront in my thoughts as I retrieve Mo and join Preston on the courthouse lawn.

Preston and I choose the Caribou County Courthouse steps for our conversation. Mo curls up on a nearby step until she spots a squirrel. The chase is on. She spends the next hour roaming the Caribou County Courthouse lawn, checking and rechecking every tree and smelling every blade of grass.

Preston begins with history by explaining:

Even though Soda Springs is a small town, it is the largest in Caribou County. I am a native of the area. The story goes that my grandfather's brother, in 1914, came to the Soda Springs area. He wrote back to his brothers in Hays, Kansas [known for tornadoes] that all the good land they could use was available. My grandmother asked my grandfather if there were tornadoes in Soda Springs. When my grandmother heard the 'no' response, she immediately began packing.

Preston's ancestors moved to Soda Springs and raised their family. One hundred years later, I am talking with their grandson.

Our conversation transitions to a time in history that marked the settlement and first industry of Soda Springs. Preston states:

The name "Soda Springs" was derived from the bubbling mineral water that looked like soda. Brigham Young came soon after the start of Soda Springs and plotted the land. The railroad soon followed the organization of the town to accommodate shipping livestock. Our original industry during the late 1800s and early 1900s included a large stockyard. Farmers and ranchers brought their sheep and cattle for shipment by train. A lot of sheep and cattle were driven to the Soda Springs area and grazed during the summer before being shipped out during early fall on the train. Farmers soon came, and open grazing became a thing of the past. Timing for the influx of farmers during the early 1900s is substantiated by the large number of requests from the Caribou County Courthouse for recognition of 100-year old family farms.

He explains that when a farm has been in the same family for 100 years, the courthouse issues a written recognition to the family. I recall this procedure to be common in many states. The 100-year family speaks clearly to individuals' love and commitment to farming. As indicated by Preston many of these farms were original homesteads.

The size of farms in Caribou County is experiencing the same fate as those in Colorado. Preston states:

Average farm size was 1,200–1,500 acres in 1970; today the average farm size is 3,000–4,000 acres. Peak population was around 3,700 in the late 1960s and early 70s. We used to have a lot of business retail choices: three clothing stores, now one; four new car dealerships, now one. We now have two grocery stores and three convenience stores. Young non-farmers are going off to the cities to work. Also, young farmers leave farming to work in cities.

Preston pauses and concludes, "The schools are becoming smaller [fewer students], and the county as a whole is less populated."

Our conversation proceeds into discussing the ramifications of increased farm size. Preston says that increasing farm sizes require more capital, which may include a significant debt. He embellishes:

The small farmers' dilemma is: Should they increase capital expense or suffer less income? Farm expenses and income may make it financially prohibitive to earn a living on a small farm. The small farm of today was a large farm for the previous generation.

He quickly changes the subject, as if it is too sensitive to dwell on the subject of small farmers being forced to make a choice to leave or continue their profession in agriculture. His words are accompanied with a slight look of sadness, which seems to be an unfamiliar expression for him.

Preston's expression brightens as he moves onto the positive thought of local employment opportunities. The main industry today is open-pit phosphate mining. Several people drive an hour from Pocatello, Idaho to work in the local phosphate mines. Of course, several residents also work in the phosphate mines. Preston offers another career option for people desiring to remain in Soda Springs: "Two or three people live here and work online. They used to live here and wanted to come back."

Preston's observation of working online surfaces an issue that can be a factor in maintaining small-town populations. Today's technology makes it possible for people to live in rural communities while working for a company in a distant city. This phenomenon increases rural population and revenue while also providing people with a choice of living in a metro or rural area. The situation Preston describes provides a meaningful option of allowing families to remain intact by living in the same area as parents and siblings.

Preston concludes his story by stating, "We are a small town. People are friendly. Neighbors take cookies to their new neighbors."

Soda Springs started as a fort on the Oregon Trail and evolved into a community that supports open-pit phosphate mining and farming industries. Preston appropriately describes his town by saying, "Soda Springs is basically Small Town USA." I agree with one additional adjective: "picturesque."

Mo

I had fun hunting squirrels on the Soda Springs Courthouse lawn. Everyone is supportive of my passion to keep the ground free of squirrels. Most people do not realize the importance of the canine mission of chasing squirrels; they believe we do it for the chase. Not true! Our mission is to keep squirrels from hoarding all the acorns. If the squirrels are successful in gathering all the acorns, there will be no seedlings to grow new trees. The result could be devastating to the ecological system. So, the next time you see one of my canine friends chasing a squirrel, be supportive like the people of Soda Springs. Also, it does not hurt to add, "You are a pretty dawg."

Randy

Mondays are great; it just takes more time than other days for the greatness to work its way to the surface. Mo and I leave Soda Springs with a more optimistic view about Mondays. I had the opportunity to visit three beautiful towns and have informative conversations with two interesting people. As we leave Soda Springs, I stop and look over my shoulder for one last view of the mountain peak at the end of Main Street. Breathtaking, simply breathtaking. That is the only way I can describe it.

A one-hour drive and we are camped in Pocatello, Idaho at a KOA. An uneventful evening, a short time in the lawn chair reliving today with the computer, and then sleep before the sun peeks over the Rockies to introduce Tuesday and another exciting day. We head west on Interstate 86 with the goal of reaching Oregon. At about the twenty-five-mile point of our drive, an old World War II type of aircraft hangar appears to the right of the highway. It grabs my attention like a magnet. Of course, we have already passed the exit to the town. I slow down, hoping to find another exit. Trailing motorists are not sharing my interest as they politely zoom by with a horn honk. A drive that takes forever leads to another sign stating "American Falls: Exit Right." I now know the name of the town that has summoned me for a visit.

The 4,500 residents of American Falls account for about on-half of Power County population. It is appropriate to call American Falls a "town on the move," as it now resides at its third location. The original town of American Falls was founded in 1800 on Snake River's west bank, the opposite side of the river from the two subsequent towns. In 1888, the town was moved across the river to what is now called the "original town." In 1925, the town was moved to its present site to make room for the American Falls Dam and ensuing reservoir. The final move, accomplished by the Bureau of Reclamation, included 344 residents, forty-six businesses, three hotels, one school, five churches, one hospital, six grain elevators, and one flourmill. It was the first town in the United States to be completely relocated.

My drive reveals many familiar small-town sights: schools, retail stores, gas stations . . . but no hint of an airfield. I finally swallow my male pride and ask someone at the 911 Emergency Operations Center for the location of the airfield. My luck is that the attendant lives in another town and has no idea about the airfield location. This should be a hint that the airfield is not a busy place. Giving up is not an option, however, so I make several stops and repeat the question until someone gives me general directions. Mo and I carefully approach what appears to be an old, deserted airfield. I park in a vacant parking lot and walk around until we find an open hangar door. I stand in the doorway of an unlighted hangar and yell "Hello!" a couple of times to get someone's attention. Of course, Mo, being inquisitive and the great protector, parks herself about a foot in front of me in the middle of the open door.

Our greeter creates a bit of a shock. Out of the dark appears a tri-colored Bassett Hound. The ears on both dawgs shoot up, followed immediately by each doing a two-step retreat. So much for Mo being a protector. Thankfully, Dick, an eighty-one-years-young pilot and aircraft mechanic, appears out of the darkness of the hangar to greet us before leading us to an office, where Mo and I will be entertained with an hour of interesting—and sometimes breathtaking—stories.

Dick begins our conversation by stating, "I soloed [an airplane] in March 1945 and received my [private pilot's] license later that year." He is very proud, as he should be, of soloing and receiving his pilot's license at the age of sixteen. It is difficult to imagine me as a high school age student, barely old enough to drive, flying solo in an airplane. It was good for the world that it did not happen. He also holds an A&P (aircraft maintenance) certification. Aviators who possess an A&P certification are not the norm. He can fly them and fix them.

Even though he began flying at an early age, he chose to not pursue a commercial pilot's license, even though it would have led to a lucrative career.

He explains:

> I did not want to be a commercial pilot. Private pilots fly when they want to; commercial pilots fly when they are told. I want to fly when I want and not when I am told. It is boring to fly cross-country. I like to take them [aircraft] up and ring them out.

His words indicate a person with an independent character who likes to push an airplane to its aerodynamic limits.

Dick adds a third certification, glider pilot, to his resume. He is a very unique aviator: one who focuses on enjoyment and serving others as opposed to making money. A rural town due to limited aviation, is very fortunate to have an aviator with his diversity.

The senior statesman of aviation remains an active flyer. He says, "I still fly my son's Stearman [older type of aircraft]." He then relays his aviation diversity by stating, "My son and I are rebuilding antique airplanes in Blackfoot [a neighboring town]. The airplanes are a Waco biplane, a Stearman PT-17 [primary trainer], and a Ryan PT-22."

I am familiar with only a few of these aircraft. The best I can do is listen with admiration, as vintage airplanes hold a warm spot in the hearts of many pilots, including my own. History of aviation, pilot risks, and rudimentary flying machines are the "wagon trains of the wild blue" that charted the course that eventually took humans to the moon.

Flying has changed in many ways since pioneer flying. The changes include issues other than aircraft and knowledge. Dick speaks clearly to the transformation. "Things are really slow now: no airplanes, no students. All the restrictions on flying have taken the fun out of it." He demonstrates his point, as he does in many instances, with an analogy. If golf restrictions mirrored flying, "Golfers would be required to check in [with a control agency] prior to playing each hole."

As a pilot myself, I share his sentiments. Restrictions and cost were what dissuaded me from continuing to participate in private aviation as a flight instructor.

Dick does not let the negative aspect of aviation damper his attitude, however. He pauses and smiles as he begins our walk down memory lane with the first of a few stories about his experiences. As a warm up, he tells me about demonstrating a J-3 Cub to a potential buyer. He explains:

This maneuver is one of his favorites to demonstrate the effect of a headwind. It is based on flying an airplane into a headwind that is greater than the aircraft speed across the ground. I showed the pilot how to fly backwards across the ground. He never bought the plane.

The second story involves a total loss of power in a single-engine airplane during approach for a night landing. He says:

I always fly high at night because it gives me extra time in case of an emergency. I always delay my descent when I approach for a night landing. The additional altitude allowed me to reach the airfield and make a safe landing [when the engine quit].

This sounds simple, but landing an airplane without power at night is at best a heart-racing task. The landing must be well executed and very accurate to ensure both landing and staying on the runway. If the pilot is lucky, it results in a complete change of clothing and the brunt of much humor from other pilots.

Dick shakes his head and shuffles his feet before stating that mice chewing through wiring in the aircraft caused the malfunction. A simple act resulted in a serious in-flight emergency.

His last story involves an emergency during a nighttime flight from Bozeman, Montana to American Falls. Dick and his passenger had been flying for about thirty minutes when an engine oil line failed, spewing oil over the windshield. He relays this account of the scary night:

The windshield was covered with oil as the engine sputtered and quit running. We made an emergency landing on a gravel road. Our aircraft spun 180 degrees during landing. The jolt of the landing and spin rendered both of us unconscious. When we regained consciousness, fuel was dripping on us. My passenger immediately passed out again. I removed the passenger and myself from the plane. Almost immediately a deputy sheriff and medical attendant were on the scene. In moments they loaded us into the waiting ambulance for a quick trip to the hospital.

Quick action by Dick and a timely response by a deputy sheriff and ambulance saved the lives of two people. Dick believes, even though both he and his passenger survived, that a safer landing, less aircraft damage, and most of all, less-serious injuries would have occurred if nearby Ennis Airfield had been equipped with runway lights. A lighted airfield would have provided a visible runway for landing.

Dick was not bashful about making his beliefs known concerning that accident and other issues of safety. He spoke to civic leaders about installing lights at Ennis Airfield. He says, "My speaking out helped influence the right people to install lights at Ennis Airfield."

Dick demonstrated his willingness to speak for safety issues after the terrorist attacks of 9/11. He recounts his actions:

> I talked with Federal Aviation Administration personnel in Salt Lake City after 9/11 about the dangers of crop-spraying aircraft carrying ammonia nitrate. I told them that all crop-dusting aircraft should be checked for explosive igniting materials. I also suggested that crop-spraying aircraft be taken out of commission during non-spraying season.

These words of restriction emanated from the same person who deplores restrictive regulations. The appearance of inconsistent attitudes is actually consistent; they represent his dedication to safety without unnecessary restrictions.

Dick is a pilot's pilot. He flies for fun and not for money. He truly loves the entire concept of aviation. I end our conversation by telling him that I am impressed with his flying and aircraft-mechanic experience. My aviation experience allows me to fully appreciate his skills and attitude about aviation. He could definitely fly and maintain aircraft. Dick approaches life with an attitude of common sense, eyes on freedom, and the conviction of his ability to fly the toughest flying bronco. His approach to flying leads me to believe that Dick is part aviator and part cowboy, as he has exemplary characteristics of both breeds. What a way to walk through life!

I express my gratitude to Dick for his time, stories, and most of all, his contributions to aviation.

It is mid-morning when Mo and I leave the airfield. I like American Falls and want to hear more about this unique town that has been completely relocated during the twentieth century. I drive straight to the courthouse.

Actually, I wander around until I find it. Why not? It worked yesterday. After posing the "who question" to a local lawyer who is leaving the courthouse, he suggests I go to Spring Creek Manor, a senior care facility, and talk with Lydia, a 104-years-young resident. I am not excited; I am ecstatic!

A few minutes after speaking with an administrator and showing her my consent letter, I am joined in the living room of Spring Creek by two gracious ladies. A comfortable couch and three comfortable chairs bracket a large coffee table. Lydia and Erma sit on opposite ends of the couch, while I sit across the coffee table in one of the big, soft chairs. The inviting atmosphere makes it seem as though I am sitting in the living room of a personal residence.

A description of Lydia and Erma's childhood hometowns will help us understand their roots. Ellendale, North Dakota was the early twentieth century home of Lydia. Her hometown was founded in 1882 as the seat of Dickey County, located in southeast part of the state. Twenty-four years later, she became a resident of that new community.

The Chicago, Milwaukee, St. Paul, and Pacific Railroads arrived during the same year the town was founded. The 1900 Ellendale population of 751 residents almost doubled by 1910 to 1,389. In 1960, the town experienced middle-of-the-century growth, peaking at about 1,800 people. By 2012, however, the number of residents had declined to 1,390: almost the exact population of 112 years prior.

Anglo-Americans comprise approximately 95% of the residents, with African-American and Hispanics combining to account for about 3%. The severe climate stretches from hot and humid summers to severely cold winters. Today, Trinity Bible College resides where the old North Dakota Normal and Industrial School once stood. Trinity replaced the college Lydia attended nearly a century ago.

Dickey County has rich farmland. The south county line is the North Dakota and South Dakota border. One county separates Dickey from the Minnesota state line. Six other towns inhabit the county.

Erma claims her home as ten miles north of Ogden, Utah, which is not the rural town or community that it was seventy years ago. Ogden, which had a census population of 82,225 in 2010, was the first settlement of European heritage in what is now the state of Utah. The settlement, originally called Fort Buenaventura, was renamed as Ogden in honor of a Hudson Bay trapper by the name of Peter Skene Ogden. It is the second-largest city in Utah and closest sizable city to the Golden Spike at Promontory, which marks where the First Transcontinental Railroad was joined to link the east with the west. Ogden, home of Weber State University, resides near the eastern foothills of the beautiful Wasatch Range.

Lydia and Erma are quite the opposites. Lydia, who is quiet and introspective, speaks mostly about life in general. Erma seems to talk as she thinks and describes events. The conversation is exciting and descriptive. Their graphic descriptions allow me to visualize the event or setting. As Lydia speaks, I visually walk in the blowing snow of the cold winter plains of North Dakota. Erma's words guide me to the mountain peaks of Utah and German prisoners of war stepping off an old, drab bus in alike attire. Their stories do not describe American Falls, but instead detail life experiences in two very different parts of America that span almost a century.

The conversation assumes the format of three people having a discussion. Both ladies are very polite and considerate of each other and me. Lydia's natural deliberate and thoughtful mannerisms were exemplified in pauses prior to her responses. Her responses were measured with few words and accuracy. On occasion she would clarify her thoughts to ensure accuracy. I found myself somewhat mystified by her articulate mannerisms. She set a standard for me to pursue. Erma's exciting and bubbly character is embedded with thoughtfulness and respect for others. She spoke with fluidity of words which exemplified her thoughts. She was very careful not to interrupt and dominate the discussion. I was somewhat mesmerized by the conversation. I hardly speak a word, just listen. The atmosphere and conversation is so comfortable and natural that I have to continually remind myself to take notes.

The best way to inform the reader about Lydia and Erma's stories is to tell each story separately. I choose to write about Lydia first. Actually, Lydia probably makes the decision when she begins the conversation with the question, "Why did you choose me?" I respond, "Lydia, several people suggested I talk with you because of your in-depth rural America experience."

Her faint smile and words inform me that she believes her life has been routine and that perhaps I am overstating my point. Her reluctance to talk about herself is indicative of her belief that her experiences of living in North Dakota during the early twentieth century and enduring the Depression are not extraordinary. Her thoughts are quite contrary to my expectations. She minimizes the hardships of life on the North Dakota Plains during the early Twentieth Century, the Depression, and travel to Minnesota to further her education.

I assumed that the strong recommendations by the lawyer and care-center attendant to interview Lydia were because of how long she had lived, but I soon find I am mistaken. The recommendations were actually because of *how* Lydia has lived those 104 years. Her story displays an amazing and yet humble lady.

The conversation continues with me asking Lydia what it was like growing up in North Dakota during the early twentieth century. She responds, "*You* know; you grew up on a farm." A period of silence that seems much longer than it truly is results in her stating that she was the youngest of ten children: seven brothers and two sisters. They lived on a cattle- and wheat-producing farm near Ellendale in the southeast corner of North Dakota. "Being the youngest, I was spared learning a lot about the farm," she tells me. After some thought, our discussion continues about not having the conveniences we take for granted today. "We had an old-fashioned windmill that pumped water from our artesian well for the cattle." She continues, explaining that they carried water to other livestock drinking locations.

Living in rural America during the early 1900s—especially as a farmer—was much harder than today due to less-effective communication and transportation and the absence of other technologies, such as gasoline-powered farm equipment and electric water pumps. Lydia frames this when she says, "Farming was done with horses. Feeding the livestock was accomplished by manual labor, such as lifting the bales of hay or shoveling the grain, then using horses to pull the load to the feeding area." Today's automated equipment precludes farmers from manual labor. Technology has revolutionized farming during the past century by reducing the labor.

I pause and think about a normal winter day in North Dakota. The wind blows, snow moves horizontal, and the chill factor is below zero degrees Fahrenheit. Labor necessities during this era required extended periods of time for a person to be outside. Life in general included a lot time outside in the weather. Placing this into context helps me to understand why Lydia considered life beyond her early years as mundane.

I, then, reflect to a time long ago when I lived in the Upper Peninsula of Michigan and Duluth, Minnesota. Our winter weather options were snowing, blowing wind, extreme cold, or a combination all of the three. I recall being dressed to fly and looking in the mirror. I saw a mummy dressed in olive drab flight suit. My five-layers of clothing made a fighter pilot unrecognizable to himself.

As I write about Lydia's experience, I reflect on my youthful years of carrying water to the hogs and how I complained. In retrospect, I realize my chores were much easier compared to hers. Today, I grew up and no longer consider my work as extraordinary. It took a few years but I made it.

Lydia changes the conversation to the social aspect of rural life, saying, "We only went to town when we had enough eggs to sell. We frequently visited our neighbors." Her experiences of infrequent visits to town and visiting neighbors are similar to those of Billie's, who I had met in Smith Center,

Kansas. He and his family only went to town on Saturday—if they went at all—and he and Lydia both claimed that they frequently visited their neighbors and attended social events in their local communities.

Communication was limited. Lydia states, "We had a crank phone, party line. People would listen [to our calls]."

I, myself, recall those days from the mid-twentieth century. Rural people's knowledge of world events was limited and certainly not current during the early 1900s. Lack of timely communication also influenced lack of knowledge about local weather and other dangerous situations. Lydia states, "We dreaded prairie fires and tornados. There was seldom any warning about fires and tornadoes. We knew about them when we saw them."

Lydia's experiences of limited news beyond the local community was very different from the people living during the second half of the twentieth century and even more so today. 100 years ago, the world of rural people was their community, coupled with untimely, sparse bits of important world events, such as war and major nature-related phenomena. Radio (with its very poor and sporadic reception), delayed newspapers, and word of mouth were conveyors of the news. Reports of major news could have taken days to receive.

Internet, television, and other immediate-communication media provide the people of today with instant news, often accompanied with video. Communication that we take for granted today was unimaginable 60 to 100 years ago. Current communication provides more than news; it informs youth about life beyond their communities, including opportunities.

As a child, Lydia had few career opportunities, due to lack of awareness and unavailability of educational institutions. Her career path, starting with a college education, clearly spoke to her strong character. Lydia broke the boundaries and attended college at a time when most young women got married and had a family. Lydia states, "I went to Ellendale Normal [college] and received a degree in home economics. In the summer, I went to the University of Minnesota to learn more." She continues, "I taught home economics."

Lydia quickly transitions from her career to the next phase of her life when she and her husband moved to American Falls. She speaks briefly of American Falls, but clearly states it has been an enjoyable phase of her life. I ask, "How long have you lived in American Falls?" She responds, "We moved to American Falls before my son was born. And he now is a senior citizen. We have lived here quite a while." She continues her remarks, stating with pride, "My son was a CPA for the Defense Department."

Lydia is a lady of few words. She is very thoughtful and reflective. Her story focuses on life as she lived it: not events, but the big picture of life. She is careful not to brag or build herself into the lady I view as a twentieth-century pioneer. Lydia broke the mold by going to college, entering the professional world, and relocating miles from her childhood home and family during a time when travel across the states paralleled today's global mobility. An aspect of Lydia's greatness is her humility.

I come away from my discussion with Lydia with some unanswered questions: Why was it difficult to get her to talk more about herself; why did she not address the Depression; and why did she not talk about difficult times growing up during World War I and living through a second world war? Perhaps future interviews will solve these unanswered questions.

Erma's story focuses on her life as a child in Utah. Her remarks about her time as a youth clearly transmit that those years with family were not only important but became the basis of her lifelong values. She is excited and ready to talk, but remains sensitive to Lydia and me while *we* are talking. Her pauses always follow a period of silence.

One of the first things she mentions is that she was the oldest child in her family. Erma and her parents lived on the family farm with her dad's parents. They lived in the same house as her grandparents. She states, "There was a big house with two apartments attached. Each apartment had two rooms. We lived in a two-room apartment until my grandfather and grandmother passed away. Then we moved into the 'Big House.'"

Her father inherited the farm when her grandfather and grandmother passed away. Their farm was located on Mt. Ben Lomond. Erma describes with great pride and affection her home life as a youth:

> Our home and view were beautiful. We had the view of the mountain and the lights of Ogden at night. There were earthquakes in the area but not where we lived. Because I was the oldest child, I had to learn everything about the farm. It was not easy because my dad had high expectations for me to master the numerous tasks that I was assigned. I had to work hard. A lot of our social life involved visiting neighbors. I enjoyed visiting our neighbors. We visited them a lot. I really liked my years growing up.

She culminated her remarks about her youth by adding that she was able to attend Weber State University, located in Ogden.

She has very vivid memories about the German prisoners of war during World War II. Her detailed recall of situations and people speaks clearly to the importance she attaches to the events. She explains:

> We lived twelve miles from a World War II prisoner-of-war (POW) camp for German soldiers. The POW's would come [during the day] and help on the farm. Most of them were nice people. Some prisoners called my mother 'Mommy.' One prisoner had one of his ears shot off. One prisoner got off the bus and stated, 'Your planes may be superior, but we will win.' My dad immediately sent him back to the POW Camp.

Her voice clearly showed compassion as she spoke about this significant event of her life.

Erma moved to American Falls in 1969. She relays, "My husband and I owned several newspapers in the area, including American Falls." She tells me this during the middle of the conversation but never mentions it again. Her story, instead, is about her childhood, her recall of which is very clear.

The interview is shortened because it is time for lunch. When an administrator tells Erma and Lydia it is lunchtime, they thank me and join their friends for lunch. A few moments after they depart, I am packing my notebook and computer, and Erma returns to make one more point. She tells me, "It was difficult being the oldest and having to learn everything and to live up to the expectations." It is very clear that she took her childhood responsibilities very seriously.

From our brief conversation, Erma seems to be a very sensitive person with a strong compassion for others. Her words about the German soldiers, even though foes in a bitter war, ring with consideration for human dignity. For her, compassion is a way of life. These feelings, which remained embedded throughout her life, appear to have been grounded in early compassion and values of humanity.

I feel very fortunate to have been able to spend time with Lydia and Erma and capture a snapshot of their life experiences. Even though the experiences of their early years were not easy, they appear to cherish those years. A commonality that exists in both stories is that, "We all knew our neighbors because we visited them frequently in their homes and in our home."

It is very interesting that neither Erma nor Lydia ever mention their experiences during the Depression. I do not pursue those experiences, however, because I have concern that the untold stories remain silent for a reason.

Lydia and Erma made such an impact on me that I later visited Ellendale. I altered my route during my return trip home from the West Coast for a brief visit to Lydia's hometown. I walked the streets, observed the strong appearing construction that allowed buildings to withstand the harsh winters. I spoke with a few people but none remembered Lydia's family. Ellendale is the epitome of a small town in the Great Plains. I saw a tall, young lady carry books on her way to greet students at the local school.

Ogden, where I had visited previously embraced a new meaning. In addition to the beautiful physical setting, I imagine the hardships of World War II and the depression. I visualized soldiers in drab clothing exiting a drab colored bus. I see a young girl watching in wonderment.

After leaving Spring Creek Manor, Mo and I venture to the city park for lunch: a sandwich for me, and a dog bone for Mo. Pondering my afternoon, I observe several mothers and their children enjoying lunch and playtime. Even though they appear to meet by happenstance, there is a lot of socialization among the children and mothers. The noise and laughter momentarily allows me to forget about the afternoon and enjoy the sounds of the children's laughter.

Snapping back to reality, I realize that I still do not have the story of American Falls. I wander to the downtown area and walk the streets. The downtown reveals a common scene from several other towns: empty storefronts and absence of shoppers.

I finally spot a thriving business: C and J Power Equipment. It is almost *too* busy, and the owner smiles and shakes his head when I ask if he has time for a short interview. After a moment, he agrees to twenty minutes. He recommends the picnic table on the corner lot next to his business for our conversation. After he finishes helping a customer, he jolts me out of my leisurely, reflective mood with a friendly greeting welcoming me to his hometown. Almost immediately I realize that I am engaged in a conversation with a man who is in love with his town and community.

Jerry, who was a teenager during the late 1970s, has lived in the American Falls community his entire life. Our conversation traverses from how his town is declining in businesses to a fun and exciting place to grow up before ending on the positive aspects and his hopes for the future. Under the shade tree of our talk is a sense of pride and love for community.

His first comment is, "American Falls is dying off." The impact of the statement is pronounced more by the sadness in his voice than his actual words. His point is substantiated by his description of how the downtown has changed since the late 1970s, with the loss of several businesses. He substantiates his point by detailing several businesses that American Falls has lost during the past thirty years.

> Our lost businesses include three lumberyards, four hardware stores, three clothing stores, a full-service animal feed store, one new-car dealership, and one coal yard. We have lost other businesses. Some businesses, such as grocery stores and pharmacies, have been reduced in numbers. We also lost the three granaries, Pillsbury, General Mills, and Power County Grain Growers.

The loss of three granaries clearly states a significant change and the plight of the agriculture industry.

Jerry continues by relating how these issues of both American Falls and other rural American cities affect today. Job opportunities in American Falls, like many other small towns, are not attracting young adults. Most of the employment opportunities for the area are in Pocatello, about fifty miles from his hometown. Many of the American Falls opportunities are low-pay, unskilled positions, which do not entice young adults. Jerry states, "Many recent high school graduates move away to seek employment. My two daughters moved to the Pacific Northwest. One lives in Portland, Oregon and another in Seattle, Washington. They, like many other young adults, moved to seek employment."

The town has maintained a positive growth by attracting several new residents. As frequently happens, arrival of new people often influences or changes the culture. It is not necessarily a negative change; Jerry states, "One of the changes is the loss of community spirit. It is different from when I was growing up in American Falls." Differences include less friendliness and decreased focus on community improvement.

Jerry embellishes the cultural change as he relates a childhood experience that demonstrates the relationship between adults and neighborhood kids:

> My father told me that I was too young to shoot my 22-caliber rifle alone. A few days later, I did some target practice alone. Not very long after I did the target practice, my dad asked me how many rounds I shot. Today, no one will tell a parent about their child misbehaving because of the repercussions from the parent. We have lost some of the small-town community feeling of adults being responsibility for the children in their neighborhood.

He adds a statement that reflects the loss of community: "Everyone knew everyone when I was a child."

Jerry connects the reduced community spirit to the "loss of a vibrant downtown American Falls." He describes his hometown, teenager years.

> American Falls was a lively, fun place. Friday and Saturday nights, when farmers came to town, the streets were lined up with people. During my teenage years, everybody knew everybody. As teenagers, we cruised Idaho Street. We hung out at the A&W Root Beer Drive-in and Arctic Circle, both of which are now closed. Roger's Restaurant, another hangout, stopped being open twenty-four hours a day.

I pause to empathize with Jerry about the closing of drive-ins. When Dutch's Drive-in Restaurant in my own hometown closed, even though I did not live in Rush County at the time, I thought the world had stopped. Actually, a piece of my world ceased to exist.

Jerry continues to talk about his pre-teen and teenage years, reliving the times of downtown. "When I was a kid walking home after school, old timers sat along a sidewalk and talked. Now this is no longer true."

Jerry believes that American Falls has a bright future. He says, "It is still a good town. American Falls is still a safe town. We experienced our last murder fifteen years ago."

American Falls experienced an entertainment void when the movie theatre burned down during the late 1970s, but after some thought, Jerry states, "We have a new dinner playhouse [theatre]." A performance of the play, *Nunsense,* was scheduled at the Little Theatre: an indicator that Jerry's dreams of revitalization are coming true.

He continues his positive feelings when he states with pride, "The chamber of commerce is back together." He believes that with the rekindled spirit of the chamber of commerce, the town will recapture some of the many aspects it lost during the past.

Our conversation concludes with a summarization of the important issues that must be solved to make American Falls the vibrant town it was in the past. "We have the same two problems that American Falls has had forever: We do not have enough money [tax base], and we need to bring retail and buying power." These two issues seem to be connected to each other, as well as to population growth.

American Falls has a history of strong people overcoming hardships. The ancestors of many of today's American Falls' citizens moved their town across the river, only to completely relocate their homes and town *again* less than a quarter-century later. Perhaps much of that survival spirit is present in today's American Falls' descendants.

I thank Jerry for his time and sharing of knowledge. I also express my gratitude for his walk down memory lane and the story of today's American Falls. He, in turn, thanks *me* for my interest in his hometown. His personal knowledge of American Falls, his youth experiences, and the account of his father making a positive out of Jerry's shooting his gun without supervision made this story very interesting. Jerry's articulation allowed me to just sit and listen. Can you picture how a 20-minute interview took over 60 minutes?

He concludes with a final statement that is repetitious of both a previous thought and other people's experiences: "Our young people move away to find jobs." Thanks again, Jerry!

Mo

Before we begin, let me say I was not afraid of the Bassett, just a little shocked. I definitely am a protector.

Once again, it is the middle of the afternoon, and my human is just getting the daily trip started. It is 3 p.m., and we have traveled twenty-five miles. This means many miles, a late or dark arrival at a campground, minimal time for a walk, and late to bed. But the evening turns out better than I expect. After a walk and dinner, we go to the campground's ice-cream social. I am the only dawg, so there is a lot petting and several comments of, "Nice dawg!" Of course, there are also a few "snooters": people who turn their noses up at the sight of a dawg. I don't dwell on them, because the big deal is ice cream: not just ice cream, but *huckleberry* ice cream. I have eaten a lot of different kinds of ice cream—all good—but this huckleberry thing is *really* good. I have my own dish, which is the only way to go. Eating ice cream out of a dish emulates chasing a squirrel, as the bowl moves around without a purpose. It goes left, then right, then straight ahead before repeating the cycle. Unlike a squirrel chase, which usually culminates at the base of a tree, the ice-cream-bowl chase often ends with bowl on top of the ice cream. Once again, as usual, Randy notices things are not going well and corrals the bowl before disaster strikes. After the ice-cream social, Randy takes to typing, and I curl up on the couch, dreaming about squirrel chases and huckleberry ice cream. Life is good.

CHAPTER 5

Oregon

This leg of the trip, as we shall learn, exceeds my expectations. Sometimes I ask the question: How can such an ordinary day lead to great events? Maybe it is attitude? Perhaps it is stepping back and taking the path that lies ahead without questing the route. Our next stop unfolds into revisiting a friendly town, situated in a beautiful setting, and talking with three fabulous people. The first story evolves from a conversation with Tabor, who invites Mo and I into his jewelry store. The second conversation is with Al, who I meet during breakfast in a small family restaurant. My last interview is with John, a volunteer at the museum. His colleagues scheduled John's interview the previous evening.

On Wednesday we are traveling northwest on Interstate 84, which somewhat parallels the Old Oregon Trail. The landscape is beautiful, with mountains, streams, and wooded landscapes marking our path. I reflect back to a period many years ago, when settlers and wagon trains dotted the Trail. I wonder what the settlers were thinking as they traversed this rough terrain to a place unknown by them. They surely were questioning their destiny and perhaps their decision to abandon the known for a life of unknowns. They certainly were not questioning the beauty. These tough early settlers opened the gates for upcoming generations, some of whom I hope will tell me stories of their beautiful, historic area.

Our destination, Baker City, Oregon, is one of four towns I plan to visit during the northwest trip. I became acquainted with the town known as Baker during a previous visit in 1982. Located near the Old Oregon Trail, Baker City is nestled in a valley of the Blue Mountains. The Powder River runs through the center of downtown on its route to join the Snake River. This picturesque town has a beautiful park near the preserved down town area.

Both Baker County and Baker City were named in honor of Edward D. Baker, who was killed during the Civil War battle of Ball's Bluff, Virginia. Baker, a friend of President Lincoln, had served in the US Congress as an Illinois representative and in the US Senate representing Oregon. In May 1846, Lincoln named his second son, Edward Baker Lincoln, for the original Edward D. Baker, who was the only member of Congress to die in the Civil War.

A discovery of gold in 1861 by Henry Griffin attracted people to the scenic area, known today as Baker County. Baker City, originally with three cabins, initiated its quest to become a trade center in 1864. A mine in proximity of Auburn enabled it to attract population, become a trade center, and act as the original seat of Baker County. Auburn, however, lost that title when its mine "played out." Baker City assumed the role of county seat in 1868, when it became the commercial center of the area. New Baker County officials confiscated the official county records when Auburn residents refused to relinquish them.

Baker City was platted by attorney Royal A. Peirce along Center Street, which soon was renamed "Main Street." The town gained one of its trademarks, a very wide Main Street, with the original platting. The wide street allowed wagons pulled by teams of horses to make U-turns. Numerous structures along Main Street and expanding trade led to the growth of the newly formed town. Size and commercialism resulted in Baker City being recognized as a town on the move. A two-story courthouse was erected in 1870, only to be destroyed by fire in 1885. A second brick structure was soon erected, again replaced in 1909 by the current courthouse.

The advent of the Oregon Short Line Railroad in 1884 thrust Baker City into considerable growth. By the turn of the century, Baker City became the largest town between Salt Lake City, Utah and Portland, Oregon. As Baker City continued to grow and develop, the citizens and local government became involved in the name game. The town became known as Baker in 1911, when the term "city" was dropped, only to be reintroduced in 1990, allowing it to resume its original name of Baker City. The turbulence of its name changes appears to have had minimal affect on the Baker County seat, as it has experienced little population change from 9,342 residents in 1940 to 9,828 in 2010 (Baker City accounted for about 60% of the county's 2010 population of 16,138).

Our route northwest on Interstate 84 brings us to the front door of Baker City. I experience the friendliness of the community immediately upon arrival when I stop at the chamber of commerce office. The first thing I learn is the 1982 town of Baker has changed its original name to Baker City. Confusion abounds. My short-term disorientation creates some shared humor between the chamber employees and the new visitor in town. Confusion continues when I ask if there is an art event in "The Park": my name for a beautiful park situated near downtown, across the street from the museum and nestled in a bend of the Powder River. Both ladies look at me with confusion until I explain the term.

Laugher continues as one attendant states, "You really are confused and confusing." She continues that an exhibit will begin tomorrow.

I thank them and start to leave. Just as I reach the door, I stop and inquire about a campground, my purpose for stopping. They provide names and locations. As I thank them, they state in chorus, "Good luck."

After a quick camper set up, Mo and I are roaming Main Street and the downtown area—but only after a drive past "The Park." A short drive and we are downtown. The first thing I recall about Baker City is the very wide Main Street. I then observe that many of the downtown stores reside in refurbished historic buildings. Several people tell me that a local organization, Historic Baker City, Inc., is instrumental in the restoration of the downtown area. Many of these same people recommend I interview Tabor.

A few minutes later I am standing behind Mo at the front door of J. Tabor Jewelers. Without walking into the store, I explain to Tabor about my research and say I will take Mo to the truck. Tabor states, "Come in, and bring Mo." Before I can move, he adds, "She will be fine. Bring her in."

I think, *I hope Mo will be mannerly*. Time will tell. Tabor's associate offers to entertain Mo and take her to the back room. As Mo excitedly leaves with the lady, I wonder how long Mo's visit will last.

Tabor begins our conversation by telling me he is a fourth-generation Baker County resident. His mother's grandparents came in a wagon train over the Oregon Trail. As our conversation continues, Tabor's comments focus on characteristics of rural Americans, sense of community, "strong pioneer spirit," and how the community has not changed—and how it has. The two statements concerning change initially appear paradoxical; as the conversation progresses, however, the differences become clear.

Characteristics of rural people, according to Tabor, coalesce around community, neighbors, and quality of life. Tabor states:

> Everyone knows everyone. Everyone knows about everyone. The idea of everyone knowing about everyone's personal life was troubling for me during my early adult years. I moved away for a good number of years, then moved back. I left because I needed to feel anonymous. I did not think I would miss it [everyone knowing everyone]. I moved back because I missed knowing everyone and the feeling of being known by everyone.

He pauses and continues, "As a kid, I felt part of the community. I still feel that way."

The people of Baker County have not changed. The feeling of belonging and knowing your neighbors remains common in the lives of the local people. These feelings are prevalent in Tabor's interaction with people entering his store. A customer stops by to retrieve a piece of jewelry that had been in need of a small repair. When the person asks what the charge is for the service, Tabor waves him away. Another lady enters and says that her grandfather clock needs a house call. Tabor tells her that he will be out next week. She then says, "I will fix dinner for you and your family." Tabor smiles and says, "We will set a date."

Tabor summarizes the importance of character among the people, saying, "Sometimes it is not about growing population, but more about growing senses [mindsets]." He believes sense of community appears to be an extension of people caring for neighbors, value of community, and strength and dedication to their basic values. Tabor continues:

> We keep doing quality projects in Baker City and help develop opportunities. Arts have never been stronger. Rural people have a strong feeling about their community. They are more engaged and feel a bigger part of what it takes to make a community.

While he believes these values are prevalent among the rural populace, people living in large areas, such as cities, could also possess a strong feeling about their community. Tabor believes, however, that community building is a more natural phenomenon in rural areas than in cities but admits it could be effectively accomplished in cities and other larger communities.

Over the years, the people of Baker City have remained resilient, community focused, and friendly. He believes these characteristics lead to a strong sense of community.

Tabor speaks eloquently of his late father and the feelings his father had about roots and sense of community. "My father believed a rural upbringing may make it easier to find roots and sense of community, but it is not a requirement, just easier. My father knew a lot people who grew up in the city that had both [roots and sense of community]."

The effects of external forces on the way of life, industry, and local economy define change in Baker County. One of the changes is a reduction of young people living in Baker City. Tabor states:

> Baker County has changed a lot in the last ten to fifteen years. The natural-resource industry is going away. We used to have fifteen milling lumberyards, saw mills, and stud mills. Now we do not have any. One of the

results in loss of industry is a shift in the age of the population. The schools are shrinking. We are becoming a retirement community. The spotted owl led to the stop of lumbering. It is difficult for ranchers and farmers to continue because of the irrigation restraints. There used to be thirty dairies; now we have none.

Even though ranchers and farmers must continually change, agriculture remains a huge part of Baker County's economy.

Tabor provides several examples of how environmental issues have led to both loss of industries and negative effects on the economy. He says, "We need to seek a balance between industry and environment. We are unable to save everything without losing everything."

His statements encapsulate a strong sense of need and potential for environmental protection and preservation of industry and farming.

As Tabor pauses, I hear an unusual sound toward the back of the store. A quick glance over my shoulder paints a picture of a well-dressed lady leaning back, holding onto a five-foot-long blue leash that is attached to a seventy-five-pound red Golden Retriever who is pulling and churning. I suggest that she drop the leash, which she does. Almost immediately Mo is lying on the floor beside my chair, where she remains for the next thirty minutes.

Unbothered, Tabor smiles and says, "Even through all the external forces of change, *people* have remained unchanged. The people's strength to remain unchanged in character has led to a strong sense of community and show of 'pioneer spirit.'"

The fabric of the people of Baker City is tough. Toughness among people is identified as a characteristic of "pioneer spirit."

Tabor continues by conveying a positive mindset about environmental issues and the economy. His concludes, "This part of the world has a lot of 'pioneer spirit.' It has never been easy to make a living in Eastern Oregon. We take great pride in making a living the hard way. We must move on."

His attitude exemplifies the attitude of people with "pioneer spirit"; he views issues as bumps in the road, not deterrents. As Tabor talks, it becomes clear that in addition to toughness, "pioneer spirit" consists of adventuress, hard work, desire to explore, and fortitude to succeed, build a better community, and not be easily dissuaded. His final statement—"People of Baker City have always possessed 'pioneer spirit' "—depicts his pride and love of hometown that pulled him back to Baker City. His words lead me to conclude that Tabor believes "pioneer spirit" has been passed from generation to generation, starting with the ancestors who came on the Oregon Trail to this picturesque setting. His statements reflect the fact that his dad possessed a "pioneer spirit" that he clearly shared with his son.

As Mo and I walk down Main Street, my thoughts are that Tabor belongs in Baker City. He is deeply rooted in Baker City and Baker County. Baker City is fortunate that Tabor returned to his hometown, and Tabor is fortunate to have returned to his hometown.

After a brief visit to the museum and some dinner, Mo and I spend the evening in "The Park," watching and talking to the artists as they prepare for the upcoming festival. They are willing to chat with a couple of strangers; in fact, many initiate the conversation, thanks to Mo. Love my dawg.

"The Park" and the people are like magnets attracting each other. Some of the people are local residents, but it is amazing how many people are visitors like Mo and me. A common thread among all is their friendliness. What a great amenity this place I call "The Park."

The next morning, I am having breakfast at the Country Cottage Café when a man comes to my table and asks, "Are you the person doing research on Baker City?" When I respond in the affirmative, he states that he grew up here and would be willing to talk with me. He joins me for an hour of interesting stories about Baker City. News travels fast in a small town. I am really excited because I got an interview without Mo's help. Things are really looking up! Luck supersedes skill, especially for me.

Al starts by telling me he is eighty years young and then laughs at my facial expression, which reflects my shock, as he looks much younger. He is a third-generation resident of Baker City. His father's parents arrived in 1870 and his mother's parents in 1874. They were true Oregon Trail settlers. Al describes the conditions of his youth as "very poor." He grew up during the Depression of the 1930s and World War II.

"My father worked with *his* father [Al's grandfather] as a scavenger [picking up trash on Main Street]," Al says. "We lived on the edge of town. We had cows and chickens on our lot. Our main pastime was to visit other people." He pauses with a smile before continuing, "When I was four years old, the exciting thing was to drive up to the depot and watch the trains come in."

Al went to the University of Oregon on the GI Bill and graduated in 1957. In 1958 he began his lifelong banking career in Baker City, where he worked his entire career, except for the eighteen years he spent in Ontario,

Oregon: a town about seventy miles southeast on Interstate 84 just inside the state line. He states, "My company asked me to transfer."

He describes Baker City through the eyes of a sixty-year resident and temporary member of the chamber of commerce:

> The quality of Baker City life is great, with four distinct seasons. The summer high is historically around eighty degrees and a winter low around thirty-five degrees. Everyone knows everyone. Every merchant and tradesman is very trustworthy. The people are extremely friendly. We help each other.

Al pauses and adds, "We have the best-tasting water." I respond with wholehearted agreement.

Al takes a moment to reflect before making a very important statement that adds credence to his comments about Baker City being an inviting tourist destination:

> Motorcycle groups or clubs have a rally in Baker City about every year. Motorcycle riders like the area for riding. They say that the citizens of Baker City make them feel welcome. Many other groups and individuals come to Baker City on vacation. Our over-seventy-years-old beautiful eighteen-hole golf course attracts golfers.

As Al talks about tourism, I mentally list the attributes that brought me back to Baker City. At the top of the list are the beautiful setting, friendly people, clean and healthy environment, and aesthetically inviting downtown.

I snap back to reality to hear Al talk with pride about Baker City's medical services. "We have very good medical amenities; we have helicopter medical service to Bend, Oregon and Boise, Idaho for serious health issues. We also have very good medical services and doctors in Baker City."

Like many small towns, they could use a couple more doctors. The population is becoming older, Al regretfully adds. This issue, he believes, can be attributed to the increasing number of retirees moving to Baker City for the quality of life. Al embellishes his thoughts:

> There are a lot of people moving to Baker City to retire. Additionally, many people who moved away to work have come back to retire. An issue that helps to alleviate the aging population is [that] some young couples move here to raise their children.

Our discussion then turns to population loss. Baker City, like the experience of several rural towns, has their young graduates move away to seek employment. Al repeats what I have heard all too often: "It is difficult for young people to find work that pays well enough."

The loss of local industries, particularly lumber, has been a key factor in job loss for young adults. Six sawmills have closed. Tabor also spoke to the loss of industry, especially lumber. The bright side is that farming has remained healthy, with several farms being operated by fourth- and fifth-generation families.

Downtown Baker City remains a showplace. Main Street is healthy, with many flourishing businesses. Al pays homage to the forefathers of Baker City, saying, "Early 1900s lumber owners made big money. They built some very good buildings downtown and made Main Street wide so lumbering-industry horse-drawn wagons could turn around." Those same buildings and a beautiful Main Street remain in good repair and are used for today's businesses. Al states with pride, "The proximity of downtown to the park, museum, and several restaurants creates an enjoyable environment for residents, as well as tourists." Al's comments make me proud of my similar assessment of Baker City's attractions. I now feel that I am an expert on tourism.

The population of Baker City has remained approximately 10,000 for several decades, even though many people have moved away while others became new residents. The number increased to around 12,000 following World War II, but then declined to around 10,000 when the war returnees sought employment. Important elements in reducing the average resident age are non-retirees returning to a notable education system that encourages an influx of families with children.

I thank Al for his time and sharing of knowledge and experiences about Baker City and the surrounding community. As he starts to walk toward the door, he pauses and says that he enjoyed telling me the story. Then he states, "I like to stop people on the street and ask them where they are from and why they came to Baker City."

As I scurry toward the museum for my appointment with John, I think, *Al not only loves Baker City, he takes great pleasure when people enjoy his town.* Al is a true ambassador for Baker City.

I arrive at the museum a little tardy, a behavior that is well grounded in my high school experience of getting to class. John, who is a volunteer at the museum, and a couple other volunteer colleagues are waiting in the hallway;

again, like my teachers. After some joking and helpful comments, John and I are off for a tour and conversation. He proudly states that he is eighty-one years young. I am amazed that John, as Al, looks so young. It must be the water.

John begins with a brief synopsis of his past. His mother, who was from Brainerd, Minnesota, and his father, who was from Chicago, Illinois, met in Bend, Oregon. They moved to Baker from Bend in 1941, when John was thirteen years old. John continues by proudly stating that he soloed an aircraft in 1945 when he was sixteen years old. I think, *What a coincidence that Dick and John soloed in the same year, and only one year separates their age.*

John continues, "I did not start flying again until 1960. I have flown ever since. I own a 1964 Skyhawk [aircraft]."

John assumes the dual role of historian and guide as we tour the magnificent building. He is so articulate on each subject that intertwining the roles of historian and guide are natural. As we begin our tour, John tells me that he graduated from college in 1951 as a pharmacist and was commissioned into the medical corps.

Tabor and Al's stories provide a personal account of their lives in Baker City and an insightful perspective of the town, community, and people of today. John, as a museum volunteer, provides a historical perspective, which complements Tabor and Al's narratives.

John begins, "Baker City and surrounding area started in 1861, when there was a gold strike about six miles from the current town. In 1864, the town was plotted, as you see it today." The gold strike and success of ensuing prospectors resulted in mining becoming the largest and oldest industry in the Baker City area. It was only a matter of time until improved transportation created an influx of people, followed by additional industries.

Railroads soon joined the history of Baker City. John continues his account of Baker City's early days:

> Soon after the town settled, it became incorporated in 1874. A branch of a railroad company, which today is named Union Pacific, came in 1884. Most of the towns during this era were located along the railroad. The railroad became so prevalent that by the mid-1880s, it replaced the Oregon Trail as the main influence for development of towns.

Presence of railroads served as more than transportation for people; it acted as a stimulus for industries such as lumber to flourish and enhance development of towns along their route.

That Baker County was situated in the midst of natural forests provided an excess of timber. An industry was born in the area, as lumberjacks came and sawmills were constructed. The forests and presence of railroads made lumbering a natural industry. John states:

> Lumbering was a large industry for several years. However, with the discovery of endangered species in the surrounding forests, lumbering has ceased to be a viable industry. Much of the construction downtown, especially construction of buildings and sidewalks, occurred during the years when lumbering was a major industry in the local area. Around town, many of the sidewalks and buildings have Baker City etched in them, which tells us they were built prior to 1911.

John switches from historian to guide as we approach a room with displays and pictures adorning the walls. One wall depicts pictures of each Baker City High School graduating class. Among the collection is a portrait with the likeness of my guide and historian, as well as ones of both Al and Tabor.

The majestic building and museum amazes me. It is especially intriguing for a town with a population of 10,000. It clearly makes a statement about the culture, preservation of history, and community spirit. I become enthralled with the structure, displays, and history of the building.

As he shows me the area, John explains, "The museum was originally an indoor pool, heated by natural hot water, where, long ago, people basked in the naturally heated pool."

John guides me left toward the stairs that ascend to the second floor. As we climb, he briefly returns to historian mode by telling me:

> Cattle are and have been a large industry for years. We grow good alfalfa. Wheat is a smaller crop for farmers. Our minimal rainfall is a detriment to farming, especially growing crops. Considering that snow contributes to Baker City's minimal [and] annual twelve inches of moisture, irrigation is required for crop production.

Half-way through the climb, I pause for another view of the inspiring first floor. The impressive view does not prepare for what lies ahead. Two steps further up the stairs present an intriguing view that adds to the wonderment of the museum. The museum's second floor is a ballroom! The ballroom, constructed years ago, is a model as a current setting. John shakes his head in amusement and says that my reaction is common among visitors. I stand in wonderment of the uniquely detailed ballroom. It seems that every element is present and in its appropriate location. I cannot pull my mind away from the accomplishments of this small town, the power of its community and commitment.

After spending time viewing the intricacies of the ballroom and its many artifacts, we walk down to the main floor. As we head toward the museum entrance, John takes the time to discuss Baker City's growth and population. He tells me:

> According to Rand McNally, Baker City, which had an 1890-1895 population of 7,000 to 7,500, was the third-largest city in Oregon, behind Portland and Astoria. Astoria had a large fishing business. Today, Baker City and Astoria each have similar populations, as they have for the last 100 years. An interesting note is [that] La Grande and Pendleton—towns located in proximity to Baker City and also on Interstate 84 in Eastern Oregon—have grown to become slightly larger in population. In 1941, Baker City was the largest of these three towns. After World War II, while other towns were expanding, Baker appeared to not be interested in growing. The [local] bankers kept the money tight.

As a result, the town did not grow during the post-World War II development era. "No one can explain why Baker City's population is not 20,000," John concludes.

Just as we reach the entryway, John tells me that the museum and many other area improvements, such as the Interpretive Center, were made possible by a $20 million gift that Leo Adler left the city. I personally think that Mr. Alder's gift has been well spent.

I thank John for his time and historical perspective. He, in turn, compliments me on my interest and effort to write a factual story about rural America. His last comment is more meaningful than I can explain: "I needed a boost."

John, the dedicated eighty-one-years-young volunteer, scurries off to a meeting. I marvel at his energy, knowledge, and dedication. The museum tour was worthy time spent. Listening and learning from John added another dimension to my life and my own story.

Mo and I make one last trip through downtown Baker City via Main Street to soak in the beauty and historic decorum one more time. I marvel at the community spirit and dedication of the people. As we leave Baker City, I ponder the interesting topic that Tabor, Al, and John all spoke of: Baker City's population. Perhaps the city planners of years past could foresee the reality of today—a beautiful, friendly, thriving town. Maybe they anticipated that limited population growth would achieve their goal and made the tough decisions to continue on the path of limited growth.

I see a beautiful picture of Baker City in my rearview mirror. Thank you, city planners from the 1860s to the 2000s, for preserving the history, beauty, and culture of friendly, welcoming people.

Soon after entering Interstate 84, a large sign appears stating "The Oregon Trail Interpretive Center Exit 302." Our 275-mile trip is interrupted by a side trip up the mountainside to the Oregon Trail Interpretive Center. As promised by John and his colleagues, the ruts from the passage of the Oregon Tail wagons are still visible. The sight of the trail remnants alone is worth the time and drive.

As we drive back down the mountainside to rejoin Intestate 84 and continue our trip northwest, I immerse myself in the scenery. The initial 123-mile leg of our scenic trip passes through the cities of La Grande, Pendleton, and Hermiston, Oregon. Our route, bracketed by mountains, takes us first to La Grande, a town named for a French explorer's description of its beauty. We then traverse the Cascade Mountains on our route to partner with the Columbia River for our westward journey. The majestic river marks the travel of the Lewis and Clark expedition over 200 years ago. I marvel at the river and the basin through which it flows, speculating how the scene has changed during 200 years of civilization. I reflect on the stories I know of Lewis and Clark's expedition and wonder what went through their minds as they passed this very point. I try to imagine the landscape without cars, trucks, trains, and power lines. I stop and pause, with Mo standing beside me. My thoughts block the sounds. I have great gratitude for Lewis, Clark, and their men for their exploration. I wonder. I imagine.

We soon turn north on US Highway 97 toward Goldendale. After a few miles, we enter the Yakima Nation. The Satus Creek welcomes and guides us for several miles. It is a quiet, friendly travel companion. The forest and landscape provide silent, peaceful moments. We go miles without seeing another person or car. The time passes quickly—too quickly—as we all-too-soon pass the town of Toppenish and join Interstate 82 northwest toward the towns of Yakima and Ellensburg.

I realize that the sight-seeing and pauses along the routes have consumed travel time. Seattle is no longer a possible destination for today. A quick check reveals that Ellensburg KOA will be our home for the night. The good news is that Ellensburg is a cowboy town, which may result in a conversation about riding, roping, and cattle.

We join IS 82 for the final sixty miles of our day's adventure. Ellensburg KOA is both comfortably and quietly situated in a valley between the interstate and Yakima River. Laundry, a nature walk, and a restful night prepare us for several days of visiting family in Seattle. I am excited; Mo is always geared for excitement.

We begin our day scouring several restaurants for a cowboy interview. No luck. They have had breakfast and are back on the ranch. I am very disappointed.

Interstate 82 Northwest provides us with another day of mountains and forests to guide us toward our destination. The peaceful drive provides an atmosphere for reflection about the people we have met, the stories we have heard, and the inviting towns and scenery along our travels. The stories and towns do more than remind me of rural America: They reinvigorate memories of my youth. I am reminded of a time when family members lived close and life revolved around community. I am reacquainted with rural America. Each town is different but has common threads. One commonality is loss of population.

Reaching the Summit of Snoqualmie Pass and descending toward the Seattle Metro area brings excitement of seeing family: my son, Greg; my daughter-in-law, Lynn; and my grandchildren, Hannah and Luke.

Snoqualmie Pass in my review mirror signals that our westward journey has ended, and a new expedition is beginning. Please join Mo and I as we visit family and journey eastward along US Highway 2, the northern-most east-and-west route in the United States.

CHAPTER 6

The Great Northwest and Family Time

Nature's beauty abounds with trees, waterfalls, and rough ledges as the mountainside highlights our descent of the western slope of the Snoqualmie Pass. At the base of the slope, we turn onto Washington 516 West. I immediately notice that Highway 516 is void of logging trucks. They have been replaced by a mass of automobiles, SUVs, a few pickup trucks, and traffic lights. The trees that once dotted small towns like Maple Valley (where twenty years ago I umpired high school baseball) are no longer visible. Instead I am amidst shopping areas, housing developments, and traffic signals. My thoughts of confusion become a feeling of being lost. A quick check of my Garmin tells me to continue westward, but my senses for an orientation-stop speak louder. The Western Washington I knew twenty years ago exists now only in my mind.

The area of present-day Kent was first settled in 1860, along the White River and Titusville. The fertile valley became so well known for the production of hops that it was renamed in 1889 for the hops-producing area of Kent County, England. Kent was incorporated in 1890 with a population of 763: the approximate number of students at Meridian Junior High School where I taught a century later. My family and I had the good fortune to live in the beautiful setting and mild climate of the Kent area 100 years following its incorporation. The infamous, continuous rain only occurs during late fall and winter. The other months are beautiful. The lush vegetation remains twelve months a year . . . at least in my mind.

Growth of the area continued beyond the first 100 years to include the twenty years since I moved from the area. For example, the beautiful natural scenery of the ten-kilometer route around the Green River where I once ran almost weekly is now laden with concrete. The rice-field setting at the entrance of our old housing development has been consumed by houses. Now you know why I need a pause in travel to reset my internal GPS, review the map, and gain the assistance of a sleeping Mo. The final fifteen miles of the drive may well be filled with sad emotions.

We drive into a large strip mall to establish our location and determine our route to Fairwood. Finding a parking place large enough for a truck and camper is no small feat. Using four parking spots does not make me popular with arriving shoppers. I finally find a gracious shopper and ask, "Where is Fairwood? Where is Black Diamond?" She confirms what the map has been telling me: "Go west on 516."

Feeling skepticism with confusion in tow, Mo and I get back on the highway and travel west. Petting an unbothered Mo reassures me that with the help of Garmin, a map, and concentration, we will find Fairwood: the town I lived in twenty years ago. I am confident that we will reach our destination.

As usual in city traffic, Mo transitions to the full-awake-and-antsy mode. She is standing on the floor of the backseat of the truck. Her head is on a swivel, except when she pauses to give me a puzzled look. City driving is not Mo's favorite sport. She dislikes stopping and vehicles cutting in front of us. I am not sure where she gets this attitude.

Mo

I really dislike being asked to assist the driver in city traffic. I checked the book called *101 Duties of a Golden*; co-pilot, co-driver, or co-*anything* is not on the list. No way am I going to "take a backseat" (non-figuratively speaking, of course). I ride in the backseat because I *want* to ride in the backseat. The fact is, we are in the city, and it is going to take teamwork to get through it. So I will be a good team player, but I am not a co-anything; I am a full-fledged troubleshooter.

My definition of "city" is the place where there are a lot of cars without dents and pickup trucks with their tailgates up. Last but not least is the baffling concept of red, yellow, and green lights. A yellow light means "go faster and look ashamed." When the light turns red, vehicles stop, and drivers fidget and tap on their steering wheels. The green light is when things turn ugly. Cars accelerate faster than a Golden Retriever launching for the food dish. The exciting part is horns blasting, drivers waving with one finger, and yelling at other drivers through closed windows. It is sort of like me barking at Randy through the front window of our house when he forgets to take me with him in the truck; he never hears me. Humans are a truly interesting species!

The next thing I notice is that we are going the wrong direction. Almost every car is traveling to where we have been. They are zooming by at the speed of heat, rushing to something really cool. Now I wonder what we missed. I nudge Randy to turn around so we can go with the crowd and check. As usual, he pays no attention and keeps going to the place from which most people are trying to escape. Duh! He sometimes is why life is so boring. I wish humans, at least mine, had some Golden Retriever DNA. Any Golden knows life is about having fun, not getting somewhere.

The boring drive continues until we trade traffic for houses and kids playing in the street. Well, this looks more promising. I even see a lake—not a big lake like where we live, but big enough to go swimming.

Finally, we stop in front of a beautiful house. I immediately recognize Greg, Lynn, Hannah, and Luke: Randy's son and family. After initial hugs, the attention turns to petting, foot-to-hand shakes, and of course, a couple of licks.

When we enter the house, I go first, as usual, and I receive an unexpected surprise. Standing in the doorway is one of my cousins: another Golden. Licking and smelling are in order. I determine we are related, but not real close. Even though Gus is a blonde Golden, we have the same values and beliefs about having fun. This is going to be a great visit! Gus and I will make our humans proud. I hope nothing gets broken!

Soon after we arrive, Lynn, Luke, Hannah, and Hannah's friend take Randy and me for a walk through the woods. Of course, Gus, the Golden, and his friend (a Chesapeake Retriever) go with us. There are a lot of good smells but no squirrels: a disappointment. After the trek through the woods, we walk on a real street until we come to a house. Much to my surprise, there is a lake behind the house. My best pleading look at Randy works. The leash comes off, and I am running to the shore. Before jumping into the lake, I decide to run down the shoreline until I hear, "Mo, come." Then I run the other way until I hear, "Mo, come." Now I know the boundaries. It is always good to do a boundary check. It saves a lot of grief and time sitting beside my human.

After the boundary check, I leap into the water, which is much colder than I expect. I swim a bit and then look back toward the shore. To my surprise, Gus and his friend, the Chesapeake, are staring at me with quizzical looks. I realize that my lake-training at home has prepared me for such activities. Encouragement! They need encouragement. Shaking water on them does the trick. I jump back into the water and swim out to check the dock. My two friends follow into the lake. The fun is on!

After about twenty minutes in and out of the water, the humans decide we should go. I run over to our hostess to show her my appreciation by shaking with all my strength. She accepts my act of gratitude by letting out a scream of joy. I then give her a big Golden hug. She again expresses her appreciation, this time by pushing. Of course, as she pushes, I push back. The greater the push, the better the hug. Lynn thanks our hostess. Everyone agrees that we have experienced all the fun we can have, so off we go. I wonder when she will invite us back. It will be soon, I am sure. Until then, I am off searching for more fun experiences, bringing joy to everyone, and making my human proud.

Randy

Time passes quickly, and it is time to continue our trip through rural America. The last six days have been filled with fun, relaxation, and most of all, love. Hannah and I maintain our tradition of playing checkers. Nothing has changed; she wins at least 75% of the games, but never gloats. Luke and I play basketball and baseball. When Luke scores a point in basketball, he makes sure I know. I kind of know where that trait comes from. Lynn and I walk or hike with the kids and dawgs, and she helps me develop my culinary skills. I am thankful for her patience. Greg and I, as always, discuss baseball and fishing, as we have for over forty years. Greg started playing baseball and fishing before the age of three; baseball and fishing are in our blood.

We see many local sights. Luke sticks with his convictions and has six pork ribs at a restaurant in Black Diamond. He insists (above all objections) that he needs six ribs for dinner. You had to be there to understand the story, but I will carry that memory forever.

Good-byes are tough, but we get through them and are on the road, heading east. I decide to travel US Highway 2 across the north of the country to at least North Dakota. Our drive in Washington takes us through picturesque apple country and the cities of Leavenworth, Cashmere, and Wenatchee on our route to Spokane. I attempt to stop and interview some apple growers, but their market stands are too busy for me to interrupt: an unavoidable decision that I regret.

As we approach Spokane, I decide to continue our journey through town to the east side so tomorrow morning's drive will not be embedded with rush hour traffic. The quality of the campground made the effort worthwhile. I congratulate myself on a great decision.

The next morning, we are ready and excited to continue our trip. A short drive on a street with no traffic takes us to a T-stop for Highway 2. Eastbound traffic is sparse, while westbound is stop and go, bumper to bumper. The wait for an opportunity to cross westbound traffic to drive east provides time for me to think about our morning drive. I realize our easterly route will be about 40 miles shorter and almost two hours quicker with no traffic.

I made a great decision last night. Suddenly reality enters the mental picture. The drive east will force us to miss 80 miles of Highway 2. My immediate thought is go east, go east! My second thought is we are going west.

Mo

Humans, humans, humans! We are in the country—no stoplights, few cars and trucks—and all we need to do is head toward the sun. Do we? No. We drive *away* from the sun and surround ourselves with fast-moving vehicles on all sides. Now I need to stand up and help my human negotiate the traffic. My head is on a constant swivel. Good! We are getting off the road that has many fast-moving vehicles.

Just ahead a light turns red. Brakes screech, and people start tapping their steering wheels. The light turns green, and everyone is off at the speed of heat. Horns are blowing, and cars are swerving from one side of the road to the other. It looks like a bunch of squirrels trying to cross a road in front of an oncoming car, unsure of their and the car's intended direction. Horns blowing, cars swerving, and the red light thing goes on and on, way into morning naptime.

Finally, it is over. I lie down on the floor and summarize the morning's displeasures with one last groan. I hope you get the meaning, Randy.

CHAPTER 7

Idaho Panhandle

After miles of driving north out of Spokane and passing many towns with no restaurants, we finally drive into Newport, Washington: a town nestled on the Washington-Idaho state line. We—or rather *I*, as Mo is still resting up for something—check every street and neighborhood. Finally, I come upon two people walking toward a building that appears to be a school. The male has a whistle around his neck, and the female has some books. Logical conclusion: They are teachers. It makes sense; I was once a teacher, and they are walking at the same relaxed gait I used to have during summer school.

They soon inform me they work at the hospital. I am too hungry to be embarrassed, so I pose the breakfast question. They give me three restaurant names, then the male looks at me and says, "The Mangy Moose is my favorite. I always go with the favorite."

Mo and I head for the Mangy Moose.

Mo

Hard to believe my human is talking education to a couple of medical professionals. Anyone, including most dawgs, recognizes a medical insignia on a shirt. Duh! It is similar to the one my veterinarian wears. I nudge my human with my nose, but he does not get it. I save the day by climbing into the front seat so the educators, who are medical professionals, can pet me. They say nice things to me and look at my human with wonderment.

Randy

My driving instructions include a caution to drive slowly because the Mangy Moose is not very visible; I thank them, and we are off. We soon pass the state line and discover that Oldtown, population of about 200, is sandwiched between the Washington-Idaho state line and Pend Oreille River. The Mangy Moose is about one mile east of Oldtown.

Per the directions, after what appears to be a drive of about a mile, we have either not seen the Mangy Moose or have passed it—probably the latter. Another mile of traveling with no Mangy Moose in sight, and I accept the challenge to find a side road for a turn-around in a mountainous area: not an easy feat with a twenty-four-foot trailer following every move of the truck. I realize that the maneuver termed "middle-of-the-road turn-around" is 25% skill and 75% luck.

Skill and luck prevail, and we make it to the Mangy Moose, which lies in the heart of the tourist area near the Washington-Idaho state line and Pend Oreille River. Mo is only able to run around the parking lot and smell, so she insists on a bacon-bit treat before I venture into the Mangy Moose alone.

My first interview on the trip east is with Lenore (pronounced "Lenora"), the owner of the Mangy Moose Restaurant and campground. Lenore came to the Oldtown area in October 1999 with seven dogs and five cats. Her husband preceded her in August of the same year. She states, "I have lived several places while growing up: Florida, Ohio, Newport, Washington, and other places. My mother lives in Newport. I went to tenth grade there, then back to Ohio."

She continues, stating that she has a lot of relatives in New York, where they gathered every year during her childhood for Thanksgiving. Lenore has a strong relationship with her family, even though they are separated by so many miles.

The Mangy Moose by itself has quite a history, not to mention the history of US Highway 2 from Newport, east to the Priest River. Lenore says:

> During the 1920s, bootleggers would run on a dirt road from Priest River, about five miles east of the Mangy Moose, to Newport. In the 1940s, the building which houses the Mangy Moose today was constructed as a bar and a brothel. Oldtown incorporated the area where the building sits so it could obtain a liquor license. Today, the property between town and the Mangy Moose is not incorporated as part of the Oldtown, even though the Mangy Moose remains part of the town.

Lenore emphatically states that the Mangy Moose does not sell liquor today; instead, it is a family restaurant that feeds a lot of loggers.

Lenore continues her story by discussing how local industry affects her business:

> When I opened the Mangy Moose, logging was a big industry. Two years ago the mills started shutting down. There used to be fifty logging trucks going up and down the road every day. Now maybe we have two [trucks a day]. Our business is down 60% from three years ago. Malloy Veneer had a plant that recently closed. The area, even though Aerocet and Aerocell have plants that make airplane parts, has always been economically

depressed. There is a lot of unemployment. It has always been hard for people to make a living. I heard Arctic Cat [a snow-mobile manufacturer] is putting in a plant.

Most of the employment opportunities require traveling. Some people commute to Spokane or Coeur d'Alene, Idaho to work. Each town is about fifty miles south of Newport.

The area (including Priest River, Pend Oreille River, and Lake Pend Oreille) supports a large tourist industry. In fact, most of the people I meet during breakfast are vacationing on the Pend Oreille River or Lake Pend Oreille. That tourism is a big boost for the Mangy Moose. Lenore says, "We make most of our money between Memorial Day and Labor Day. A lot of 'snowbirds' who live in Arizona and California spend their summers in the area. Many people also come from Spokane to Priest Lake as tourists."

The local community residents are strong supporters of local businesses. "There is great community spirit. The community helped keep my business surviving during my husband's illness," Lenore claims. She explains that the people of the town assisted her in many ways to keep the restaurant operational not only during the illness but also during another untimely event. The unfortunate event, which occurred two days prior to Labor Day, involved an old truck and the Mangy Moose front wall. She tells about the accident:

> A 1930-something truck was driven through the front wall. The truck had been converted from a manual transmission to an automatic that required the driver to count slots when shifting gears. There was a miscount while shifting gears. The truck, to the amazement of the driver and restaurant customers, advanced *forward* as opposed to the intended *backwards*. The Mangy Moose front wall became the brakes.

Even with the untimely accident, which adversely affected her holiday business, Lenore loves her community and its people. Her final comments tell the whole story: "I love to live in a small town. You get to know everyone. Everyone helps each other." She pauses, smiles, and states, "I inherit a lot of pets because everyone knows I will take care of them. This is a fun place to live. I like living in a small town. I do not miss the traffic."

I thank Lenore and tell her that I have spent over an hour eating an omelet while talking with her. I emphatically state, "There is so much food I cannot finish. The food is great; I just cannot eat it all." Lenore smiles and says that the Mangy Moose is a logger's restaurant; the servings are big.

She then jumps up. "Wait here," she says. "I am going to get a homemade dog bone and go meet Mo." Needless to say this turns out to be an exciting event.

I thank Lenore for an interesting story and a very different insight into rural America. I add, "I really appreciate you taking time from a busy schedule and the special treat for Mo." Lenore is truly a rural American.

Mo

On our way to breakfast, I see a picture of a moose. It seems rather obvious that it might be the Mangy Moose. We drive right past the restaurant, which means another one of those exciting turn-arounds. Oh well, we make it. The parking lot has some cool smells. But the big deal is that Lenore brings me a homemade dog bone and the accompanying irresistible pet. She is a real dawg person! You talk about good chow. I will go back to the Mangy Moose anytime. This is going to be a great day!

Randy

With the Mangy Moose and good memories in our rearview mirror, we follow the Pend Oreille River east-northeast. A one-hour drive takes us to Sandpoint, which I *assume* is a small town. The first hint that I am wrong is a traffic jam; each of the several traffic lights takes three cycles to get to the next three-cycle traffic light. The second clue is masses of people walking along the sidewalk carrying shopping bags and cups of Starbucks coffee. Please do not get me wrong: I love Starbucks. But it is not normally a small-town amenity. The final conclusive clue is Mo when she wakes from her morning nap to offer her version of assistance for the city driving.

Patience and perseverance leads us to the north edge of Sandpoint and open road. My mind is occupied with traveling north on US Highway 2. A roadside sign informs me that Bonners Ferry is about a thirty-minute drive. Bonners Ferry becomes the goal for our next stop.

Our drive on the highway provides the view of a small town in a pristine setting. The attendant at a convenience store suggests that I interview Mr. Pace, a past mayor and realtor. As I depart the gas station and once again view the town from the higher vantage point, I marvel at its beauty and realize how it attracts residents.

Edwin Bonner, a merchant from Walla Walla, Washington, established Bonners Ferry in 1864 when he opened a ferry business to cross the Kootenai River. The ferry served to accommodate the surge of prospectors heading for the gold rush in the east Kootenay Rockies of British Columbia. As the mines flourished in the 1880s, the area of Edwin Bonner's ferry became a supply point for the miners. In 1893, Bonners Ferry (now located in Boundary County) was established as a town on the south bank of the Kootenai River. Bonners Ferry, like many other rural America towns, been has located in more than one county during its history. County boundary changes resulted in Bonners Ferry originally being part of Kootenai County, then Bonner County, and now Boundary County. Today, the town is home to an approximately 2,500 people.

The mountainous, forest-covered terrain of Boundary County ranges in elevation from 1,745 to 7,357 feet above sea level. Its lakes and rivers are an invitation for fishing and other water sports. The forests are an invitation to hunters. Nature provides a lovely setting for the county's over-10,000 residents. The 1,269-square-mile area is inviting to development, as can be realized by the 9% growth from 2000 to 2012. Bonners Ferry experienced a 14% growth during the 1990s and a negative 1.7% growth from 2000 to 2013. The decline in growth may be related to an increase of unemployment from about 6% in 2000 to over 14% in 2010. The 2014 rate, however, decreased to approximately 5%.

Our slow walk down Main Street is halted numerous times by people stopping to pet Mo and talk with me—in that order. I have moved up on the respect chain, however, as people actually greet and talk with me about something other than Mo.

As we continue our walk, I cannot erase the friendliness of the people and picturesque view of Main Street ending at the Kootenai River and scenic mountain peak. Only a sturdy chain-link fence stands between cars and the river. The Kootenai is a major contributor to the Columbia River.

I have been in Bonners Ferry less than thirty minutes, and I am in love with the town and its people. I see our destination. Upon entering the real estate office, Mo takes over and saves the day.

Mo

It is nice to enter an office that appears friendly from our first step inside the door. I feel important, so I act important. The friendly receptionist tells Randy that Mr. Pace is out of town for several days. I sense the anxiety in my human. The receptionist responds by calling an associate, who states he does not have time for an interview. It is time for the big, brown, sorrowful eye look.

I abandon the eye thing and walk over and sit in front of an associate named Joe. He, of course, pets irresistible me. I raise my right front paw (always put your best foot forward!) for a hand-foot shake. Joe shakes my foot and responds to Randy, "I will give you twenty minutes."

I have to do better; twenty minutes is not enough time. So I give Joe my best "heel position" walk, right by his left leg. Am I cool or what?

He sits behind his desk. I lie down between his and Randy's chairs and give Joe "the look." He calls Tanja (pronounced "Tonya"), his associate, and says, "Come to my office. This going to be fun!"

I move over and lie by Tanja's chair. Now that the public relations stuff is complete, I will let Randy have the pen back. I am so cool.

Randy

The story of Bonners Ferry is told through the eyes of two people who have different backgrounds. Their dissimilar experiences merely allow them to tell a similar story from different points of view.

Joe grew up in San Francisco, and Tanja is a lifelong resident of Bonners Ferry. Joe left San Francisco in 1970 when he was twenty years old. "I decided that I did not want to live in the city. I was off to Oregon." He summarizes his living locations: "The first twenty years were in California, the next forty years were in Oregon and Idaho, [including] twenty years in Bonners Ferry." The last statement carries pride: "I moved to Bonners Ferry and lived for six-and-one-half years during the 1980s." He then moved back to Oregon, only to return to Bonners Ferry, where he has lived for the past fourteen years. I enjoy listening to Joe's pride when he speaks of Bonners Ferry.

Tanja grew up and attended school in Bonners Ferry. She surpasses Joe's pride, which I would have thought was impossible. She says, "It was great growing up in Bonners Ferry. Everyone knew everyone. I worked in a gas station and grocery store." Then she speaks of the important things. "We cruised Main Street [and] spent summers at Herman Lake and Dawson Lake. Pretty much everyone was in sports." She describes school as "fun" and expresses pride in her achievements as a student.

The spirit of community, like many small towns, is healthy. Bonners Ferry is a town where people help each other. Tanja and Joe agree that the people of Bonners Ferry embrace and help each other in times of tragedy. Tanja relates this phenomenon as happening throughout her life, while Joe discusses it in the context of one very special occurrence: While he and his wife were living in Oregon, his wife became ill. "People from Bonners Ferry came to Oregon to help us." He states, "We needed the support of the Bonners Ferry Community." He and his wife moved back to Bonners Ferry because his wife believed it was a better place to recover from her health issues.

The conversation transitions to how new residents have affected the social climate. Joe emphatically states, "Support and help for each other remain true, even though several new people have moved to Bonners Ferry."

Tanja does not disagree, but offers a differing twist as to how the social climate has changed with new residents: "There have been some changes in closeness, but closeness of community still exists."

Tanja speaks with the longevity of a lifetime, which reflects back to her youth, whereas Joe addresses a shorter frame of time.

Small, rural town amenities become the next topic. Joe's synopsis about living without some amenities describes the difference between Sandpoint and Bonners Ferry. He states, "If a person cannot live without such things as airports, malls, and other urban-type amenities, you live in Sandpoint. If you *can* live without these things, move to Bonners Ferry." Tanja very calmly adds, "It's definitely a slow-pace life here."

Tanja reflects from the standpoint of a native. "We are losing the old, established people of the community, like farmers." In the next breath she states, "Bonners Ferry is definitely a kid's town. Everybody watches for everyone's kids."

Joe's daughter backpacked for eight months through Australia, New Zealand, and Fiji. Tanja states, "Everyone flocked to see her when she returned."

Joe and Tanja talk about Sandpoint and in some instances compare it to Bonners Ferry. They appreciate Sandpoint's growth, but it seems they have some concerns that Bonners Ferry could become like their neighbor thirty miles to the south. Sandpoint experiences some conflict between resort and rural community. Tanja states, "We get more full-time retirees; Sandpoint gets more seasonal people. Sandpoint used to be a family town. Now it's a resort town."

Northern Idaho is a beautiful part of America. If the people of Bonners Ferry are representative of the northern Idaho people, it is a very friendly place. Joe and Tanja conclude by telling me that in 2003, Bonners Ferry won the "Friendliest Town in Idaho" award. I am not surprised. If they have only won it one year, then I am anxious to visit the other recent winners.

I thank Joe and Tanja for their time and interesting stories. Joe and Tanja express their appreciation for my interest in their town and community. Mo receives departing pets from Joe and Tanja. Our exit is accompanied by my final statement: "Bonners Ferry has a beautiful setting and very friendly people." Joe and Tanja smile and wish us well.

Mo and I, without thinking of the consequences, wander around town, soaking up the beauty and friendliness. Finally, we are on the road heading southeast on Highway 2 toward . . . I don't know where. A quick check of the map reveals that Kalispell, Montana is the closest town: large enough to have a campground. The Garmin reveals 125 miles of mountainous roads, which means more than three hours of driving. My trusty iPhone, which I use for researching campgrounds as well as for communication, does not have reception in the national forests.

It is 3:30 p.m. This appears to be another case of poor planning. The town of Libby might have cellphone coverage.

An hour later as we come over the mountain into Libby, I see two bars on my phone. I have never been so happy to see two bars, phone or otherwise! The internet search identifies a campground. I call and reserve the last spot. Another example of good planning!

The remaining two-and-a-half-hour drive through the mountains is exhilarating. Finally, we arrive at the campground just in time to set up camp in the rain. Reflecting on the day, writing field notes, and sleeping to the tune of soft rain brings us to another day with new people and thrilling places. Our goal for tomorrow is Shelby, Montana. As we depart the campground, I am hardly prepared for the day.

CHAPTER 8

Montana

Today's travel takes us through the country of Glacier National Park. The landscape is pristine country, except for the paved roads and railroad tracks. The setting seems to look the same as I expect it would have to the original trappers who traversed the area while hunting and trapping over 150 years ago. The railroad tracks are built along mountain ledges. After several miles of mountainous driving, we come to Marias Pass, where the sign states "Elevation: 5,216 feet."

John Frank Stevens, principal engineer for the Great Northern Railroad, and Coonsah, a Blackfeet Indian guide, made the expedition to discover the pass in December 1889, one month after Montana became the forty-first state. Marias Pass, which connects the eastern and western United States, has served in this capacity since its discovery over 120 years ago.

Stevens, who was working for James J. Hill, was known for his western railroad route expeditions. Canadian-born Hill, the key person in the development of the Canadian Pacific Railroad, was determined to find the most expedient route to connect the eastern and western United States. He hired Stevens to make his dream a reality. The explorer realized that assistance from the local Native American tribe members, who lived on a reservation, would be necessary to find a traversable pass. He experienced difficulty convincing a member of the Blackfeet tribe to accompany him to the current Marias Pass, due to the tribe's belief in evil spirits in the area. Coonsah eventually agreed to guide Stevens.

The December trip, laden with snow and extremely cold temperatures, caused Coonsah to stop short of the pass. Stevens went on to discover Marias Pass without his guide. The decision to disregard the sage advice of Coonsah, a Native American familiar with the pass, terrain, and severe December weather, speaks clearly to Stevens' resolve and determination to find a route to unite the eastern and western halves of our nation.

After the two reunited, Stevens and Coonsah traveled to the agency and made their report. They originally measured the elevation of Marias Pass as 5,200 feet above sea level, with an east-west grade of 1.8% and a west-east grade of 1%. Their discovery shortened the trip to the west coast by 100 miles.

Coonsah was not the first regional Native American to meet the European Americans. Members of the Lewis and Clark expedition were dissuaded by hostel Native Americans from returning to further establish fur-trading routes. Yet in 1846, the regional tribe members traded at the newly constructed Fort Lewis, located on the banks of the Missouri River. Fort Lewis, later named Fort Benson, is considered by many to be the birthplace of Montana.

As we traverse the area now, my attention is directed to how the railroad, rippling mountain stream, and highway all jog shoulder-to-shoulder through the pass. The original fixture, the stream, is bracketed on each side by the railroad and highway. I fixate on the serenity of the scene and how the three tributaries lie in peaceful coexistence. The rippling sound of water and fresh mountain air create a serenity I have not felt for a long time. Thank you, Mr. Stevens and Mr. Coonsah.

Several miles after Marias Pass, we depart the mountains as quickly as we entered them. A small town, Cut Bank, clearly identifies the demarcation of mountainous forest from grassland pasture. Our destination, Shelby, looms twenty-five miles southeast on Highway 2. Shelby is one of four rural towns I have planned as a stopping point during this trip. Doug, a friend and basketball-coaching colleague from Kentridge High School, Washington, had once served ten years as high school principal in Shelby, his wife's hometown. During our time together, he told me so many nice things about Shelby, I knew I had to one-day experience it for myself.

Traveling now, I learn that even though Doug could spin a yarn, he actually had not over-used adjectives in his description of Shelby.

Our trip from the mountains to Shelby takes a little over thirty minutes. Completion of our short drive is a good time to provide information about Shelby and Toole County.

Life does not get any further north in the United States than Toole County, as it shares its northern county line with the southern Canadian border. We cross Interstate 15 on its route from the Mexico-United States border at San Diego to the Canadian border, where it joins with Alberta Highway 4 on its northerly path to Lethbridge and Calgary. Travelers on these two highways are exposed to some of North America's greatest beauty, especially the American and Canadian Rockies. I resist the temptation to turn north and just drive until sunset; Shelby and Toole County's beauty and new people are a stronger attraction.

Shelby, incorporated in 1910, is the seat of Toole County, which was established in 1914. In 1891, the general manager of the Montana Central Railroad,

Peter Shelby, unknowingly created the beginning of the town that bears his name. He established a small train station along the railroad route to Marias Pass at the site that grew into the town of Shelby. The settlement area attracted ranchers and farmers, and the rich grassland in surrounding Toole County enticed the development of cattle production. The late 1800s saw Shelby as a cowboy town and Toole County as a land with very few fences.

Toole County is named for Montana's first governor, James K. Toole. Governor Toole and his family owned a ranch in the county, as we will learn from an interview participant, who later purchased and lived on the Toole Ranch. Shelby and Toole County acted as support for each other as they developed and grew in harmony.

Shelby and Toole County experienced significant growth during early statehood and through the decades of the 1900s. In 1921, the discovery of oil by geologist Gordon Campbell fueled the attraction of people beyond farmers and ranchers. Shelby and Toole County's continued growth is revealed by the 2010 Census report. Toole County grew to a 2010 population of about 5,300 people, while Shelby had slightly less than 3,400 residents the same year.

Mo and I enter town from the west and turn north on Interstate 15. We exit after about a mile to select one of two campgrounds as our home for the next two nights. An easy decision and we—well, one of us—is busy setting up our camper. After a quick camper set up in the municipal recreation vehicle campground and the retrieval of a wandering Golden Retriever, we are off to town for a restaurant check. My walk down Main Street, Highway 2, gives me the impression of a healthy downtown. Most storefronts are occupied. The Montana Club appears to be a favorite gathering place. The Griddle Café is my eatery of choice on this Friday afternoon. At 2:30 in the afternoon, business is slow. The twenty-seven-year-old server decides to join me in a conversation about Shelby.

Jessie is a bubbly young person with a passion for life. She begins by stating that she is a nurse's aide at the hospital and works at the Griddle Café during busy times. She continues, "We moved here from Arizona in 1988 because my mother's mother lived here. We wanted to be close to family. The move was easy because I was young."

She continues by explaining that Shelby is a great place to live. "It is in a great area for people who like the outdoors. Glacier Park is not far away. Lake Shelby is good for fishing and water skiing. Shelby is a good place for kids to grow up. It is safe." She smiles and adds, "I was told that back in the 50s, the town [Shelby] was a hopping place."

Jessie pauses before discussing a topic that appears to be sensitive:

People in Shelby are very close-knit. People feel safe. They do not worry about being judged. A lot of young people express themselves with their dress. Several kids have dreadlocks. The older generation is accepting of the younger people and their culture. The adults are not judgmental of young people.

Sense of community and acceptance of others, especially between younger and older adults, is a very special topic for Jessie. It seems to speak clearly to her feelings of accepting people for who they are.

The conversation changes to Jessie's high school years. She states:

When I was in high school, a lot of kids hung out at the park. Some kids went down to the river and drank. I graduated high school in Great Falls because I only needed a few classes to graduate. Shelby High School would not allow early graduation [less than four years], so I went to Great Falls and graduated early.

She values her high school classmates and their success. She claims, "Quite a few Shelby High School graduates go to college. A lot of graduates move out to town. Out of our class of twenty, only three live here." She closes her discussion of high school classmates by saying that she sees a lot of her classmates at school reunions.

The people remain the same, even though the town has changed over the past several years. I observe that downtown has very few vacant stores, even though Jessie informs me that several businesses have changed owners. Jessie looks around and says, "The Griddle Café has changed owners four times during the past five or six years. Many businesses have been bought and sold, but the new owner usually continues in the same business."

People tend to cling to their old practices and names of businesses. Jessie elaborates, "Noon's, a gas station, was Circle K several years ago before change of ownership. People still refer to Noon's by its previous name, Circle K. The town basically stays the same, even though there is a new industry."

A newer prison, which is part of a national organization called the Crossroads Correctional Association, was built twenty years ago. Jessie states, "The prison brought in a lot of new people." The new employees and families account for much of the 1,000 additional Shelby residents. She adds, "They are constructing a new subdivision in town. The subdivision will change the appearance, but the people will not change."

Jessie changes the topic to her future. "I will soon be moving to Havre [Montana] to attend Montana State University–Northern [and] to attain an associate degree in nursing. After completing my associate degree, I plan to complete my bachelor's degree [and] become an RN [registered nurse], with the final goal of becoming an anesthesiologist."

Jessie is a determined young lady with a great attitude and social skills. I thank her for her time. After a pause, I add sincerely, "You will accomplish whatever goals you set." She thanks me for the compliment and the opportunity to talk about her hometown. She smiles and says, "My grandmother just retired and is moving to Arizona. It is ironic because we moved here from Arizona, [and] now she is moving to Arizona."

I walk down Main Street and find a sleeping Golden Retriever. A yawn and a stretch, and Mo is ready for a walk around town. We pass the Montana Club, where people are beginning to gather for an end-of-week rendezvous. Downtown has a few people enjoying the weather and shopping.

As Mo and I eventually begin our drive to the campground, I think that interviewing someone who has lived in Montana for several years and experienced the earlier days of statehood would make a terrific story. I pose the question to a supervisor at the Marias Care Center, who turns out to be much more perceptive than me. She suggests an interview with a small group of three to five residents, and the smile on my face is my answer.

She guides me to a small room and says I will have some volunteers in there at six o'clock, following their dinner. I thank her and state that I will be back at a little prior to six.

I return to the Center a few minutes before six o'clock to discover the people gathered in the designated room. Four will participate in the discussion. Three other people are spouses, and one middle-aged man with two children is the son of one couple. He is anxious to hear the stories. I am more than delighted.

After introductions and explanation of the research purpose, four people are anxious to tell their stories. The early Montana historians include four experts with differing backgrounds who assemble to make an interesting account of Montana that includes the first-half century of statehood. Tom, a book author and historian, is very detailed and articulate in his descriptions. He frequently would rise from his chair and walk toward me to make a point. I appreciated Tom's passion for early northern Montana history. Lloyd, who was born in North Dakota and came to Montana as an adult, was the owner, operator of a local grocery store with a full service meat market. He moved to Montana during his adult life. Robert and Ethel, husband and wife, were ranchers. They described Montana ranching and life in in a manner that made me feel part of the time. I pictured myself as a traveler joining them for lunch. My challenge is to do justice to the words of these four people.

Posing a question concerning "change in rural America" to the residents of Marias Care Center surfaces an array of perspectives and thoughts. They reflect on how things have changed since the middle of the twentieth century. They immediately addressed progress and their ancestors. Lloyd states, "The hospital where our daughter was born was so small, it is now a house." The participants are all very proud of the new hospital, of which Marias Care Center is attached. The current hospital replaced the older one mentioned by Lloyd.

The topic of change quickly transfers to ancestors and how farming has replaced ranching. Tom very articulately describes the prairie, stating, "My grandfather told stories of how the prairie was once a wave of grass when he came in 1887." In addition to imagining the beauty of miles and miles of grass, the idea of someone talking to their grandfather about a time of pre-statehood causes me to sit on the front of my chair. Tom concludes, "Now the land is mostly farming. When people first came, it was all grass." Robert quickly adds to the issue of increased size of farms and ranches by explaining, "Farming is more modern and uses more technology with bigger machinery. A family now owns over 2,000 acres. The Homestead Act granted 40 acres." Adding to the topic of homesteading, Ethel says, "Both my grandfathers each homesteaded here in 1914 [prior to Toole County and during the first quarter century of statehood] and raised their families." Robert and Ethel purchased and lived on the Toole ranch.

Immigrants and foreign investors contributed to the settling of Shelby and Toole County. Ethel's great grandfather migrated from Odessa, Ukraine. Tom's grandfather came from Italy. The narrow-gauge railway that ran from Lethbridge in Alberta, Canada through the current location of Shelby and on to Great Falls, Montana was financed by Holland and constructed with steel from Germany. Tom informs me, "A man named Shelby built a train station in 1891 where our town now stands. The town was named for him."

For several years, ranching was dominant; now farming has consumed the prairie. Tom states that he came back from World War II and started ranching.

"We raised Hereford cattle, sheep, saddle horses, and grain. Now it is mostly farming. When people came, it was all grass." In addition to the change in agriculture, the stores have changed. Lloyd states, "Stores are now huge and have a variety of everything. Large variety stores replacing locally owned stores has resulted in the loss of owners personally knowing each customer."

The story was not all about ranching, although I admit I am mesmerized to this point about one of my favorite topics. Lloyd, who has been relatively quiet, adds a whole new perspective to our story. He explains that his grocery store was very oriented to serve the customer.

Lloyd expands on the topic of service by focusing on the old time meat market that has virtually been lost with time. He states:

> We carried groceries and men's clothing. Our store included an *open face meat market*. We butchered, aged, and packaged the meat for farmers, ranchers, and other customers. They received one-half and one-quarter beef sides that we cut up and packaged. Today, the meat comes from market cut up and packaged. There are no longer butchers at meat cutters.

Lloyd pauses and continues with pride and a smile, "Each month we gave each customer a bag of candy for their kids."

I have faint memories of neighborhood groceries with full meat markets. My faded memories tell me that the butchers wore white clothing and a hat. I do have more vivid memories of the *Milroy Meat Market* with a large freezer room and a room with big, individual meat drawers where people would store their meat. Lloyd ushered me down memory lane.

The underlying message is that everything from farms, ranches, and stores has become larger at the expense of being personal and friendly to neighbors and customers. It is obvious by the number of statements that the increase in farm size and the transition of ranching to farming are very important.

The end of the conversation with Lloyd, Tom, and Robert, and Ethel is a sentimental experience for me. I shake hands with the four interview participants and the other residents who have sat in on our conversation. I then turn to thank the administrators and one of Robert and Ethel's sons who has joined us. My voice breaks a little as I state how overwhelmed I am talking to four people who were instrumental in the early development of northern Montana. Their voices rang with humility and grace.

Prior to leaving, I make a stop in the social gathering room to say hi to my old friend Doug's mother-in-law. We had met twenty-five years before, during a social event at Kentridge High School in Washington, to honor Doug's retirement from coaching. She exhibits today the same grace she had then. I regret that I failed to request that she be included in the interview. I would have liked to heard her story.

My conversations with early Montana residents, as well as with Lydia and Erma of American Falls, did not mention the Depression. Only Erma spoke of World War II and it was during her discussion of the prisoners-of-war. Their absence of comments seems to state the lack of relevancy to the story of their life.

My time at the two Care Centers was gratifying and memorable, the conversations help put life into a meaningful perspective. I appreciate the Centers' employees and the four persons who shared their stories. My trip would not have been the same without them.

Mo

Finally, we are at the campground. This has been a *high-time day* in the truck. First, we drove. Then we drove some more. I got out of the truck in the mountains, only to be told not to jump into the stream. At the campground, I cannot wander around and hunt.

The only fun was walking down Main Street. One place, the Montana Club, had a bunch of people talking loudly and laughing. Of course, we walked right past it. I bet we missed something.

As soon as we park by the camper, I am out of the truck and on my way to hunt. I am in the full nose-down, no-hearing mode. Usually, squirrels and rabbits are the main attraction, but not this time. New friend! I spot a man, a bicycle, and a tent that is too small for a pup. My new friend has an accent and uses new words like "*nein*." The faster I run toward him, the louder he yells, "Nein! Nein!" I know "nein" is a welcoming call, so I decide not to jump, but instead hit him with my shoulder. You guessed it: another "Nien" as he topples backward.

Randy comes running, saying, "I'm sorry, I'm sorry!" I am not sure what he did, but it must have been really bad. The cyclist and Randy talk. I am able to understand most of it. The cyclist is from Germany and riding his bicycle across America from San Francisco to New York, where he will meet his girlfriend in the fall. They talk about the trip and other boring stuff, so I ease off to checkout the campground. A lot of good smells, and of course, there are a few dogs tied to picnic tables, barking at me. They are just jealous that I am running and hunting while their humans keep them tethered. They probably are not disciplined like me. I like running close to the little white dog, which always causes a lot of barking and maybe some yelling from the humans. After all, it has been a boring day. Someone even yells, "Get that dawg on a leash." Here we go with another, "I'm sorry." I wish my human would stop the "I'm sorry" stuff and just tell them to mind their own business.

We finally go back to town. This time the people talking loudly and laughing are out front of the Montana Club on the sidewalk. Of course, they all want to pet and talk to me. Inevitably, they want to tell us they have a dawg just like me, only it is about a foot-and-a-half shorter and has black hair and ears that stick straight up. I look in the window at myself. Sure enough, I am still two feet tall, have red hair, and my ears lay flat against my pretty face. What is wrong with the human species? How can a black dawg, whose ears point to the sky, look like me?

Eventually, we go back to the campground. It is getting cold: not colder, *cold*! Randy tries to light the furnace. No success. Getting colder. Oh boy, here comes the book. After several minutes of reading, Randy messes with the furnace. We still have no heat and are getting colder. I cannot believe this. Randy's solution is to get inside the sleeping bag, chatter his teeth, and say four-letter words about the furnace. Me, I am not going to sleep on the cold floor. Too cold. I am aware of the "no couch" rule. Rules, however, are intended to be broken. With great gusto and authority, I jump on the couch, roll into a ball, and cover my ears. I say to myself, "I can't hear you," as I nod off to sleep listening to a chorus of "dumb furnace." He never once considers, as it turns out, that it might be operator error.

Finally, morning comes. Trailer teardown is exciting. It is wet, it is cold, and I love it. Guess who is *not* a happy camper . . .

I hunt; Randy tears down the camper. Dawgs rule! We are off to town, where Randy goes to the Griddle Café while I guard the truck. It is always a good idea to make your human have a guilty conscious. I give that big mournful, sad look, even though I am one happy dawg. The "Grouch" is gone, and I can sleep in the warm truck.

Randy

To say that breakfast time at the Griddle Café is crowded would be an understatement. Many regulars are sitting drinking coffee, eating, and discussing the major events (as they view them). I find a table next to a couple of men who are real without-a-doubt cowboys. After I order, I start a conversation with them and explain my travels and aspirations to write a book about rural America. They invite me to join them, and the conversation focuses on their stories—and rodeo cowboys. This conversation is not about Shelby and could have occurred anywhere in rodeo country. The Griddle Café in Shelby is a fitting place for our conversation.

Lee and Cody are on their way to Butte, Montana to participate in a rodeo as Team Bulldoggers. "Bulldogging" is often called "steer wrestling." We sit at a small corner table, which is covered with plates of eggs, bacon, sausage, hash browns, toast, coffee, and pancakes. Guess who was the light eater in the crowd?

The food, like yesterday, is good, but the conversation is extraordinary. I always enjoy talking to rodeo participants. It may be that I love the sport, but more than that, I am always happy talking about dawgs and cattle. Well, dawgs who don't believe they are the boss and actually work.

Lee, the senior partner of the team, introduces himself, followed by Cody. The first words out of Lee's mouth are, "I am seventy-four years old." Before I can respond, he is smiling as if he knows I am going to say, "You look fifty-five." His quick response: "I *feel* fifty-five."

I judge Cody to be in his late twenties or maybe early thirties. Cody smiles and states, "I am the hazer; Lee is the bulldogger."

The bulldogger is the one who jumps from his horse to grab the head or horns of the steer and wrestle him to the ground. The hazer rides his horse on the other side of the steer to keep it going in somewhat of a straight path. Bulldogging is a timed event.

The conversation quickly and briefly turns to hometown and weekday living. It seems Lee and Cody want to get the mundane aspects discussed first and then get on the topic of the rodeo: the fun aspect of life.

Cut Bank in Glacier County, the town and county Mo and I passed yesterday, was the childhood home of Lee. He now makes his residence in a larger town in southern Montana, where he owns a gravel pit. Cody adds, "From Monday through Thursday, I work cows in the mountains near the Idaho and Montana state line. I sleep at home every night. Then, on Friday, I leave for the rodeo."

At this point Lee diverts the story to the past, and Cody keys on how he became involved in the rodeo.

Lee focuses on his rodeo experience in the 1950s:

In the 1950s, three guys could each throw $20 into the "kitty," and the money would take them across country. We went from Montana to Texas on $20 each. Gas was twenty-one cents a gallon; most motel rooms were $2.50. If you were lucky, you might find one for $1.50. There were mom-and-pop restaurants in every small town. Now there are none. It's not the same. Fast food is not as good. In the 1950s, if you won $30, it was as good as winning $300 today. There are very few, if any, $25 motel rooms, and the last time I purchased gas for $1.90, I had a full head of dark hair; clearly not true today.

He concludes, "I have rodeoed most of my life."

"Rodeoed" is not in the dictionary, but it clearly is in the vocabulary of those who count: the rodeo cowboys and cowgirls.

Cody had a totally different and very unique path to rodeo. He grew up in Solon, Iowa and played football for his high school. He states, "We were perennial state champions." His cousin played for the New York Jets, and Cody had a scholarship to play in college. Cody's football life began to unravel, however, on a Friday night under the bright lights. "During the fourth quarter, I fumbled. It cost us the game." Even though he was a member of a football family, "I started losing interest in football after the fumble. I gave up my scholarship."

But his desire to compete remained strong. Cody turned to rodeos to satisfy the hunger of competition. He says, "I received a scholarship to Laramie College in Cheyenne, Wyoming to participate in rodeo. After college, I just moved to Idaho." The rest is history. He became a real cowboy who works cattle and rodeos. I use the term "real" because a lot of folk wear the hat, Wranglers, and boots, but have never seen the backside of a cow from horseback.

Cody stops talking and focuses on his plates of breakfast. Lee picks up the story. "During the Korean War, a recruiter signed up eleven boys from Glacier County. Nine of the eleven were killed. I reported for the draft twice. One time I had a broken leg; next time I had a broken arm."

Eventually, the conversation turns to financing the habit of rodeo participation. Cody states, "A car dealer sponsors me by giving me a discount on truck purchases. Participating in rodeos is hard on trucks." Lee shows me his 1995 Medicine Hat Saskatchewan, Canada Senior Rodeo Finals belt buckle. He smiles and says, "There is no money in 'Old Timer' [rodeo]. I had to get back to competing with the young guys."

Lee says that it is time to go so they can make the Butte rodeo. We shake hands and say our good-byes. They wish me luck; I return the goodwill. We walk out of the "Griddle" and head for our trucks. Lee and Cody have a big heavy-duty truck with a two-horse trailer attached; I head for my half-ton truck with the camper. I reflect on the fun I have experienced during the past eighteen days and the time I have spent with some great people. Their stories are fascinating. I would not trade these experiences for anything, but I would have liked to experience just one day around cattle and horses and to hear more rodeo stories.

Oh, well. Mo and I have a lot more people to meet and stories to capture.

Mo

Randy comes out of the restaurant with two men. They are dressed like the men who are employed by dawgs to herd cattle and sheep. Please don't misunderstand me: Work is not a bad thing. But too much does not leave enough time to hunt and play ball.

We leave Shelby on US 2. A few miles from Shelby, I am still navigating to make sure we are traveling toward the sun. I see a man on a bike. Hey! It is my friend from the campground. Randy honks the horn; I bark. The man waves. He undoubtedly recognizes my bark. All horns are the same, but not all barks. It is morning naptime.

Randy

Our uneventful drive across the northern plains of Montana allows time for reflection. This section of Montana is drastically different from the western part we have visited the past three days. The land is flat with few trees and is considerably hotter. A notable thing about today's drive is that the best radio reception is a station from Regina in Saskatchewan, Canada. We listen to a Regina radio station for miles. The towns are small and separated by miles of highway. The drive, however, does provide time for me to reflect on the similarities and dissimilarities between the comments about Shelby and Toole County made by Jessie and the comments made by Marias Community Care Center residents Lloyd, Tom, Robert, and Ethel.

The differing comments allow me to gain a perspective about dissimilarities between life during the early and middle twentieth century, as compared to the late twentieth and early twenty-first. The four Care Center residents frame their thoughts from experiences embedded in the early years of Montana statehood, whereas Jessie forms her thoughts from recent times. Jessie's experiences focus on living in a town with minimal consideration for farming and ranching. The Marias residents speak from immersion in an agriculture-based society. I realize that comparison of the two sets of interviews requires the recognition that over a half-century in age separates Jessie and the Marias residents. Together, they afford close to a century of Toole County history.

The culture described by the Marias residents during early and middle twentieth century emulates the culture described by other senior citizens who were alive around the World War II era and prior. All five of the interview participants from Shelby spoke clearly to the friendliness of the people and a culture deeply steeped in acceptance and respect for others. Change in the view of the Marias residents referred to farm and ranch size, as well as ranching and livestock giving way to farming and crops. Jessie referred to change mainly regarding the turbulence of downtown store ownership and the increase in residents that had resulted from the addition of a prison opening about twenty years prior. Young adults leaving Shelby were a significant issue to Jessie. The senior residents, Robert and Ethel, spoke only of two daughters who had left. They added that their four sons remained in the area to work in the agriculture industry.

During the last half of the century and beyond, Shelby has experience minimal change among the people and culture. Stores may change owners; people working the land may increase their operation size; and they may change the commodities they produce. But when someone needs help, it is always available.

Residents of Shelby provided a very enlightening view and comparison of two completely different eras and lifestyles. The two rodeo cowboys added the needed understanding of a seemingly romantic life style I have viewed only from the periphery. Shelby and its residents provided a warm welcome and acceptance. I am very grateful to the residents and staff at Marias Care Center.

The view of Havre in my windshield snaps me back to reality. I am hopeful that Havre, one of the largest towns in the northeastern section of the state, will provide a campground with hook-ups and laundry facilities for a restful remainder of the weekend. A few minutes' drive on US Highway 2 leads me the campground and a greatly needed area to walk and rest.

Mo

After a long ride, we stay in a campground behind a motel and do one of my least favorite things: wash clothes. Randy spends a lot of time in a building with machines, and I am expected to lie by the door for hours, and hours. Well, maybe not quite that long. Eventually, I wander off to check on security or food. Then I hear Randy pose the same question he always asks when I take the initiative to hunt: "Did I ask you to stay?"

I always think, *Why does he ask me that?* If he said it, he should know. It makes me wonder whether he really said it or if he just *thinks* he did. Why not say, "Mo, please come over here and lie down." Of course, I would not do it, but at least it would sound better.

After putting clothes in bags, we go uptown. Randy goes to eat; I stay in the truck. When he returns, a lady with a big dish of ice cream is walking with him. I mean *really* big. I know it is for me! The door opens, and I am out of the truck. No time for greetings. Get on with the eating! Greetings later.

With ice cream dish completely clean, I now have time to greet and thank the lady. I give her some ice-cream-coated tongue licks, then comes the leaning and hand-to-foot shakes. She pets and talks to me. She wipes her face where I licked her and says, "I must get back to work." A great ending to a great day!

Randy

What a way to end the day and another chapter of our journey. Since we departed Seattle, I have experienced conversations with ten people and traveled through beautiful mountains and several rural towns. The people of Idaho and Montana possess a certain degree of independence, appreciation for their environment and people, and love for freedom and life. They have a sense of values that keeps "the main thing, the main thing": people, land, and environment.

It is beautiful country with a breathtaking environment. But the "main thing" remains the *people*. I hope two things: One, that they stay true to their values, and two, that *that* way of life becomes contagious.

It is early Sunday morning, and Mo and I are traveling east. We bid farewell to Idaho, Montana, and the Rocky Mountains. Each time I leave the Rockies, I pose the same reflective question: "When will we meet again?" My answer is always the same: "Soon, I hope."

Our arrival in North Dakota forces a tough decision about continued travel on US Highway 2. Further travel east on US 2 limits our interview area to the northern segment of North Dakota and a small sector or possibly a complete miss of South Dakota.

The consequences are too great. We bid farewell to Highway 2 and turn south on US 85 at Williston, North Dakota. I say good-bye to Highway 2 in my rearview with a pledge to one day drive its over-2,500 miles from Everett,

Washington to Holton, Maine. The stories of the people with differing lifestyles along that northern highway would be fascinating and intriguing.

Mo

A good night's sleep, a five-mile walk, and we are off for new country. My human, as always, is anxious to get on the road. My human's story conveniently omits an important aspect of the Sunday travel story involving poor judgment and a little dumbness. The story begins with one of his bad habits of being in a hurry. (The only thing worse than his hurrying is trying to make *me* hurry. It never works.)

He stops at a fast-food restaurant and grabs a breakfast biscuit to eat as we travel: mistake number one. When he gets back into the truck, he mumbles something about slow service and cold food sitting on the counter. He eats the biscuit: mistake number two. About an hour down the road, Randy starts sweating and bends over the steering wheel, saying unrepeatable words. I only hear these words when bad things happen, such as when he hits his thumb with a hammer or trips over my tennis ball. I try to cheer him up by laying my chin on his arm and giving him a big lick to moisten his nose. More words that make my ears burn are followed by, "Mo, cool it!" No appreciation for my kindness: mistake number three.

The day's drive through eastern Montana and western North Dakota gets better with time. Finally, we stop at a campground. Parking the trailer is an event to behold. Randy pulls up. He backs up, then tries another spot. Four times he repeats the three-step routine of pull-up, back-up, and try another spot. Finally, we go back the original spot and repeat the pull-up, back-up routine until he gets tired. All day long I thought his stomach was sick, but now I know it was actually his brain.

A long walk along the river makes me feel better, as it does Randy. I cannot wait for tomorrow and new adventures. I have had all the fun I can handle for one day.

CHAPTER 9

Dakotas

It is amazing what chicken soup and a good night's sleep can do for a person. Monday morning, and we are on Interstate 94 heading east. Our plan is to eventually travel a highway south, spend some time in a North Dakota small town or two, and sleep in South Dakota. Two-and-a-half hours later and twenty miles east of Bismarck, we turn south on US Highway 83. The first thing I notice after a light breakfast is that I am working up a big hunger; the second thing is that the towns are small; and the third thing is that most of towns do not have restaurants—or they are closed on Mondays, which happens to coincide with today.

A little over a half-hour's drive, and I see a large sign along the highway stating "Restaurant." A quick drive through the empty parking lot at noon creates a suspicion that is confirmed by a sign on the door stating "Closed Mondays." Good luck had turned to bad luck in a heartbeat. Not to be detoured, I head for downtown Hazelton, population about 250.

The municipality, situated amidst fields of grain, radiates the portrait of a rural town. The streets are arranged in squares. The houses, large but not fancy, are neatly situated on larger-than-normal city lots. The pride of the people is evident by maintenance of their homes and property, as well as the one-block Main Street, which fronts the post office, a couple of stores, and a larger building called the "Mall." The Mall houses a grocery, hair salon, and the Senior Center.

Most of the residents drive less than ten minutes to work, with a few traveling sixty minutes. The two main industries are related to construction and agriculture. The school district, located on the edge of Hazelton, serves the two additional small communities of Moffit and Braddock.

North Dakota gained statehood on November 2, 1889, about twenty-eight years after both it and South Dakota were organized into the Dakota Territory in 1861. Arrival of the railroad in 1889 stimulated population growth and the development of numerous towns, including Linton, the seat of Emmons County, which was organized as a town for the sole purpose of providing a central location for the county government.

With no restaurant in sight, it is time to improvise. Lunch is beginning to seem like cheese and crackers, which, of course, I do not have in my possession.

When things appear really dismal, I see a middle-aged man exiting the Senior Center. Trying to hide my panic, I query where a traveler could eat lunch in Hazelton. He responds to the hunger question with a smile and says that the Senior Center serves lunch on Monday. My original thought is that I am not a senior citizen. Well, I guess might be by definition. Anyway, hunger pains override age and pride. Hunger trumps pride!

Much to my surprise, the Senior Center has the aura of a restaurant, with many folks chatting and sitting around tables. The ladies of the Senior Center prepare and serve lunch on Mondays to fill the gap of the closed restaurant. Good luck is back! There is no way I could have had a better ham dinner at a restaurant. Home cooking is difficult to beat.

I am greeted with smiles and welcoming words as I walk beside a long table filled with food. I think: *This is better than good.*

Food in hand, my attention focuses on several people sitting around a table, chatting and eating. I sit at the vacant end of the table so I will not interrupt conversations. It does not work. I am immediately engaged in a conversation that makes me feel part of the group. When I explain about my and Mo's rural America research, there is a lot of interest, which evolves into three interviews.

Ellen, who reports her age as 83 years young, gives me a historical perspective of Hazelton and why and how it became a town. Arlene chooses life in Hazelton during current times as her focus. Herman takes a whole different approach and conveys issues of farming and how retirement in Rural America can be exciting.

Ellen, who is cleaning tables, sits down and introduces herself. She begins by telling me that Hazelton became a town during early twentieth century, when the railroad changed its projected route. The track had been planned to run in the approximate area of Williamstown but was relocated west about three-and-a-half miles, to the approximate location of Hazelton. Ellen is steadfast about the distance. "It was not four or three miles; it was three-and-one-half miles," she adamantly states. Ellen says, "Williamstown was abandoned when the railroad did not go through their town. It was all moved to where the railroad ran. A man named Ropy, the founder of the new town, named it after his daughter, Hazel."

Ellen's family helped settle Hazelton. "My family was among the founders of Hazleton. My father had the keys to the Williamstown jail door. After the jail was torn down, we used the door to haul rocks." Ellen's story reveals that she was born about twenty-four years after the founding of Hazelton. I continue to be amazed that I have been talking with people whose lives so closely approximate the settling of towns, communities, and even states.

Arlene, who I met in the serving line, has wandered out of the kitchen and heard some of my conversation with Ellen. She joins us at the table and picks up the conversation after Ellen has finished talking.

Arlene begins by telling me that the Senior Center has a lot of activities. "We have dances, holiday happenings, rummage sales, [and] breakfast for the community. Breakfasts are served at the Senior Center for everyone. We usually have pastries or doughnuts and coffee."

The Senior Center was very involved in the centennial celebration, which occurred in 2003. Arlene quickly leaves the table and scampers across the room. I think I must have said something wrong, but in moments I realize all is well. She is returning with a big smile and a very thick, hardbound book, which turns out to be the 500-page *Centennial Book*.

As we leaf through its pages, Arlene proudly gives me a verbal picture of the contents. The book contains a picture of every Hazelton High School graduate, significant events for each of the first 100 years, the name of everyone buried in the cemetery, and numerous other items. "It took three years to research and develop the book," Arlene says. She concludes her thoughts about the centennial by stating, "We made $20,000 for the city from the centennial by selling books and doing other projects. Everything was free, including the entertainment."

As quickly as the review of the *Centennial Book* began, we are off on another topic, and I suddenly realize that Arlene moves at a pace that is challenging to my note-taking skills.

We switch gears to the amenities of Hazelton. "We have three churches: a Presbyterian, Catholic, and Lutheran. We call this building our 'mini shopping mall.' It contains the Senior Center, hair salon, and grocery store."

She then looks at me thoughtfully and says, "The courthouse was moved to Linton. They are the county seat of Emmons County. They moved it from Williamstown during the late nineteenth century. There were hard feelings between the people of Williamstown and Linton." She pauses before continuing with an anecdote about how feelings have mended over the years. "We had a *Hee Haw Show*. Linton asked us to present the show for them." With these comments, Arlene jumps up and says that she enjoyed our talk and the opportunity to tell me about Hazelton. She then hurries back to the kitchen to finish cleaning.

Emmons County, where Hazelton is situated, had a late nineteenth-century dispute over the location of the county seat. The North Dakota legislature established Emmons County in 1879. The county board named Williamstown the seat soon after the county was organized in 1883. As residents began to populate the southern portion of the county and Hazelton developed near the railroad, Williamstown began to lose population and thus popularity as a county seat. A vote was taken and passed to create a new, more centrally located town to be the county seat. The town named "Linton" was born.

The residents of Williamstown, however, would not relinquish the official county records and filed a court order to set aside the vote that had been made to move the county seat. In February 1899, "the southerners" formed an armed group that went to Williamstown and took possession of the records. There was no resistance to the armed group. The irony of the battle over the county seat is that Williamstown ceased to exist during the early 1900s. It is now buried underwater: the result of a dam built to create a lake.

Arlene's departure leaves only Herman and I at the end of our table. Herman is a retired farmer who has a very clear view of the changes to rural America. He begins the conversation by stating that farming has really changed since he retired nineteen years ago:

> Farms have increased in size by ten times. One farm has 18,000 acres, and the owner is looking for more acreage. A very common farm size is 6,000 to 10,000 acres. Small towns in North Dakota are losing population, but the state is slightly increasing in population. People are moving to the cities. Schools [rural] are suffering because of the loss of population. Some counties have only one school district.

Herman pauses to think and shifts his sitting position. He then looks directly at me. "I farmed all my life. Retired when I was sixty-three. I am now eighty-two. Due to better equipment and chemicals, farmers have doubled their yield in the last ten years." He pauses and reflects while arranging his silverware on his empty plate. "Years ago we shipped grain in 2,500-bushel lots. Now trains transport grain in 110 cars, carrying 4,700 bushels each. There are only a few market terminals in the state. We used to have one in every town." His thoughts about farming conclude with, "Machinery has become so computerized [that] you almost need a college degree to run them."

Herman smiles, sits up, and leans forward. He proudly says, "People in little towns gather. You know each other. Strangers are made to feel welcome. We have a top-notch school." I interrupt by adding, "I can vouch for strangers feeling welcome." A bigger smile and a degree of self-assurance is demonstrated by his body language. He grins and states, "I have ridden 750,000 miles on a Harley since I started in 1947. I rode 50,000 miles the year I turned eighty."

He pauses and continues with the question, "Do you see that Corvette parked out there?" I say that I could not miss it on the street with the two other cars. "It's mine," he says. I respond, "Herman, you are my hero!" We laugh and shake hands. This turns out to be a great lunch.

I thank Ellen, Arlene, and Herman for taking time to talk with me. I pause, then add, "I thank you more for making me feel welcome. Actually, you made me feel like I live in Hazelton." My final words, "The ham dinner was extraordinary. Home cooking is difficult to beat."

They bid me farewell with smiles that are as big as my own and give me words of encouragement for my research.

For the first time on the trip, Mo and I walk down Main Street without a leash. The people are few, but friendly. Mo receives a lot of pets and comments of "pretty dawg." Main Street terminates at a soybean field. Most Main Streets go on and become a highway—not in Hazelton.

The soybean field at the end of Main Street is the current home of a rabbit. The chase is on. Mo gives the bunny a run. The bunny gets the thrill of outrunning a dawg. While Mo is doing her thing, I reflect on the prowess of rural America. I drive into a small town: only restaurant closed, no place for lunch. The people of the Hazelton Senior Center turn my bad fortune around 180 degrees. They make me feel welcome, talk with me, provide knowledge about their town and community, and offer me an opportunity to have a good lunch. All I have to do is show up.

After I finally rescue a panting Retriever and convince her to get into the truck, we head south on US Highway 83, then east on North Dakota 11 for an intermediate stop at Ellendale, North Dakota. Ellendale was the childhood home of Lydia, the 104-years-young resident of the Spring Creek Care Center in American Falls.

I have no reason to stop, other than it is on our route, and I want to see how Lydia's town looks today.

We continue our drive south for about forty miles on US Highway 281 to Aberdeen. Our home for the night is a large campground adorned with many recreation facilities, such as miniature golf, a swimming pool complete with water works, and other amenities. It is refreshing to see kids everywhere, having fun. I have dinner on the patio of a steakhouse. The fun part of the evening culminates with Mo and I hiking. Then, as every night, I relive the day as I write interview field notes.

The next morning, Mo and I are headed east on US Highway 12 without a planned destination. Some of the creek beds appear to have a lot of salt residue that is naturally excreted from the soil. These soils have a content level of sodium. A thirty-minute drive east through corn and wheat country provides an early morning boost more wakeful than any first cup of coffee.

The thought of breakfast and talking with a local farmer takes center stage in my mind as I approach the town of Groton. The small town in Brown County lies on the southern edge of the highway. The thought of leaving a landscape of grain fields for streets, traffic lights, cars, and businesses is not appealing.

Groton, organized in 1881 as a railroad stop, was incorporated in 1888. Well situated at the intersections of two well-traveled highways—US 12 and South Dakota 37—Groton is less than twenty miles east of Aberdeen: the Brown County seat and the third largest city in the state. Population in Groton has shown a nearly 40% increase during the past fifty years: from 1,063 in 1960 to a 2010 total of 1,458. Groton is one of five small towns in South Dakota with an increasing population. Growth may be attributed, in part, to its proximity to the large population of Aberdeen and its location near the two well-traveled highways. Many of the residents make the twenty-five-to-forty-minute employment commute to the Brown County seat of Aberdeen.

The town, like many other railroad towns, was named after a familiar New England town: in this case, Groton, Massachusetts.

Brown County, officially developed in July 1880, is the home of the recently developed Granary Rural Culture Center: a part of history and a tourist attraction. Dorothy Wallace Sieh, farmwife and artist, developed the project by crafting paintings well into her nineties. During the 1990s, her son eventually solidified the project by turning his parent's farm granary (built in 1928) into a museum. The Center has hosted numerous events, while keeping farm history alive for the future.

Mo and I drive into a parking lot behind a Shell gas station and convenience store. The number of pickup trucks and a sign stating "Red Horse Salon" commands my attention. Mental gymnastics leads me to conclude that either there was one big party last night, or the Red Horse serves a really great breakfast.

Several pickup trucks, mostly with dents, signify this is as *the* breakfast place. My grey truck, also with a few dents, and camper find a spot amongst the other Chevy, Ford, and Dodge trucks. Mo guards the truck (or naps) while I venture toward the Red Horse.

The surrounding view as I walk across the parking lot portrays streets lined with large trees and small homes that assume the architecture of several past decades. The homes and lots are neat and well maintained. The nondescript building that houses the Red Horse Saloon has a flat storefront.

Inside, a long bar, which appears to seat between twelve and fifteen people, follows the L-shaped room, as do the tables and chairs. Eight men, obviously regular customers, sit at the only occupied table. I select a table next to them with the hopes that maybe someone might wander over to talk. The chances look slimmer as two more men join the occupied table.

I am about to give up on the Red Horse and start to formulate a plan. Should I go into downtown Groton and look for another restaurant that is serving breakfast? Or write Groton off all together and travel to another town?

My thoughts are hindered, not interrupted, when everyone greets a man called Gilbert with a "good morning!" Gilbert distinguishes himself from the other coffee drinkers by his hat. The men sitting at the table either wear clean, well-shaped, one-size-fits-all baseball-style caps or are hatless. Gilbert breaks the mold with his old, beat-up straw cowboy hat. His hat rivals my own, in fact, as being the most beat-up hat in town—maybe in South Dakota. Gilbert's hat looks as if a horse has walked on it, then drug it a mile through a wheat field. My hat resembles a rag that had been chewed by a dawg, rolled on, and drug through a cornfield. Every morning my hat receives a couple squirts of cologne, which actually has minimal affect on the odor.

As Gilbert receives his morning greetings, I take a moment to ponder the "old hat syndrome." I cannot help wondering why some people, mostly men, wear hats until they are well past decency. Perhaps we dislike change; maybe it is comfort. I like to think I am frugal.

But that is all really bull. It is a style, a fashion statement: sort of like my jeans with holes. It is who I am. Old hats have character, which makes me feel that *I* have character.

Dirty hats are not a new phenomenon for me. Years ago, my hat usually ended up being pinned to the wall identifying it as the dirtiest, most worn hat in the fighter squadron. I cannot recall feeling any shame. My hat and I had character.

As Gilbert approaches the tables, a man pulls a chair from my table so Gilbert can join them. This is a defining statement that the stranger in town—me—is unnoticeable. To my surprise, Gilbert grabs the chair, pulls it back to my table, and says, "I am going to join this guy. I want hear his story." I will gladly swap my story to hear his.

Gilbert and I talk over coffee, sharing our life experiences and philosophy on life. He is enthused about my research on rural America, and I immediately realize he is actually the considerate person he demonstrated by making a stranger feel welcome. He begins, "Life is what you make of it. Everywhere you go, you get good people. I am seventy-one."

Gilbert's story has two distinct concepts: The first clearly transforms his philosophy into action, and the second describes how Groton and rural life has changed during the past fifty-plus years.

Gilbert moved to Chicago in 1962 because there was no winter work in the Groton area. In 1963, while living in Chicago, he joined the army to serve his country. During his two years of military service, he lived in Germany and traveled throughout Europe. His time in France made a lasting impression on him. "In Paris, if a person got sick, everyone helped." He continues by stating that the attitude there reminded him of his childhood days in South Dakota.

Gilbert connects the attitudes of South Dakota farmers during the first half of the twentieth century to the people of Paris. He states, "In the community around Aberdeen, when the first farmer got done with [harvesting] his crop, he helped the next one closest to being done. This practice went on until everyone helped the last guy finish his crop work." His statement about both the people of Paris and the Aberdeen-area farmers during the first half of the twentieth century verifies his view that good people are not fixed to a location. His ensuing comments relate that a person's attitude, more than the person, finds good people.

Following his time in the army, he lived in Chicago a few more years before returning to Groton. He returned to Groton because someone from his childhood community needed help. An elderly farmer, who could no longer manage his land, contacted Gilbert and asked if he would return to Groton to help him. Gilbert explains:

> I returned to Groton to help a neighbor and friend in need. He had too many acres to farm alone at his age. Today, I farm the 160 acres my dad bought years ago. One-half of the land is underwater because salt coming out of the ground blocks the James River water flow.

Gilbert transitions his thoughts to describe a situation when a small contribution made a large impact. The person assigned to play "Taps" was unable to attend the burial ceremony of a person who had served in the military. Gilbert volunteered to ensure that the deceased military person received the appropriate honor. He recounts the story in these words, "I sang 'Taps' during a funeral because there was not a bugler. When I forgot the words, someone gave me a harmonica. I played 'Taps' on the harmonica." His actions may seem minor, but to family, friends, and military, they were monumental.

Gilbert's need to help others is not limited to humans. His heart-warming story concerning the purchase of a horse demonstrates his kindness and consideration for animals. He becomes serious and speaks from the heart. He does not portray his actions as extraordinary, but ones that anyone would do for an animal in distress:

> I went to the sale barn to purchase a riding horse. I entered a pen to have a closer look at a particular horse. I discovered that the horse had a cut on its front leg from knee to hoof. I thought if I bought her she would die. As I attempted to leave the pen, she stuck her head in the gate and blocked my way out. I bought her and took her home and treated her wound. She healed and tamed down and became friendly. I can walk up to her in the pasture and hug her. I don't try to ride her because I am concerned of reinjuring her leg. She knew I could fix her leg. I don't have a pet dog; I have a pet horse.

I sit in silence as I soak up the meaning of a man's kindness to an animal. Finally, I am able to find words, words that are hollow compared to Gilbert's description of kindness. (Later, when I write the account of his story, I will tear up.)

We sit and sip coffee as we reflect and discuss cruelty to animals and how he saved a horse's life. The pause ends when I pose the question, "How has Groton changed?"

"This will be tough. It will take a while to tell you," he says.

I sit back and drink more coffee as he pulls a folded paper from his pocket and starts writing. His frown reveals concentration. He says he wants to ensure that he paints an accurate verbal portrait of his town and community. I smile at his concern and actions to ensure accuracy. It is the first time during my trip that anyone has made a list of changes. About five minutes later, he says, "I am ready."

He begins by stating that the population of Groton has increased over the past fifty years, while the number of businesses has significantly decreased. He adds, "Marketing of farm products has become more difficult, as the number of grain elevators in Groton has decreased from five to none, and the number of butcher shops has diminished from two to none." He pauses, then places the absence of grain markets into perspective when he relays that he has not been able to take his wheat to the grain elevator in Aberdeen because wagons are not allowed to drive on the expressway. He explains, "Everyone uses semis; I still use gravity feed wagons."

Gilbert transitions his thoughts on change from farming to the town of Groton and its loss of businesses. The time and effort Gilbert took writing the list becomes apparent as he explains the change:

> Back in the 1940s, we had five grain elevators, two butcher shops, three grocery stores, one drugstore, three bars, two cafés, three doctors, three new-car dealerships, four farm machinery dealers, and one newspaper. Today, we have zero grain elevators, zero butcher shops, one grocery store, one drugstore, three bars, several restaurants and fast food places, two new-car dealerships, zero farm machinery dealers, two newspapers, and one clinic with one intern. Every town used to have a dairy; now milk is trucked to the supermarkets. Milk is not fresh, as it was when we had our local dairies.

He concludes that during the 1940s, about one-half of the farmers used horses: a statement that has implications well beyond farming.

As autos, trucks, and tractors replaced horses, travel became easier and faster. Groton residents could make the less-than-thirty-minute drive to Aberdeen for greater selection and lower prices. Large market centers, such as Aberdeen, expanded. Consequently, smaller shopping areas, like Groton, lost their stores and downtown market area. Due to the inevitable loss of public revenue, the effects reach well beyond the loss of retail stores and into infrastructure.

I hope to gain a sense of Gilbert's personal thoughts concerning how the changes have affected life in Groton. I prompt the discussion by posing the question, "What is life like in Groton?"

He responds with a grin, "I like it. It is too hot in the summer and too cold in the winter. People are really good." His short, but meaningful statement portrays that things change, but the important things—namely people and community—do not necessarily follow the path of change. He believes in the power of people.

Gilbert and I shake hands and express our gratitude to each other for the conversation. Then on a lighter note, we share a compliment for making the other person's hat look better. The reality is that there is not a thing we can do to make our hat or the other person's hat look better or even assume an aura of anything other than a beat-up, dirty head cover with self-acclaimed character.

The drive east on US 12 provides time for me to reflect on our conversation and the future of rural America. That seventy-one-years-young man, who returned home to Groton and assumed the task of helping a farmer friend, continues to farm his dad's acreage purchase over sixty years later. Gilbert demonstrates an enduring commitment to his community, his family, and to farming. The questions that beg to be answered are the ones I continue to pursue: Is Gilbert a member of a dying breed, and what is the future of the towns like Groton?

CHAPTER 10

Minnesota

Our planned stop is Willmar, Minnesota, for a couple of interviews and a good night's rest. Traveling back roads often does not provide a direct route, so we just aimlessly drive southeast in the general direction of Willmar. After a little over two hours of driving, we discover the beautiful, quiet, small town of Appleton, Minnesota, located about twenty miles across the South Dakota-Minnesota state line on US 59. By happenstance we discover a town with a great community spirit and a big heart.

The economy in Appleton, located in Swift County, experienced a rapid population decline with the 2010 closing of the Prairie Correctional Facility.

We drive around town on the backstreets, eventually stopping to briefly talk with a group of about fifteen high-school-age students, who are fixing up an older home. They are excited about their project and its obvious success. A young lady among the group directs us to the grocery store.

During our meandering in search of the grocery store, we come upon a small, well-groomed park, nestled in the crook of the Pomme de Terre River. The park is the setting of a military memorial for people who lost their lives during a war. Four smaller statues, each depicting the four branches of the military, flank the larger statue dedicated to the persons who lost their lives. A brief conversation with a proud resident reveals that Appleton's streets are named after military personnel killed in combat. The process began with World War II military on May 21, 1947, and extends through today and the wars in the Middle East.

After spending some time absorbing the beauty and meaning, Mo and I cross a "walking bridge" to walk along the banks of the swift Pomme de Terre River. Mo, of course, thinks a swim is appropriate. She obviously did not comprehend the characteristics of swift water. Thankfully, she heeds my call to return and forgoes the swim. Begrudgingly, we depart Appleton and drive toward Willmar.

My drive from Appleton toward Willmar provides time to reflect about war and loss of life. I think about how humans can sometimes be cruel to other humans. I am not anti-war. But I know all to clearly the ramifications of war, loss of life, life-sustaining injuries that people carry for the remainder of their lives, and the trauma to families. I think about the friends I have lost. I wonder what happened to their children.

On a totally different level, I think about Gilbert's story of saving a horse. I recall the many times I have seen animals being treated cruelly. I consider his attitude toward humanity as he saved one animal. I wonder why this humanity does not spread to human beings and make them more considerate of animals. As I drive, I consider the question, "Why?"

Mo

I think it is time I take over the storytelling. Randy will not tell you the details of how a great day "turns south," and I do not mean by the compass. First, I really like Appleton; the people are friendly and pet me. The park is beautiful. I sit by Randy's left side for a long time as he stands in silence before the memorial. I see the tear in his eye. I know to sit quietly. I also know that my role as a dawg is to make my human happy. I will . . . in due time.

We leave the memorial and walk toward a river. It is time to brighten his day. The river is filled with rapid-running, clean water. I know better than to jump in, because it is too swift. Dawgs are smarter than most people think. My feint toward the river causes my human to think I am going jump off the steep bank for a swim. Not me; I am brave, but not stupid.

Randy reacts. It is kind of fun watching my human when his blood pressure rises.

I immediately make a short run through the park for a smell check. It is a great run until I hear the famous words, "Let's go, Mo." A little more smelling and a slow walk toward the truck results in another, "Let's go, Mo." My slow walk gets me one of Randy's looks of disgust, which improves when I jump into the backseat. Everybody is happy as we continue our journey.

A one-and-a-half-hour drive brings us to Willmar, Minnesota. I immediately sense my human is confused, because he says, "This does not look like Willmar." He remembers Willmar as a friendly small town where he once camped . . . over thirty years ago.

Even I know things can change during a period of thirty years. Duh! We are basically lost, but not everyone in our group of two is aware of it.

In an attempt to save the day, he stops at a vegetable stand and inquires about a campground. The short response from the male attendant is, "There aren't any."

That is followed by Randy's second question: "Where is the *closest* campground?"

The attendant's even more curt response? "I don't know." (The unspoken words are, "And I really don't give a . . .")

Then the questioning reverses. The attendant asks, "Don't you have a campground book?"

It would have been a great time to say "thank you" and move on, but that seldom happens. Instead, Randy gives him a look that always makes people say words I hate to hear. Before the attendant can respond, Randy's mouth kicks into overdrive, "A campground book would ruin the whole idea of our trip."

Thankfully, before Randy can embellish the comment, the attendant turns, walks the other way, as if to say bother someone else. The good news is that we stop for ice cream before we point the truck toward Mankato, Minnesota. But the afternoon does not get any better.

We arrive in Mankato and drive on the bypass, looking for a campground: like one might just be waiting for us. This type of exploration never works, so we stop at a gas station/convenience store. The sky is getting dark, the clouds are getting darker, and the wind is blowing, which are all bad indicators. A young man takes up our cause and searches the phone book. He goes one step further and makes a suggestion and actually *calls* the campground. It is settled; we are going to Madison Lake.

We point the grey truck east and travel. I spend the trip with my head on a swivel, looking back to watch the dark clouds chase us. Then I gaze forward to ensure we are not heading down the wrong road. After a thirty-minute drive and a twenty-minute parking escapade, we are setting up camp—and constantly checking the progress of the dark clouds.

The sky becomes lighter; the clouds move away from the sun and us. I eat, then we walk the hiking trail. My kind of evening!

Randy announces that it is dinnertime for him, which usually means me sitting in the truck and waiting. He drives the truck a short distance to a bar and grill just outside the campground entrance. He parks close to the patio of the Trail Blazer Inn: very appropriately named. He enters the bar and reappears out the backdoor to sit on the crowded patio. He and the waitress talk; she brings him a beer. He then climbs over the short split-rail fence and lets me out of the truck. He asks me to walk beside him and lay *by* the fence, with instructions not to move or crawl *under* it. I do very well. It only takes three or four reminders. He shares some of his hamburger with me. Finished eating, he jumps over the fence to walk me to the truck. The waitress yells something to Randy. He looks over his shoulder and responds, "I will be right back. I am putting my dawg in the truck." The patio crowd laughs and shakes their heads as Randy jumps back over the fence. The waitress tells Randy, "You are my favorite customer tonight," followed by, "Do you live around here?"

It is important that I tell you about the patio experience. Randy forgets to tell people about some of his well intended actions that turn out less than expected by him. Me, on the other hand, or foot, know that embarrassment is on the horizon.

With the patio experience over, we walk some more before returning to the camper. The sky once again becomes dark, and the wind blows stronger. A few people gather and tell war stories about the storms they have experienced. Finally, it rains. All the heroes go inside their campers for cover. The rain quits, we sleep, and another great day is in the book.

Randy

It is morning, and we are having a disoriented drive on county roads heading toward Owatonna, Minnesota. Eventually, as we approach US Highway 14, we enter a restaurant-sized town. The sign states "Waseca." A drive on State Street leads us through an inviting, clean, well-maintained downtown. Waseca, like many Minnesota towns, has lakes—Loon Lake and Clear Lake—within its city limits. The Waseca County Courthouse, historic buildings, and lakes make for a scenic town. The well-maintained town shows the pride and self-respect of its citizens.

Waseca County, prior to being organized in 1857, was inhabited by Dakota Native Americans. In Dakota language, "Waseca" means "rich in provisions." Today, the county with a population of slightly greater than 19,000, has a reported land mass of 433 square miles. The county seat, Waseca, was platted in 1867 on the Winona and St Peters Railroad. It was incorporated as a town in 1868 and as a city in 1881. Today, the town population of 9,345 represents a little over half of the approximate 19,000 county residents. Population increased from approximately 6,800 in 1970 to about 8,500 in 2000: a 25% increase. The most common industry of manufacturing and other local businesses provides significant employment opportunities, as most people travel less than ten minutes to work.

A gas-pump conversation reveals that the Maplewood Restaurant serves great breakfasts. A short drive east on US 14 leads us to the Maplewood Restaurant parking lot. The large parking area clearly signifies that farmers with pickup trucks are valued customers.

I enter the restaurant to join nine people, none of which are farmers, for breakfast. I assume the farmers have already eaten breakfast and are in the fields. The waitress confirms my thought when she says, "The farmers start coming in around 5:30 for breakfast before they go to the fields."

It is a slow time for customers, so the cook walks from the kitchen to join our conversation. After listening to the waitress and me talking, he adds, "My family bought this fifty-year-old restaurant thirty-two years ago. This is truly a family restaurant that employs only family members."

After the server brings my food, the cook asks a couple of questions to ensure my omelet has all the right ingredients.

Following my dialogue with the two employees, I have a conversation with three senior women drinking coffee at the table adjoining mine. The conversation evolves into an interview with Marilyn, plus input from her two friends.

Marilyn begins the conversation by describing Waseca. She paints the picture of Waseca as being a friendly town that has changed very little during her life. Marilyn informs me that she and her recently deceased husband were married fifty-five years and lived in Waseca their entire lives (over seventy) years. She continues, "Ethnically and religiously, the town is homogenous, with most people being of German descent and Catholic and Lutheran religious persuasion." One of the ladies immediately informs us that she is Norwegian. The other two women laugh and confirm that she is unique, which creates laughter and additional humorous comments.

People in Waseca, like in most small towns I have visited, help each other. The mindset in Waseca is to ensure respect for others' privacy. Marilyn firmly states:

> We help each other; you just have to ask [for help]. It is being insensitive to help others without being asked. If you offer to help someone without being asked, you are interfering with someone's business. When I lost my husband, a lot of people said, "I will help you, just ask."

The other two women nod in agreement that asking for help is appropriate. This mindset shows a sense of independence and respect for others. As a result, I attempt to show sensitivity by making myself available for assistance, stating, "If you need help, please feel welcome to ask me." It is a work in progress.

Independence and respect is accompanied by the importance of responsibility and dependability. A personal story confirms Marilyn's belief that responsibility, dependability, and learning from mistakes are important. She operated a lemonade stand at the county fair for fifty years. "I hired a young boy for three hours a day because he needed work. He showed up every day until Saturday, our busiest day. I would not let him work Sunday, because he would not learn responsibility [if allowed to work]." Marilyn believed that this young boy would not learn responsibility, if not held accountable for failing to meet his commitment to work the previous day. She looks at me with a thoughtful expression and states, "The government is too easy giving money away." Marilyn exhibits a strong resolve that people should be responsible for themselves.

The conversation transitions from individual responsibility and sensitivity to the health of Waseca as a town. The three women agree Waseca has grown approximately 50% (from 6,000 to 9,000 people) during the past fifty years. They agree that most of the growth occurred during the 1970s, with much less growth occurring since. With the issue of population growth established, Marilyn's friends excuse themselves for a scheduled event. I bid farewell and thank them for their comments. They laugh and tell me they enjoyed it. One lady states, "Without my help, the Norwegians would not have been included." I agree.

Increased farm size and availability of rental cropland contribute to the reduction in the growth of population. Marilyn states, "Farms have become much larger. Land rents for $400 per acre." The $400-per-acre rental land, with the current crop prices, allows the landowner and farmer to make a reasonable profit. Rental land allows farmers, especially large ones with bigger machinery, to rent additional acreage to grow crops. Larger farms and leased acreage allow one farmer to work more acres, thus reducing the number of farmers.

Reduction of farmer population results in fewer jobs and requires less support people, such as businesses and school staff. Marilyn states, "Car dealerships, restaurants, clothing and hardware stores, and services stations have [all] been among the lost businesses. Waseca has experienced the loss of several jobs and an increase in home foreclosures during the past two years." She believes that corporate stores locating in the area have added to the loss of jobs.

Marilyn changes her focus to the positive aspect of businesses in Waseca. There are three main industries that employee several people. She embellishes, "Winegar, the oldest, has operated for over thirty years. It is a contract machining-manufacturing company. Browning Printing, the largest employer, prints magazines. The third industry, Birds Eye, freezes corn and peas." The three companies greatly contribute to the employment of people in both the town of Waseca and Waseca County.

Marilyn has a lot of resolve and pride in Waseca and its people. She believes in the necessity of individual responsibility, and the determination to improve one's self translates to responsibility, determination, and health of the community as a whole. The lifetime home of her and her late husband remains a sense of pride and commitment, as do the residents of her town. Marilyn holds herself to the same standards as she does her community by exhibiting self- resolve and pride.

I thank Marilyn for her time and insight into individual responsibility. She completes our conversation by thanking me for taking the time to learn about Waseca. Marilyn then scurries off to attend the funeral of one on Waseca's residents.

If any of my readers want a good home-cooked meal in a friendly atmosphere, I highly recommend Maplewood Restaurant. There clearly is pride in service, as demonstrated by both the cook and the server. While I was talking with Marilyn, the cook took my breakfast to the kitchen. He returned with a smile and said, "Your breakfast had gotten cold. I reheated it."

As I am leaving, the clock's train whistle sounds to inform me that it is 11 a.m. I have enjoyed my visit to a friendly farm town.

Mo and I are driving to Owatonna, one of four preplanned visits during our northwest tour. The drive to Owatonna is about twenty minutes east on US 14. Jim, a close friend and hockey coach, grew up in Owatonna. We once brought our team of thirteen- and fourteen-year-old players from Colorado Springs, Colorado to play a weekend series in Owatonna. The competition was good, and the people graciously accepted us into their homes for social gatherings.

Later, Jim, in his early forties, died unexpectedly from natural causes while playing hockey. I just need to visit his hometown.

Owatonna, the seat of Steele County, has a 2010 total of approximately 25,000 residents. The most common industry appears to be manufacturing. Owatonna contains over 65% of Steele County's 2010 population of approximately 36,500. The county has a landmass of 430 square miles.

Mo and I walk around the uniquely beautiful downtown. Attractions include a large park situated in a downtown square. The park is framed by two historic buildings: one built in 1908 that now houses a Wells Fargo Bank and the other, the Owatonna City and Firemen's Hall, constructed in 1906–07. The park is busy with people sitting on benches, chatting, or having lunch.

A candidate for mayor recommends that I talk with Elmer, the county fair director. Mo and I leave the serene setting of the park for the Steele County fairgrounds, located south of town.

We easily locate the fairgrounds. As usual, we wander around the area looking for the office. Another common event that always impedes our progress is that my interests and Mo's are not closely aligned. Mine is to find the office; Mo's is to smell, hunt, and chase a squirrel. My interest eventually prevails, but not until Mo leashes up.

I enter the office unannounced, with one Golden Retriever on a short leash. The secretary's smile and warm greeting provides a welcome mat. Elmer immediately appears from his adjoining office. After a handshake and a friendly pet for Mo, he says, "Take her leash off; she will be okay." A short hesitation, a smile, and I respond, "It might be good to keep the leash on Mo." Elmer insists that we let her do her thing, so off comes the leash.

After a couple of pets, Mo's first action is to check for food, which includes going into the wastebasket from her nose up to her ears. Within seconds, Mo's scavenger hunt for food results in success and an over-turned wastebasket with trash on the floor. While Mo chews remnants of food, Elmer immediately picks up the trash and says, "It's okay. Let's go to my office." Me, I feel fortunate to not be headed for the truck. Mo wags her tail and proudly leads the way.

Elmer's office is very large, with a desk, credenza, and furniture that facilitate meetings. The environment is very relaxed as we both sit on swivel chairs that lean back. We begin our conversation with Elmer's embellishment of the local history. The story transcends back to a time when Native Americans and European-American settlers shared a rich, fertile land.

Elmer begins the story of the local community by intermingling the written account of Steele County Historical Society's website with his personal knowledge. During the 1850s, the settlement began with two log cabins, a railroad station, combination general store/post office, fire station, farm machinery building, blacksmith shop, and country school. Elmer adds that the town was named after Owatonna, an American-Indian princess, who came to drink the mineral water from the springs. It cured her illness. The Owatonna Chamber webpage embellishes Elmer's account by stating that Owatonna's father, Chief Wabena, was the one who brought his daughter to the springs to cure her illness. In contrast, the Steele County Historical Society's website states that a more likely scenario is that the name originated from a river the Native Americas called "ouitunya" ("straight river"). Today, the river reflects that origin and is named "Straight River."

Both scenarios make for interesting conversation around a campfire. I will probably tell both, and let the listener decide which is true.

Elmer smoothly transitions the conversation to a brief synopsis of his life: why and how he happened to come to Owatonna; the recent history of Owatonna and its community; and an in-depth background and current events of the fair. It is almost like he is reading my mind about my need to make a meaningful story.

As often happens, my attention is diverted to the unexpected behavior of my dawg. Just as Elmer starts to talk, I notice Mo doing a belly crawl under a desk, headed for the credenza. I decide to treat the situation as I used to with my kids: don't ask or say anything, because you might not want to know or hear the answer (i.e., ignore it with the hope it will go away).

I did, and it did. Mo captures the three peanuts under the credenza and returns to sleep beside my chair.

With the drama gone, I am able to give my full attention to Elmer's story. He was born and raised in Fertile, Minnesota, in the northwest part of the state. His hometown is located about thirty miles from North Dakota. He taught at Crookston and East Grand Forks, in the northwest part of the state. He came with his superintendent to Owatonna in 1965. Elmer was the principal of the elementary and intermediate schools until he took an early retirement in 1994 to become manager of the Steele County Fair.

Our conversation immediately turns to Elmer's interpretation of Owatonna's interesting history. The history and growth of Steele County, I soon realize, is linked to the success and growth of the county fair, which directly affects the growth of the county. Location, as always, is important.

Owatonna is located on Interstate 35, about sixty miles south of the Twin Cities: Minneapolis and St. Paul. Elmer states that the interstate has greatly influenced the growth of Owatonna. Elmer attributes Owatonna's doubling of population since 1965 to being located on IS 35 and his town's proximity to a large metro area. He is also clear that the development of shopping areas and businesses contributes to the growth.

Mr. Kaplan, a real estate developer, and two others were instrumental in purchasing and developing Three Corners, a large shopping area located at the intersection of IS-35 and US Highway 14. Elmer states assuredly, "The opening of a Cabela's [retail] store about ten years ago was instrumental in the shopping-area growth." He summarizes the value of an interstate highway, saying, "Development of towns was first attributed to rivers, then railroads, and then interstate highways."

My own experience, especially during this trip, confirms his beliefs about development of settlements, with one addition: Migration trails such as the Oregon and Santa Fe Trails also were significant factors for the development of towns.

Owatonna and Steele County are examples of the changing demographics in rural America. The dairy industry was a large component of employment during the past. In the early 1960s, there were several butter makers/creameries in Steele County. Elmer states:

> Steele County was once known as the butter capital of the world. Now the lone butter maker/creamery sells to local restaurants and candymakers. In the 1960s, there were thirty-two butter-maker exhibitors at the fair; now there is only one.

Employment has shifted significantly. Federal Insurance, with about 16,000 to 18,000 people, has replaced agriculture as the largest employer. "Farming, mostly soybeans and corn, remains a large industry, even though the size of individual farms is much larger than they were thirty years ago," Elmer states. There are approximately the same number of acres, but those acres are operated by fewer farmers.

The fact that the farms are larger but fewer in number has influenced a change in Steele County during the recent decades. The local economy has shifted away from being primarily agricultural to become increasingly oriented to manufacturing and retail shopping. Even with the changes, a diminished focus on the number of agri-businesses, and decreased employment in the industry sector, the Steele County Fair has continued to grow: a phenomenon that strongly suggests the fair is embedded in a strong, historical foundation.

The long and distinguished history of the Steele County Fair becomes immediately apparent after I ask Elmer, "Can you tell me about the Steele County Fair and why it has continued to grow?" His initial response is, "The success of the fair has been a combination of city planning, location, and aggressive pursuit of developing the fair."

The fair, which began a few years after Owatonna was settled in 1860, has been held every year except 1943, when World War II interceded. Prizes given for the 1860 fair included $6 for the best yoke team, $3 for the best wagon, and $1 for the best washing machine. It was a street fair until the early 1900s, when land was purchased to hold the event south of town.

In the 1880s, early in the local fair's history, state officials recognized the insightfulness and ability of the Steele County Fair Board to conduct a successful fair. They chose Owatonna, a small town, to host the 1883 and 1884 Minnesota State Fair. The success of the Minnesota State Fair in Owatonna could be attributed to local effort, expertise, and support from beyond the area. Elmer adds, "Trains contributed to the success of the state fair in Owatonna by providing free transportation for entrants."

In 1827, when the Steele County Fair Board traveled to Michigan to observe a "free fair" (i.e., no admission fee was charged), members illustrated willingness to aggressively move from the norm. Free fairs were non-existent in Minnesota at the time, and the implementation of a free fair in Owatonna caused quite a backlash from other Minnesota county fair boards, who attempted to have legislation passed to terminate funds for free fairs. The free-fair movement became common in Minnesota, thanks to the Steele County Fair Board's initiative to introduce the concept. The compensation issue was solidified several years ago, with legislation passed to compensate county fairs per animal entrant.

The purpose of county fairs is to promote agriculture. Elmer states:

Our county fair is a true agriculture fair. We usually have 2,000 animals each year at our fair. The livestock shows consist of 4-H members, as well as breeders and other farmers. The reduction in [the] number of farmers has minimally affected total livestock exhibitors. Out-of-county exhibitors and attendees have minimized this effect in other areas of the fair. One out of three of the 275,000 attendees [in 2010] came from out of [the] county.

He concludes that the fair annually adds about $9 million to the local economy.

The Steele County Fair webpage revealed that 306,000 people attended the fair in 2012. The average daily attendance of the six-day fair was approximately 46,800 in 2010 and 51,000 in 2012. To put the size of the Steele County Fair into perspective, it exceeds some state fairs in both average daily and total attendance. Also, many state fairs last anywhere from ten days to two weeks. Elmer states, "The landmass of Steele County is the second smallest county in Minnesota, but has the largest fair."

The Steele County Fair maintains a healthy reputation. Elmer claims:
If your county fair is big enough, people will come to you with requests to be an exhibitor. The same family with its taffy-making company is coming back for the eighty-fifth year. The same company donated an old taffy puller for the museum. The company's reputation allows them to focus on large fairs, but they come back because of tradition. Two of the largest exhibitors are the US Air Force and [the] army. Next year, the US Army is bringing a seventy-foot display.

The Steele County Fair is an example of a small town refusing to remain small and accept what the future brings. The people instead decided to build their future. Growth and a healthy future are seldom about one event or business. Instead, they require an infrastructure that promotes and supports the event or events, such as fairs, businesses, or tourist attractions. Deeper yet, growth and a healthy future are about people like Mr. Kaplan and his associates' development of a shopping area. Or Ken Austin, my friend Jim's father, who was instrumental in getting a new fair building.

Owatonna, Minnesota is a town, which has decided to shape its future.

We conclude our visit with a tour of the Steele County Fair Museum. The size of the museum and number of display items far exceed my expectations. The old taffy-pulling machine is one of many examples. Some items retrieve memories from my youth. I also recall how the Rush County Fair brought my own community to life with its midway, livestock, and other 4-H exhibits. The Rush County Fair was five days of excitement and work for the exhibitors and many other people, both participants and attendees.

As Elmer states, "The Steele County Fair is an agriculture-based event with fun for everyone."

My conversation with Elmer is very enlightening. I am impressed with how a small town with strong leadership has developed over the past few decades. They have used their resources very effectively. I thank Elmer for his time, sharing, and willingness to let Mo have fun. He, in my mind, represents the rural American attitude.

Follow up of the 2014 annual Steele County Fair revealed that the Fair Board estimated that slightly less than 340,000 people attended the six-day event.

Mo

My fair experience starts in Elmer's office in Owatonna. Soon after we enter, the administrative assistant introduces my human and me to Elmer. That starts things off on a good note, because most of the time, I am not included in introductions. Things only get better. Elmer pets me and tells me I can run loose. Actually, he tells my human it is okay to remove my leash. So that five-foot barrier to my freedom is suddenly gone, and so am I.

There are a lot of good smells. Whoops! There goes a wastebasket. In the process of smelling its contents, and perhaps food scraps, the wastebasket tips over. Not a big deal. If the stuff was in there, it can surely be put back.

As Elmer and my human go into Elmer's office, being polite, I lead. They sit and talk; I become bored and stretch out on the floor. Wait! There is an interesting smell. If I move slowly and crawl on my belly, no one will notice. Sure enough, there are a couple of peanuts under a credenza. Not any more. I did my work to help clean up a little bit. Isn't life good when we all work together?

After a long time, Elmer and my human walk toward the door leading to the Fair Museum. As my human reaches for the leash, Elmer states, "Mo will be okay." What a guy! I walk around, smelling scents that appear to be from a time long in the past. It is interesting to smell about times I did not know existed.

After a long time, even in dawg years, we express our thanks: the humans with words, and me with a lick and a lean. I hope, as my human does, that we can go to a fair during our trip.

Randy

Thirty minutes of driving and the time of day make the KOA at Austin, Minnesota the obvious choice for our destination. While sitting around the campfire and reviewing a map, I decide to spend two nights in Austin and do an exploration of local communities. The Iowa-Minnesota state line is only a few miles south, which will allow us to spend time in the Hawkeye state.

CHAPTER 11

Iowa

The next morning, Mo and I head south about twenty miles on US Highway 218, which leads us to St. Ansgar, Iowa: the northern-most Iowa town located on US 218. Residents estimate the population to be slightly grater than 1,100 people. The eight-mile drive in Iowa leads us to a large grain mill sitting adjacent to US 218 and a railroad track. Soon after passing the mill, Highway 218 turns left at Fourth Street and proceeds out of town to the east and eventually south, about twenty miles to the Mitchell County seat of Osage.

The quiet rural town of St. Ansgar began when Claus Lauritz Clausen (who was originally from the island of Aeroe, Denmark before he moved to Muskego in Racine County, Wisconsin) explored the areas of northern Iowa and southern Minnesota. In 1852, Reverend Clausen's desire to explore led him and five companions to the area where Cedar River and a river he named "Deer Creek" joined the waters. He named the site "St. Ansgar," meaning "God's spear," after a French monk and bishop who was a missionary to the Scandinavian countries during the ninth century.

The following year, 1853, Reverend Clausen returned with seventy-five settlers and thirty wagons to settle the area. This very same year he was instrumental is starting First Lutheran Church of St. Ansgar. It is remarkable that only nine pastors have served First Lutheran Church during its over one and a half history.

Later, around 1867, Clausen helped start St. Olaf Lutheran Church a few miles north in southern Minnesota. St. Olaf eventually became two churches serving the separate communities of Hayfield and Byron, both in Minnesota.

Back to the reality of driving, my trip continues until I make a right turn that takes us into the small-business district of town. At nine o'clock in the morning, the town is quiet, except for a few businesspersons opening their stores. At the intersection of Fourth and Washington Streets, several parked vehicles, mostly pickup trucks, tell me that the Sportsman Lounge is our breakfast spot in St. Ansgar. I take a chance that it is the latter and enter the front door. It *is* the breakfast spot, filled with good food and several lively discussions, most of which are unburdened by facts or data.

While drinking coffee and perusing the menu, Norbert and Don enter and sit at the booth next to me. I immediately realize they either are bored or like to pick on strangers, because they invite me to join them. I soon recognize it is both. After a bit of fun and harassment, we start a conversation about St. Ansgar. Norbert and Don are both farmers and have lived in the community their entire lives.

Norbert begins with a humorous perspective of the history of the community. He says, "St. Ansgar was founded in 1854 by a bunch of Norwegians. They got lost. People are friendly. We invited you to talk to us." Norbert then abandons his humor and become serious when he states:

> The Lutheran Church started in 1852, two years prior to the founding of the town. There were a lot of onions, cabbage, and potatoes grown from the 1920s until early 1940s, when the industry moved west to drained swampland. The cattle industry was large, but now it has moved to larger operations and feedlots. Now the main agriculture products are corn and soybeans and limited dairy operations.

Norbert takes a breath, giving Don a chance to add, "There is very little dairy in our community. Mennonites have moved here and started a few dairies. They do a little of everything, such as chickens and nurseries."

The discussion transitions from farming to St. Ansgar's very important companies: Grain Miller and Malt-O-Meal (frequently called "Horizon Foods"). "Grain Miller started twelve years ago [around 2000] as a silo. It is a Swedish owned company, with locations in Oregon and Canada. The Multi-O-Meal building connects to Grain Miller," Norbert states.

Don picked up the explanation by stating that Grain Miller purchases most of it is grain from Canada and North Dakota. He continues, "They process it here and ship it out. Malt-O-Meal uses a lot of the grain to make cereal. They process the hulls into heating pellets for stoves and furnaces. Our local school heats with their pellets." Much of St. Ansgar's local economy and slightly increasing population can be attributed to the two companies.

St. Ansgar's webpage states that their 2010 population was 1,107, which is a 7.3% growth since the 2000 census. It further claims to be the fastest-growing town in Mitchell County.

Don and Norbert become bored with the history and industry and enthusiastically convert the conversation to today's quality of life in the St. Ansgar community. Don begins, "Very few people milk the system for money and support, unless they need it." Norbert nods his head in strong agreement and states with pride, "Good little town to live in. You do not see any empty buildings [in the downtown area]."

Norbert makes a comment that triggers a rapid succession of verbal thoughts between he and Don, each building on the other. The conversation that ensues makes me feel like a professional interviewer.

Norbert: "People help each other when asked."

Don: "People are very loyal. There are a number of benefits here, such as fundraisers for children with cancer."

Norbert: "People really help and support the community and people."

Don: "There was a benefit for cancer walk at Osage [the Mitchell County seat]."

Norbert: "They had over 400 people attend the omelet breakfast, sponsored by the American Legion."

Don: "People help each other."

Norbert nods in agreement.

Again, the boat changes its course in midstream. The two farmers are testing me to see if I can keep up with them. Norbert states, "We are twenty miles from the closest town that has a Walmart." Don adds, "We have four churches. The people are great!" Norbert nods in affirmation.

Our conversation ends as quickly as it started. Norbert and Don have other things to do. I thank them for their time and expert knowledge. My comment about "expert knowledge" creates laughter. Norbert concludes, "We are experts; it just takes a stranger to realize it." I am happy to be the stranger who provided the opportunity for Norbert and Don to show their expertise.

I wake up a sleeping dawg for a walk through downtown on Fourth Street, while hoping Mo will use her charm to find another unsuspecting person. We end our travel at the other end of town without meeting anyone.

I notice the local barbershop, which is always a good place to meet talkers. The door is locked, even though the sign clearly states that it is normal business hours. As I stand there scratching my head, thinking that the barber must be running an errand, a friendly voice from behind asks, "Which one of you needs a haircut?" Before I can respond, the woman informs me that the barber is at the county fair in Osage, watching his daughter show livestock.

I immediately ask, "Where is the fair?" She explains it is in Osage: "Just follow highway 218."

As fast as I can walk two blocks to retrieve a truck, Mo and I, with great anticipation, are heading south about twelve miles to the Mitchell County Fair in the town of Osage. Twenty minutes later, we are walking through the main gate, taking in the sites of a small county fair. We follow the crowd, which I assume to be a good idea. Our path leads to the only food court. Much to my surprise, Mo handles the food situation well—probably better than the customers.

As a stranger with a camera, a folder full of papers, and a seventy-five-pound dawg, I create a vacant area around our table. A friendly, inquisitive couple is brave and joins us. Well, they are not completely brave. They sit across the table at the furthest corner, in case they need a rapid egress. Their friendliness might have been influenced by the fact that all the other tables are taken. Nonetheless, Mo and I stick to the notion that they are friendly. I start a conversation with them.

Jim is wearing a cap with the inscription "Korean War Veteran 8209th MASH 1951–53." MASH is the acronym for "Mobile Army Surgical Hospital," which was depicted in both a movie and long-lasting television series. Our conversation begins with his military experience. He speaks briefly about his army service. "Talk to anyone around here between the ages of seventy-nine and eighty-three; they were in the service." He elaborates on his duty with the 8209th MASH unit by stating, "We did not wear GI [army government issue] clothing, but instead dressed in such clothes as loafers and jeans." Their attire appeared to emulate that of the movie and television series *Mash*.

He introduces me to Jan, his wife of six years, proudly informing me that they were married in The Little Brown Church in the Vale, as were he and his first wife (who he was married to for forty-eight years). He continues by stating that the church does not have Sunday services, but is used for weddings. "They shut the doors for weddings and allow only invited guests."

The Little Brown Church in the Vale, located in Nassau, Iowa, will host its fifty-eighth annual reunion this year. "This year will be my fifty-sixth one to attend," says Jim.

He then transitions to talking about his childhood, ancestors, and how Osage has changed. He proudly claims:

> My father's parents came from Kentucky. My grandmother was married when she was sixteen years old. She brought her horse with her when she came from Kentucky. My grandfather put the horse down [killed it] when it was forty-two years old. He tanned its hide. The hide has been around for seventy years. I still have it. I remember the day he put the horse down.

After a long pause, I pose the question, "How has your town changed?" Jim's immediate response is, "Now [today] businesses are mostly what you call"—he pauses—"antique stores." His pause reflects the sorrow embedded in his next statement: "There is no way I can explain to you. We don't have anything anymore. We have to drive thirty-five miles to Mason City to trade."

He continues by summarizing how Osage has changed during the past several years. Examples of the diminishing number of businesses are reflected in his statement, "We had eight supermarkets; now we have one. We have one new-car dealership and two used. In the past we had six."

Jim transitions his thoughts to the human aspect of Osage. Even though the population has remained rather constant, the characteristics of the people have changed. He recounts:

> The population is approximately 3,500, which is about the same as it was when I was four years old. When I was in the sixth and seventh grades, I was related to 60% of the other students. We are now a bedroom community, with most of the people traveling to Austin, Minnesota and Charles City and Mason City, Iowa to work. About one-half of our people work for Winnebago.

The loss of businesses, minimal reduction of population, and the fact that this rural town is not in the proximity to a large populated area, yet has become a bedroom community, all cause me amazement.

The three towns of Austin, Charles City, and Mason City have a total population of about 60,000, and each is located about thirty miles from Osage.

Jim's business fell victim to the lost retail in Osage. "I owned a meat market for twenty-six years. I shot the animals and butchered them," he states. He then turns and looks down the midway. His final comment summarizes his interview: "There is no Ferris wheel this year." The sadness in his voice and shake of his head clearly expresses his emotions of how Osage has changed over past several years.

His statement reflects his feelings about a town that once served it residents with businesses. Jim is a man with a great sense of pride for both his service to his country and his hometown: a hometown that is no longer a thriving, self-sustaining business center and does not have a Ferris wheel at the Mitchell County Fair.

I thank Jim and Jan for their time and the informative interview and bid them "farewell."

As Mo and I depart the food court without an incident and head toward the cattle barn, I give her a pet and hug to show how I appreciate her being a good dawg. A little positive reinforcement can go a long way with a Golden Retriever.

Mo

I am excited to get out of the truck and walk. Our walk starts on a shady street and progresses to a place with interesting sights and smells. First and foremost, food. I smell food. Second, there are a lot of potential petters—people. After passing small buildings, wooden statues of people, and horses galloping in a circle with kids on their backs (all to the tune of music), I smell food. In front of us are several tables with seats attached and a small building on wheels with lines of people facing a window. A person stands at the window for a short time and then receives a box of food. I tug toward the window, but to no avail. I just don't understand why we miss all the food deals.

We talk with some folks and then walk toward a barn, where I see a surprising thing: Some dawgs are telling sheep where to go. I have herded geese off my yard into the lake, but I never dreamed dawgs could herd *sheep*. I ask myself the same question I pose when I move geese: "Why does the higher species never help herd?"

Dawgs move sheep and cattle through a gate and into a pen while their human watches. The human usually sits on a horse, in a pickup truck, or stands with his hands in his pockets and a toothpick in his mouth. All the time the human has a mystical facial expression like he is learning something, but he never acquires the skill. Next time, same dawg, different cattle, different pen, same human, same expression, and same results. I do not know about the rest of my fellow dawgs, but I am going to teach my human to herd geese.

Randy

The walk to the cattle barn took less than three minutes. As we walk, I reflect on my youth, when I showed dairy cattle. My thoughts are focused on having a young person tell me his or her story of preparing and showing cattle. I become more excited with each step. Mo is watching a Border Collie work around the sheep. Her eyes are glued on the dawg, who is herding sheep toward an open gate. I am not certain if Mo wants to play or is mystified that life consists of more than fetching and keeping the world free from errant geese and squirrels.

As we approach the livestock barn, I observe a young man walking with an empty bucket and a cattle hairbrush. In moments, I am sitting with Justin on bales of straw and talking about life, cattle, country living, and change. Justin is an eighteen-year-old high school graduate of three months. His perspective, as you will read, is mature for a young person.

His first comments describe his community and town as a friendly and comfortable place to live. "Comforting. You don't have to worry about violence or somebody breaking into your house. Our community is good. Everybody knows everybody. It is one of those towns where anyone will help a person, if they ask," he relays.

I am amazed to again hear "if they ask" in the context of neighbors helping neighbors. It has become obvious to me that the approach is a common one to neighboring in this northern region of the central United States. It further supports my beliefs that state borders and county lines are primarily geographic and political boundaries, with minimal social significance. We certainly have our state and community pride, but as people we share many similarities with others across geographic or political lines. Distance is a greater determinant of social behaviors than borders and boundaries.

Justin then transitions his thoughts to youth activities, with a focus on sports and more pointedly, football. "You feel good about yourself growing up here. If you do something good, everyone recognizes you for it." He describes Osage High School's trip to the quarterfinals in football with these words, "We got to play in the UNI [University of Northern Iowa] Dome. We had between 2,000 and 2,500 fans at the UNI Dome. This was the first year we have done well in football since the early 1990s." His voice dropped some of its excitement "The last game, which we lost, was in Osage."

I pose the question, "How have Osage and the community changed?"

He explains with pride:

A lot of kids go to bigger cities to find a job. Some kids fall in love with it here: go to college and come back in ten years. It is a town you know you can come back to and still feel important. Osage is a great place to raise a family. Northern Iowa young people are learners. It is a great place to grow up and raise kids.

Justin's expression clearly reveals his pride in northern Iowa and Osage. After a quick look for Mo to determine if she has made any new friends (or more pointedly, new enemies), I ask, "How do you prepare to show cattle at a fair?" He states that it is "easy" to get ready to show. I immediately think, *Where did I go wrong all those years ago?* I recall, however, how fun it had been to train the cattle and help them show how cool they were, but getting ready to walk into the show arena was a difficult task.

It was always the hour *prior* to showing that I had not relished. I related it to getting ready to go to a formal dance or party; I had to make myself into someone I was not. The same was true for the cattle; we polished their horns, combed out their braided tails, touched-up their hooves with shiny polish, and clipped the hair in their ears. I would then trade my ragged jeans, T-shirt, and boots for a white shirt, white pants, and white shoes. I looked like Mr. Clean.

Back to reality, I refocus on the now.

Justin begins:

It is a long process [to get the cattle ready] that takes about a year. A major issue is getting them to lead with a halter, settle them down, and get [them] used to people. I believe the most important thing in training is to handle and treat the cattle positively. If you are having a bad day, they sense it, and make it [the showing] miserable.

He shows his pride by stating that two years ago, while competing with seven older showmen, he won "showmanship." His pride elevates even higher: "I have seven cousins in northern Iowa who have won 'showmanship.'"

We then transitioned to show day. He explains in detail:

It starts at about 5 [a.m.]. You feed and scrub them. It is hard work grooming them. You clip their needed areas [and] spray them with various solutions to acquire a perfect appearance. In the ring it is nerve-wracking, with one eye on the judge and one eye on your animal. You may not know the judge, but you communicate like you know each other.

I then ask him to compare being in the ring to being on the football field. He responds, "Each one prepares you for the other." He adds that it is competition that requires focus and concentration. "You practice for the event. The difference are your teammates; one is people, [and] the other is cattle."

I query him about what he sees as his future. "After attaining a degree in agriculture from Iowa State [University], I would like to move out west and buy a big cattle ranch." He then reveals his reflective side: "When I was a kid in school, my friends stayed inside and played video games; I wanted to be outside." He culminates his interview with a pause, looking me in the eye while stating, "I don't name my calves because I would get too attached to them." I share that I know the feeling all too well. I, myself, was unable to show beef cattle or hogs because at the end of the final show, they would have been sold. Instead, I took my diary cattle home to show again the next year.

I thank Justin for our conversation and his candor and maturity. He thanks me for my interest and for listening to him. Mo and I retrace our steps toward the main gate. Our path leads us by the ice cream stand. I pause to decide if a milkshake at three o'clock in the afternoon will suffice as "lunch." Mo knows ice cream when she sees and smells it. Her decision about the ice cream lunch thing is a done deal. Without eye contact, she gives a light tug on the leash in the direction of the ice cream stand. I conclude she has been good and deserves a treat. Actually, I decide that a milkshake is in order.

It is a popular place, and standing in line takes a few minutes to get served. There is not a lot of patience on the other end of the leash. Mo thinks lines, delays, and ice cream are not compatible. She is not a patient dawg, but we endure and everyone is happy.

The only uneventful part of the remaining fair visit, however, is our walk to the truck . . .

Mo

I was on my best behavior for the entire time at the fair. Why? Because I saw a very small building on wheels, with people gathered around it, eating ice cream. As I had hoped, my human gives me a cup of vanilla ice cream: probably because I have been so good. I chase that cup all over the area until the ice cream is gone. Just as I finish, I spot a little girl holding a cup like the one I have just licked clean. She is undoubtedly eating ice cream. I wonder if she would like to share? Oh, what the heck. It won't hurt to ask. With a mighty jerk, I am off. My human drops his milkshake cup, the little girl screams, and her momma yells some awfully ugly words. This pretty well wraps up the day at the fair.

It is a nice walk to the truck, except for a few people pointing and saying, "There is that dawg again." I guess bad notoriety is better than no notoriety; at least, today it is.

Randy

The walk to the truck is rather sedate. I keep my eyes on the pavement, checking for cracks, while Mo holds her head high and looks at every person, as if they should be petting her. Sorry to tell you, Mo, but people view certain incidents differently than dawgs.

A campfire, good night's sleep, and our morning walk allow me to laugh about Mo's quest to share ice cream. Mo may be correct about taking life too serious. Maybe humans, especially me, should lighten up and see the world through the eyes of a dawg. The world might be a better place. I decide I will let Mo be my mentor. I wonder how this will work out?

After packing the camper, we are off for a two-hour drive to visit my daughter, son-in-law, Neil, and grandkids—and their two black Labrador Retrievers. Our home for the weekend is a public campground near Waterloo. We spend the weekend reminiscing, relaxing with family, and walking trails. Kerri, my daughter, is preparing for a sixty-mile cancer benefit walk later in the month.

The dawgs, after re-acquaintance, play and struggle with the concept of sharing toys. There is little progress, even though there is much encouragement. We do take time to eat at my favorite Waterloo restaurant, Morg's Café. It is a rural restaurant in the middle of a town of over 100,000 residents. The employees, guests, eating counter, and decorum all exude *rural*. It is a tradition that we eat breakfast at Morg's every time I visit the area.

All too soon, Mo and I are driving south on US 63, going home to Missouri. The trip encompasses three highways: Highway 63 from Waterloo to Columbia, Missouri accounts for six hours of the eight-hour trip; and Interstate 70 and US Highway 65 account for the remaining miles. The non-complexity of the drive allows me time to reflect on the trip and consider what lies ahead.

Miles pass as I drive through rural America. Highway 63 takes me amidst green fields of corn and soybeans, herds of cattle, and homesteads. I mentally return to the scenery and nature settings of the small towns Mo and I have visited during the past month. The beauty of a town surrounded by mountains or fields of grain is a photograph etched in my mind. Our route also takes us through numerous small towns and people meandering down the streets or accomplishing life's tasks, such as going to the bank, purchasing farm supplies, or heading to the hardware store. I particularly observe people greeting people, and people stopping to briefly talk. In essence, I see people interrupting life's necessary tasks to talk with a friend or be neighborly.

I decide that our next trip, which will occur during early October, will take place during corn- and soybean-harvest season. Our travels will include Illinois, Indiana, Kentucky, all ancestral states, and the surrounding states.

Our continued drive south on US 65 passes the Missouri State fairgrounds. A large sign informs me that the fair will begin in ten days. A state fair, with its concentration of rural Americans, is a must. Plus, I have never seen a fair I did not like. This means livestock barns and show arenas will precede the Midwest trip. Life is good.

Thanks to all the readers for accompanying us on our trip west. You are welcome to join us on our visit to the Missouri State Fair, as well as my childhood home in Indiana and my dad's, grandfather's, and great grandfather's home in Illinois.

Missouri State Fair

CHAPTER 12

Missouri State Fair

Sedalia, the home of the Missouri State Fair, began in 1857, when George R. Smith bought and platted 503 acres. He began selling lots the following year. In 1860 the land was re-platted, and the town became official, with its name changed to Sedalia. Growth of the town and the surrounding area escalated in 1861, when the railroad arrived, bringing people, cattle herds, and drovers. Mr. Smith and the citizens were proactive to make their small town the market center of Central Missouri. The plausibility of the Missouri State Fair being located in West Central Missouri began, some 40 years prior, with the desire and aggressiveness of Mr. Smith and others to make a Sedalia viable market center.

Every year for eleven days in the middle of August, the town of approximately 22,000 people bursts at the seams when it hosts the Missouri State Fair. Sedalia has been the home of the state fair since the fair's inception in 1901. The people of Sedalia, fair employees, and volunteers all approach the fair with the same resolve as their forefathers did 150-plus years ago.

The Missouri State Fair began to grow roots in 1899, when Representative R. E. Clark of Mexico, Missouri introduced a bill creating the fair. Discussion for having a state fair began in 1897. That same year, N. H. Gentry of Sedalia offered 150 acres for the state fair grounds. Sedalia offered the most land and won the six-town competition to host the Missouri State Fair.

The Missouri State Fair Mission Statement is:

The Missouri State Fair promotes excellence in Missouri agriculture, cultivates and supports future leaders in agriculture, and provides opportunities for agriculture community to deepen consumers' understanding and appreciation of agriculture's role in their daily lives and economy of our state.

The mission is a living document that is supported by numerous activities. Examples include Missouri 4-H member competitions; recurring live-agriculture-related displays (e.g., live-calf berthing); live formal and informal presentations; and one-on-one discussions conducted by such group members as Farm Bureau. The fair also is the big stage for other fun activities, such as concerts, midway rides and games, a rodeo, numerous vendors, enticing food and beverages, nightly concerts, and a rodeo.

Proximity of the Missouri State Fair and the potential to talk with a variety of rural Missourians makes the thirty-five-mile trip an easy decision. My experience of meeting friendly people during several previous state fair visits substantiates my decision. There are a couple of issues that afford a slight detraction of pursuing interviews. One, Mo will need to stay home. I can find my way and talk without Mo. The issue is Mo convinced all the people beyond restaurant walls to talk with me. Second, the fact that I have tickets for three concerts creates a question of how much fun can I have at the fair. Weighing the issues, I decide to pack my interview material and go to the fair. The forty-five-minute drive and ten-minute walk to the gate gives me time to build my confidence.

I get strange looks as I approach the Missouri State Fair entrance gate with my camera, folder of consent letters, and tablet, not to mention the ballpoint pen clipped to my T-shirt. My ragged, dirty cap seems to attract more second glances than other well-worn hats entering the gate. But I am one of the few people entering the east gate on a mission: to hear stories about rural America, Missouri-style. The question that begs to be answered is, where do I go to accomplish my mission?

The few number of fair attendees on a mid-morning Friday presents a good time for me to stand in wonderment and look around. I do a couple of 360-degree circles, a maneuver that usually accompanies my time of indecision. During my second gyration, I recognize the Coliseum, which houses a livestock show ring. I stride the short distance to the building while thinking there should be a lot of people watching the 4-H youth show their cattle. To my surprise, most of the observers are parents and grandparents gathered around the show ring, watching their kids show beef cattle. I am a little anxious about interrupting parents or grandparents, because an interruption will likely be intrusive and result in a "No!"

I abandon the idea. It is important to have success in gaining the first interview. Success breads success, and failure breads failure. Plus, the big issue: Mo is not here to bail me out if everyone says "no."

My choice of a seat is located toward the top of the bleachers, well beyond the circle of parents. I start a conversation with a well-dressed man in faded Wranglers, a worn one-size-fits-all baseball cap, and scruffy boots. I think maybe the similarity of our clothing will be a positive point.

Mike responds to my greeting by informing me that one of the female beef-cow handlers is a 4-H and FFA (Future Farmers of America) student from Pleasant Hill School. I explain my research with caution so as to not interrupt him. He says that he can talk with me and watch at the same time. He immediately informs me without a prompt, "We have great kids at our high school. We did not have locks on our lockers until two years ago." This interesting and proud statement is the beginning of a conversation that speaks clearly about a teacher who has a positive attitude about education, kids, and life.

Mike continues, "We [he and the other agriculture teacher] instruct 210 of the estimated 750 Pleasant Hill High School students. Of those 210 students, 187 belong to FFA. We [agriculture] are the biggest 'at-risk program' in the school. Our kids range from top to bottom of the class."

He stops momentarily to watch his student show, then turns to me and says, "I focus a lot on expectations. If you set high expectations, kids will live up to them. They work hard and are respectful. You can change kids. The kids can use math, but they cannot do math in class." He describes how students used math to determine if specifications had been met on the recently built school. Their conclusion was that the builders were very accurate.

We turn our attention to the show ring, where the judge is examining his student's animal. Mike adds:

> A small percentage of the kids [agriculture students], about 2% to 4%, will farm. Most will have day jobs, but will [also] have agriculture roots, such as horses [and] family gardens. I want kids to be ready for the workforce. If 30% to 40% of the kids go to college, what does the other 60% to 70% do?

He then responds to his own question: "We must serve all the kids."

Mike claims there is a trend of high school graduates leaving Pleasant Hill, only to return. He says:

> Students who graduated ten years ago are trying to reestablish back in their hometowns. They are trying to buy small farms of about 40 acres. Some will have gardens, a few animals, or crops, such as hay. Their agriculture classes and the FFA and 4-H programs prepare them to begin their small farming operation.

In addition to teaching agriculture and sponsoring FFA and 4-H, Mike is in charge of the Pleasant Hill Community Education Program. The program assists adults in expanding their life skills. His agriculture-teaching colleague, who was one of his previous students, teaches gardening, greenhouse, and other horticultures in the Community Education Program. Mike states:

> Small-animal production, fruit-tree production, as well as blackberry and raspberry production are [all] part of the community education curriculum. Missouri Agriculture Department staff teaches community gardening. This program creates knowledge that enables landowners to rent small plots of land to people for gardening.

Attendees learn how to manage the plots and provide gardening skills to renters. It becomes obvious from Mike's comment that the community education program meets the needs of the local adult community, as well as providing a service that attracts people to purchase land and move into the Pleasant Hill community.

Mike then transitions to his personal life. "I have taught agriculture for twenty-two years, seventeen of those at Pleasant Hill." His path to becoming a teacher was not easy. "I grew up in the small town of Frankenstein, Missouri. There were eleven kids in my middle-school class. My transition to University of Missouri was an overwhelming challenge. But I was determined to successfully achieve my chosen career." He adds, "My two high school agriculture teachers influenced the path for my chosen career. Charles Parkes and John Haselhorse motivated me to become an agriculture teacher."

Mike redirects his attention from the show ring to me and says with a big smile:

> We have two elementary-age daughters. My wife grew up in a metro area, but quickly adapted to rural farm life. She did not know what to do with the bushels of vegetables that I grew the first year of our marriage. Now she makes a mean salsa and cans green beans, among other vegetables.

His statement reflects pride in his family, as well his wife's ability and desire to become agriculture-oriented. Her transition is a model for people desiring to adjust to farm life.

He transitions our conversation to the family-operated farm and rural, agricultural lifestyle. He states:

> We own and operate a small farm of 96 acres, plus a rental farm of 200 acres. We raise "Beefmaster" cattle and hay. We feed and sell square bales of hay. We deliver hay to people who do not have a means to transport the bales.

Their business requires hiring part-time employees. Mike proudly claims, "We hire only FFA students, because they are hard workers and are responsible." The kids have an opportunity to extend their learning by working in the agriculture industry. In a way, students' jobs become an internship for their agriculture class.

Mike summarizes his beliefs about learning and people in one simple statement: "Every kid in my class has something to offer. It may take a while, but we figure it out."

Our conversation clearly illuminates Mike's vision. It is a vision that people can be empowered to make a difference.

The three facets of his professional life integrate into a system that connects teaching high school, facilitating adult learning, and practicing his related knowledge as a small farmer. Each of these three practices informs the other two, which enables him to improve each aspect of his professional life. Mike has a busy workload, which, from our conversation, appears to be actively supported by family involvement. On a personal, professional note, he touches and positively influences the lives of many young people and adults.

Thank you, Mr. Parkes and Mr. Haselhorse. A teacher may not realize until many years later—or perhaps never—the positive affect she or he has had on someone's life and the lives of following generation members. I stand and say, "Hats off to our teachers."

Mike and I bid farewell. He scurries off to the cattle barn to see his student. I amble around various cattle barns until I meet Ryan, sitting on a lawn chair and taking a break from working with his Angus heifers. He gladly agrees to talk with me about rural America and his preparation of cattle for the big show and competition at a state fair.

My comfortable chair is a square bale of straw. There was a time when a bale of straw beside my cow served as a chair, lunch table, and afternoon nap spot. Showing livestock can bring out the best in a person.

Ryan begins by informing me that he is a spring graduate from Mexico High School in Mexico, Missouri. He adds, "My hometown is the seat of Audrain County, which has about 11,000 people. We are approximately twenty-four miles northwest of Columbia, Missouri. Highway [US] 54 runs through town." The interesting US Highway 54 becomes East Liberty Street for a couple of miles through Mexico, passing a small lake, golf course, and other businesses. The short route adds to the intrigue and beauty of the route along US 54.

The city called "New Mexico" received its name because it was a favorite stopping point for settlers heading to the Republic of Texas. "New" was dropped from the name when Texas became part of the United States.

Mexico is embedded with agriculture industry. Ryan works for Fox Run, a large Angus breeder. "Fox Run breeds about 500 cows per year. It is one of the two largest Angus breeders in Missouri. Sydenstricker, the other breeder, also is located in Mexico, along with an ADM soybean plant.

"We are definitely an agriculture community," Ryan states. He elaborates, "One reason I chose Angus as a breed is [that] I work for Fox Run. Another reason [is] I met and made friends with lot of people who prefer Angus cattle. Missouri is the leading state for Angus."

Ryan is truly a person dedicated to agriculture.

He continues his comments by describing the elements of preparing his heifers for the show ring.

I bought my two heifers last September from a breeder, about eleven months prior to the state fair. I work with my cattle one to two hours each day. I start working them with a halter, next walking them, then washing them. After these steps, we start getting them around people. Next, we trim [their] hooves. I first showed these two heifers at the Audrain County Fair during the second week of July. I took third place and Reserve Champion. After the county fair, we modified the feeding process.

The sequential process for training cattle allows the cattle and Ryan to grow accustomed to each other while building confidence. Beginning with low-threat tasks minimizes the element of fear among the cattle while building trust and learning expectations. Trimming hooves first would undoubtedly start a rodeo scenario that would take months, if ever, to undo. One small step at a time is the foundation for learning, not a lot different than humans, actually.

Ryan's twin brother shows crossbreed hogs, which he raises. "We live on an eighteen-acre farm," Ryan states. "My twin brother will show one heifer, and my dad, who has never shown cattle, will show the second heifer."

It is obvious from his statements that the livestock operation and farm are very much a family affair. Ryan transitions his thoughts from the present to the future. "I am going to keep my heifers and breed them. [Then] hopefully start a herd."

Ryan expands his thoughts about the future by discussing his education plans, relaying, "My immediate future includes pursuit of a degree in junior agriculture this fall at State Fair Community College here in Sedalia." Following his studies at State Fair CC, Ryan plans to work in agriculture. "Hopefully I can live in Missouri and work with cattle. When you work with cattle, there is something new everyday," he states with a broad smile.

Ryan concludes with his determination to gain knowledge through his studies at State Fair Community College, applying that knowledge by continuing to work at Fox Run on weekends.

He tells me that it is time to prepare his cattle for the afternoon show. I express my appreciation for his time and dedication to the pursuit of a career that will help feed the citizens of America and the world. Our conversation also brought back some of my old memories of showing dairy cattle.

He smiles and thanks me for my interest.

As I reflect on Ryan's story, one element becomes very clear: He is in the process of accepting a leadership role of his operation by delegating the showmanship duties to his brother and dad. At his age, I could not have handed the halter of my cow to anyone. His maturity is impressive to me.

A side note that made my day occurred five years later in the same barn. I seek and find Ryan. True to his character he is helping a young man with his show steer. Our brief conversation tells me that Ryan met his goals: an associate degree from State Fair Community College, he manages a section of bull production for a large breeder in Missouri, and he owns a few cattle. An additional goal which he never mentioned, but I knew would be an element of his character. Ryan is a leader.

I head off to the pork producers' restaurant for lunch and some reflective time. I have a quick lunch while reflecting on my youthful years, Jersey dairy cattle, and friends. I take my reflection time while listening to farmers' conversations about crops, weather, and hog production. The question of where to go next is answered: the swine barn to watch 4-H members show their hogs. My dad was very knowledgeable about hogs. I never gained his expertise or passion, but I always enjoyed watching my friends show their swine.

The swine show barn is a beehive of activity. Young adults and adults scurry around, conducting the sequence of preparing hogs for the show, showing hogs in the competition pen, or bringing hogs from the show pen to their holding pens. I carefully make my way to the pen and watch a show in progress. I lean on the top rail of the show pen, attempting to look as if I am knowledgeable about what makes a championship hog. No one is fooled, not even myself.

The man standing beside me explains that he is watching a couple of his students show their hogs. He is a high school agriculture teacher and FFA adviser at North Harrison High School, located eight miles south of the Iowa-Missouri state line. After I explain my research, he recommends Wyat, who is currently showing one of his barrows, a neutered male hog.

Wyat and his hog work as a team, resulting in another ribbon to add to his collection. When Wyat pens his hog, he joins me next to his hog's holding pen. He immediately informs me, "This is my twentieth year coming to the state fair, and I am only nineteen [years old]." In response to my quizzical expression, he states, "I came before I was one [year old]."

Wyat speaks with confidence and a sense of timeliness. His urgency relates directly to the busy schedule of preparing his hogs to show. I am grateful and impressed that he can balance his numerous tasks and still speak with me for thirty minutes.

He begins his story by talking about the process of animal selection, then moves on to the feeding and care regimen. Finally, he discusses the process of preparation for showing. The order of his comments speaks clearly to his priority of first purchasing and then developing a healthy, marketable hog. Wyat explains:

> In April, we go to several Iowa hog sales. We look at about 300 head of swine in the weight range of forty to fifty pounds. Show quality and reasonable price are two primary factors. We usually buy five barrows. The newly purchased hogs are taken to our family farm and placed on the "elite swine program," a locally developed feeding regimen. We weigh them every week to monitor gain and ensure proper development. When they weigh about 200 pounds, we start adding nutrients to their feed. The desired show weight is around 240 to 250 pounds. Our show hogs are kept inside until the weather warms.

He pauses before changing subjects to make a quick visual check of his hogs. Deeming they are okay, he turns back to me and collects his thoughts before continuing.

The training process of hogs parallels (in philosophy) the training of cattle: Start with a nonthreatening activity, proceed slowly, and gain confidence with each step. Wyat continues:

Training the hogs is a regimented process that does not begin until the hogs each weigh about 150 pounds. They are then placed in the show barn, which separates them from the remainder of the herd. We start training by walking them every day. The training of the hog includes becoming comfortable around people, walking with guidance, responding to being guided by a cane or show stick. The cane or show stick is merely an instrument to guide by lightly touching, not hitting, the animal.

He ensures I understand that a hog is not hit. Animal handlers exude patience and treat their animals with respect and therefor assume patience and respect from the animal, in turn. Respect and patience usually occur from the animal. It is almost certain, however, that disrespect, coupled with lack of and/or rough handling, will result in an unmanageable animal.

The training process requires showmanship knowledge and patience by the handler. How can I best display my animal to the judge? How can I get the animal to go where I want without using force? These are questions that must be answered throughout the training process and in the show arena. Development of showmanship behavior requires hours, days, and weeks of training, until the animal and human are on the same page, thinking alike. Wyat's knowledge and expertise makes the explanation of the process seems easier than the actual task of training a 250-pound hog. Frustration of training an animal can be very high. When frustration peaks, a good show person becomes calmer, followed by a calming affect on the animal.

Without a prompt, Wyat relates showing hogs to playing sports. He explains:

> You practice daily. Training hogs is similar to drills; you must do them right. Improvement is a constant goal. Adrenalin pumps in the show ring like it does during a game. Time in the show arena is like time on the court or field. The person and animal needs to perform at their highest level. Mistakes are critical to the outcome. The biggest difference is your teammate. In sports, it is a person. In the show arena, it is an animal. Preparing and showing an animal require the human player to also be a coach.

It is interesting that both Wyat and Justin (at the Mitchell County Fair in Iowa) use the same analogy, comparing the playing of sports to the showing of animals.

Wyat and his hogs participate in a series of shows, including county fairs, state fairs, and a sale show. He discusses the routine by saying, "We hit a few county fairs to get them [the hogs] used to being shown. County fairs prepare us for the Missouri State Fair, the big show. We concentrate on the state fair. From purchase to state fair is about four months." After a pause he says, "The hogs are then shown one more time at a sale show and sold to a local butcher."

Wyat will soon be too old to show as a member of 4-H, but he plans to remain involved with showing hogs. "My goal is to start a breeding operation to sell show hogs. I plan to run my operation on the family farm, which is about 250 acres," Wyat states. He is preparing himself for his dream by studying animal production at Kirkwood Community College in Rapid City, Iowa. He has completed one year of the two-year program.

Wyat and I quickly exchange a "thank you," as he hurries off to attend to show preparation. As I walk from the swine barn, I reflect on our interview and Wyat's professionalism. His formal education in high school and at Kirkwood Community College, in conjunction with his experiences of purchasing, feeding, training, and showing hogs, will shape his dream business. Wyat's intensity, personality, and dedicated work ethic will certainly be his partners during ventures into the world of business.

After leaving the swine show barn, I gather a glass of lemonade and my paraphernalia and sit on a bench. I sit for a few minutes, aimlessly observing people passing in both directions on their way to destinations unknown to me. As I reflect, two things become clear: First, the three people and their stories were amazingly informative about rural life, and second, I must return another day to seek additional stories.

Four more trips to the fair may qualify me as "frequent visitor." My friends believe that *five* trips to the fair is absurd, but then they were not farm kids. They mentioned expulsion from their group. Oh well. I have been expelled before and lived. Plus, with a friend like Mo, well . . . whatever.

On Tuesday, August 17, 2010, I am headed back to the fair. Since my Friday visit to interview three people, I attended two concerts at the fair Grand Stands. At the gate I purchase a ticket and start walking and gawking like I have never seen these sights. The anxious feeling that no one will want to talk with me nags once again. I receive an immediate uplifting of spirts as a couple of gate employees and an attendant immediately inside the gate smile and greet me like an old friend.

Eventually, I walk into the Farm Bureau building. My family has deep roots in Farm Bureau: Farm Bureau operated the grain elevator in New Salem, where my aunt, my mother's sister, operated the office and eventually became the elevator manager; my uncle, dad's brother, operated the Rush County Farm Bureau chicken hatchery; and we purchased our insurance from Farm Bureau, as well as supplies from their store. Farm Bureau, or just "Co-op" as we called it, accommodated a major part of our marketing needs.

My purpose for visiting the Farm Bureau building now is to learn about today's operations. I know it has changed, but I want to know *how* it has changed.

I meet Don, a Farm Bureau services representative. The conversation soon becomes an enlightening interview. As we talk, Don continues to perform his duties of answering questions for people visiting Farm Bureau displays. I literally kneel on the floor to take notes. I would appreciate a bale of straw right now, as old baseball-catcher knees are very opposed to kneeling and getting up. My knees speak clearly to me.

Don lives an interesting life, balanced between running a turkey farm and his service to the people of Missouri as both a former state legislator and current Farm Bureau lobbyist. He served in the Missouri House of Representatives for the maximum-allowable eight years (4 two-year terms). His service now is primarily dedicated to ensuring equity for the agriculture industry. "The farms are getting larger," he states. A ramification of larger farms, which I have not considered, is less representation in the state government. He expounds:

> Of the 163 Representatives in the House, only five or six represent rural people. In the Senate, only one or two of the thirty-four senators represent rural communities. Over 50% of the Missouri citizenry live in the St. Louis and Kansas City metro areas.

When stated in those terms, it seems that the rural citizen is a dying breed. "My job as a lobbyist is to educate and influence representatives. The issue of under representation is clearly becoming worse," he adds.

Don smoothly changes the focus of his comments to Farm Bureau as a service organization. "Farm Bureau is a grassroots organization, with representation in all 114 counties in Missouri. The chain of representation is from county to state to national. Membership ranges from 200 to 400 members per county," he explains. Farming has suffered in both representation and public knowledge about how food is grown, specifically what is entailed to raise grain, meat, and dairy products. Don clearly states, "A lot of the Farm Bureau representatives of the past were farmers or children of farmers. Today, many representatives are more distant to agriculture. The firsthand knowledge of representatives is lacking; they are not knowledgeable of the day-to-day farming routines." Even though representation has become more remote, he claims, "Farm Bureau is the sixth-most influential group behind such organizations as AARP and teachers' unions."

Don is a strong believer in agriculture and the need for it to be a major producer in the United States. He is committed to supporting the cause. He closes our conversation with an statement of great concern for loss of land and confidence in technology: "We are losing a lot of agriculture land to urban sprawl. Farmers and technology are making up for loss of production land by increasing yields and production."

People like Don will continue to carry the banner to ensure that the American public will have homegrown food. It is frightening to think what might happen if there ceases to be farming advocates like Don and other Farm Bureau representative and agents.

I thank Don for his time. He smiles and states that he enjoyed the opportunity to talk about Farm Bureau and agriculture. He then hurries off to meet and greet more people. My best decision today is that I am going to become a member of Farm Bureau.

I wander around with the goal to talk with someone who is unique to my experience. A half-hour of wandering leads me to the "bee expedition," which meets my criteria of uniqueness.

My knowledge of bees and beekeepers is non-existent, at best. Speaking with several people behind a display counter of various honey products seems to be the best choice to enhance my knowledge. Good choice! I not only gain some knowledge and purchase some honey, but they all insist, "You need to talk with Bob."

An overwhelming recommendation of someone to speak with usually creates skepticism, as I never know if the person is truly knowledgeable or if his or her friends are getting even for some previous prank. After some salesmanship by me, Bob consents to a conversation about bees and the production of honey. My concern about any lack of expertise is immediately dismissed after a few comments from Bob.

I know entering into a conversation with Bob, or any beekeeper, that I am walking the path of ignorance. Bob keeps beehives, plus he has an orchard of apple, peach, and pear trees on his ten-acre farm near Odessa, about twenty miles east of Kansas City, Missouri. He also has beehives on fifteen others farms in his area. His operation center is a sixty-foot square barn, which serves as the processing and marketing center.

Bob has been a beekeeper for fifty years. He says, "I started keeping bees as a Future Farmers of America project when I was thirteen years old [and] living in Florida." He moved to Kansas in 1960 and then to Missouri in 1967. Bob nonchalantly states:

> A hazard of being a beekeeper is stings. Being stung by bees is an accepted hazard of working with bees. If a person gets stung 150 to 200 times a year, he or she is immune to the sting. I get stung all of the time.

This statement certainly does not put me at ease. I always wanted to be immune to bee stings, but not at that price!

He changes his focus with a startling statement: "95% of the wild bees are gone. Last year I lost 143 out of 300 beehives. The year before I lost more. These types of losses are unprecedented." If he is trying to get my attention, it works. I sit on the front of my chair and listened intently for the next forty-five minutes.

The thought of bee extinction is frightening. It is not just the absence of honey but also and more importantly the loss of bees to the ecological system. Peter Senge stated during a presentation at an American Association of School Administrators conference that the loss of ants would break down the whole ecological system. I cannot image that losing bees would be any less devastating.

Bob adds, "I am not certain of the causes for the losses." After a short pause he continues, "I found parasites in the bees' gut. It was *Nosema ceranae*." Even with parasite evidence, however, he is not comfortable naming it as the cause for the loss. Bob is a researcher in the field of beekeepers and has published several articles in professional journals. His background in research and publishing dissuades him from making conclusions unsupported by data.

Bob continues the topic of parasites and the threat to bee existence by stating, "There are two types of parasites, both of which came from Asia. One is trachea mite. These mites chew holes in the trachea. The other one is vorae mite. This mite has similar behaviors of ticks in that they are blood suckers."

A pause and wrinkle of his brow indicates his concern for the mystery of losing bees. He continues his discussion of mites by adding:

The trachea mite was blamed for the big die-off of bees in England during the 1920s. They [the mites] were discovered in the United States in 1985. Originally, they effectively used strips to control them in England and Italy. Now the trachea mite has developed a resistance, and there are no alternative methods. The vorae mite was first seen in the United States in 1989.

Bob lowers my anxiety with a positive statement about bee survival: Beekeepers will be able to save the bee species by making beehives. Without new beehives, we will run out of bees. We live in a very fragile system [ecological]. Beekeepers in the past were counted by the hundreds; now they are discussed in terms of thousands. The beekeeping industry has experienced significant growth.

Two elements of maintaining bees are developing and moving hives. The dynamics of moving bees is a very complex operation, much more intricate than I realized. Bob meticulously explains, "You move them at night, when the bees are in their hives. You move them at least two miles, or they will come back to their original hive. If you move them more than two miles, they will remain in their new hive." I am so mesmerized that note taking has become a difficult task. I am simultaneously fascinated and burdened by the new knowledge.

Bob emphasizes that both agricultural uncertainty and risk in commodity production extend beyond bees to other crops, such as corn, soybeans, and apples. He explains, "Apples are a real challenge. Last year, my McIntosh dropped all their apples. Farming is uncertain, with weather and bugs. Some of the best entomologists are puzzled with what is happening to bees. Research remains an important factor."

The phenomena of insects, disease, and weather are large factors in grain farming, which affects animal production because of the feeding process. Farming is fragile. The farming process, whatever the product, is dependent on weather and science to help in our battle against insects, bugs, and parasites.

Bob philosophizes a bit as he claims, "What we do not know makes what we know absurd. Considering how life has changed during the past 100 years, what will people think of us 100 years from now?"

To me, this is a great question. How will our ancestors a century into the future consider us?

You will find Bob—the beekeeper, fruit farmer, and philosopher—every Saturday from March to Thanksgiving at the Old River Market. The Old River Market, an open-air market with a roof, is the largest market in a six-state area. It is situated in the Old Historic area of Kansas City. Missouri. Maybe I will see you there?

In the meantime, I depart from my conversation with Bob as a much richer person. Actually, my interviews have *all* been informative, but I entered them with some basic knowledge. I walked in to my conversation with Bob, however, knowing only two things: one, I like honey, and two, I do not like getting stung by bees. I was knowledge-bankrupt about bees and honey production. Bob's information about the number of bee stings it takes to bring on immunity was enlightening but not comforting. I will not feel any better when a bee stings me.

My conversation with Bob was educational: not only about bees and fruit production but also philosophically. I thank Bob for his time and sharing of knowledge. He is a proud, knowledgeable person with a strong sense of privacy and self-assurance. He triggered thoughts about my knowledge: What do I *not* know?

I classify knowledge into three categories: I know what I know; I know what I don't know (in essence, I am not interested in pursuing it); and finally, I don't know what I don't know.

My goal now is to enhance my listening and reading with an open mind. Thanks for the wake-up call, Bob.

I have a new appreciation of bees and beekeepers, as well as a heightened awareness that what I do today will affect my grandchildren's grandchildren. I do not want my lax or selfish behavior to create conditions that my ancestors and their peers must repair in order to achieve a quality life, the same quality I experience today.

Maybe a starting point is to place clean air and water, along with healthy food, as priorities over issues of self. Perhaps a guiding question should be, what value will this program add to the greater good, environment, and enduring quality of life?

Bob is more than a beekeeper and philosopher; he is a teacher.

My visit to the Missouri State Fair and the conversations with five people exceed my goals. A fair, for me, is always fun. The 2010 Missouri State Fair, however, is also a valuable learning experience. And it is not over for me; I have another outdoor concert tomorrow night.

In about six weeks, Mo and I will leave for our trip to the middle states to visit the hometown of my dad's family, plus New Salem and Rush County: my childhood home. Please join Mo and I for those visits and a few other unexpected adventures.

Middle States

CHAPTER 13

Illinois

As a fourteen-year-old young man in 1868, Ernest Turk left Germany for the United States to settle in Earlville, Illinois. 142 years later, on October 5, 2010, his great grandson and a dawg called Mo depart Missouri to visit and talk with residents of Ernest's American hometown.

The second trip of my journeys to talk with rural Americans and write their stories will include Illinois, Michigan, Indiana, Ohio, Kentucky, Tennessee, and Arkansas. I have planned to visit two towns: Earlville and Rushville, Indiana, the town of my roots.

I am excited and can hardly wait to cross "The Big Muddy": the Mississippi River. Mo is taking the trip in stride. To her, it is a chance to meet new people, smell new scents, and chase squirrels. I love her simple life!

The first 125 miles of our trip is four-lane highway. Four-lane travel ends as we turn onto US Highway 54 about 25 miles east of Columbia, Missouri. US 54 is one my favorite highways, which I have nicknamed *The Main Street of rural America* because it is the main street of many small towns such as Eldorado Springs, Missouri and Eldorado, Kansas. The highways' winds its way from the western terminal of El Paso, Texas to about five miles northeast of Pittsfield, Illinois, where it ends in the middle of cornfields at the intersection of US 36 and Illinois 107. The approximate 120-mile drive completes my lifetime 1,197-mile tour of US 54.

Our journey via the back roads, passing fields of harvested and non-harvested corn and soybeans, presents an opportunity for me to provide the reader with a brief history of Earlville. Settlers began arriving in the area between the years 1835 and 1840. Garden vegetables, the primary product, were marketed in Chicago. The rich soil brought more settlers, and a village by the name of "Earl" became the market center where people purchased retail goods. The town incorporated in 1863 under the name "Earlville." The area grew, resulting in construction of a seventeen-mile plank road south, connecting the community with LaSalle, the Ottawa County seat. Residents estimated Earlville's population to be about 1,600.

The story of Earlville can be more effectively conveyed as a single scenario. The three interviews, which include four people, intertwine very realistically into one story. Michael, who I meet at the Sunshine restaurant during my first night in Earlville, appears to be about 50 years of age. Kenneth, who I meet the next morning, is an 83-year-young retired farmer and truck driver. Ken and Norma, a retired farm couple, invite me into their home for our around the table discussion. They are the parents of a close friend and colleague as a graduate student and later a professor at Wichita State University. Denise scheduled my interview with her parents.

We arrive at the campground in time to set up camp, walk, and go to the Sunshine Restaurant for dinner. I sit at the counter, a couple of stools from the other lone diner. The norm of my previous trip was to introduce myself and perhaps gain an interview. Not so at the Sunshine. Michael introduces himself and begins telling me, with great pride, about his hometown of Earlville. I quickly explain my research and gain his approval for the interview. Michael's reflections about the past, coupled with positive feelings about the present and future, make for a very interesting and informative conversation.

The next morning after breaking camp, walking, and preparing for a ten o'clock interview, I am back at the Sunshine, having breakfast in the dining room. I meet and interview Kenneth, who many years ago played cards with my Uncle Oscar and knew my Aunt Gertrude. We reminisce and share stories about Oscar and Gertrude. He tells me that Gertrude had spunk. I smile and respond, "You are kind and have political savvy." Aunt Gertrude was not shy about explaining her thoughts on an issue.

After my conversation with Kenneth, Mo and I drive less than a mile to a recently developed housing area on the outskirts of town. Ken and Norma greet and welcome me like an old friend into their home for a discussion around their dining room table.

The small town of predominantly German heritage, where my great-grandfather made his American home, is experiencing issues similar to those of many small American towns. Farm size has transitioned from approximately 250 acres to anywhere from 2,500 to 5,000+ acres. Livestock, mostly cattle and hogs, which were prevalent on the 250-acre farms, are absent on today's farms. Most Earlville community farms are limited to grains such as corn, soybeans, and infrequently, wheat. The transition began in the middle 1970s, but accelerated during the early 1980s, and is continuing to be the norm.

Decreased population and reduced number of local businesses accompany larger farm sizes and the ensuing population loss. "Earlville's number of businesses has diminished to eight; we once had three grocery stores," Michael claims. He continues that there had been "two car dealerships and two implement dealerships, Massey-Ferguson and International Harvester." Ken adds a more historical description of lost businesses when he says, "We had four groceries and five auto dealerships: Nash, Kaiser, Chevy, Ford, and Plymouth. There were four implement dealerships. Now there are none." The auto names of Nash and Kaiser date the dealerships, as those auto companies vanished during the early-to-middle 1950s.

Michael believes that corporate headquarters' demands for an auto dealer's building, facilities, and sales, as well as dwindling population, were factors for the closure of car dealerships. He claims that personnel from the auto dealers' corporate headquarters told the dealers to increase their physical size and increase sales—or close. "The dealerships could not meet those demands, so they went out of business," he states.

The loss of businesses began during the 1950s, but has accelerated during the past thirty years. Ken's description more closely approximates my own childhood memories of the 1950s, when I visited Earlville with my grandfather and dad. My 1989 visit coincided with Michael's analysis.

Ken continues that there used to be two pharmacies, then adds, "Now Ellis Pharmacy orders prescriptions, which we receive the next day." Michael states, "When I was a kid, the Sunshine [Restaurant] where we are sitting was a Dairy Dip. There was an A&W Root Beer across the street. We had five gas stations; now there are two."

Michael, Ken, Norma, and Kenneth all discuss, in various ways, how farms have become much larger. Michael states, "In the 1980s, there were sixty-five farms [in the Earlville area]. Everyone farmed around 250 acres. Now there are very few farms." Michael's family stopped cattle production in 1981 and quit farming in 1982. Kenneth, who farmed 600 acres, states that someone informed him that he needed 1,200 to 1,500 acres to make a living. He says, "I told him I would rather quit." Kenneth adds that he would need to hire help if he expanded operations to 1,200 acres. "Hired help on the farm does not do the same quality of work as the owner, because it is not their property," he claims.

Ken and Norma approached larger farms from a different perspective. Larger farms, which are consolidations of smaller farms, create vacant homesteads from the previous smaller, independent farms. Ken says, "A lot of people are moving from the city to the old farmsteads, which have been separated from the land."

Kenneth transitions his thoughts to Earlville's current community. "A lot of people work in the city and rent or buy farmhouses. They live in a different world," he says. With a wrinkle of his brow, he expands his last statement, explaining, "The people, who have moved from the city, spend most of their time outside the Earlville area to work and shop. In reality, it appears to me that they do not typically socialize into the community." Kenneth's statements reflect a significant cultural change in the community.

The process of increasing farm size and loss of agriculture-based homesteads follow a simple pattern: A local farmer expands his operation by purchasing an additional farm in the community, and in most instances, the new owner sells the unneeded homestead buildings from the newly purchased farm. Selling the buildings allows the farmer to recover some capital, as well as to reduce property taxes. These capital gains create funds for expansion of operations through the purchasing of more-productive equipment or additional land. The new homeowners are usually new residents of the community. Many of these new families maintain their jobs, shopping preferences, and family and friends from their previous community. The new families are residents with little interaction and commitment to their new community, as Kenneth explained.

The separation of my father's childhood home from the land occurred by this very process during the late 1980s. It was difficult for me to view remodeling of the house, but not nearly as difficult as it was for me to tell my dad that his childhood had been sold and was no longer connected to the farm.

The influx of new residents has changed the culture of the Earlville community. Michael, referring to the time of his youth in the late 1960s and 1970s, says, "We had great people, [and] everyone knew everyone. Today, I do not know my neighbors. People come and go." Ken cites another example of loss of community: "There used to be 100 kids in Sunday school; now there are thirty. Churches are becoming smaller."

The local school has also become much smaller. Michael states that from 1970 through 1972, Earlville won twenty-nine consecutive football games and three district championships. "We stopped football in 1979. We became too small and had to change classifications." He continues with a degree of sadness, "We lost our football program."

Michael's lifelong friend, Al, who recently joined us at the counter, chimes in and states that Earlville is still a great place to live.

Kenneth, discussing the days when Earlville was a vibrant town, shakes his head as he says, "There is no shopping in Earlville now. There used to be stores all around the downtown area on Main and Ottawa Streets. We had a theatre on the corner."

Michael brings reality to the old days in Earlville: "When I was a kid, we did all of our shopping here. Friday was fish night at the B&L Bar. People came to town and ate and shopped. You could hardly find a place to park."

Kenneth speaks with melancholy about the social aspect of Earlville during his youth: "Earlville had dances every Thursday night in the hall above the tavern. The dances started around ten o'clock, after the card game broke up. My brother and I went to the dances." He goes on to state that he played cards every Friday uncle Oscar.

My own dad often spoke of attending those dances as a child, accompanied by his parents.

Michael emphasizes the closeness of the people and sense of community responsibility for raising the local kids, saying, "When we were kids, Ben, the policemen, would always give us one warning. One night I threw a beer can out of the window while riding in a car going into the drive-in theatre. Ben warned me." He pauses and continues, "Today, all six of us would have gone to jail."

Kenneth offers yet another example of the past, when smaller farms surrounded the market area of Earlville: "Tractors used to line up to get into the grain elevator [to sell their harvested crops]. There were arguments about who was first. Now there are big trucks." Larger farms allow, or perhaps dictate, larger equipment, including trucks. The cost of bigger equipment dictates continued farming on a large or larger scale. The cycle continues, resulting in competition for the fixed commodity: land.

The closeness of the Earlville community forty years ago (or longer) could partially be attributed to its heritage as a single-ethnic culture. "Earlville used to be a predominantly German Lutheran town," says Ken, whose parents were from Denmark. He adds that there also "were a lot of Swedes and Norwegians." Norma's family lived in Rolla, nine miles north of Earlville. Her two grandmothers were from Germany.

Ken and Norma's reflections allow me to recall a childhood story of my own, which I share with them, relaying how my dad and grandfather addressed the same topic with different meanings. My dad explained that his own father "did not speak English until he went to school." My grandfather chose different words when he told me the same story during the same frame of time of my youth. He clearly stated, "I spoke only German until I went to school." My grandfather's words reflect pride in speaking German. My conversation with Ken and Norma allow me to realize a strong meaning to my grandfathers' words

Ken and Norma laugh, and Norma states, "Very typical of your grandfather's generation!"

Earlville does have a future. Everyone mentioned one amenity with great pride, something not only a part of the past but also the present and future: the drive-in [theater], one of only two in the state. "When there is a good movie, the place is packed," Michael states with great pride. He adds that during bad weather, there is not much of a crowd.

The town and community, even though they have changed and lost many businesses, still retain a commitment to serving their citizens, with several amenities that go well beyond the drive-in. Ken states, "Earlville has a nice park. We had a big fundraiser to get money for the playground equipment. Walmart was a contributor." Norma adds, "Earlville has a good library with good children's programs. They have reading contests."

They also discuss with pride that they still have a doctor and dentist. Mendota, about ten miles west, has a good hospital. Peoria and Rockford are available for serious medical care. "We have a locker where you can buy fresh meat or have an animal butchered and package to your choice," Ken states. Norma adds, "The Dollar General has milk, eggs, and other essential food items." Their remarks summarize the spirit of the past that continues into the future with many similar amenities, even though on a smaller scale. They approach the current services in a positive manner that meets their needs. Ken and Norma share a very positive outlook for Earlville. The apple does not fall far from the tree; Denise shares the same positive outlook about life.

The story of Earlville's history can best be summarized by Michael's concluding remarks about Doctor Fisher, his childhood physician. "Doctor Fisher was one of the best doctors in the world. He made house calls. If you did not have money, you did not pay." After a pause and a supportive remark from Al, Michael concludes, "Doctor Fisher took a day off and went to observe one of my many childhood surgeries." Michael makes a long pause. He turns to look me directly in the eye and express that corporate companies have influenced changes to small-town America.

After saying good-bye and thanking Ken and Norma, Mo and I head into the late morning sun with Earlville in our rearview mirror. Our drive provides time for reflection. I think back to a time almost 150 years before, when a fourteen-year-old young man—my great grandfather—first stepped onto the rich Illinois soil. He was alone in a new country, with the thought of never again seeing his family. The stories of Michael, Kenneth, Ken, and Norma helped me gain insight beyond family stories. An unexpected talk with Kenneth about Uncle Oscar and Aunt Gertrude made my day. Earlville was a great visit for me. The accounts of life and culture of the once-German town of Earlville were enlightening, but more importantly, the story of that character is embedded in friendly, community-oriented people. My great-grandfather Ernest chose the correct community.

CHAPTER 14

Michigan and Ohio

The drive from Earlville to Crown Point, Indiana provides time to reflect on family and the past. As we become surrounded by traffic in the Chicago metro area, I am snapped back into reality. With Mo's help, and after an eternity of stop and go, we arrive at the home of Bob and Chrissie. Bob was my college roommate. We eat, drink a bit, tell stories, reminisce about college life, and inform each other about our lives since we last saw each other over a decade before. Our conversations reveal that our memories of academic prowess are much greater than our transcripts depict.

All too soon, morning arrives, and Mo and I are heading east. We travel about two hours, arriving at Jack and Diane's house in southern Michigan. Jack and Diane are friends from the lake. They owned the BB Bar and Grill, a local hangout close to my home.

Mo

I see an old friend, Jack. I am out of the truck in full tail-wagging mode, giving a Golden hug, a few licks, and (why not?) a big jump. Both humans yell, "Down!" Life is great; two people yelling. They just don't get this excitement thing. Jack and Randy get in the Gator. No room for me. I am stopping this! A quick pass across the front of the Gator, screeching brakes, and a "Mo, get out of the way." Once again, they don't get it. I am going to ride! I grit my teeth, take a chance, and stop in front of the Gator. Randy gets out, I get on the seat, Jack drives, dawg rides, Randy walks, and Goldens rule.

After we get to the house, I run back and greet Randy, and we walk together. It is not about being lazy; it is about who has the right to ride.

Diane joins us. I give her a big greeting, with a lick and a lean. Diane is cool. She used to bring me people food when I was guarding the truck at the BB. The people talk, laugh, and eat. I make a couple passes by the kennel, just so I can hear a Jack Russell bark. Jack yells to the dog, "Be quiet!" I'm so cool!

Soon, it is time for pictures, which means we are getting ready to leave. Jack and Diane line up. Jack calls Randy a familiar name; everyone laughs. Eventually, the picture taking is complete, and I get in the truck, and we head down the road.

Randy looks different. He forgot his hat. I nudge him and look at his head. Once again, a great hint goes unnoticed. After a short nap, we are driving along a lake in town, around a school, down narrow streets with cars parked on both sides. I detect that we are lost. I should have awakened sooner.

After many narrow streets and several bad looks from pedestrians and drivers, we find a wider road that leads to a campground. At last, I am out smelling and chasing a squirrel. Life is good.

Randy

The next morning, I am enjoying a quiet breakfast at the Coldwater Garden Restaurant when three people of retirement age belly-up to a table fairly close to mine. My quiet thinking time is over. They are talking and laughing and having fun. There are things you can ignore, and there are things you cannot. This is one of those *cannots*.

Coffee cup and paper tablet in hand, I walk over and ask if I can join the fun. They introduce themselves and excitingly invite me to join them. They are three longtime friends getting together for breakfast and catching up on each other's lives. I am grateful they are willing to share some of their time.

Molly and Sally grew up in Jackson, Michigan, which is about forty-five miles northeast of Coldwater. Mike lived as a youth in Marshall, which is about thirty miles west of Jackson and twenty-five miles north of Coldwater.

The three friends estimate Jackson's current population at 30,000, while Marshall has approximately 7,000. Marshall and Jackson are both located on Interstate 94, approximately in the east-west middle of Michigan's Lower Peninsula and about thirty-five miles north of the Indiana-Michigan state line.

Mike, whose wife is a teacher in Jackson, claims that Main Street in her teaching town has many vacant stores. He goes on to say that Marshall, which has been economically pro-active, has a more flourishing downtown area. Mike relays the story of how Marshall has a governor's mansion. During the early years of statehood, Marshall and Lansing were the two finalists for state capitol. A governor's mansion was constructed in Marshall prior to Lansing being selected for the capitol. Today, the mansion is an unused landmark.

The three friends speak mostly about their teenage years. They consider their respective towns as rural communities. Molly and Sally speak about "cruising" [in autos] between two drive-in restaurants. Sally says (as Molly shakes her head in agreement), "We cruised the avenue between Bea's Drive-In and the Dome, another drive-in." Mike claims, "We cruised Main Street. We always had a hangout with a jukebox." Molly states, "We sat on hoods of cars, turned our radios up, and danced. We called the dancing to car radios 'Grassers.' " Mike adds that they had dances every week. They all conclude that kids today do not have hangouts like the three friends experienced as teenagers. Mike states, "We had more fun than kids today." Kids of today might take exception to his statement.

Teenage life during the 1950s was simple. It was a fun era for teenagers. Most activities of the 1950s, which we all fondly recall, were either self-planned or happened spontaneously. Mike claims that growing up in the great times of 1950s is substantiated by the popularity of Dick Clark's weekly radio show, "Rock, Roll, and Remember." The 1950s teenage years lives on with the today's version of the traditional sock hop. The current version is celebrated with certain modifications. The attendees no longer have dark hair groomed in ducktails or curls. Instead, the dancers of today relish thinning, grey hair. Blue jeans of today fit tight but for a different reason. With all the differences there remains some very pronounced similarities: the music, crowded dance floor, and many attendees masquerading in similar attire. The 1950s lives on with senior citizen teenagers.

Did we have more fun than kids growing up during other eras? I cannot answer yes or no with great conviction. I can, however, state that I had fun. I equate my teenage environment as both 1950s and rural. It was fun, filled with fond and lingering memories.

Following the interview Sally, Molly, and Mike join Mo for a short pet. As always, Mo is excited to meet new people and has no difficulty displaying her emotions. I thank Molly, Sally, and Mike for sharing their fond memories and their time and table. They express their appreciation for an opportunity to share.

Their youth hometowns stretch the definition of a small town. Sally, Molly, and Mike, however, believe their youth towns were rural when you consider highly populated area of Detroit, its metro area, and the southern part of the Lower Peninsula. Perhaps concept of "rural" is relevant to the area.

Mo

It is nice to meet three new people. Until I met Molly, I did not realize that people use dawg names. Of course, this brightens my day . . . but not as much as a bite of biscuit and the chasing of the dumb squirrel that struts close to us. "See you in a bit. I have to chase a squirrel up the trees where he belongs. Solid ground is dawg territory."

With my work complete, I sit by Randy patiently for a few seconds, then give a nose nudge: my signal that it is time to do something different, like travel, see new things, and meet new people.

Randy looks weird without his hat. The glare of sun off a spot of a thin hair dome is blinding. Love my human!

Randy

I get the hint. The impatient dawg is bored, so Mo and I are soon on Interstate 69, traveling toward Auburn, Indiana. I am not sure why; we just are.

An hour of interstate driving causes my "fun meter" to peg out at zero, so we drive east on US Highway 49. A few minutes later, I see a "Welcome to Ohio" sign. Visiting Ohio has just become part of our plan.

A short drive and we are wandering around a beautiful little town called "Hicksville." One stroll down Main Street clearly informs me that the name is not reflective of the town or its people.

Hicksville was named for one of its founders, Henry W. Hicks. The treaty of 1795 and Ohio statehood in 1803 brought fur traders, loggers, and land developers to the rich, fertile area. In 1836, Hicks Land Company of New York sent an agent named Alfred P. Edgerton to purchase land at $1.25 per acre. Tribes of Potawatomi and Huron had vacated the land due to many settler coming to what is now Hicksville and Defiance County. The timber-laden area was host to thickly populated trees with enormous circumference. Today, Hicksville has grown into a market center with approximately 3,600 residents.

Edgerton became powerful and influential in the areas of eastern Ohio and western Indiana. He became an Ohio state senator in 1845 and a member of the US House of Representatives in 1852. In 1845, he successfully petitioned the Ohio General Assembly to build a wooden road from Hicksville to Antwerp, thus facilitating transportation to the Miami and Erie Canals. He later used his influence to persuade the Baltimore and Ohio Railroads to run tracks through Hicksville, which was deemed influential in saving the community. Edgerton eventually moved to Fort Wayne, Indiana, keeping his Hicksville home as a summer residence.

The first thing I notice today is several friendly "Good afternoon!" greetings from people on the street. The second thing is an opera house. Mo and I immediately return to see that the name is Huber Opera House. I peruse the list of upcoming events, which answers my question as to whether or not the opera house is operational. I then marvel at the inside décor, partially visible from the street.

A few steps and I am in the newspaper office with the goal to ask about the opera house. Mike, editor and owner, and the two-lady staff are so friendly and conversational, I soon find myself in an interview with Mike, while his two associates act as coaches.

Mike first became acquainted with the newspaper business when he had a 100-customer paper route in Auburn, Indiana, where he lived and went to high school. After high school, he obtained a business marketing degree from Ball State. He met his wife, who was from Cincinnati, while she was working in Fort Wayne: a large town located a short distance from Auburn. In 1990, they moved to Hicksville and purchased the weekly newspaper from his grandparents. The newspaper has a 125-year longevity with quite a history.

Mike's positive comments about Hicksville and its comparisons to Auburn clearly inform me that he enjoyed his childhood in Indiana. "I chose Hicksville because it had the same background I was accustomed to in Auburn." They are both safe places to raise kids. He states, "I could not do anything wrong as a kid, because I knew everybody, and they would tell my parents. Hicksville, like Auburn, is a safe, caring, friendly community." He then qualifies his statement, adding, "Even though Hicksville is safe, I cannot allow my kids to ride their bicycles down the street after dark. As kids we stayed out at night. I cannot allow my kids the same freedom. It is the change in culture over time."

The story transitions to life and times in Hicksville. Farming is a large industry, "but the town does not depend on it for an economic base. There are several other industries, such as Apex Tool Group, which manufactures pneumatic grinders, sanders, and screwdrivers. We have an industry that makes equipment for restaurants. Parker Hannifin Corporation, a third company, makes hydraulic controls. There are other, smaller shops that make such products as countertops, tool and die, and woodworking tools and offer hydraulic repair. The downtown and surrounding area has several retail stores. Mike says, "There are four banks, a grocery store, [a] bulk food store, hotels, and four dry-goods stores. Things are not the same as they once were; downtowns of county seats are going away."

Mike then switches topics and becomes more enthusiastic as he starts explaining about the civic amenities. "Hicksville has a brand-new fire hall, our own police force, mayor, and city council, of which I am member. We also have an American Legion and Fraternal Order of Eagles, plus a hospital and a great park with seven baseball fields." He then looks at me with a smile as he states with pride, "We have a warehouse with wheelchairs, scooters, lift chairs, [and] hospital-type beds. The equipment is loaned free to people. Equipment is returned when no longer needed. There is an annual fundraiser to support this project."

The school district, as it is in many small towns, is an institution of great pride. There are about 1,000 students housed in the recently constructed building. The grand opening was in December 2008. Mike pauses and states, "Our school boundaries encompass about a five-mile radius." With a reflective look, Mike captures the feelings of small-town residents across rural America: "People do not want to consolidate school districts."

I thank Mike and his staff for their time, sharing of knowledge, and positive mindset about the future of rural America. Mo and I walk a couple of laps around the downtown area, just to soak up the good vibes. Hicksville is a rural town with civic spirit, manufacturing businesses, and agriculture that all appear to support the local economy.

CHAPTER 14

Back Home Again in Indiana

Mo and I, once again, are en route to another town and more stories about rural America. This leg of our trip is different, however, because we are traveling to a planned destination. Our drive on Ohio county roads leading south soon moves southwest, crossing the Ohio-Indiana state line. The roads are flanked by fields of corn and soybeans. Our open truck windows allow the roar of combines, tractors, and trucks to keep us company. Harvest season causes my mind to wander back to my youth. The process appears the same; the equipment and scale of operation, however, are much larger.

Our planned stop is Rush County, my childhood home. Rushville, the county seat, is the primary business center in the county. East Central Indiana is flatland, black-dirt farming country. As such, green fields of corn and soybeans normally fill the countryside. The fall season, however, transitions from dark green to brown, intermingled with a tint of yellow, and the fall-dyed corn and soybean fields and brightly painted tree backdrops make for a breathtaking picture that follows us south on Indiana Highway 3 to Rush County, Rushville, and New Salem, my hometown.

From the view of small aircraft, the picturesque Rush County would depict a checkerboard landscape, with the county road structure marking one-mile squares of land. These squares are called *sections* of land, 640 acres. Many areas in the Midwest are designed in the same manner as Rush County. Clear streams, such as the Little Flat Rock River, traverse the farmland and run through sparsely located small patches of wooded areas. The larger Big Flat Rock River flows predominantly north to south through the eastern half of the county, picking up water from various streams along its route. "The Big Flat," as it is often called, navigates east of Rushville and then turns west to mark the southern outskirts of town. As the river continues flowing southeast, it once again picks up water from the Little Flat Rock River and other streams as it heads south on its eventual path to the Ohio River.

The majestic Rush County Courthouse, constructed in 1896, marks the drive down Main Street. The large multi-story building accents the downtown square along Main Street between First and Second Streets. The courthouse is located amidst a colorful city square adorned by flowers, shrubs, trees, and grass.

US Highway 52 and Indiana Highways 3 and 44 intersect at the courthouse front door. The building with its architect marks a county steeped in history and pride.

New Salem, Rush County, and Rushville all began the settlement process during the early 1800s. Prior to European-American settlers, the Delaware Indians occupied Eastern Indiana and Western Ohio. The Delaware Native Americans were a hostile tribe for the good reason that they had been driven out of their homeland on the east coast. William Penn had treated them justly, with a treaty during the late seventeenth century, named the Friendship Treaty. The Friendship Treaty, signed under a large oak tree, established neutral ground where the Native American tribes could hunt, fish, and trade. The honorable relationship ceased with Penn's death. The Native Americans were forced to give up their land and move to what is now western Pennsylvania, followed by relocation to Eastern Ohio and the Indiana Territory. Their hostility came with a cause. The treaty at St. Mary's in October 1818 ceded the land, which is now Rush County and other areas, to the United States by the people of the Delaware Nation. By January 1819, they once again were being forced to relocate, this time moving west of the Mississippi River to land promised in a treaty signed by United States commissioners. The move of the Native Americans opened the door for the new European-American settlers.

Some of the land approximately twenty-five miles west of Ohio began to be organized into what is known today as Rush County. Noble Township, the home of my ancestors and my youth, began to be settled the very year that the Delaware Nation moved west.

The most southeastern area of Rush County—Noble Township—made it inviting for settlers coming from Cincinnati and eastern Kentucky. Evidence of early settlement indicates Noble Township was an enticing area to begin a new life, in a new home, in a new land: the place we now affectionately call Indiana, the Hoosier State.

There is strong evidence that the first settlement in Rush County occurred in Noble Township, one of the six original townships. Later, six townships would be added to form the current twelve townships of Rush County. Isaac Williams became the first Noble Township area settler in September 1819, when he built a cabin. Conrad Sailor, who was appointed by the legislature to organize Rush County, is believed to have been the first Rush County merchant when, in 1821, he built a store in Noble Township. Rushville and Rush County, founded in 1822, were named in honor of Dr. Benjamin Rush, a signer of the United States Constitution. Rushville was named the county seat the same year of county establishment.

William B. Laughlin hosted a meeting at his house on June 17, 1822, that began the movement to legally form Rush County and its seat, Rushville. The primary factors in choosing seat location were its exact geographic center in the county and proximity to the Big Flat Rock River.

A document on July 29, 1822, announced the official decree to sell lots. Rushville was frequently referred to as "The Town in the Woods," and Mr. Laughlin was called "The Father of Rushville." A livery stable, bank, merchandise stores, tavern, and homes soon lined the streets.

As time passed, Noble Township and Rush County, with its rich, black dirt, grew into populated farmland. Rushville grew, too, with businesses and other amenities to support the county and itself.

The story of Rush County would not be complete without recognition of some notable citizens who left their mark on society. Wendell Willkie housed his 1940 presidential campaign headquarters in Rushville. Others include Joe Cotton, a World War II veteran and NASA test pilot who flew the XB-71; Knowles Shaw, composer and author; Carmelita Geraghty, silent-film actress; and NASCAR legend Tony Stewart.

Rush County, as we are about to learn, is also the home of proud, hard-working citizens who, without fame, have left their own marks on the local culture.

This narrative of Rush County is the story of two towns—Rushville and New Salem—told through the voices of Wayman, Dale, Ed, and me. Rushville is the primary market center of Rush County

The Rush County interviews occur at the Rushville McDonald's, one of the local gathering place for morning-coffee drinkers looking to receive the latest local news. The Local Mac News Network (LMNN) is timelier than the *Rushville Republican*, a local newspaper. Perhaps not as accurate, but you cannot have everything.

I do not seek friends to interview; they find me. It's a small town.

I see Wayman and Dale during most of my visits to Rush County, which also speaks to how often I visit the Local Mac News Network or "Restaurant in the Park." My relationship with Wayman has been life-long.

As a fourteen-year-old, Wayman moved with his family to a farm that my own parents were leaving (they were going to assume the operation of our current farm). I was one-year old and have no memory of that time. Rather, I heard stories later in life from my parents and from Wayman.

As a preschooler, I knew Dale through Little Flat Rock Christian Church and the neighborhood. During my first school-bus trip to New Salem Elementary, I recall feeling certain that both Dale, who was six years my senior, and my sister would make sure I did not get lost. They were obviously successful; I graduated twelve years later.

The interviews occur during two visits about four months apart. The first visit occurred in June, when I was in Rush County to attend my fifty-year New Salem High School reunion. During that visit, Wayman and I had a conversation as we toured his farm and surrounding area. The second interview with Dale and Ed took place in October of the same year, during my trip to the surrounding states.

Wayman is a slow and deliberate waste-no-energy person, who I more closely emulate. Dale is a high-energy, perpetual-motion person. I always observe him with marvel.

My June visit to Rush County begins with an unexpected surprise after having coffee with Wayman and another acquaintance Marvin, also several years my senior. I came to know Marvin in my youth as a fast-pitch softball competitor and a relative to my cousin's husband. On more than one occasion, Marvin taught one young a high school softball player a well-deserved lesson in humility on the diamond.

Back in the present day, a beige truck stopping beside me interrupts my walk back to the motel. A familiar voice rings out, "Get in. I want to show you something." A short pause allows me to realize the voice is Wayman's. I hesitate to respond because I have plans for the morning. A second request assumes the force of a military command to which I am accustomed.

The good second lieutenant in me takes over, and I follow orders to jump into Wayman's truck. The surprise Wayman has in mind provides a significant learning experience. It is as if he knows that I am naïve to the reality of today's farm sizes.

Immediately, the tour is in progress. Wayman tells me that he once farmed the land that is now home to Walmart, McDonalds, my motel, and other retail businesses. We drive about a mile to his family farm. Sadie, his dawg, greets us. Wayman explains that Sadie had to stay on the farm when he moved to town. My immediate response is, "If being separated from my dawg is progress, I will pass."

Standing among the large machinery—tractors, combines, and a semi-trailer truck loaded both with gigantic tanks and a shower—is mind-boggling.

Wayman explains, "The shower is for safety in the event that a person has contact with chemicals."

My recent experiences of climbing on large tractors at state fairs never brought to reality the size of the equipment I see now in the tool shed. The large tractors do multiple times more work than my old dawg, Bird, and I did on our 1951 John Deere A (model). We farmed 250 acres, including about 100 acres of corn, each year. The remaining acres were rotated with wheat, hay, and grass for cattle grazing. Today, the same farm annually produces 215 acres of corn and soybeans. We no longer have livestock, such as hogs, dairy and beef cattle, and chickens. Thank goodness for the absence of chickens.

Wayman and his son have also abandoned the raising of livestock for a total grain operation.

The world of farming has changed significantly in the capacities of labor and production. The advent of the gasoline powered tractor in 1924 began modernization of farming that greatly enhance efficiency. Technology has continued to improve, larger equipment enables one person to farm significantly more acres than two or three people could have operated during the 1950s and 60s. Technology and research has greatly increased crop yield per acre, as well more efficient, improved production of livestock.

The shower on the semi trailer marks both progress and improved safety. When I was young, we took very few precautions while handling fertilizer and other potential hazards. Granted, today the chemicals are more prevalent and used in larger quantities. In my opinion, however, the shower is one of many indicators that farming has shifted to an operation with greater semblance to a business than fifty years ago. The progress is dynamic, and the reality is that farming, which has become larger and more complex, will continue to evolve.

As Wayman and I continue our tour around the community, I reflect back to a time over thirty years before, when I leaned on the wheel of an ex-high-school classmate's tractor that sat on the same land as the motel where I am staying today.

In thirty years, the land has changed ownership from one farmer to another before becoming part of rural America's version of urban development. I am well aware of urban development around Indianapolis, Kansas City, Wichita, and other similar *metro* areas, but never considered it being associated with Rushville and other *rural* towns.

I turn to Wayman and explain how informative our last 45 minutes have been for me. I realize the magnitude of large in the context of farm and equipment. I more clearly understand operation costs of a large farms. I become more acquainted with the required level of professionalism and knowledge in today's farm operation. My time with Wayman has also enhanced my understanding of how community development contributes to lost acres in farm production.

A handshake and a "thank you" results in a smile and Wayman's response, "It is good to help a friend. Your mom and dad meant a lot to me."

My five-minute walk to the motel is filled with reflection and memories. I ask myself what the reaction of my dawg, Bird, would be if she had to ride in a tractor with a *cab*. The answer would undoubtedly be no because she would loose her ability to jump off and chase varmints.

The second element of our story occurs four months later in October, when I see Dale, an old friend, at the Rushville McDonald's. Dale true to form is dressed in worn jeans and a well-worn one-size fits all baseball cap. He introduces me to Ed, a relatively new resident in Rush County. The time has changed, but the topics remain the same, and Dale's first comment relates to change of farm size and the ensuing loss of population in rural America. "Today, there are less farms and less people in rural America," Dale states. Ed agrees that both larger, more efficient machinery and better technology have made larger farms possible. Dale continues by claiming that larger farms and reduced number of farm employees have created longer work days during crop planting and harvest seasons. "I remember times when I would be in the field until midnight and be back the next morning at six [a.m.]," Dale recounts. Of course, this brings a laugh and comment from Ed: "Maybe *one* time." Dale rebuts with humor. I listen and laugh, but refrain from refereeing.

Our discussion turns to Saturday-night shopping in Rushville during Dale's and my time of youth. Dale says, "Rushville was so crowded that you could hardly find a parking spot. The streets were packed, with people everywhere." I quickly add, "There was more socializing than buying." Dale laughs and nods in agreement, then excitingly adds, "Stores were packed. The Princess [movie theater] was full."

Dale and I laugh while Ed looks at us in amazement. I continue the conversation by saying, "We used to 'curb sit' around the courthouse square." Dales counters, "You got the curb because we got too old and gave it up." I do not admit it, but Dale's statement is true.

We continue our walk down memory lane, discussing how Rush County and things in general have changed since our youth. I say, "The greatest loss may have been Dutch's Drive-In." Dale agrees, "You are right." I then recant my statement:

The loss of Dutch's may have been the greatest loss in Rushville, but the overall greatest loss for me was the closing of New Salem School District. When the Eagle [our mascot] no longer soared over Noble Township, we lost more than a school with caring teachers; we lost the feeling of community. It is a time that cannot be recaptured.

Dale nods his head and says, "It was a great place and a great time. The loss of farm families probably was the largest factor in school closings. The people made New Salem and Noble Township a good place to live and go to school." I add, "New Salem is no longer considered a town. It was a full-market town when my mother and father were in school. Now it is just an 'unincorporated housing area.'"

We continue to reminisce about the Fifth Wheel gas station and restaurant, the grain mill, and our teachers and friends.

When Dale and I run out of stories, Ed picks up the conversation with some intelligent remarks. He states, "Many farmers are operating on borrowed money." Dale says, "The borrowed money is used to expand operations by purchasing additional land and larger equipment." We all agree that using land as collateral is good *if* properly managed, but it can be devastating if the practice becomes too aggressive. Our discussion continues about how excessive borrowing resulted in many farmers losing their land during the farm crisis of the 1980s. I add, "Mom and Dad's neighbors lost their farm, which had been in the family for generations."

We all conclude that the 1980s were a tough time we never want to experience again.

Our discussion transitions to the increased size of farms. Dale expands on previous statement by adding, "Today, there are less farms and less people in rural America. The acreage has remained practically constant. Larger equipment allows less people to work more acres. During harvest time, the days are usually longer." After a pause, I add, "It seems that the loss of people and increased farm size began during the 1950s and 1960s. Half of my graduating class left Rush County; only about 25% of our class became farmers or wives of farmers."

Dale remarks, "You were one of the 50% [who left]." I respond, "You are right. I was one of the 50%."

The conversation has a long pause. I say, "Guys, I have to go some place." Dale asks, "New Salem?" My head nod confirms his suspicion. Dale adds, "You miss it. Every time you come home you go to the school and elevator."

With a big smile, I respond, "Yes I do! I am making the seven-mile drive down 52 [US Highway] to walk around the grain mill and the school grounds." Dale says, "Don't get lost!"

I thank Dale and Ed for their time, insight, and walk down memory lane. My final words are, "I cannot get lost at home."

I depart McDonald's for the seven-mile drive to New Salem. I drive around the elevator parking lot, pausing to remember the fun, the interaction with farmers, and my aunt Betty, who was once the office manager. I then make the short drive to visit the site of the school. A walk around the school area is always accompanied by a feeling of emptiness. When I spend time at the brick commemorative wall, located near the site of the demolished school, I hear the sounds of laughter and kids playing; I hear teachers' voices; I hear the sounds of fans cheering the New Salem Eagles onto victory. I imagine George, Carp, Rosebud, and me sitting on the hood of Jerry Carpenter's old truck. I *see* progress.

The visit to the school grounds also brings back memories of high school basketball, when all the schools, large and small, competed for one championship. My mind flashes back to 1954 and "the shot": when Milan, a high school of less than 200 students, defeated Muncie Central, a high school of over 2,000 students. It was a last-second, David-beats-Goliath, win for the Indiana High School Basketball State Championship.

I suddenly decide that Mo and I are going to make the fifty-mile trip to Milan. Mo, for some reason unknown to me, jumps into the truck without me ever saying a word. Love my dawg, she reads me like a book.

The picturesque small town of Milan is nestled among the hills of southeastern Indiana. Located in Ripley County.

The town and its people will never forget a Saturday night in March 1954, when ten high school basketball players, along with Head Coach Marvin Woods and staff, pulled off the high school basketball upset of the century when a small high school beat a large high school. They accomplished the dream of every small-town high school basketball player in Indiana, including me.

Until the late 1990s, all high schools in Indiana competed for one championship. Every October we would enter the gym for the first practice, knowing we could be the next team to repeat that once-in-a-lifetime achievement.

Mo and I drive the back roads south for about an hour and a half, until we find the town of Milan. I have no idea what remains of the town and school, or who I can talk with about the great feat of fifty-six years before.

I roam around town until I see a sign marking the museum of the Milan Indians. Appropriately, it is the *old barbershop* and gathering place of the "downtown coaches," which consist mostly of ex-basketball players. When they gather, they all become first-rate coaches, replaying every play of last Friday night's game.

Mo and I wander into a maze of memorabilia. Mary Lou (not her real name) greets us with a hearty welcome. Before I ask, she says, "Your dawg is welcome." As always, I am the guy with the pretty dawg.

As Mary Lou tells me the personal stories of the players and their family lives, I realize they were just a team of boys with everyday issues like anyone else. The one thing that separated them from other teams was the high level of caring and commitment to one another, a necessary element in any high performing team. Mary Lou tells me that the players also helped each other with family and other personal issues, as well as sharing work on their farms. They were a team both on and off the court. "This caring attitude exists today," Mary Lou states. The players, managers, and cheerleaders still meet annually for a reunion. The coaches were a part of this reunion until they passed away.

As she continues with the story of the games and tournament, my memory fades to a Saturday night in March 1954, when I watched the game on a grainy TV screen. The score was tied at 30, with only seconds remaining on the clock. Marvin Wood, the Milan coach, called a timeout. Players returned to the floor with a play. Bobby Plump, a Milan guard, drove from the top of the key to the right elbow of the free-throw circle, pulled up, and shot a *jump shot* that got *nothing but net*. The picture on a grainy-pictured TV when Bobby Plump hit nothing *but net* will be forever ingrained in my mind.

At the time, I had no idea the impact those few seconds would have on history. The next day, however, I was on my limestone basketball court in the barnyard, replicating the play that had allowed David to defeat Goliath. I would repeat the play until I made two shots in a row. Then I would do it again and again. My actions were not unique. Many young, aspiring, Hoosier basketball players were doing the same thing in alleys, barnyards, asphalt courts, and gymnasiums. It is more than the shot, the win. The momentous victory created an ongoing belief, "I can achieve." Such was the power of Indiana basketball.

The name "Milan" will always be synonymous with small-town high school Indiana basketball. It will forever be the last time David slew Goliath in Indiana basketball, because the teams are now classified for competition by size of school. Some claim that is good for Indiana basketball, while others maintain it ruined the game.

Our path back to Rush County consists of many side trips, weaving our way through every feasible small town the Eagles played in during my high school years, as well as unintentionally touring some towns my dad and mom had mentioned as existing during *their* high school days. Many of these ill-fated towns identify themselves by weathered signs telling their name and marking the streets.

Many small towns of my parents' time have been claimed by history. The vision of these towns speaks clearly to the history of rural America. The questions that haunts me, even as I write this, are: Does the fate of these towns predict the future of rural America; will the towns of my childhood become only remnants of the past; and will some county seats become extinct?

My day soon changes focus as I visit with family. The remainder of Saturday, which is spent on the farm with my sister, Sandy, and her family, provides time to catch up on the lives of my nieces and nephews. We visit and talk about old times. Sandy and her husband, Larry, add to the stories, some of which I have tried to forget. My great-nephews, all six of them, are growing, which reminds me that some of us are getting older. Life is good on the farm.

The next day, after saying farewell to family, Mo and I are on the road. Our route to Kentucky takes us through historic Brown County in southwestern Indiana. The travel is slow, as the roads are hilly and winding. The scenery, however, is breathtaking. Multi-colored leaves on the trees approximate the beauty of New England during this time of year. No place equals the uniqueness of New England. I am learning during my journeys that uniqueness of people and places is a great attribute of the United States. At times, we drive through tunnels formed by the trees reaching across the road to touch their counterparts.

The countryside presents a totally different perspective than New England. Towns, churches, houses, barns, and fenced fields with horses and cattle present a flavor of America's deep south. We have not crossed the Ohio River, where most Hoosiers believe the South begins, but the people of Brown County fortunately either missed or ignored this perspective.

Brown County has the definite flavor of a slower lifestyle than other parts of Indiana. Ironically, people from Indianapolis and other larger cities own some of these houses for weekend retreats.

Mo

The trip to Indiana, as always, has been fun. People in Rush County know me. They know Randy as my human. They always pet me and tell me I am a pretty dawg before they shake Randy's front foot. I, of course, already know I am a pretty dawg, but it is always nice to hear.

They always ask me how I am doing. Randy believes they are asking him and answers. I treat it nonchalantly with a lick or "Golden hug," so I do not burst his ego.

I walk with Randy around New Salem and the farm where he lived when he was a pup. It is a sad time for him. I know because he spends a lot of time with his head down like I do when I have been a "bad dawg." I even get a few extra pets and hugs. His sadness makes me realize why I never go back and visit my mom and brothers and sisters. For dawgs, some things are better forgotten. We are a special specie.

On the bright side, I get to see Skeeta, Sandy's dawg. I have known Skeeta since I was eight weeks old. I would jump crossways on her back and go for a ride. We don't do this anymore! We still play, but less frequently. She even tries to block me from going into Sandy and Larry's house. I go anyway.

Milan is cool. I go in the famous barbershop. I have my picture taken and check out every piece of memorabilia. I even meet some tourists. They are quite impressed that a dawg is the official greeter of the barbershop museum.

Our drive today through Brown County keeps me from my afternoon nap. The scenery is beautiful: the trees, winding roads, and horses. I am surprised to see very few squirrels. There are thousands of trees with nuts but few nut-hunters, which confirms my suspicion that squirrels are not the brightest creatures. I am lost for an explanation of squirrel behavior.

We eventually cross the Ohio River into Kentucky. Our trip south of the river consists of driving east on a highway, followed immediately with a drive west on the same stretch of highway, then another, shorter drive east. I am thankful when we finally turn south on another road and drive without turning around. It is an indicator that the phenomenon of being lost is over . . . at least for a while.

We finally find a campground, walk, eat, and sleep. Humans have some weird behaviors, especially when driving. Tomorrow will be another day. I can hardly wait to visit people in Kentucky, Tennessee, and Arkansas. New friends!

CHAPTER 16

Kentucky

Mo and I spend the night at a campground near Calvert City, Kentucky, a town of a little less that 3,000 people. Calvert City is situated between the Ohio River near Paducah, Kentucky and northwest of the Kentucky Lake Dam. Its proximity to the Land Between the Lakes makes it a haven for fishing, hunting, and water sports.

Potilla Calvert gave land to the railroad in 1860 to encourage much-needed transportation to serve the small settlement nestled along the Tennessee River in western Kentucky. The new transportation enabled the settlement to thrive and become incorporated as Calvert City in 1871. The natural beauty of the area also provided encouragement for new residents. Today, transportation remains a vital asset, with interstate highways connecting Calvert City with St. Louis to the west, Louisville to the east, and Nashville to the south. The area is host to sixteen manufacturing plants, most of which are chemical-producing, with some steel and metallurgical.

Additional assets are Calvert City's proximity to the Land Between the Lakes and its southern charm. President John Kennedy created the 170,000 acres known as the Land Between the Lakes National Recreational Area in 1963 that added to a previous dam. The project began in 1938, when construction on the Tennessee River Dam began to preclude future flooding as had occurred the previous year. Thus, Kentucky Lake, with a length of 184 miles, became the largest man-made lake.

Development of the area continued in the early 1960s, when construction of a dam on the neighboring Cumberland River Dam began to form Lake Barkley. The second lake would have a length of 118 miles. The ensuing peninsula between the lakes became know as the Land Between the Lakes. I had the good fortune to camp and fish LBL two times, including once with my then-seven-year-old son. The fishing *had* to be defined as good, because we were able to hook a few.

Calvert City has shown some population growth during the past forty years. Population increased from 2,104 people in 1970 to 2,566 in 2010.

Our morning drive reveals a scenic setting of rolling hills, trees, fields, and rivers. His donation and encouragement for a town was a significant factor in the location of Calvert City. Thank you, Mr. Calvert, for selecting such a beautiful area.

Monday mornings are sometimes just that: Monday mornings. The world does not spin at the normal speed or is, perhaps, a bit off balance. Such is true with Monday morning, October 11. I always begin the week wondering if I will find someone to talk with about his or her rural American town or community. This Monday morning starts with a big doubt.

I stop at a fast-food restaurant, usually a good place to find some unsuspecting person for an interview. The first hint should have been the absence of pickup trucks in the parking lot. I obviously miss the first clue. Inside, the sight of two men in suits having breakfast gives me another clue I am in the wrong place; suits, ties, and country folk are an oxymoron.

Not to be dissuaded and not to let Monday morning defeat me and set the tone for a bad week, Mo and I begin a driving tour of Calvert City. With trailer in tow, we visit what seems every backstreet in town. The designation of "City" attached to "Calvert" is somewhat misleading.

Finally, I see a restaurant with several pickup trucks and a few cars in the parking lot. My first thought is, *This must be the breakfast place in Calvert City.* The sign above the front door stating "Smokies' Bar-B-Q" creates breakfast doubt, but it is, after all, Monday mornings when strange things happen.

Five of the six tables are occupied. My two primary choices are a table with two men talking or a table with five people laughing, bordering on the edge of "out of control." Normally, the table with two people would be more likely to accept an interruption than a table of five. But it is Monday. Plus, I cannot miss the fun. I sit down next to the table of five: three guys and two gals. Everyone is fair game for a little humor. I soon realize that the stranger—me—is also fair game.

Following an introduction and explanation of my research, the people at the table state emphatically that Bub and Don, who appear to be in their middle sixties, are the persons of choice for interviews. They both consent to tell their stories.

I start with a grave mistake; I call Bub "Bubba." My time in Texas led me to the mistake. As a middle school principal, if I had called for "Bubba and Bo" to report to the principal's office, one-third of the male population would have joined me.

But back to the story. I ask "Bubba" a question, which is immediately followed by a chorus of five voices, saying, "It is not 'Bubba,' just plain 'Bub.'"

I am uncertain if this is part of the humor or for real. I go with "Bub," which turns out to be my third good decision of the day. Now I am gaining confidence. I am on a roll! Three good decisions: the correct restaurant, correct table, and correct name.

Bub begins the conversation by immediately making certain I am on the right page of basketball when he states, "I am a Kentucky Wildcats basketball fan." He will never know the importance of this statement. The Ohio River is the demarcation of basketball loyalties, which I tend to forget. Growing up north of the river, I am a Butler University (my alma mater) and Indiana University fan. Those loyalties go back sixty years. Both Indiana teams are big Kentucky rivals. Plus, my Kentucky cousins and their relentless negative Indiana University comments make being a Kentucky fan difficult, at best. Without a doubt, I would have stepped in the bucket of whatever and created tension.

I brag on UK basketball with a slight, hopefully undetected tinge in my voice.

Bub continues the conversation by stating that he is a lifelong resident of the Calvert City area. He says, "My parents owned a business in Calvert City, and I attended Symsonia, a small, rural school district." Symsonia, even though located in neighboring Graves County, is a few miles from Calvert City. Don then informs me that he came to the area in 1960 and to Calvert City in 1975. Don states, "I worked much of my life for a trucking company. I also was a private pilot. I enjoyed flying the Cessna 172. I tried a lot of things and had a good time traveling the country. Now I repair train cars."

Bub changes the subject to the interesting history of Calvert City, saying, "The lakes, Kentucky and Barkley, have made a huge difference in the surrounding communities. Kentucky Lake was built in the 1940s and Barkley Lake in the 1960s." Don immediately adds, "I really agree that the 'Land Between the Lakes [National Recreation Area]' has made a big difference in our town and community."

Bub uses the concept of crop harvesting during his childhood to explain one means of crop transportation in the 1950s and 60s. He recounts:

> I saw old steam-engine boats on the rivers. They were our main source for transporting crops. The steam-engine boats carried a lot of cargo, including corn and strawberries. I remember horse-drawn wagons being used while picking corn by hand. We picked five rows at a time. The same laborers would come back every year. They would help with corn and strawberry harvests.

Bub, in a moment changes the course of discussion when he smiles and states, "I still own a 1957 pickup truck, which has only 34,000 miles on it." Don and I look at each other in wonderment. Don expresses our question, "What made you think of your old truck?" Bub just smiles and states, "We were talking about 'old times.'" With puzzled looks, Don and I nod our heads in agreement.

Don changes the subject to the economy of the Calvert City area. He states, "We have a lot of jobs." Bub agrees, "The economy is good. It took a long time to get here [strong economy]. We have a lot of heavy industry, such as construction and chemical plants on the Tennessee River. Most of the jobs are good-paying." He qualifies the employment situation by stating, "More people would like to have jobs."

Bub humbly discusses his company, stating, "I have a rail-car [train] repair company that employs forty-eight people. I own 112 acres, which is located on both sides of the tracks [railroad]." It is obvious that Bub is proud that his company supports the Calvert area economy.

Bub and Don claim that the people of the Calvert City area are very oriented toward community and helping each other. Bub states, "Neighbors gather to help each other." Don and Bub immediately turn the conversation to how people help each other in times of need. They both agree that the little things make a big difference. Don states, "My neighbor, who is a nurse, interrupted painting her house to give a shot to a neighbor. She would not take any money." Bub states that he had brush-hogged the nurse's lot. Their comments depict the belief that the circle of community is not only present but strong. The small acts of kindness and support make a huge sense of community.

Our discussion of community leads to how mass media has changed the concept of community in Calvert City. The discussion piques Don's passion:

Mass communication has changed the world. I believe that communication media of today have moved the focus of community from local to the world. The world as a community is an improvement, but the result has lessened the focus of local communities. When I was a kid, life was our community. We knew if a neighbor was ill or had a problem. Now, with the world as our community, we know less about our local community. Our focus has changed to world issues as opposed to local matters. Local is still present. Maybe not like it was forty to fifty years ago, but it remains present.

Don's remark about the impact of mass media on small towns and rural communities is not a unique perspective.

Mass media (e.g., television) has flooded the market with international news. Local TV news represents a large metro area many miles from the small, rural town. Radio stations for most rural communities are located in larger towns, representing another area. Many small, rural newspapers are usually published weekly, which informs readers of events and activities but lacks timely coverage of news. Communication of local news is dependent on word of mouth. The caring about neighbors remains a common thread among rural populations, even though news spreads slowly by person-to-person communication.

People still care about each other. Residents still deem rural America as a great place to live. Don speaks clearly to his feelings for the Calvert City area. Even though he did not come to the area until 1960 and spent much time traveling with his employment, Calvert City is his home. Don concludes the conversation with the comment, "This has always been my home."

I thank Don and Bub for taking time to talk with me. I also express my gratitude to the other table members for their hospitality. Bub and Don, as well as the other table occupants, thank me and say that they enjoyed our conversation. Everyone scurries off to work, while I proudly walk to the truck excited about a Monday.

Mo and I drive southwest to an unknown destination. I am feeling confident that the Monday-morning blues have faded into the unknown. With little guidance, the truck takes us to US Highway 45. Our southwest course guides us through the beautiful hill country of Kentucky. I am in dreamland because the scenery reminds me of the farms of my cousins, which are located in north-central Kentucky. I spent several of my teenage Augusts helping them cut tobacco.

Back to reality, I see a highway sign announcing the town of Mayfield. It becomes our next stop. Mayfield, the county seat of Graves County, has a maintained a consistent population of approximately 10,000 since 1970.

The "Jackson Purchase" of 1818 included Mayfield and Graves County at the center of the land bought from the Chickasaw Native Americans. The settlement began three years later, when John Anderson became the first settler. Completion of the Memphis, New Orleans, and Northern Railroads in 1858 connected Mayfield to markets and travel to the world beyond western Kentucky. The railroad facilitated marketing of locally produced commodities, such as wool and tobacco. The town received its name from a kidnapped gambler named Mayfield, who carved his name in a tree during his captivity. He drowned in the Mayfield Creek while attempting to escape.

A slight left turn onto North Seventh Street immediately places us amidst a street lined with houses and tall shade trees. In minutes we are parked on South Seventh Street between East Broadway and East Second Streets, across from the town square and Graves County Courthouse. The immaculate town square, lined with well-groomed storefronts and the old brick courthouse situated in the middle, lures Mo and me to the join the few people leisurely walking along the streets.

A trip around the square and a four-sided view of the courthouse makes an interview secondary to a visit of the historic building. The intriguing courthouse deserves a visit. In moments, with Mo in the truck, I am wandering the hallways of this historic building.

How and why, I do not know, but I end up in the sheriff's office. The secretary introduces me to the sheriff, and our conversation begins. The sheriff introduces himself as John and immediately begins telling me about Mayfield:

> I have lived my entire life in Mayfield, a town of about 14,000 people. I have lived here for sixty-one years. It is my home; it is home to my kids and now to my grandchildren. Friends I grew up with from junior high and high school are still my friends.

John quickly transitions to the story of his youth and proximity to downtown. His narrative of growing up in Mayfield is so interesting that I listen and forget to take notes, which leads to a requested pause so I can capture the story on paper. John continues:

> The courthouse is the center of town. I was born two blocks from the courthouse. Originally, I lived one-half block from the courthouse, then two-and-one-half blocks from the courthouse, then three-and-one-half blocks, then three blocks, and then across the street from the courthouse. I recently moved one mile away from the courthouse.

He spent most of his life in proximity to where he works today as an adult. Other than church, family, and friends, both downtown and the courthouse are the focuses of his life.

Our conversation transfers to a description of downtown life and childhood days during the 1950s and 60s.

As a kid, we did not have a car. We walked everywhere; groceries were in the neighborhood; we walked to church and school. There was not a bus system. My parents did not own a house or a car. My friends and I were poor, but we did not know it. It did not matter what your friends' parents did for a living. Family, friends, and community were important. Cousins lived in the neighborhood. People sat on their porches. I even remember our neighbors' names: Milnor and Mable lived next door.

He stops and smiles before talking about the movie theater's role in his life. He says, "Every Wednesday morning was 'Junior Jamboree.' We [kids] could go to a business and get a free movie pass. On your birthday, you would be recognized on the stage by a radio personality." The way he tells the story, it is obvious that the Wednesday-morning movie was very important to John and the other kids in town. Downtown was more than his neighborhood while growing up in Mayfield; it was the center of activities for kids living in other neighborhoods.

John fast-forwards his remarks to his years in junior high and high school: In 1950 there were three elementary schools, one junior high school, and one high school. Now the three elementary schools have consolidated into one school, and the junior high school is now a grade[s] six-through-eight middle school. School-age population has not decreased, because the boundaries have expanded.

John sits back and pauses with a smile before he speaks briefly about high school. He continues, "Three hangouts marked the stops for 'cruising.' In the southern part of town was Storgy's Drive-in, which became Hill's. Next, we went to Hick's Drive-in and then to the Dairy Queen." He pauses and concludes with emphasis, "Our high school years were fun times."

John's experiences in the 1950s and 1960s are his version of "Happy Days."

Prior to commenting about more recent times and how downtown has changed, he pauses and reflects. Then he states:

The south side of the square is the only section intact. Since the 1970s, two buildings have gone. One burnt. It hurts to see old buildings torn down. The downtown area has always been the downtown area. Since Walmart came to the area, some downtown businesses have closed.

Remarks by John allude to the demise of mom-and-pop stores downtown in lieu of businesses located in strip malls at the edge of town. This phenomenon appears prevalent throughout rural America. It is part of the change process.

Our discussion moves to the present time and a more diverse population. The schools and town population have become more diversified since John was in school. He speaks fondly about the diversity, support, and success:

> We now have a diverse population that did not exist in the past. We have a Hispanic population because of the chicken-processing plant. We have a small Asian population, some Somalia residents, and a few people with Middle-East Indian heritage. Our biggest challenge has been to meet the needs of the Hispanic population. Language is no longer a barrier. I feel comfortable that we provide good services.

He shows his commitment to diversity by stating, "All people deserve to have services if they are going to live here." He concludes his thoughts on diversity by stating, "Our church has a Hispanic minister and service."

Another example of successful services is Hispanic student achievement. He cites the example that Hispanic-student scores were below their Anglo peers. He states with pride, "Now the trend has been reversed. The Hispanic-student scores are higher than the Anglo-student scores."

Another example of change is agriculture. Tobacco farm size has increased dramatically from the time he was in high school. John describes childhood memories of working on farms. He says, "As a kid, I helped cut some tobacco, but worked more with baling hay. Tobacco farm size was 1 to 2 acres when I was a kid; now tobacco farms are around 100 acres." John explains that there is a lot of contract labor from Mexico to cut tobacco. "Usually, only the father comes to work without their families," he adds.

I personally recall when, as a teenager, I worked on relatives' tobacco farms in Central Kentucky. Their tobacco acreage was about 1½ acres each. It seemed it took us forever to cut and house the tobacco of those three farms.

John concludes his story with some personal issues. His mother passed away when he was twelve. His two older sisters, fourteen and nineteen years his senior, were influential during his childhood. He states, "Kids now grow up differently." His commitment to his town and service and civic activities are very strong.

He gives a summary of his professional experience and intentions for retirement years. "I have been sheriff for twelve years. Previous to being sheriff, I had a career with the Mayfield Police Department." During those years of service to the public, he had time to be involved in civic activities. During retirement, he plans to expand his collection of memorabilia. He claims, "I am the unofficial, self-appointed historian."

As I depart, John takes time to walk with me down the hall. I express my gratitude for his time and informative interview. I add, "John, you have lived an interesting life, all within walking distance of downtown Mayfield, small-town America."

He nods and says that it has been good and plans to continue his enjoyment of life during retirement. It seems that commitment and service to Mayfield and community will not end with retirement, but will simply assume a different path. It will, however, stay on the course of both contribution and improvement to the people of Mayfield, his lifetime hometown.

His story is distinctive as illustrated by his living most of his life within a few block of the courthouse, where he now works. His lifetime focus on his hometown has enabled the town to reap the benefits of a dedicated servant.

Mo and I walk one more lap around the courthouse square, imagining Mayfield fifty years before. As we walk, several people greet us a neighbors instead of strangers.

Some things change; some things just live on.

CHAPTER 17

Tennessee

Mo and I travel southwest on back roads for about two hours. Our drive takes us through a mix of hills and bare fields, which have seen the harvest of their crops. A town suddenly appears in our windshield. Mo needs a break because my back is hurting, so we stop in Dyersburg, a small Tennessee town that is actually larger than I realize.

Our voyage down US Highway 51, which parallels West Interstate 155 for the final few miles, becomes Saint John Avenue. I chose US 51 to view rural scenery versus saving time. Saint John Avenue is adorned with older homes, large trees, and of course, some retail businesses.

Dyer County was acquired in the same 1818 land acquisition as the counties of Mayfield and Graves, only it was termed a "treaty" as opposed to a "purchase." The current county population is a little less than 40,000.

When we stop a few blocks from the town courthouse square, Mo is out of the truck like a bolt of lightning. As soon as her four feet hit the turf, she is in nose-down, tail-up mode, working a zigzag pattern. A great hunt is in progress. No one, including Mo, knows the goal of the hunt; it is just the right thing to do. Finally, with the assistance of a leash, Mo abandons the hunt to checkout the town square and courthouse. The Dyersburg town square maintains its beauty, even with the large construction project on its surrounding curb.

We are obviously in a southern town, well steeped in tradition and culture. A few people are sitting and enjoying the warm October afternoon. A realtor standing at his front door recommends that I interview Darrell, who was born and raised in Dyersburg. The lawyer adds that Darrell has lived some of his adult life away from Dyersburg, but has returned and writes a lot about history. My iPhone allows me to make an appointment while I continue my second trip around the square.

A businessman stops, and we talk briefly about the town. When I ask him whom I should interview, his immediate response is, "Dave Crockett. He has lived in the town several years and was a successful businessman. He is also a descendant of Davey Crockett, although he will not tell you unless you ask him."

I immediately call Dave, who invites me to meet with him on his patio.

A quick retreat to my pickup, and Mo and I are making the short drive to Dave's house. Dave's home is on a street lined with tall, mature trees, well-established lawns, and flower gardens. Even parallel parking with a trailer is easy on the sedate street. As our truck doors slam, a voice calls out, "Come around the right side of the house!" Dave is waiting on the patio with two glasses of iced tea and a bowl of water for Mo. His hospitality and warm, welcoming handshake assure me this is going to be a friendly, productive interview.

We start the conversation with a little background from each of us. He is interested in my background, as I am in his: another good indicator.

When he realizes that I had been on the graduate faculty at Wichita State University, the conversation takes a heartfelt, unexpected turn. He relives the 1970 University of Arkansas versus Wichita State University football game. The game occurred six weeks after the October 2, 1970, plane crash that killed about of half of the WSU players and many university faculty and staff. Dave states that due to depleted WSU player roster the game was a very lopsided Arkansas win. He commends the players, coaching staff, university staff, and fans for even continuing the season. He states, "The Arkansas players, as well as coaches and fans, gave WSU a standing ovation for their fortitude and valiant effort."

My time at Wichita State University gave me the opportunity to learn about the accident and meet some families of those whose lives were lost. I attended several annual memorial services for the victims. Dave's recounting touches me about as deeply as my WSU experiences, themselves.

After a short pause, we continue our conversation. Dave informs me, "I am from Memphis, but I had lived for a while in 'cabin cotton country.' It is exactly what the term describes." He moved to the Dyersburg area in 1973, which was considered a small town at the time. He states, "You had to watch what you said, because everyone knew your business." His home was considered part of the county and not Dyersburg. He now lives immediately behind a strip mall, which he terms "Hamburger Row." The serenity of his backyard does not reflect proximity to numerous small business. The thick backyard's grove of trees creates an ambience of country living.

Dyersburg and Dyer County had a 1970 population of about 14,500 and 30,000, respectively. The 2010 number of residents was about 17,000 for the city and 38,000 for the county.

Dave begins our conversation by stating even with the growth of Dyer County and Dyersburg some important things remain with the culture. "It is now a little faster pace, but old timers still sit around the square. Most of them gather to drink coffee."

Dave was a partner in Colonial Spring, a manufacturing company. He says, "Colonial Spring, several years ago, was the largest employer in Dyer County. We employed 1,500 people. The company split into thirds. Each third employed 500 workers." He never states what happened to Colonial Spring or his subsequent company.

The conversation about his company and work lead to an interesting story. One that I am excited to hear. Dave says with a smile, "I used to have a Black Labrador Retriever. He routinely flew on an airplane and went to San Antonio on business trips." I thought I had dawg fever. It is good to hear I share the fever with someone else.

The economy in Dyer County and Dyersburg has suffered, like the rest of the country. He mentions two recent company closures: Dyersburg Fabric [mill] and Caterpillar. He continues, "The economy during the downturn was hit hard. Kids go off to college and do not come back unless their family has a business."

It is time to pose the question; my curiosity can no longer be contained. I ask, "Are you related to the Davey Crockett?" It opens a floodgate of knowledge. He smiles and begins an amazing story: "My aunt traced the family back to France. Originally, the name was *Crockattaine*. The Crockattaines in the late 1500s ended up in the UK. They later came to the America. Davey's brother was my great-great [unknown how many times] grandfather."

The explanation that is more understandable to me: Davey Crockett was Dave Crockett's great, great, great . . . uncle.

Staying true to his modesty about being an ancestor of Davey Crockett, Dave tells only one story about the Crocketts, plus a little family history. The story is about Jamie Walkup Crockett, who Dave believes to have been about one-half Cherokee. "At the time of his death, around 1844, Jamie Walkup Crockett, the high sheriff of Decatur County, Georgia, left each of his children a slave, one hog, and a table and chairs. They later found $80,000 under his mattress."

Dave and I laugh about his ancestor's monetary wealth and how Jamie placed more value on the basics of life than money. $80,000 from 1844 would equate to several million dollars in today's currency.

Dave continues by telling me about his heritage. "My grandfather was born before the Civil War. There were fourteen children in my mother's family. I only have one cousin younger than me. My mother's oldest aunt was born in 1861."

As he presents the ages of his grandparents and great aunt, it is difficult to understand—until I consider the number of his ancestors' per family and relate that to my own ancestors. One of my grandfathers, who was a middle sibling of sixteen kids, was born in 1883. My genealogy research revealed that some of my great grandparents were born prior to 1850.

When I think of Davey Crockett, I visualize a tall, very strong man. Dave, however, is not a large person in stature. His strength is in his character. He is a proud person who exudes strength without expressing it.

I would like more time to talk with Dave. He is very interesting, as well as a classy person. His closing statement creates a small commonality between us: "I am one-sixteenth Cherokee." I then share that I, myself, am one-thirty-second Cherokee, reflecting that my Native American heritage is very small, but enough to make me proud.

I thank Dave for his time, stories, and hospitality. As Mo and I are making a short drive to the other side of town, I realize we are chasing my fourth interview of the day. The ten-minute drive across town gives me some time to clear my head and think about the upcoming talk with a local historian.

The leap from Dave to Darrell is greater than I expect. Dave is a storyteller, an art unto itself. Darrell, however, is a factual historian . . . with a *science* degree.

Mo and I follow the Garmin to a small building in what appears to be in an industrial section of town. After introductions of both Darrell and his wife, Darrell, Mo, and I head down the hall to a small office with a desk and a couple of chairs. I take a position across the great grey desk from Darrell.

Mo wanders around, doing her routine safety-and-security check. She soon decides all is clear and chooses a position next to my chair for a well-deserved rest: not for her but for me.

Darrell begins the conversation by telling me that he was born in 1942 in Dyersburg, where he lived until pursuing his bachelor's degree in nuclear engineering at the University of Tennessee, Knoxville. He eventually sacrificed income to return to his home county of Dyer and assume residence in a small, rural town. He further relays that history is now his passion. He has written and continues to write about the history of Dyersburg and Dyer County. Darrell's local historical knowledge and organizational and verbal skills result in my being enthralled by his stories of the community. It becomes difficult for me to continue writing and not just listen (an affliction that is becoming too common).

I continue my note-taking as the conversation transitions to a focus on the history of the cotton industry in Dyersburg and Dyer County. As we talk, it becomes clear that until the early twenty-first century, cotton was not only the main financial base but also the lifeline of the economy. Darrell begins by stating, "Dyersburg was and remains strictly a rural farming community. Schools let out [closed] for cotton-picking season until the 1950s." He further explains that during his childhood, Dyersburg was a low-income area. He explains, "When I was a kid, very few families in Dyersburg owned a car. Most people used the bus for transportation."

To make a point about the local financial system, he regresses to a time when the primary job opportunities consisted of sharecropping and day-labor employment. Darrell states, "Most people worked day labor or sharecropped [grew cotton on rented land]." Sharecrop farmers usually have very small profits, because expenses for growing the crop account for a considerable amount of their 50% share of the income.

The financial picture began to change in 1929, when Adrian Mills/Oswego Mills, from Michigan and New York, respectively, built a cotton mill in Dyersburg. Employer-employee union issues occurring among mills located in the north made moving production to the south a very popular solution.

Construction of the mill's building began during the summer of 1928, with operations commencing on March 25, 1929, with about 1,500 employees. Thus, Dyersburg Cotton Products began operations six months prior to the advent of the Great Depression, which struck the nation on October 25, 1929. Bad timing had a distressing affect on the success of the mill. A second issue hampering the local economy was the hiring of immigrant employees. Workers from England, Germany, and Italy were hired due to their specialized expertise in cotton milling.

The year 1932 saw reorganization of the mill and new leadership. Mr. Wheeler convinced Mr. Amis, the accountant, that he could make the mill profitable. The actions of Mr. Wheeler saved Dyersburg Cotton Products, as Mr. Amis had recommended liquidation of the mill's assets.

Wages were low, but the mill remained open throughout the Depression and World War II. Darrell states, "The workers had low income, which allowed the company to control the employees. Mr. Wheeler offered script [certificate of money offered by Dyersburg Cotton Products company] when United States currency money was not available because of the Depression. They owed all they earned to the company. The people were subservient."

Low income was prevalent across our nation during the Depression years. People considered themselves fortunate to even have a job. Company-owned housing and retail stores were prevalent among milling and mining towns and companies. Frequently, these areas of residents became known as "mill towns" or "mining towns."

During the era of Depression, people throughout the United States and beyond suffered from hardships and uncertainty of the future. Mr. Wheeler realized how the hardships of the Depression and low income affected employee morale. The threats of the European war becoming a global issue further distressed the spirit and optimism of people. Mr. Wheeler realized on a local basis that employees of Dyersburg Cotton Products suffered from the same issues of morale and uncertainty. With the assistance of Mr. Amis, Wheeler initiated an aggressive employee-relations program to alleviate the emotional impact on workers and their family members. The employee-relations program orchestrated a strong plant and community affiliation during the end of the Depression years and World War II that remained intact until plant closure in 1999.

Mr. Amis, the secretary-treasurer, also assumed the role of employee-relations director. Among other programs, in 1940 Mr. Amis created the *Spinnit*, a company newspaper that provided company news, event listings, employee want-ads, and articles containing self-improvement (such as tax-filing instructions), as well as cartoons and pictures. The *Spinnit* took on a life of its own. By the company's fiftieth anniversary in 1979, thirty-nine years after it's inception, the newspaper had grown from four pages to fourteen.

Other employee-relations programs included a company bowling league, a once-a-year pancake breakfast, four weeks paid leave for employees with twenty-five years or more of employment, and annual employee-recognition dinners. The company also sponsored a very successful semi-pro baseball program that began during 1940. Ray Weidner, head of the knitting department and a former semi-pro catcher, coached the team until 1948. The team folded in 1949, but only after three players signed professional contracts. Two of the players competed in the Major Leagues. The company ballpark, built in 1941, was donated to the city for youth baseball.

During its seventy years of operations, the cotton mill experienced several renovations in products, as well as owners. Darrell states, "During the 1960s, the business was sold to new owners." They continued to support employ relations and community projects. He embellishes:

> The mill owners donated land to build a school. The owners earned loyalty. There never was a union. They [mill owners] went out of their way to help people. Many young adults graduated from college who would not have been able to afford the educational opportunities without the help of the owners. Three or four generations of family members worked in the mill. The mill became known as "Fleece Fabric" and [was] eventually titled "Dyersburg Fabrics."

The mill went out of business on 1999 due to price competition from international manufacturing plants. Dyersburg by that time had attracted several other manufacturing plants and businesses, however, such as Dave Crockett and associate's Colonial Spring.

Darrell now takes us on a walk down memory lane. He begins our walk with Saturday nights in town. It seems to be a favorite topic of many adults our age. Saturday-night shopping was more a social activity than one of actual purchasing. Darrell's story reflects the hardships of low income and the simplicity of the era. He reiterates:

> In the 1940s, kids and parents came to town on Saturday nights. Kids sat on the town square, while parents did their shopping. Stores stayed open late, [and] [their] closing [time] depended on shopping. It has totally changed. We now have shopping centers and malls; they are not as friendly as other shopping stores. I did not know what it was like to eat in a restaurant until I was in high school. Dyersburg was a very friendly, neighborly community. Most people today do not know their neighbors.

Many adults who were kids during the 1940s and 1950s mention the loss of downtown stores and Saturday-night shopping. We all remember the shopping night as a fun time. I wonder: If *we* had been the adults doing the shopping, instead kids going to the movies, eating ice cream, or just playing with friends, would we be as sad as we are today? I then question how our parents perceived Saturday-night shopping. I like to think their feelings would emulate ours.

Our next topic, as usual, includes changes in farming. Darrell shakes his head and says,

"Farms are getting larger. Today, they are 2,000 to 4,000 acres. There is quite a bit less cotton. Our main crops, in order, are soybeans, corn, and then cotton. It [farming] has become mechanical."

He then changes the subject with a very proud statement: "During World War II, we had an Army Air Corps field for training B-17 pilots." Dyersburg, like many rural towns, was the site of temporary military training facilities. Many of the bases accommodated flight training, as the need for pilots and aircrews grew immensely to support the World War II effort. The training facilities, which were economic boosts, changed the culture for a short period of time.

Darrell pauses and then says, "I feel very fortunate to be raised here in a rural setting. There is a sense of closeness not present in cities. I was offered more money, but did not leave again because of lifestyle."

I am lost in the moment, as I reflect how fortunate I was to spend my youth in a rural environment surrounded by people with strong character.

We stand and shake hands. I thank him for his time, knowledge, and willingness to share. I say, "You are the local historian." He smiles and responds that it was his pleasure to share. As we walk down the hall, he offers a last comment that sums his feelings: "Things we take for granted now, we did not have then." His concluding statement summarizes much of my first six weeks and over 7,000 miles on the road, talking with rural Americans.

Mo leads the way to the door and truck. As always, she is ready for new adventures. The drive west and search for a campground is just that: an adventure. Highway construction results in momentary disorientation. Finally, with the help of my iPhone and the Internet, we locate a campground in southeast Missouri, "boot heel country."

The campground is part of a gambling casino, which requires a drive through narrow backstreets to get to the Mississippi River. This portion of the trip is not disorientation; it is plain and simple *lost*. Having a trailer in tow makes it extremely difficult to recover from mistakes. As always, limited common sense and perseverance prevail; we find the campground. It is well worth the trials and tribulations.

Mo

What a day! What a *couple* of days. Yesterday morning, I was playing with Skeeta on her farm. During two days of travel, I have seen four beautiful states and am now in a cool campground with high-class amenities. I know it is high-class because the leash comes into action—until I convince Randy I will be . . . not *good*, but *discreet*. There is a difference. "Good" requires unfamiliar behaviors, which I do no like to practice. "Discreet" is not letting people know I am going to apply my normal behaviors. You may be confused, and I hope you are, because confusion is a large part of being discreet.

The three towns were fun, with nice people and cool smells. Dave's yard was full of great scents, some of which were unfamiliar. Randy's friend at home claims that when I am in the nose-down mode, I am reading the newspaper to ascertain the daily news. Hey! I used another big word: "ascertain." Am I cool or what? It is great to be loose and not attached to my human with a leash.

As we walk around the campground, I am confronted with decisions. Should I chase that squirrel? "Yes" means I will be on the leash. "No" means freedom, no leash. But chasing squirrels is my job; I have to do it. Short chase, and the squirrel scurries for the protection of a tree. Job well done, I go and sit down in front of Randy with my head down to show remorse. It works! No leash! Sucker. I really *am* in control. I cannot brag by strutting, because then he knows that *I* know. It is tempting, though. But freedom is more important than bragging. Goldens rule.

CHAPTER 18

Arkansas

A good night's sleep and a morning walk, and we are navigating (in reverse direction) the streets that had humbled us during yesterday's evening drive. We keep the sun at our back, which leads us westward on US Highway 412. A sign just ahead indicating "Walnut Ridge" reminds me that it is approaching noon, and my light breakfast is leaving me, moving me into full-fledged hunger.

Our short drive on US Highway 412 brings us to Walnut Ridge, population approximately 5,000.

When the first European settlers came to the area in 1873, Native Americans, most likely members of the Osage Nation, inhabited the area. Later that same year, an announcement that the railroad would be coming to town caused people to abandon the original higher-ground site that was more suited for farming. They began moving closer to the tracks. The area prospered with the arrival of the railroad and as farming thrived with hard work and rich soil.

Today, the original site is now called "Old Walnut Ridge." The current location of Walnut Ridge was founded in 1875 by a Missourian and Civil War veteran, Colonel Willis Miles Parker.

I decide to not follow the sign for the direct route to Don's Steakhouse, but instead tour the downtown area. The great choice leads us to a homey downtown and the site of the beautiful, historic train depot. The train station requires a drive around the block for a second look, which results in stopping for a walking tour. The beautiful, well-preserved station serves as the offices for the Lawrence County Chamber of Commerce and Tourist Information Center, as well as an Amtrak passenger station. The red 1910 Mediterranean-style structure dominates its area of the town. The train station's presence speaks to its importance to both the town and the area, which includes the small town of Hoxie, about two miles south.

With great reluctance I leave the station for the drive north on US 412 in search of Don's Steakhouse. The short drive provides time for me to reflect about what the train station has seen during its 100 years, from the sad departures to the happy reunions of friends and family. Undoubtedly, some departures were young women and men going to serve their country. Placed in perspective to the people in the station's history, my departure is simple. The Walnut Grove Train Station is a memorial to the people, the town, and to history.

My drive north on 412 leads me to a large parking lot jammed with a ratio of five pickup trucks to one car. The sign tells me this is Don's Steakhouse; the parking lot tells me it is *the* place to eat. I find a seat at the corner of an occupied table, with the permission of the other diners, of course. Soon I am talking with Greg at the next table, which leads to my moving across the narrow aisle between the tables for a conversation. When I ask about an interview, he pauses, turns to his friends, and tells them to "go on"; he will catch up soon.

Greg, who is about fifty years old, starts by telling me that he grew up in the country, rode bikes and horses, built a tree house, and dug a cave. The conversation continues, "I rode motorcycles with my brothers. We built a ramp and turned an old house on our farm into a motorcycle garage." His enthusiasm clearly transmits his love for family and country. The topic of cruising Main Street enters the conversation when he says, "We cruised Main Street. Our big hangouts were Hoxia Green Lantern and PF, [the teenage hangout] that was located in Walnut Ridge."

Walnut Ridge and the surrounding area have changed, but Greg's love for the community is clear. He states, "This was a great place to grow up. There used to be several department stores to buy clothing. We lost four or five service stations and a lot of the mom-and-pop places. He reminisces about the relationship between merchants and customers by saying, "A store owner [once] gave me a pocketknife."

After a pause, he continues, "To show how it was, I was delivered in Dr. J. B. Elder's office." Forty years ago, the small-town doctors made house calls, delivered babies in their offices, and welcomed walk-in patients.

Greg changes the subject with a pause and a thoughtful look. He says, "Farming changes every day. We used to raise cotton; now there is none grown in Lawrence County. We grow rice, soybeans, wheat, some corn, and milo. In addition to the change of primary crops, farms have become much larger. I farm 7,200 acres." He continues, "Changes in farming, such as crops and size of farms, have been a result of technology. Technology has produced improved nutrients for crops, as well as better seed and better machinery." Greg's statements concerning large farms and technology define the changes in farming throughout the United States during the past half century.

For Greg (and most farmers), farming is a family operation. Children farm with their parents, then grandchildren join the operation. Grandparents retire, and the operation perpetuates itself with the next generation. Greg clarifies the process by stating, "I live on the farm where I grew up. I built a house in the middle of a field. My oldest son lives in my parent's house. My parents retired and moved to Cherokee Village." Greg further substantiates the family affair of farming when he relays, "My wife drives the combine." It is obvious by Greg's comments that farming is not only a lineage family affair, but also one that transcends gender.

Giving back to the community is a passion of many rural people. They love the community where they grew up, where their children reside and work, and the people who they have known all their lives. Relationships are enduring and embedded in family and community. I am not surprised at Greg's closing statement, "I just got elected to the school board. My first meeting is tonight." His calm demeanor transforms to slight anxiety. He says, "I hope it goes well." He explains that he wants to serve the people well. We shake hands, and he is off to the fall harvest.

I sit and quietly eat lunch, or "dinner," as the noon meal is often called in rural America. The crowd dissipates from the steakhouse as I linger, contemplating my drive home. A couple sitting at the next table are completing their meal. JD, whose age appears to be in the mid-seventies, begins a conversation with me about my interest in rural America. He is interested in why and how I am telling the story of rural America. I respond that it is a time in history that will be lost if not captured from the people. The true stories are viewed through the eyes and spoken in their voices of the people who have lived the life. He nods in agreement. As our conversation progresses, I realize he has an interesting story that includes childhood during the Depression.

JD begins his life story with a description of his childhood years in northwest Lawrence County. He recounts his early years by stating:

> I was born during the Depression in the small town of Imboden, which is located eighteen miles north-northwest of Walnut Ridge on US Highway 63. We lived there during my early years. When I was young, we moved about nine miles south of Imboden to Black Rock. We did not have electricity or a car. We walked everywhere. On Saturday, we would "flag" a ride to town with the mail carrier. When I was fifteen years old, we moved ten miles southwest of Imboden to Annieville. My dad built a house on the 87 acres that he purchased.

As JD speaks of his early years, he does not express any negative feelings about his life of immobility or the absence of amenities. His explanations and mannerisms transmit that his youth was a seemingly positive experience.

JD experienced a great transformation of his life when he graduated from high school. His world changed from the local geographic setting of Lawrence County, Arkansas to a life beyond the shores of the United States. He explains:

> I graduated from high school in 1953 and joined the army. After my army enlistment, I transferred to the coast guard, where I served eighteen years. During my twenty-one-year military career, I served two tours in Vietnam, with eighty-seven combat patrols on the rivers. Today, I suffer health issues from those two tours.

I am impressed by his two tours of duty in Vietnam, especially the number of combat patrols on the rivers. While he is very proud of his military career, he is not boastful. His not elaborating on health issues, to me, indicates his deep pride is from duty and not external accolades.

After his military career ended, JD returned to his roots in western Lawrence County, where he and his wife purchased a home in Smithville. He then resumed a second life of service on a local scale. He recounts his experience by explaining:

> When I returned to Lawrence County, I served on the police department. Later, I became a member of the Lawrence County Sheriff Department. My last job was being the city recorder of Black Rock. My wife and I are now retired. We have a nice home and a small garden.

A brief reflection leads to the philosophical side of JD. He says, "I have seen a lot of progress. Walnut Ridge has become larger than when I was a kid. When I was young, people from the hill country could not be elected to public office. Now that is no longer true." The last statement reflects a significant issue for JD and not only addresses progress in Lawrence County but also clearly recognizes his own lifetime of service and achievement.

As we both prepare to leave, JD looks me in the eye and states with great pride, "The 87 acres my dad bought in 1949 for $4,000 sold in 1968 for $20,000." With a smile, he concludes our conversation with one final statement: "Ten years ago, I gave away the house my dad built." His effort and success in life has enabled him to help someone with a need for housing. The act of kindness to help someone is a way of giving back. My smile is an internal applause for him remembering his roots after a life of significant accomplishments. He exemplifies the statement if you are humble you will be made great.

I bid farewell to JD and his wife. As I walk through the parking lot to the familiar grey truck and trailer, I reflect on the stories and lives of both Greg and JD. An almost-empty parking lot seems like a good place for Mo to check out the smells. Her time of investigation is my time of additional reflection about the future of rural, small-town America. What will future generations bring to the lifestyle I call my "roots?"

I further reflect that JD's experiences are unique compared to many that I have heard during my trip. His twenty-one-year military career and service to his country instilled a motivation to serve. He came home to his roots and served the people of Lawrence County.

Mo and I are on the road, headed northwest on Highway 63, with the goal of sleeping in our real beds tonight. The drive through hills and farmland is serene and beautiful. We make it home. The drive provides time to consider the next trip. Each trip increases my motivation and determination to meet more people, see more communities, and hear more stories. I decide spring will take us to the southwest.

Southwest

CHAPTER 19

Oklahoma

It is a bright, sunny day as Mo and I drive out of our driveway for a trip southwest to visit new towns and people. We are heading for "cowboy country." Our drive begins in the same way our previous two excursions did, traveling through familiar, previously traveled country. Our four-hour drive on mostly back roads takes us to Interstate 44 and Oklahoma.

I notice that the novel 1965 restaurant over the interstate has aged since my first trip forty-five years before. The second thing I notice is that the tollbooths, once staffed by humans, have been replaced by technology. I misread a sign and take the wrong exit. Quick mental gymnastics tells me: wrong exit, lost, insufficient money change for the toll, a turn around is inappropriate, and pride leads me to the decision get out of here. The get out requires a lengthy retreat to the highway. The 50 yards of distance to the highway provides me an opportunity to practice my backing skills with a trailer attached to the truck. All bad news! The good news is that I have improved my trailer-backing skills, though I still gain notoriety from drivers honking their horns.

Eventually, after six-and-a-half hours of driving, we are camping east of Oklahoma City. The drive after the wrong exit made the remainder of the trip seem mundane.

Wednesday morning navigation through Oklahoma City determines our route for the day. I take the easiest, quickest route out of city's rush-hour traffic. The highway takes us west on Oklahoma Highway 152, which leads us to US Highway 81. Eventually, the battle of hunger causes me to think about giving up the beautiful farm-country scenery to find a town.

Our drive soon leads us to Minco (pronounced "Menco"). As I approach the town driving south, I am greeted by a large sign stating "Welcome to Minco, The Land of Milk and Honey." I feel welcome. Later, I learn that the sign depicts the large number of dairy farmers and Oklahoma's largest beekeeping company, Gibson-Ross Clover Bloom Honey [officially named Ross Honey].

Minco, named for the Chickasaw warrior and chief, Itawamba Minco, was settled in 1890 as part of the Chickasaw Nation. Even though there were three previous expeditions through the area, Minco did not become a town until the

Chicago, Rock Island and Pacific Railroad (CRI&P RR) ended in the area. The railroad was constructed to facilitate shipping cattle from the Chickasaw Nation's abundant grazing lands.

Minco, the railhead from 1891 to 1894, became the site for cattle shipping via rail. The disturbance of large cattle herds driven through the streets of town and the rowdiness of people staying in the wagon-yard campgrounds, which were larger than the town, caused ill feelings and contributed to a lawless atmosphere. Numerous gunfights and stabbings resulted in one hotel being called the "Bloody Bucket Hotel."

Modern-day peaceful Minco hardly reflects its past. Today, Minco has an approximate population of 1,600. Proximity to both Oklahoma City and Tinker Air Force Base provides Minco and its host county, Grady, employment opportunities in a large urban area. Most residents earn their living in manufacturing, followed closely by construction.

I enter town on US 81 and North Oklahoma Highway 37, which become Third Street. About halfway through town, Third Street intersects with Main Street, where Highway 37 turns east. The southwest corner of the intersection marks the home of the Coffee Cup Café, the place for today's breakfast. The restaurant consists of five tables, each with four seats, and a seven-stool counter. I become the lone counter patron.

My country breakfast leads to a conversation with Audrey, a server and the manager of the café. Audrey is a twenty-six-year-old graduate of Oklahoma State University. She tells me, "I attended El Reno Community College for one year and then Oklahoma State University, where I graduated. After graduation from OSU, I just decided to come home. I missed the country life." Her story continues by describing a second reason for returning to Minco:

> This is mostly cattle country. I was in Future Farmers of America and showed sheep. My brother won Grand Champion for one of his hogs at the Grady County Fair [local fair]. My involvement in FFA and showing livestock made me feel part of the community. We [my brother and I] both feel part of the community.

Audrey proudly transitions to Minco: its growth, local businesses, and other commutable employment. She explains:

> We have grown quite a bit during the last ten years, [by] maybe 200 to 300 people. Our population now is about 1,600 people. We are a little farming town with a lot of community involvement. The downtown

storefronts [either] have been or are being renovated. The box store[Uline], a local business, is expanding and will hopefully add new jobs. The Braum's Dairy is located in the community. We are a farming community, but diverse, with oil fields and people working at Tinker Air Force Base. We are a little politically divided.

I ask, "How?" She replies, "Some residents like new people moving in, [but] some do not. We are still a close community. People stay the same, pretty much." Her statement reflects the fact that the original residents have established a strong culture, which the new populace has accepted as needing little change.

Minco events are instrumental in creating a healthy community environment. Audrey excitedly tells me, "Every December we have the [Minco] Honey Festival. It is a large event that attracts many people. The festival is one of several events that adds to community life in Minco." She smiles and says, "You can always go to Oklahoma City if you get bored. I do not go very often." She informs me that Oklahoma City, which is only about a half-hour drive, has shopping and several venues for entertainment.

Audrey explains the importance of family, both immediate and extended. She proudly states, "My mom owns the Coffee Cup, and my grandmother has her real-estate office next door." As if right on cue, Audrey completes her sentence just as the front door blows open, and a storm of energy named Lori enters the restaurant. The restaurant comes to life with talk, laughter, and bubbles of excitement.

Audrey exclaims, "Lori is always like this. She is my cousin. We live together." My question, "How is that working out for you?", leads to both women excitedly describing how much fun they have sharing a home.

Lori then tells me that Audrey is getting married next month, which kicks off another new conversation filled with laughter and excitement. Then, as quickly as Lori enters, she says her good-byes and leaves. I tell Audrey that being close to her family appears to be a large aspect of her having returned to Minco. She responds, "You should interview my Grandma Verna! I will call and tell her you are coming over. You can take your dawg. Grandma would like to see her." I am happy and grateful that she recommends her grandmother for an interview. I am also in awe of her high-energy enthusiasm and excitement.

I thank Audrey and tell her how meaningful our conversation was for me. She responds that she is happy to talk about her hometown. I wish her the best and head out the door to retrieve Mo.

I make the short walk to find an alert dawg who is ready to get out of the truck. In less than a minute, Mo and I are sitting with Grandma Verna, her husband, and their adult son. I immediately know by the family pictures adorning the office walls and desk that Verna and her husband are proud grandparents. Her and her husband's enthusiasm and vigor give the impression of a much younger couple charging onward to build a business and community.

Verna begins by stating, "This is a wonderful community. When someone has a problem, everyone helps. If someone does not like someone, they will help him or her anyway. You know everyone, their children, and their grandchildren." Verna pauses and looks me in the eye: "A small town is the only place that you can call the wrong number and talk for thirty minutes." The statement, in a few words, clearly describes a small community. She continues by stating a phenomenon that I have heard about several times: "A lot of couples have moved back, bought 5 to 10 acres, and built a house." The statement indicates that several young couples with families are raising their children where they, themselves, grew up a few years before.

This is going to be an exciting interview! Verna has read my mind. She has addressed my interests before I ask a question. I am infected by her excitement and enthusiasm about her hometown, Minco. She continues without a prompt. My only tasks are to listen fast and write faster.

Her family and their closeness are extremely important to Verna, as she sums up by saying, "It is nice to live near to our children and grandchildren." The statement reflects an obvious appreciation that her family is very close, physically and emotionally, to her. Verna's next story about her son clearly depicts her feelings of pride for her children, specifically: "My son has eight children, including a fifteen-year-old who moved in with them when both his [the fifteen-year-old's] parents passed away. The young man hyphenates his name with my son's name, even though he is not adopted." She pauses with a smile directed at her son.

> Verna continues with a description similar to many small towns. She says: Our town has several amenities and retail stores, but lacks a few, such as a grocery store. Our closest grocery store is in Tulla, eight miles from Minco. Minco has a Dollar General store, which carries milk and bread. We need a meat and vegetable market in Minco.

Her son enters the conversation by stating, "We need a Braun's." He definitely values good ice cream. He and I are on the same page.

Verna continues, "We have a hardware store and a flowers shop. There are plenty of good restaurants, but we do not have a steakhouse." I can understand the rationale for a Braun's and a steakhouse: Minco is located in cattle country and in proximity to a Braun's dairy herd. To me, a novice in marketing, it seems intuitive that steak and ice cream are natural choices for Minco. Actually, I believe they are natural choices for *any* town.

Our topic of discussion quickly transitions from food to a comparison of churches and farm-equipment dealers in Minco. I can hardly wait to see where this conversation is going to take us. Verna states, "We have not lost a church, except for maybe a Catholic Church, since the beginning of the twentieth century. The John Deere dealer had not been as fortunate." She explains:

> We lost our John Deere dealer about twenty years ago. It was one of the top three in the country. When the owner retired, John Deere would not let him sell the dealership. They would allow only one [dealership] per county. There were several interested buyers.

She shakes her head indicating that she does not understand the logic of closing a successful dealership. The negative thought lasts only a moment, however, as she immediately transitions to a positive aspect of Minco.

As almost a second thought, it seems, Verna adds, "We have a cotton gin and a weekly newspaper called the *Millennium*." She gives me a copy of the paper. Then she adds a statement that is a surprise and contradictory to what Audrey told me. Verna claims, "Most of the people work in town." Audrey had informed me that many people worked in Oklahoma City and at Tinker Air Force Base. The discrepancy between the two statements seems to represent differing opinions, until I consider that the persons making the conclusions represent two very different age groups. Verna is speaking about her contemporaries, while Audrey is considering her own peers. The two statements depict behaviors dissimilar to the age group of the communicator.

Verna, her husband, and son share a few laughs and small-town memories. Mo is getting bored. She lets me know by the familiar nudge with her nose. We thank each other for the conversation and say our farewells.

Mo and I walk down Main Street, soaking up the small-town sights and friendliness of the people. I receive several "hellos," where as Mo receives warm greetings, pets, and yes, some people food. Mo is soaking up the attention, while I am relishing the friendly people and culture of a small town.

Mo

I always enjoy walking around small towns. It is a chance to build my ego after sleeping in the truck while Randy is in a place where people gather to talk, drink coffee, talk some more, eat, and talk even more. I have listened at the door of some of those places and know they are not all they are cracked up to be. People sit around tables, with each person believing his or her story is captivating (whatever that means) to the others. In reality, what usually happens is that while one person is talking to the other three people, at least one gets tired of listening and starts telling his or her side of the story—or maybe even a whole different story. Soon, the third person decides to join the conversation and talks even louder than the other two. There is always a fourth person, who just sits there but does not talk—and from his or her expression, does not listen.

You put four dawgs at a table with food, however, and there is no barking. We get busy with the eating process! You might hear a low-order growl from time to time, if it is possible to do so with a mouth full of food. But otherwise, when we are done eating, we lick the plates, maybe burp, check our neighbors' plates, and then go about our business. At least, all of us but one: the lone jack. The real dumb jerk that has to jump down and lift his leg and mark the table. He thinks the other dawgs really care. Why is there always that one dawg who gives the rest of us a bad reputation?

No matter how bad peoples' manners are early in the morning at coffee, it does not compare to their night behaviors. People gather at a place where the music is really loud. Everyone is yelling instead of talking. They drink out of a bottle filled with a "voice potion" that causes them to talk even louder. Then eventually, two people (usually a man and a woman) go out onto the floor, grab each other like a fight is brewing, and they prance across the floor while counting, "One and two, and one, then one and two, and one . . ." They continue counting and stomping across the floor and back—and then back again!—until the music stops.

You know, dawgs can walk across the floor, around the floor, and back *without* counting. I can even hunt birds, squirrels, and rabbits, and never count one number. Who is the superior creature? I believe we need to rethink this whole thing we call "hierarchy."

Randy

I finally convince Mo that it is time to trade the attention and people food for travel, not an easy task. We drive about twenty-five minutes south on US 81. Just as we are about to enter the town of Chickasha, I see an old

World War II-style aircraft hangar. By the time I realize what I am seeing, I miss the turn to the airfield. Not a problem. I can make a turn-around. In fighter-pilot language, we call it a "low-speed yo-yo."

Following the successful "yo-yo," I find the turn. We are headed for an old World War II airfield. This day just gets better and better! Mo and I wander around, looking at the sights. Eventually, we find the old base ops (operations) of Wilson-Bonfils US Army Air Corps Flying School, which operated from 1941 to 1945.

The walls are decorated with memorabilia of World War II pilots. Pictures of the seven Wilson-Bonfils graduates, who were "Aces," hang on the wall. Aces are pilots who have shot down five or more enemy aircraft. Three framed quotations by General Chuck Yeager adorn the walls. General Yeager is the famed fighter pilot who was the first to break the sound barrier. He was not a Wilson-Bonfils graduate, but his fame earned him a spot on the wall and other notable venues.

George, who is an instructor pilot and sky-diving instructor, enters base ops and introduces himself. I explain my research and background as a fighter pilot. Then I say, "I am uncertain how a World War II airfield fits my rural America research, but a magnetic force pulled me into the airdrome."

George gives me a quizzical look and a quick verbal sketch of the Wilson-Bonfils Airfield operations. The quizzical look resulted from the technical aviation questions that I asked him. An aerial view of the airfield, along with his explanation, reveals that there was one asphalt strip (runways 17 and 35) and three grass strips (runways 02 and 20, 17 and 35, and 13 and 31). The three grass strips intersected at midfield. One grass strip and the paved runway paralleled each other. (Runways are identified by two numbers, which indicate their magnetic direction, rounded to two digits.)

George explains that the airfield was activated during October 1941 and deactivated in May 1945. He further explains that hangar 2 was destroyed during the tornado of 1999. "Hangars 3 and 4 still stand," he adds. I was remiss for not asking about Hangar 1. Failure to determine the fate of Hangar 1 haunts me every time I read this interview. My response is, No excuse."

I walk outside with him as he heads off to fly. George points to the many trailers parked between the airfield and the road. He said, "The trailers now sit on the concrete where cadet housing stood during airfield operations."

We shake hands, and I thank him for his time and sharing of knowledge. He hurries off to the airfield, while I divide my focus among the old cadet housing area, airfield, and hangars.

My mind wanders back in time to the early 1940s: a time and place where numerous young aviators preparing for war descended on the small Oklahoma town. How did their arrival and residence affect the people of Chickasha? How did the town change during the four years, with so many young airmen residents? What was it like as a student pilot, flying on a small strip of earth covered with four runways, three of which intersected at midfield? Did any of the aviators return to Chickasha after the war to live, maybe to marry a local girl? How many of the young men did *not* return from the war? What was the impact on local citizens when they learned that one or several of their friends was not coming home? Was Chickasha changed forever, or did they return to life as it had been before the young pilots had come to their town?

Due to the passage of time, those questions are difficult to answer.

One question I believe *can* be answered is, how were young men treated during their time in this little Oklahoma town? I am certain that patriotism and small-town hospitality reined supreme. They were certainly made to feel welcome.

I trained in west Texas during the mid 1960s. The citizens more than made us feel welcome; they accepted us graciously. Big Spring citizens made us part of their community, as well, for which I will be forever grateful.

Mo

I had a great time exploring. Randy was mentally occupied, so I had free reign to go and do what was important. I hunted. I checked the smells for clues to whatever. I was a free dawg!

All good things must come to an end, however. Randy, my human, must be ready to travel, because he says, "Come on, Mo! Let's go!" He then opens the truck door. Guess what? I am not ready. He should know I am not ready because I am in the nose-down, tail-up mode. Plus, I do not hear well when my nose is on the ground.

Randy calls again. Ok, I will play the game. Step 1: I take a few steps toward the truck. Step 2: I keep my nose down as I walk. Step 3: I stop and smell. Step 4: Randy repeats, "Come on, Mo." Step 5 after a pause: He repeats, "Let's go!"

His "Come on, Mo" is supposed to be a reminder to me that I have stopped—as if I am not aware of that already! I repeat steps 1 through 3. *He* then repeats step 4 and 5. After a few repetitions, usually six or eight, I jump into the truck's backseat. Everyone is happy. Randy thinks he won because I jumped into the truck. I know *I* won because I completed my hunt.

We are off again to a place called "west."

We travel two-lane roads, avoiding the interstate. Our route takes us through many small towns, a larger town with several of those red-yellow-green lights, and then back on the open road. My afternoon nap is interrupted by noise above my head. After a post-nap stretch, I realize that big birds with engines, some with their tails on fire, are flying over our heads. Randy, who is oblivious to the unique birds, is on the phone, talking with someone about a place to camp. I hear him say, "The campground is one mile from the bathroom, and it is closed from midnight to six in the morning?!" I can see one unhappy camper in the mirror as he utters, "Only campground within 100 miles." The reality is that he really can get us into some bad camping situations.

We arrive at Altus Air Force Base campground. This is a "great place!" There is a big field with a track around it. I run and check new scents, roll in the grass to scratch my back, and just generally be a dawg. We eventually drive to a big store. As usual, I guard the truck. He spends some time in the parking lot, talking to guys in drab olive coveralls with patches. Randy calls them "flight suits." They always shake hands and say to each other, "Thanks for your service." Must be some kind of fraternity.

We park by a building that omits the great smell of food. After an eternity, Randy returns, saying, "First time I had to cook my own food at a restaurant." I can tell we are really having fun!

During the course of events, we find the bathroom, which is located in a "fitness center." New term! I do not know what "fitness center" means, but I receive a hint that it is more than a bathroom when I see soaking-wet humans with red faces exiting the building. It might be a place to chase squirrels.

We then tour the base on our way back to the camper, where I immediately take my place on the couch and dream.

At 11:30 p.m., when we should all be sleeping, Randy jumps out of bed and announces, "Time to go the bathroom!" I utter, "No, thanks. I have been."

He shakes me awake, and off we go in the truck. It takes a short time to get there and *forever* to get back. "One-way streets make life difficult," I hear from the front seat. I ask myself, *Was he really a pilot?*

We drive around, just like this afternoon during our return from the "fitness center." If I did not know better, I would think we were lost. As we pass the street to the campground, I hit him with my nose and look toward the campground. He does not get the hint, however, because we drive a while before stopping in front of the camper.

I exit the truck, in the camper, jump on the couch, and am asleep before we take another tour. After what seems to be a short nap, I am awakened by the words "it is six o'clock!" Off we go for a short drive, followed by the same long drive back to the camper. After our five-mile walk, we make another trip to the "fitness center," this time with Randy's backpack over his shoulder. After forever, he returns smelling much better. Interesting why dawgs never smell bad.

After another tour of the base, we are at the camper, packing to travel. You guessed it: "west." Randy drives, and I finally take a well-earned nap.

CHAPTER 20

Texas

Our forty-five-minute drive west on US Highway 62 leads us across the Oklahoma-Texas state line. A few miles further, I am confronted with the first major decision of the day: a T-road. Should we go north or south on US Highway 83? A rolling West-Texas stop, a left turn, and we are heading south on US 62 and 83, with Childress, Texas in our sights.

The first thing I notice is friendly angle parking for pickup trucks. My second observation is men wearing wide-brimmed western hats. Childress, with a population of around 6,000, is unmistakably a western cowboy town.

The West Texas town of Childress was originally settled in 1887 and incorporated in 1890. Childress and Childress County are named in honor George C. Childress, author of the Texas Declaration of Independence. As is normal of many rural counties, there was conflict during selection of the seat. Childress and Henry, separated by four miles and the OX Ranch, were vying to become the seat. An election, later deemed illegal, selected Childress as the seat. Additionally, R. E. Montgomery, a railroad agent, considered the Henry location preferable to Childress because the rough terrain made Childress unsuitable for tracks. Montgomery proposed the successful compromises of locating the county seat at the Henry location, changing the name of "Henry" to "Childress," and giving landowners from the old Childress lots in the new Childress.

Conflicts for county seats become a part of history and result in interesting stories. The story of Hazelton, North Dakota, from Chapter 7, involved armed persons during the establishment of a new county seat. If our own twenty-first-century town was competing for a business that would boost our economy, would we be less intense?

The Childress Bakery Sandwich Shop & Deli, located at the intersection of Avenue F Northwest (US 287) and 10th Street Northwest, is the breakfast choice this morning. I sit at a vacant table next to four men who are having way too much fun. Three of the men are around the ages of forty-five to fifty, while I guess the age of the humor guy to be about eighty.

We talk for a few minutes, and I explain my pursuit of rural America stories. I then pose the proverbial question: "Would someone like to tell me about life in Childress?" The unanimous choice is Floyd, the humor guy. The other three label him as "The Storyteller," which I soon learn to be a fitting name. The conversation evolves into a conversation with Floyd and three cowboys encouraging him. I am well aware that this conversation may take the aura of riding a verbal bronco.

I think it is appropriate to caution the reader that the following stories may contain some truth, while some may be *just* stories. To me, they are fun and tell a larger story about old-time cowboys, namely that they have fun and do not take life too seriously. Readers beware: The following content contains humor.

Floyd begins by telling me he was a "horse trader" most of his life. He says, "I told a man who wanted to buy one of my horses that the horse was twelve years old. The man looked at the horse's teeth and said, 'This horse is at least twenty.' I said, 'He is my horse, and I say he is twelve. When he is your horse, he can be as old as you say.'"

Momentarily, Floyd becomes serious and talks about life and Childress, Texas: "I have lived here twenty-five years. I moved from Matador, Texas, which has about 700 people." He embellishes:

> The smaller the town, the friendlier the people. I had cancer surgery while I lived in Matador. The people all signed a big piece of butcher paper and sent it to me. The doctor could not believe it. Matador is becoming very small, but Childress is growing. Childress has a lot of industry, such as farming, ranching, and the location of a prison in 1992. The prison employs several people. Cattle and cotton are the big farming crops. The people are very friendly and helpful. People help each other when they need it.

He follows with a caveat: "People of Childress are not quite as friendly as they used to be. I think it is caused by people moving in and out." After a pause, he then adds that Childress has a "good school system."

His big grin gives away that his time and patience for seriousness has run out. He says, "If my wife caught me with another woman, she would send her a sympathy card." The laughter from his friends spurs him on. "I used to know a lot of people; now they are not as friendly." A pause for more laughter, then he continues, quipping, "I am taking applications for pallbearers."

Floyd takes time to tell a couple of more stories before he has to leave. "When I was a kid, I rode my stick horse from Matador to Stanford. I felt like I ran all the way." He then tells me, "Jack Daniels sold more horses than I did."

I thank Floyd as he prepares to leave. He tells me that he must go because, "I have a deal on some tires." Floyd seems to be a man of deals.

Floyd represents a vanishing breed. He is an old-time cowboy and horse trader, as well as a storyteller. His stories are about his life and the people and places that were present along the journey. He is also a bit of a philosopher. I have read about many old-time cowboys, but Floyd is one of a very few with whom I have had the opportunity to engage in conversation. It is quite a treat.

The other three men leave, too, after we talk a bit more. I order breakfast and enjoy some quiet time. Naomi, my server, stops to ask if I need anything. She is interested in my pursuit of the life stories of rural America. I ask her if she would be interested in telling me her story. She replies, "I need to think about it." Pretty soon she returns and says that she would like to talk with me. She explains, "I am now on break."

> Naomi begins by telling me that Childress is a good town. She explains: I have lived here since 1959. Gas was nineteen cents a gallon then. People of Childress take care of each other. If someone needs help, everyone pitches in. If a house burns down, it does not take long to replace it. I have worked at the Childress Bakery for twenty-five years. Prior to the bakery, I worked at the Dairy Mart until the late 1970s. It was a high school hang-out, but not anymore.

She believes her employment of serving the public allows her to meet a lot of the residents and be knowledgeable about the people, specifically their behaviors, attitudes, and activities in town and the local community. Naomi enjoys her work because it allows her to interact with a lot of people. She is definitely "a people person."

As she talks about Childress, she speaks with surety and confidence. She is a proud citizen of her town. She says, "Everyone knows everyone. [But] it has changed somewhat since the prison was built." There was a large influx of people to work at the prison. Even with the new residents, however, she believes that the people of Childress remain committed to community.

She pauses and clarifies her remarks by adding that the prison brought in a rapid influx of people. They were good people but the numbers changed the culture. The face of the town also has changed somewhat, with many new buildings. Yet many of the older ones remain. She embellishes:

> US Highway 287, called "Avenue F Northwest," has always been the main street. Probably ten of the twelve buildings on the street remain standing.

This donut shop has been here since 1950. We have always had a lot of motels. Two were torn down during the last five years. Four new ones were built in the last two years. The two Phillips gas stations still stand, but neither is used as a gas station. One is a souvenir shop.

Naomi's huge smile indicates pride and importance. She adds, "The drive-in has been here since I was a kid, at least sixty-five years. It is still run by the same family, the son-in-law of the original owner. It was also a high school hangout, but it is not anymore."

She ponders a moment before she continues:

There is not as much for kids to do as there was in the past. There are a lot youth baseball and football teams for kids up to high school age. We have enough seven- and eight-year-old kids to field fourteen baseball teams.

The pride in the way she makes this statement reflects her belief that Childress has a substantial, non-decreasing population.

Naomi cites pride and commitment to community and residents as she speaks of the passing of two of Childress' favorite citizens:

Auto mechanic Dilbert Wilson died last year. Six months after he passed away, we had a car show with all of his old cars. When a "good old boy" passes away, they carry him to the cemetery in a horse-drawn wagon.

The two events are very meaningful to Naomi and reflect her strong belief about the core values of the people of Childress.

She pauses and reflects for a few seconds, then concludes her story with, "Childress is still pretty much a cowboy town. My father-in-law was an old-time cowboy. My husband is a pretty good roper. He still works some [as a cowboy]."

The cowboy culture appears to be very much alive and deeply steeped in the people of Childress. I am a bit overwhelmed by the deep rooted caring for community and others. It brings back memories about one of my youth mornings at the grain elevator. After I thank Naomi, I walk to the truck and give Mo a big hug. I need to hug someone, and "Mo," I tell her, "you are the lucky one."

I have deep beliefs that the people of rural America are a strong breed. Childress has maintained its cowboy culture and commitment to friends and neighbors. This has been a great morning.

Mo and I head south on US Highways 62 and 83, then turn west on US Highways 62 and 70. Our planned destination is Muleshoe, Texas, which is about a three-and-a-half-hour drive. There is not a direct route, so I chose the route of US highways, as opposed to Texas "farm roads." I have traveled and enjoyed many trips on Texas farm roads. With a trailer, however, I usually choose highways.

Our 2:45 afternoon arrival provides time to drive around and find a restaurant with pickup trucks in the parking lot. It is not about eating. It is about finding someone to tell me the story of Muleshoe.

I locate a bunch of pickups surrounding an eatery. Once inside, the friendliness of the people makes it easy to initiate a conversation with four unsuspecting souls sitting around a table. The conversation informs me about the name of Muleshoe and why it became a town in West Texas. In 1877, Henry Black purchased the original ranch in the area. The ranch was Muleshoe" because—you guessed it—a mule shoe was found on the land. About forty years later, a settlement began on the proposed railroad line from Farwell, Texas to Lubbock. A few years later, the original settlement was abandoned in favor of a replacement town, due to the revised routing of the railroad. The town, Muleshoe, borrowed the name from the neighboring ranch.

Muleshoe originated in 1913, when the Pecos and Northern Texas Railroad installed tracks through the county. The town became incorporated in 1917, when Bailey County was organized. Muleshoe, the market center for the county, has maintained a population of approximately 5,000 for the last forty years. The number of businesses however, as with most rural towns, has decreased in numbers.

After our round-table discussion, a man named Gene states he would be happy to talk with me, but adds, "You will need to ride around town in my pickup while I make a few farm errands." I respond that a guided tour of Muleshoe would be great. My remark creates some laughter and the comment, "You may be getting the first ever guided tour of Muleshoe."

Gene is obviously a cowboy. Clothing is the first hint; his rugged, well used pickup is the second. The big clue is his attitude and mannerism. He talks plainly with a realistic approach to each issue. He is not judgmental about people and issues. Plus, our tour is focused on dealing with cattle supplies.

In minutes, Gene and I head up the road in his pickup to a farm store. As we drive he says, "Agriculture has always been our big business. Farmers used to make a living on [anywhere from] one-quarter to one-half sections of land:

160 acres to 320 acres." (Note: a section of land, one mile square, is 640 acres.)

As we pull into the parking lot of a farm-supply store, Gene tells me there were four periods of enormous growth in both Bailey County and Muleshoe. The first three booms focused on agriculture, where as the fourth was due to a different industry. He explains:

> The first settlement in Bailey County did not have water, so the first boom resulted from digging irrigation wells. The second boom was the beginning of feedlots in the mid-1950s. The third boom occurred with the raising of corn during the mid-1970s. Corn, because it is used to feed livestock, supported the feedlot operations and made it economically feasible to relocate dairies from East Texas and California to Bailey County. The ten to fifteen dairies employ several people. The fourth boom was due to the Tolk electrical plant, a coal-burning, electricity-generating plant.

As Gene excuses himself to go into the store, I rewrite my scribbling into readable notes.

Following a brief interlude of business, Gene returns and continues my guided tour:

> During our history, a lot of people with different backgrounds have moved to Muleshoe. People working at [not only] the prison [but also] Tolk and [the local] dairies have provided a diverse population. In the early 1960s, we started raising vegetables. A lot of Hispanics came to help harvest, then went home. After a few years of seasonal work, they brought their families and stayed to work on farms and other businesses. The workers and their families now own farms and businesses. About 40% of our population is Hispanic.

He speaks with pride about the new citizens progressing from migrant workers to full-time employees to finally owning their own farms and businesses.

As we continue our tour, Gene says, "Muleshoe and Bailey County is a fine place to live. I am seventy-four and have lived here my whole life. People help each other. If someone gets sick, everybody gets together and harvests his crop." He pauses while waving to a person in a passing pickup, then continues, "The new residents have socialized well into the community."

In addition to the changing population, Muleshoe, itself, has changed quite a bit. It has experienced the plight of many small towns. After some deep thought, Gene states:

> We have only one dry-goods store and two implement dealers, a John Deere and Case IH. At one time, [there were] five car dealerships; now [there are] none. [There used to be] four or five grocery stores; we now have two. We lost our two movie theaters. As a kid, we would come to Muleshoe on Saturday night with twenty-five cents. I could go to the movie, buy popcorn and a toy. A really big night was to go to Clovis.

Clovis, New Mexico is a town of about 35,000 people located thirty miles west of Muleshoe.

We have completed my guided tour or more explicitly, Gene has finished his business. Sitting in the truck in the restaurant parking lot, the subject changes to the schools. Gene states with pride:

> We have good schools. Muleshoe is the only school district in Bailey County. There used to be eight school districts before consolidation in the 1970s. We won State in [the] football championship during the early 2000s. Winning the championship was the biggest thing in town.

He continues that the school district is one of the largest employers, then adds, "The school district just completed a $26 million construction project last year."

We sit in silence as Gene thinks. He says, "Our largest employer[s] [are] grain farming and beef cattle, followed by dairy, then the school district, and [the] fourth is the Tolk plant."

We talk a bit about how life, community, and towns have changed. He summarizes his thoughts as he repeats a previous statement: "I really enjoy living Bailey County and Muleshoe."

Gene turns to me and says, "I enjoyed talking with you about Muleshoe and Bailey County." I respond that during the six years I lived in Texas, I heard the name "Muleshoe" several times. I add, "I really learned a lot and appreciate your knowledge and willingness to share. I especially liked the guided tour." He laughs as we shake hands. I thank him again as I step out of the truck.

I watch as he drives down the street in his well-worked pickup. My thoughts focus on cowboys, and I ask myself, "Are they a dying breed?"

Muleshoe is rural America in values, pride, and lifestyle. The afternoon I spent in a town exceeded my expectations. I learned about Muleshoe, West Texas culture, and talked with man well steeped in cowboy culture. Plus, I received a guided tour!

Mo is patiently waiting in the truck. As always, she has some time to run and check the local terrain. When she is ready, she returns, jumps in the truck, and looks at me, as if to ask, "Where next?" The afternoon sun is slipping low in the western sky as we drive toward it, heading west on US Highways 70 and 84 toward Clovis, New Mexico. After the thirty-minute drive to Farwell, we say farewell to Texas. It is always good to spend time in Texas and revisit the many good memories I have of my seven-year residency spanning a thirty-year period, not only in the west but also in the north, east, and Brazos Valley areas.

CHAPTER 21

New Mexico

We cross the Texas-New Mexico state line as the sun approaches the beautiful New Mexico horizon. A one-minute drive takes us to Texico, the first town in New Mexico. We continue our drive on US Highway 84 for eight miles before setting up camp in Clovis. An uneventful evening, a good night's sleep, and morning walk, and we are ready to begin our tour of New Mexico.

Our early morning drive with no planned destination leads us onward into New Mexico. The beautiful countryside accents my high expectations for our visit to this enchanted land. Our plan is to find a parking lot full of pickup trucks, have breakfast, make new friends, and hear a story about rural New Mexico. My second goal for the day is to visit Santa Rosa, a scenic small town with a southwest motif. It is situated at the intersection of US Highways 84 and 54. Intentions beyond Santa Rosa are as muddy as the Mississippi River.

The sign along the highway states "Melrose." Good news! I know the town. We continue our drive until I observe a parking lot full of pickup trucks gathered around a building that hosts a combination restaurant and gas station. Our short morning drive exceeds my expectations with an early breakfast, a restaurant with several people, and the appearance of an inviting small town.

Melrose, the smallest of the three towns along the thirty-three-mile corridor of US Highway 84 in eastern New Mexico, has experienced a decrease in population, while the other two towns of Clovis and Texico have realized a slight increase in residents.

Clovis and nearby Cannon Air Force Base are the primary sites for employment in the area. Commute time from Texico to Clovis is ten to fifteen minutes, where as, the commute from Melrose to Clovis is a little greater than thirty minutes.

The numerous pickup trucks are like a magnet pulling us into the parking lot. The sign identifies the combination gas station and convenience store, while the trucks distinguish the restaurant as *the* breakfast spot. At the order window inside, I ask, "What is good?", then order the recommended breakfast burrito. I am not disappointed.

I sit at a table near three men who are discussing and solving major world issues. After listening for a while, I wonder why we need heads of state; solutions to problems seem to be best solved at the local level during coffee hour—at least on this particular Friday morning. I join the conversation, which evolves into an interview with Wendell, who is in the fifty- to sixty-year-old age group.

Wendell begins our conversation by stating, "In the mornings, the guys show up and drink coffee and talk. We solve the problems of the world. We do not always agree, but we agree to disagree, agreeably." They all agree when I explain my theory that solving world issues is better accomplished at the local level.

Wendell transitions our conversation to family, friends, and people. He begins by stating, "I have visited family in Melrose since the 1950s, when we lived in Lubbock, Texas." The 250-mile round trip was quite an expedition during the 1950s. Just to jog the memories of my contemporaries and enlighten the younger reader, in the 1950s travel was much slower, more difficult, and did not include air-conditioning.

As if reading my mind, Wendell explains the obstacles of his dad's travel during the 1930s. "My grandparents, father, and aunt came to Lubbock during the Depression. The trip included my dad and his sister, [along] with their parents, my grandparents. They drove from Cooper [Texas] to Lubbock during the Depression to pick cotton."

It was a time when people would do extraordinary things to find work. The drive from Cooper, which is northeast of Dallas, to Lubbock was over 425 miles. The Dust Bowl closely coincided with the Depression, so Wendell's family may have experienced a dust storm en route, and if not while traveling, then certainly while living in Lubbock.

The 1930s trip was a significant challenge. He continues:

> They had a flat tire en route to Lubbock. Because they could not afford a spare tire, my grandmother rolled up a scarf and placed it inside the tire to allow them to complete the trip. People did what they had to do to get by.

After a pause he proudly states, "My dad is eighty-seven and still square dances twice a week."

Melrose has been Wendell's home for twenty-five years. He explains, "I raise Limousine bulls for breeding. I keep the heifers to replenish the herd. My granddad told me long ago, 'If you have money to feed your cattle, you will not go broke.'"

Even though he became involved in farming later in life, Wendell gained knowledge from family members and childhood experiences. He smiles and recounts a long ago experience: "When I was a kid, we had three milk cows. The first time I drank store-bought milk, I swore I would never drink it again."

I, myself, recall a similar personal experience and the same declaration about purchased milk.

Wendell changes the conversation to an issue that causes him to frown:

We have lost a lot of population since I moved to Melrose. It is much smaller than it was twenty years ago. Demographics have changed; farms have become larger. It is a natural thing with improved technology. Larger farms and decreased school population [are] a problem throughout New Mexico. It is a challenge to maintain rural schools. Only about 10% to 15% of our graduates find good employment locally.

I personally pause to reflect on how many times that I have heard a similar statement with the same sense of concern.

Wendell quickly bounces back to the positive side of Melrose. He strongly believes that the Melrose schools are very good. He says, "An advantage to rural schools is that we graduate 95% of the students who enter ninth grade. And 70% of our graduates continue their education at a university, community college, or vocational training program." The numbers are impressive for any school district.

Melrose schools not only have a good reputation for educating the youth; they are also the center of most activities. Wendell proudly states, "School is the hub of our community. Most everyone has a kid or grandkid in school, so everyone attends activities. We do not have movie theaters and other things to do, so people focus on school events." He pauses and ponders the words to make his next point: "If a kid thinks something is important to his or her parents, grandparents, or other adults, then he or she will do the best that they can. Involvement is the key. And time is the key to involvement."

Wendell's insightful words are the topic of many school meetings involving both staff and parents.

As in many small towns, a phenomenon in Melrose is declining population, resulting in lost businesses. Wendell details the losses by explaining:

We had three grocery stores; now we have none, just a convenience store. There used to be two implement dealers; now we don't have any. We now have one hardware store; we used to have two. The good news is we have improvement in medical services and banks. We built a new health clinic, which will have a nurse practitioner and staff. We have two banks.

He concludes with a historical statement, "In the 1920s, we had twenty-one bars, now we are a dry county."

New residents have mitigated Melrose population decline. Wendell pauses as he searches for the best words to describe his next thoughts:

Melrose has become a bedroom community. Many people have moved into our community but work at Cannon Air Force Base and in Clovis. The number of new residents has minimally affected the prevailing culture of friendliness and community spirit. The people are very friendly and helpful, even though we have a lot of new people. New people influence the culture but do not change it. They socialize in pretty well.

As our conversation continues, it becomes obvious that Melrose maintains several commonalities of small, rural towns. Adults are concerned about the kids and their safety and behaviors. Wendell defines these thoughts by stating, "It is a great place to raise kids. There are a lot of eyeballs around town. Parents often know what kids have done before they [the kids] get home. If not, [then] they will find out during morning coffee."

I, myself, have heard and experienced this phenomenon.

Adults even treat recently arrived kids the same as if they were longtime residents. Wendell tells the story about the daughter of a newly arrived Air Force pilot. The expert ballet dancer transferred her athletic skills to basketball. Wendell recounts a pleasant experience, explaining, "During her third basketball game, the fans gave her a standing ovation when she scored her first points." This statement and many others define a common thread throughout our conversation: Adults strongly support students and schools.

Melrose is a small town, not just striving to exist but motivated to achieve a level of excellence that will attract new residents and promote growth. Because of their proximity to Cannon Air Force Base and the town of Clovis, they have a viable resource of potential new residents. The noteworthy school performance, new health clinic, friendly people, and small-town community mindset all make it appealing to living in Melrose. In many instances, it seems to be a choice between proximity to amenities and work versus daily travel and small-town American values and lifestyle.

After thanking Wendell and bidding farewell to the remaining coffee drinkers, Mo and I head west and then north on US Highway 84. Our intermediate goal is Santa Rosa, New Mexico, a beautiful town I have visited a few times before. Since we are in eastern New Mexico, I cannot pass the opportunity for a revisit.

The hour-and-a-half drive provides time to reflect and consider our weekend camping spot. The two frontrunners are Santa Fe and Las Vegas, New Mexico. I drive northwest, thinking about the five towns we have visited during this aspect of the trip. The memory of each person brings special thoughts and a smile.

The Southwest is unique in that it is cowboy country, reflected in an attitude more than the presence of a horse. Their attitudes exude a special type of freedom, one that is difficult to explain but that I have respected since my first introduction to it in Big Spring, Texas, forty-six years before. I think the true experience can only be gained by living it.

As I turn left from US 84 onto US 54, I make my decision about our weekend visit. I choose Las Vegas because I believe it will more closely represent rural life. With the burden of decision lifted from my shoulders, I pull into a busy truck stop on the southeast edge of Santa Rosa.

Santa Rosa, with a population of approximately 3,000 people, is situated on the Pecos River at the intersection of Interstate 40 and US Highways 84 and 54. The elevation of Santa Rosa is listed at 4,616 feet. People, hospitality, and Mexican food have all been very good during the two previous times I spent the night there. The scenic downtown and surrounding terrain, both wrapped in southwest motif, as well as people, hospitality, and food all make return visits mandatory.

Don Celso Baca founded the town in 1865. The town was originally Aqua Negro Chiquita" or "Little Black Water." The founder of the town built a chapel in 1890. The town was renamed Santa Rosa to honor Baca's mother, Rosa, as well as Saint Rosa of Lima. During the early 1900s, the railroad connected Santa Rosa to Chicago, El Paso, and the rest of the world.

We stop at a large gas station situated at the intersection of three highways. Mo, as always, is anxious to get out of the truck. After a brief investigation of the small area of grass, she is ready to make new friends. An African-American man about fifty years old looks at our truck and trailer and asks about our trip. A little interest is all it takes, and Mo is wholeheartedly pursuing a new friend. It is an instant friendship. I caution the man that Mo can be a pain, to which he quickly responds, "She is okay." He continues to pet her, and she continues to respond with the Golden hugs and hand-to-foot shakes.

In response to his question about our trip, I try to be brief with my explanation so that I don't receive a look of "I am sorry I asked the question." It sometimes appears I provide more information than is needed or wanted by an inquisitive person.

I notice the man's car is packed very full. He tells me that he is moving from San Diego, California to Fort Leavenworth, Kansas. I ask, "Why?" He laughs and explains that jobs are scarce in San Diego. He continues by explaining that he is going to live temporarily with his daughter and son-in-law and find a job. His son-in-law is stationed at Fort Leavenworth in the army.

I caution him there will be a bit of culture shock going from southern California to the Midwest. The fast-moving lifestyle, along with having a lot of things to do, will be replaced by a slower pace. "The Midwest is great," I say, "we just have a slower pace."

He says, "People of all areas are good; they just have different beliefs. You cannot hold it against them. They are all good people."

We continue to talk for a while. His experience in the navy and life in general is interesting. He and I decide that we had better continue our journeys. We share a firm handshake and well wishes for each other. We are both off in opposite directions.

We may never meet again, but I am influenced by his optimistic attitude and positive beliefs in people. He gives me incentive to pursue self-improvement. I reflect on the value of taking time to talk with—and more importantly, listen to—people I do not know. Please notice that I shied away from the term "strangers." A person is not a stranger; they are just someone I have not yet met. Maybe they think *I* am a stranger.

Mo and I are heading west, with Santa Rosa in our rearview mirror and Las Vegas, New Mexico on the horizon. Our trip continues west on Interstate 40 until it turns north to pursue Interstate 25. The welcome sight of Las Vegas finally looms through the windshield.

Las Vegas, the seat of San Miguel County, has been experiencing a slight population loss since the year 2000, when it had 14,568 residents. The ten-year period from 2000 to 2010 saw a 7% population decrease to 13,753.

The rich history of Las Vegas dates back to a Mexican government land grant given to a group of settlers in 1835. The town was designed around a central plaza, the traditional Spanish Colonial motif. During its early years, Las Vegas flourished, as it became a stopping point on the Santa Fe Trail. For eleven years of the town's history, the Mexican-American War presented a precarious issue, which finally eased in 1846 when Stephen W. Kearney delivered a speech in the plaza claiming New Mexico as part of the United States.

Presence of the railroad in 1880 enhanced development that allowed Las Vegas to gain notoriety: Some good and some not so good. Regis University gained its roots in Las Vegas, when a group of exiled Italian Jesuit priests founded Las Vegas College. The college later moved to Denver and became Regis University. The shady side of notoriety can be attributed to the city having been a hangout for several notable men (some lawmen and some outlaws), including Billy the Kid, Jesse James, Wyatt Earp, and Doc Holiday. Ralph Emerson Twitchell, a notable local historian and New Mexico public figure, once claimed that Las Vegas, New Mexico harbored more outlaws than any other town.

Fast forward to the present day, and we see a town marked by several noteworthy amenities, including New Mexico Highland University (originally New Mexico Normal School), which provides educational opportunities for students, both local and statewide. We also see many facilities that are not only unique but also carry national prestige, including the Duncan Opera House, a Carnegie library, and the historic Major Fred Harvey House, now known as The Hotel Castaneda. Las Vegas has earned worthy state and national recognition.

Las Vegas, with its beautiful, peaceful setting of today, once experienced a period of time that discouraged the development of its citizenry, hampering its drive to become the thriving town it is today. The impressive Gallinas River acted as a barrier, separating two separate cultures and municipalities: West Las Vegas and East Las Vegas. West Las Vegas was called a "town," while East Las Vegas was termed a "city." The municipalities and the Gallinas River separated the two major populations of Hispanics and Anglos.

A paper account of history cannot describe the two separate entities as well as a man I meet named Donata, who I will soon introduce.

Mo and I continue our seventy-mile trip from Santa Rosa to Las Vegas, which takes almost two hours. Mountains and curves, plus the natural beauty, increase the driving time. I drive slower than normal, even though I am anxious to complete the week's drive. The majestic, colorful scenery cannot be absorbed with flashes of passing glances.

We finally arrive at the KOA campground, park the trailer, set up, and take a well-deserved walk. The campground owner welcomes us and makes certain all is well. I am already impressed with the friendliness of the people, as several other people give us friendly greetings.

While Mo and I are walking around the area, a campground attendant, who I guess to be in his late sixties, is doing some routine cleanup. During our brief conversation, he tells me that five years before, he departed from Vermont to walk across America. He says, "I stop and stay when I find a place I like."

I ask, "How long do you stay in one place?" He responds, "I stay anywhere from one night [to] a weekend, [a] few days, a month, six months. I just stay as long as I want."

He continues, adding that he has been at the KOA campground in Las Vegas since the fall [about six months]. After a pause, he states that he is about ready to hit the road again.

I have read and heard stories about people walking across America, but have never talked with a person who is actually undertaking the formidable and exciting journey. From his brief description, I glean that he did little, if any, planning. Rather, he just loaded a backpack and started walking away from the early morning sun.

My lingering thought is that I am missing something. The experience and freedom to cross our great nation, or other nations, at a pace that allows total freedom to experience places and interactions with people. The freedom to roam and explore.

Later in the evening while having dinner at the Hillcrest, my thoughts keep returning to the man and his walk across America. My dining experience clearly shows that you do not judge food by a restaurant's physical appearance. The restaurant is nice, but not fancy: no flashing lights, no fancy building, and not located in a strip mall. Rather, the Hillcrest is located on a side street, with a historical western appearance that would be well-suited for hitching posts. The food is authentic, however, and the service is extraordinarily homey.

The next day, as Mo and I drive to Las Vegas, I spot the "walk across America" gentlemen toting his backpack as he walks toward town, a one-way trip of at least five miles. It is easy to know that offering a ride would be an intrusive gesture. He walks for physical condition and to experience the freedom of uninhabited travel.

Mo and I take a driving tour of Las Vegas. A backstreet bracketed by angle parking full of pickup trucks signals a great breakfast restaurant. A sign stating

"Charlie's Spic and Span Bakery and Café" marks the spot. Like a magnet, I am drawn to the front door.

As I step inside, I see two large rooms, the tables surrounded by people—and a Starbuck's sign. I immediately know I am living right: a great breakfast *and* Starbuck's coffee!

A latte in hand, I find a small, unoccupied table. While leisurely eating breakfast, I observe the people: tables filled young adults, older adults, mixed-age adults, and adults with kids. Tables host family dining, as well as breakfast clubs, which can be defined as "people who gather to socialize, solve world and local problems, or share news" (or perhaps all of the above).

Charlie's Spic and Span definitely caters to a mixed crowd. The people, ambience, and culture all provide an inviting experience worthy of a return trip to this beautiful town.

Two people at one table intrigue me. They appear to be a grandfather and grandson having breakfast. I pause to think what a treat it must be to drive down the street and pick up your granddaughter or grandson and share time over breakfast. As I sip a vanilla latte, my thoughts are drawn to the positive interaction between a Hispanic grandfather and grandson. A high level of energy makes it difficult for the youngster to sit still. The grandfather, however, relaxingly eats and calmly talks with his grandson. The grandfather's demeanor has a calming affect on the child. I decide that the grandfather must have a great story to tell.

I am caught in a dilemma. Should I interrupt or not? My decision is to allow the grandfather to make the determination as to whether we can talk without ruining his morning. I pose the question in a manner that allows him to easily say no. Fortunately, he responds that he would like to share the story of his hometown, which I soon learn is much more than a place to live. Rather, Las Vegas, along with its people and his family, is his true love.

Donata's conversations, actions, and expectations of his grandson all obviously make the six-year-old feel valued and honored. Donata's treats his grandson with respect while maintaining the grandfather and grandson relationship. His grandson responds with polite mannerisms without losing his childlike behavior. Saturday morning breakfast for grandfather and grandson appears to be a common experience. I am intrigued by the interactions and relationship.

Donata's story is about passion for family, hometown, and law enforcement—as well as creating opportunities for all people. These are the things that make his story special.

Donata begins by reflecting on his childhood: "We lived in West Las Vegas. My father worked at the New Mexico Hospital, an institution for mentally challenged persons. He also worked part-time as a bartender, and my mother worked as a waitress. Together, they raised eight boys and one girl."

As our conversation continues, I become intrigued by his thoughts about family, hometown, experiences, and positive beliefs.

Donata continues, saying that with the exception to naval duty and a tour in Vietnam, he lived his entire life in Las Vegas, New Mexico. He tells me that he has been married to his high school sweetheart for forty-one years. I estimate his age to be in the middle sixties. Donata then returns to his career, adding, "I was an officer with the Las Vegas Police Department. I graduated from high school and did not get a college degree. I went through the ranks and ultimately became the chief of police, retiring at the age of forty-one."

New Mexico has a law that police officers must retire after twenty years. The law was passed, Donata tells me, after research came to light that policemen who work too long die within five to ten years of retirement. He follows the explanation by commenting, "I was too young to retire. I did criminal investigation for the district attorney and others, plus I ran the jail." After a brief pause, he looks me in the eye and says:

> I could have left Las Vegas and worked as a policeman in another state and made more money. I love Las Vegas. Why should I leave the place where I want to help the people? I decided to stay in a friendly town. I have seen violence in other cities; some have almost one homicide a day.

Today, Donata keeps occupied by serving the public. "I am the drug-law enforcement coordinator for nine counties in northern New Mexico. Our money for the program went to [reallocated] homeland security." There is a shortage of personnel and training for drug-law enforcement. Donata adds, "If we share our resources, we have ten people working on drug enforcement. Our personnel need more training. Drugs cause us to lose a lot of talented kids."

Donata has a passion to both *get* and *keep* kids off drugs. Our conversation obviously accents his feelings about drug control for both kids and adults. His enthusiasm, however, is targeted specifically toward young people and drug issues.

Until 1971, Las Vegas, New Mexico was two towns: East Las Vegas and West Las Vegas. The Gallinas River divides the towns. Donata lived in West Las Vegas, a place he terms the "Hispanic side." He says, "East Las Vegas was home to the Anglo. As a boy, we lived a semi-segregated lifestyle. I do not remember any violence." Each town had its own city council and mayor.

Not wanting to linger on the past and segregation, Donata immediately speaks of the positives that occurred after Las Vegas became one town and one community: "Hispanics got more opportunities and started to get more responsible jobs. I became the second Hispanic chief of police in 1983. We have more Hispanics running for mayor." He continues that there are a lot more Hispanic attorneys and judges. Job opportunities for Hispanics in northern New Mexico have increased since the early 1970s.

Educational opportunities also have increased for everyone. Four years ago, the vocational school became Luna Community College. New Mexico Highland University, located in Las Vegas, provides four-year-degree opportunities. Donata says, "A lot of kids work their way through Highland University."

Donata believes that growth in Las Vegas is hampered by "lack of economic development and limited water supply." The three largest employers in Las Vegas are the city, New Mexico State Hospital, and New Mexico Highland University. Even with three large employers, job opportunities for young people are limited. A lot of kids leave because of the lack of jobs. On the positive side of population growth, however, Donata states, "We are seeing a lot of retired baby boomers coming back and building homes."

The limited water issue has contributed to restricted farming. Some people garden farm and sell their produce locally.

As we reached the end of our conversation, Donata reflects on some cultural issues and how life in Las Vegas could be improved. Some of the issues extend well beyond Donata's hometown:

> We need to deal with domestic violence, especially aimed toward Hispanic women. Sometimes they think it is the way it should be. Also, kids, with [the] use of technology, are much smarter today than the past. We need to make sure there are no barriers for youth seeking employment.

Donata encapsulates his proactive passion with a story of a teenage boy who experienced domestic problems. He tells the story about a fifteen-year-old runaway from Albuquerque:

> The boy told his dad that he hated him—had no time for him. I asked the teenager if his father had hit him. The boy replied that his dad did not hit him. I told him, "The next time your dad gets mad, pretend you are your dad. Then tell him you love him." Six years later, when the kid was

twenty-one years old, he came by and thanked me. The young man said, "My dad and I became good friends. I am entering graduate school." The young man wanted me to know that he took my advice, and it helped him to be friends with his dad. I was happy for him.

Donata ends with two philosophical statements and a reflective thought: "We can never give up. You have to know where you come from, or you do not know where you are."

The reflective thought and ending statements are completely unexpected from a man with Donata's accomplishments and strong character. Donata tells me, "I never thought forty years ago [that] an Anglo would be asking me my opinion on anything."

I am at a total loss for words. I thank Donata and shake hands, saying, "Our conversation—your words—were very powerful."

I shake hands with his grandson and thank *him* for his patience. He replies, "Nice to meet you." He has a great mentor.

One last time, I thank Donata for his time, insight, and sharing of time. He responds, "I enjoyed talking with you and sharing about our great town."

Mo and I walk around Las Vegas, not only to take in its culture but also to have time to reflect on my conversation with Donata. I need time to process his powerful words. Eventually, we drive back to the campground, where I meet a male in his early twenties. He explains that he is from Germany and on a thirty-five-month international internship. He says that to become a licensed carpenter in Germany, you are required to have thirty-five months of learning—in countries other than Germany. He continues by telling me that he helped construct a cedar hot tub, with no liner, in Japan. He has worked in Australia and many other countries. He and his lady friend are hitchhiking cross-country from Miami, Florida to San Francisco, California. They camp in their tent wherever they end their day: in a campground, wooded area, park, or wherever.

I am amazed at my good fortune of meeting so many people with unique stories. Las Vegas seems to be the crossroads of people who are unique and interesting.

Saturday afternoon with nothing to do, Mo and I make a day trip to Santa Fe. We spend all afternoon at The Plaza. Luckily, there is an art show. After way too much deliberation, I purchase two small paintings. Mo meets a lot of people and a few new canine friends. When we meet a large German Shepherd dawg, I suggest to Mo that humility would be a smart tactic. Nope. Humility is not in her playbook. She walks right up to him and does the nose-to-nose thing. Thanks to nice people and an understanding dawg, all goes well.

Our drive back to Las Vegas is uneventful, as is the evening. We walk around the campground, after which I have dinner at a small, very authentic Mexican restaurant. The people and atmosphere add to the tasty Navajo taco, a first for me.

When the lights in the trailer are turned off, there is a race to see who can get to sleep the quickest. I lose because the last thing I hear is a dawg snoring.

Mo

On Sunday morning, I wake up to the smell of coffee. I stretch and hear the familiar, "Good morning, Mo." I turn to see Randy putting on his walking shoes. Walking shoes! I am standing here, staring at my bag of food and my bowl. I continue looking from the bag to the bowl as he says, "Ready to walk?" He obviously did not get the hint. When I nose the bag, then push the bowl, I hear, "Oh, Mo! You should eat before we walk."

As I eat, I think, *This is not going to be a great, or even good, day. I am going to need to be at the top of my game all day.*

The walk goes well. We do not get lost. Back at the campground, I think Randy is making progress. He is back from the shower, only to sit at a picnic table and talk with some campers. He and the German apprentice carpenter have a long talk. Finally, we are ready to travel. Off we go on the highway, with signs stating "25." We drive. Then we drive some more. We are chasing the sun.

We climb up a forever-hill, only to come down the other side. Randy says, "We reached the summit of Raton Pass and are now in Colorado." Like I need to know this?

Finally, we grow weary of chasing the sun and stop for lunch, which includes a walk and hunt. As we continue our drive, the first thing I notice is that while we were stopped, the sun passed us. Hard to believe, but now the sun is chasing *us*.

We drive off the wide highway onto a narrow road, with cars traveling two directions. We pass many small towns, stopping at a larger town that is beside a big river. At last, we set up camp and walk.

CHAPTER 22

Arkansas Valley of Colorado

Arrival in La Junta is the beginning of our drive through the fertile Arkansas River Valley in southeastern Colorado. This mighty river originates near Leadville, Colorado and flows through the states of Colorado, Kansas, Oklahoma, and Arkansas on its path to Napoleon, where it joins the Mississippi River. Use of the Arkansas River's water has resulted in federal legislation to settle legal actions between states. Water from the Arkansas River is a precious commodity, not only between states but also among Colorado citizens. Through all the turmoil, the peaceful river flows and provides water for agriculture and residents along its lovely valley. It represents livelihoods for farmers and the existence of many rural towns.

Towns along the Arkansas River in Southeast Colorado provide an example of the trend of shifting population from rural America to larger cities. The five small, rural towns of Holly, La Junta, Las Animas, Rocky Ford, and Lamar experienced a total decrease of 2,233 residents during the ten-year period from 2000 to 2010. The lost populace accounted for 9.5% of the inhabitants. The same time period saw Pueblo, a town of 106,595 residents in 2010, has an increase of 4,474 (or 4.4% growth). The decrease in population of these five small, rural towns and the growth of a larger town in the same area follows the recurring trend throughout America.

La Junta, the seat of Otero County, had a 2010 population of 7,077 while Otero County had 18,572 residents.

La Junta, Spanish for "junction," sits at the intersection of the Arkansas River and the Santa Fe Trail. Fort Bent, a historical site, was a major trading post along the Santa Fe Trail 150 years ago. The town and surrounding area are the location of several western movies, such as *Badlands* and *Mr. Majestyk*.

La Junta served its country with an Army airfield during World War II. Today, Otero Community College, which began in 1941 as La Junta CC, serves its students on its modern forty-acre campus. The metro area of Colorado Springs, which has a population of about two-thirds of a million people, sits approximately ninety miles northwest of La Junta.

Monday morning, with trailer in tow and heading for Kansas, I have breakfast in La Junta at the Copper Restaurant, where I meet Dexter and Ruth.

Both have doctorate degrees (PhDs). Three PhDs at one table is dangerous in any setting, but especially in a small-town diner filled with breakfast customers. It is important that we stick to the task of learning about rural America and not start philosophizing. I keep a close watch for local law enforcement personnel.

Dexter and Ruth are transplants to Colorado: Dexter was born and raised in Rome, Georgia, while Ruth was born in Albuquerque, New Mexico and raised in the Chicago, Illinois area. Professional positions brought Dexter and Ruth to La Junta. Dexter came to La Junta in 1958 to take a teaching position at Otera Community College. It was his first job after earning a doctorate degree in biology from the University of Colorado, Boulder. He has held several positions, mostly in industry, since teaching at Otera. Ruth came to La Junta in 1986 to work at a school for boys. After earning her doctorate from the California School of Professional Psychology, she had a private practice in San Diego, California.

The path to La Junta and educational and professional success was not an easy or smooth path for Dexter and Ruth. Dexter dropped out of college at the end of World War II and joined the United States Air Force. He was stationed in New Mexico, serving as a weather-service specialist. His time in New Mexico created his affection for the southwest. After completing his bachelor's and master's degree at Duke University, he returned to Colorado and has never left.

Most of Ruth's childhood was spent in foster homes. Turmoil surrounded her family prior to Ruth's birth. Her father, who was in the US Navy, was one day short of being in Pearl Harbor aboard his aircraft carrier on that fateful day in December 1941. His ship returned to a California port, where Ruth's mom and dad were married. Ruth was born in 1942 with a congenital heart condition and was given only seven years to live. After Ruth's mother abandoned her, Ruth's life became filled with turmoil. "My father raised me until I was three-and-one-half years old; he abandoned me on the courthouse steps. My mother's family took me to a Chicago orphanage. I lived with fourteen families until I was in seventh grade," Ruth recounts.

Fortunately, she spent her high school years in Lamont, Illinois, where she had a couple of good mentors. Ruth pauses and continues, "I was placed with one foster family through high school. Michael Galati and the Methodist Church members became my mentors." She adds that their mentoring encouraged her to gain a BA from North Central College in Naperville, Illinois and become involved with an organization called Up with People. As a high school student, Ruth became involved with loving and supporting people. In the words of Robert Frost, she "took the road less traveled." She continued that path by moving to California and gaining her master's degree, completing her studies at the California School of Professional Psychology Studies and earning her doctorate of philosophy. Ruth never gave up on life.

Dexter's and Ruth's separate paths, although a winding and difficult road, led them to La Junta, where they have found happiness while meeting the challenge of making contributions to their new hometown. Dexter is very much at home in La Junta. He says, "The small-town rural life fits my personality. I spend a lot of time chasing wildflowers." It offers him an environment to explore and enjoy wild plants.

For Ruth, the small, rural-town environment is not quite as comfortable. She states, "In La Junta, I will always be viewed as an outsider." She attributes some of her discomfort to her abstract thinking: She believes that her way of thinking is not always understood. Another issue she believes contributes to her lack of acceptance is being a female with a doctorate degree. On a positive note, she adds, "The community came together to fight for changing an institution that I was hired to change."

People in general, and perhaps more so in small communities, resist change. Persons that represent change are remembered and often shunned, even though the outcome is recognized as being positive. Discomfort and turmoil resulting from the change becomes the remembered issue.

The conversation shifts to population and age of residents. As a town, La Junta appears to remain fairly steady, although it has some indicators of population shift. Dexter claims, "The population is fairly stable, with a small decrease. A lot of young kids leave to get a job for which they have been trained. The school system focuses on technology, but there are no local technology jobs." Ruth states the inevitable: "The age of our population is increasing. We used to have four elementary schools; now we have only two."

Sustainability of the agriculture industry may be another influence of population shift and loss. Dexter adds an encouraging perspective when he summarizes, "Outside companies, which have come here, usually stay." Dexter seems to believe that new industry a offset the population decline apparently caused by changes in the agriculture industry.

Water supply to support population growth in Colorado has been an issue for many years. It was even an issue in the middle 1970s, when I, myself, moved to Colorado Springs. The front range continues to grow even though availability of water remains an issue in Eastern Colorado. La Junta and the Arkansas

River Valley are feeling the crunch. Ruth says, "The Valley is losing more and more water to the urban areas." Dexter supports this statement by stating, "Urban investors are buying farm land for water rights. There are [a] lot of farms located along the river."

Availability of water contributes to the concept that crop farming may not be feasible east of the Rocky Mountains, either in eastern Colorado or western Kansas. Dexter believes that the land around La Junta is more inclined to support cattle ranching than growing crops. He claims, "There is an imaginary line running north to south in Kansas. Land east of the line support crops, and land west of the line supports grazing." Dexter then brings to light an issue concerning the appropriate use of natural resources to produce food, asking, "How long will the dwindling water supplies last?" His question reflects the need to monitor and regulate water usage.

La Junta and the Arkansas River Valley is a unique setting of Colorado. It is historic in nature and an integral aspect of the settling of the west. Towns such as La Junta, Rocky Ford, Lamar, Las Animas, and Holly all depend on the agriculture industry, whether it is raising grain or feeding cattle. There is an argument for each side of the issue. The issue appears to be the maintenance of food production—while protecting natural resources.

Agriculture is and will remain an integral aspect of the Arkansas River Valley region, unless replaced by other industries. Maintaining population in the area is dependent, as always, on the availability of jobs.

Dexter comments, "La Junta is losing its downtown": a statement that is always troubling to hear. I fear the people of small towns must reverse the trend of vacant Main Street businesses or run the risk of losing their town: something that happened to my hometown of New Salem.

After I relay my appreciation for their unique view of small-town America, Dexter and Ruth go on their way to a meeting.

Mo and I travel east on US Highway 50, passing a large reservoir in John Martin State Park. A two-hour drive leads us to a large sign stating "Welcome to Holly." The inviting sign makes Holly a welcoming town for lunch. Like most of my noontime stops, this one focuses more on the prospect of an interview than eating.

Located along the Arkansas River in Prowers County, Holly was incorporated in 1903 and named for Hiram S. Holly, a local rancher who settled in the area during 1871. In 1905, two years after the town was incorporated, Holly Sugar was created to use the locally harvested sugar beets. The company grew and eventually, in 1988, merged with Imperial Sugar, ending the famous industry's home in Holly, Colorado.

Agriculture, the main industry of Holly, has experienced two disastrous weather phenomena during a three-month period. December 2006 saw a terrible blizzard, causing a massive loss of livestock. Three months later, in March 2007, a devastating tornado killed one lady and seriously injured ten other people. The resilient people and community fought back from human and property losses, and Holly became stronger.

Holly, I learn from a parking lot conversation, has a declining population that is currently around 800. Even with declining population I also learn Holly is a vibrant small town, with the determination and community spirit to grow.

Many of the businesses in Holly are located along Highway 50. My lunchtime dining is a choice between pizza at the gas station on the south side of Highway 50 or Porky's on the north side. I choose Porky's Restaurant, as do two ranchers and what seems to be half of the Holly High School student body. I feel like I am back monitoring a school lunchroom, only this time I am not responsible for controlling student behavior. The ethnicity of the students at Porky's is about 50% Anglo and 50% Hispanic, which is representative of the town's demographics. It is enjoyable watching the students joking, laughing, and having a good time while taking a break from academics. I seem to recall that my friends and I had less than exemplary behavior 50 years ago. I am not proud, but truthful, to say that the Holly students' behavior is much better our behavior.

I go to the counter, try to make sense of the menu, and order lunch like I know what I am doing. Actually, I am mimicking the actions of the person in line in front of me. I cannot fool the servers, however, so they walk me through the menu. The slogan on the wall states, "Pig out at Porky's."

As I eat, Denice, the owner, walks by my table and checks to see if everything is okay. Our conversation leads to an interview, which is delayed until the departure of the lunch crowd. The stories of Denice and the town of Holly, Colorado are ones of perseverance, commitment, and dedication to a way of life. The story of Holly, as told by Denice, clearly speaks to the elements of small towns. One issue is dealing with family separation and hardships.

Denice expresses her deep feeling for Holly, her hometown:
I left Holly and went to Texas Tech University for my education. I lived in Texas for ten years before returning to Holly in 1979. I am deeply committed to Holly. I like it here. My parents live here. There is not the

"big-city rat race" in Holly. Everybody knows your business, but you can control that some.

Holly, like most small towns, has lost some population. Denise states, "We have lost some people. A lot of kids leave after graduation because there is a lack of jobs." The Hispanic population has grown significantly since Denise's return in 1979. She estimates that it has increased from 20% of the total population in 1979 to about 50% in 2010. The percentage of Hispanic growth indicates that during the last thirty years, a lot of families have relocated to Holly from other towns. The migration could also indicate family separation for many of the new people: the same type of family separation that occurs when young adults leave their hometowns to seek employment in other areas, which has been the case for many young adults in both Holly and La Junta.

The citizens of Holly are resilient, however. They help each other in times of emergency, even if they, themselves, are experiencing difficulties. Denice tells me:

> We had a snow blizzard during December of 2006. Snow blizzards can be devastating to herds of cattle and other livestock, as well as to people. It was followed in three months by a tornado in March 2007. The people rallied to help each other. If you lost your home, you received help. But if you lost your business, it was difficult to receive much help [i.e., financial assistance]. It was very difficult for businesses—agriculture and non-agriculture—to recover from the two devastating losses.

The financial losses to farmers and ranchers resulted in the necessity to sell some land in order to continue operations. Urban investors purchased the land for the water rights. The result was farmers going out of business and less land for food production.

Denice states that there are a lot of dairies in Kansas, just across the state line. She claims, "Many of the employees live in Colorado. The dairies [are] located in Kansas because of Colorado's strict laws." She adds a positive, hopeful thought: "If an electrical plant locates in our area, it will increase the population."

Denice believes that the future for Holly is as bright as the Colorado morning sun. She would like to see Holly grow in the number of available jobs, as well, to keep young people from leaving her hometown. "Even a farm cannot support more than one family."

I thank Denice for her time and perceptions about Holly and all small towns. The lunch was very good; the new knowledge was great. I highly recommend Porky's for good food, ambience, and down-home conversation.

After some parking-lot hunting time for Mo, we drive east on US 50 toward the Colorado and Kansas state lines. It is always difficult for me to leave my home state of seven years. Colorado is the home of many good friends and fond memories.

CHAPTER 23

West Kansas

*D*riving east on US Highway 50, I am confronted, as usual, with the choice of our nightly destination. A brief stop and quick map-check reveals two options: Dodge City and Garden City, Kansas. I have spent a lot of time in Garden City while working at Wichita State University, but minimal time in Dodge City. The decision is a no-brainer. Even though it is not the most direct route to Stafford, tomorrow's interview site, tonight we go for the new experience of Dodge City, a town with about 30,000 residents. The 130-mile drive, followed by the search for a campground, a walk with Mo, some sightseeing, and dinner all complete a long, fun, productive day.

The town began in 1847, with the construction of Fort Mann to protect civilian travelers on the Santa Fe Trail. In 1865, Fort Dodge, an army-constructed fort, replaced Fort Mann. The new fort added support for Indian Wars to its original mission of protecting settlers. Fort Dodge soon expanded into a town with the same name.

Dodge City was constructed just in time for the arrival of the railroads, which brought cattle drives from Texas and the ensuing people and businesses. One of those early businesses was the first bar in town: George M. Hoover's, which opened in a tent. Dodge City soon became a town notorious for its presence of many famous gunfighters, including both Wyatt Earp and Bat Masterson.

An account written in 1882 by a drover named Andy Adams provides some insight into the early cattle-drive days. Adams was a drover in a group of cowhands on a five-month cattle drive from Texas to Western Montana. His account tells of a day in Dodge City that regressed into a gunfight between Quince Forrest, a member of Adams' drovers, and the bouncer at the Lone Star Dance Hall. The fight began with a confrontation and ended in angry words between the two men. Afterward, during the short horseback ride from town to the drovers' camp, Forrest stopped the men he was riding with and invited them to return to the dance hall. According to Adams, Forrest stated, "I'm going back to the dance hall and have one round at least with that whore-herder. No man who walks this old earth can insult me as he did . . ." Adams continued the story by stating, "The bouncer [who was] struck with the 6-shooter fell like a beef. Five 6-shooters turned on the ceiling. The lights went out . . ."

Adams' brief eyewitness account of his days in Dodge City brings to life real history, which has been portrayed in several movies about Dodge City and the Old West. Dodge City is definitely a cowboy town with a history, a history that is brought to life annually during Dodge City Days and the Dodge City Roundup Rodeo. These events provide a return to the roots of the Wild West and early cowboy culture. I could not pass through Dodge City without relating its story to my readers.

The next morning, our easterly route to Stafford, Kansas on US Highway 50 soon becomes familiar territory. Wichita State University students, their towns, and respective schools of employment create many fond memories for me. Our travel into the morning sun is filled with thoughtful reminiscing.

I chose to visit Stafford school district because during the past two decades they have displayed a practice to be innovative in implementing progressive educational programs, as well as forming partnerships to effectively use resources. They were one of the first to provide free laptops to high school students, open a recovery center for high school dropouts, and open an entrepreneur center.

Both the town of Stafford (founded in 1878) and Stafford County (established by the Kansas State Legislature in 1879) were named in memory of Kansas Militia Lieutenant Lewis Stafford. He was a Civil War casualty, killed during the Battle of Young's Point at Port Madison Parrish, Louisiana. The county was at its inception then and remains today an agriculture-based economy of cattle and winter wheat. Beginning during the early twentieth century, the addition of oil and gas wells made a noticeable financial contribution.

The county was organized in 1873, but almost lost its existence in 1875, when the state legislature gave away all its land to surrounding counties, except a strip twelve miles long and six miles wide. In 1879, the United States Supreme Court found the legislative act unconstitutional, and the original territory was restored as "Stafford County."

Stafford, like many rural counties, has experienced a fluctuation and overall decline in its number of residents. The county's original population of 4,755 is similar to the 2010 census of 4,437 residents.

There are three school districts in Stafford County: Stafford, St. John, and Macksville. Stafford and Macksville each have a few less than 300 students, whereas St. John has a few more than 300. Stafford's approximate

1,100 residents ranks it between St. John, which has around 1,300, and Macksville, which has around 550.

The town of Stafford with a population approximately 1,100, like most small towns, has experienced slight loss of residents. Stafford, one of six towns in Stafford County, is located about eighty-five miles northwest of Wichita (population of 385,000) and approximately thirty-five miles west of Hutchinson (42,000 residents).

We arrive on Main Street in Stafford during early afternoon for an interview coordinated by the superintendent of Stafford schools, Mary Jo. Mary Jo is a former WSU graduate student and friend.

It is not difficult to find a parking spot on the once-busy Main Street. I walk about a block to a building that previously housed a furniture store. The retired furniture store is now a beehive of activity as the Stafford High School Entrepreneur Center. As I step through the doorway, I am immediately impressed with the high-energy activity of six students and a teacher. The Entrepreneur Center is part of the high school curriculum of Stafford Unified School District 349 [henceforth termed "Stafford school district."]

Natalie, the teacher, and her students are expecting me. Natalie asks, "Where is your dawg?" Evidently, Mary Jo has told Natalie that Mo would be with me. I respond, "Mo is in the truck." Natalie immediately says, "Mo will be fine in the Center!"

A few minutes later, Mo becomes the honored guest, with the run of the large, old furniture store showroom. Each student spends time petting Mo, which she, of course, soaks up. I stand in awe as I attempt to process the activities.

Natalie introduces me to each of the six students. We decide to begin with a tour, allowing me to visit each student at her or his business area. The complete tour takes place in the old, large furniture showroom. First, Taylor shows me the equipment he uses for his business of digital transfer, where he converts music and videos from cassettes to digital format on CDs.

Our second stop is with Brandi. She is the office manager for all the businesses. She does invoices and billing, as well as all other administrative functions. The students and teacher praise her for her work. As I listen and observe, it seems to me that she is qualified to assume an office manager position in a true business; I am envious of her organizational skills.

Bo's business, "Xtreme Customs," entails working with leather. His service includes both treating leather to change colors and engraving. He also makes key chains and coasters with designs. Bo played a key role in a shop project of building a house on Main Street. He escorts me to the showroom window to see the beautiful house that was constructed by the shop class. Thanks to their project, a fortunate family has a new low-cost home. He also was part of a project to remodel a room at a church into a coffee shop.

Bo introduces me to Michaela, who has an engraving business. She engraves on wood, glass, acrylic, and metal. Samples of her engravings and designs show meticulous work and artistic skills.

The next business is a partnership with Taylor N. and Ross. "Tay-Ross," their business, does logo design and shirt printing. Ross pulls me aside to tell me about his racing career. He says, "Last year I finished third in the Kansas Adult Dirt Track racing association." Impressed by a teenager taking third in the adult association, I pose the question, "NASCAR?" He responds, "It is a possibility someday."

All the Entrepreneur Center businesses sell on the Internet. The online sales bring in revenue from beyond the Stafford area. The student-operated businesses not only provide experience-based learning but also help boost the local economy.

The tour and individual conversations with the students helps me develop an understanding of the entrepreneur program and enables me to better learn about each student and his or her business. I can hardly believe the accomplishments of these six high school students, their high self-confidence, and their individual readiness to tackle the world. Their skills transcend well beyond any knowledge learned in a classroom setting and/or measured by a standardized test. The Entrepreneur Center allows students to gain *experience* and enhance academic skills by learning in an authentic business environment.

We gather around a large oak table for a round-table discussion. I join Ross, Taylor, Taylor N., Michaela, Bo, and Brandi, as well as Natalie, the teacher for four of the Center's six-year existence. Taylor, who is African-American, is the only minority in the group.

Mo makes a trip around the table to ensure that everyone is comfortable or more likely, to see if they have a stash of food. After the check, she chooses to lie beside my chair. Good choice. This way she might stay out of trouble.

I begin by explaining my research and why I stopped at Stafford. I ask the broad statement, "Tell me about Stafford, the Stafford school district, and the Entrepreneur Center." Each student enters the conversation. I am amazed at the politeness and consideration they have for each other. I have the feeling of being in a senior-military-officer staff meeting. The difficult task is not directing verbal traffic but capturing the conversation on paper. The students seem to understand my dilemma of note-taking, and they pause to allow me to "stay in the game."

Our conversation begins with the students describing Stafford and living in a small town. Ross says, "Small town. Everybody knows everybody; you cannot get away with much." Taylor quickly adds, "Everybody welcomes you into their home." Taylor N. contributes, "I can walk into anyone's home." All seven participants agree that Stafford is a very friendly town. Ross concludes, "I like small-town life."

Stafford is a farm-based community, along with other, smaller industries, such as oil. Taylor N. says, "We have a lot of oil. We have good hunting and good fishing. There are four hunting guides living around here." Ross quickly notes, "We have a good grocery store."

During my conversations with residents of small towns, I have found that having a grocery store is not only a convenience but also a large factor in morale for the people of the community. Entertainment such as movies, dances, and teen-centered activities are huge factors, especially for students. Ross proudly states, "We have a new movie every other weekend." Taylor quickly adds, "We have Elroy's Pizza. Michaela works there."

The students redirect the conversation to school programs. Bo says, "In shop class, we built a new house [and] tore down the old one." Ross picks up the story, adding, "I learned about wiring [electrical] and other things, such as plumbing." Bo proudly continues, "They auctioned off the house."

I tell the students, "I saw the beautiful one-story home located in a nice setting on the corner. It is an asset to the community and the product of a great learning experience for the student builders."

Natalie states, "We have a FFA [Future Farmers of America] program. We also have a forensics program; Michaela is a member of it." Ross states, "Sports in small schools are not big. [There is] not a lot of involvement. Only seven [students] went out for basketball." He immediately counters the remark by stating that the football team was one win away from the district playoffs.

The students continue by discussing service activities, such as cleaning along the highway and working with younger kids. Michaela talks about tutoring elementary students after school. She says, "We do several academic activities, including playing games." Taylor N. states, "We work with younger kids on learning and academics." All six students have worked with elementary students in the academic program. The students are proud of their community service, especially their involvement in developing academic skills among elementary students and other community centered work.

I ask the students about their future plans. Bo says that he plans to join the navy. Taylor plans to relocate to Wichita, Kansas. Other students plan to go to a university or community college, while some intend to enter the workforce.

The students then reflect on what the entrepreneur program has meant to them. They all agree that it has been a great experience about management, marketing, inventories, month-end reports, and how to work with people. Taylor N. proudly discusses the financial aspect of the program and how their businesses support the overall costs: "We received a grant five years ago. We do not pay rent for the building; it is donated. We split the utility bills. We get 70% of the profits, and the school district gets 30%." All students nod their heads in affirmation. They are proud that income from their businesses enables them to pay their share of the expenses.

Students transition their thoughts to current events in Stafford and Stafford County. They begin by mentioning the Stafford County Rodeo and Fair. The PRCA Rodeo, sponsored by the Stafford Saddle Club, is held on Friday and Saturday nights during the second weekend in July. Community garage sales, a parade, and bar-b-q accompany the event. The topic then turns to the Stafford County Fair. Student involvement in the fair is immediately apparent, as their words reveal ownership in the activities. Various students randomly present comments like, "We have livestock shows" and "We have 4-H exhibits, a wheat show, and birthday cake competition." The events focus on agriculture competition for youth and adults.

The students' comments about the fair are followed by talk amongst themselves concerning their participation and projects. As the excitement subsides, a student proudly states that the town of Stafford also hosts an Octoberfest every year, which attracts several out-of-area people to their town.

Residents of Stafford are active community builders. Preparing and hosting local events provides an opportunity for people to proudly work together to showcase their town and community. Their work not only creates fun events; it boosts their local economy by attracting visitors. Citizens of small towns, who fashion tourist attractions and special events, not only generate an excellent opportunity for people to gather but also enhance appreciation of rural American communities.

As the discussion ends, I thank Natalie and the students for their time and valuable information. The students thank *me* for visiting with them. Their pride in community, school, and the Entrepreneur Center has been obvious during our conversation. I am most impressed by their maturity and self-confidence. It appears that their accountability for themselves and businesses, as well as assuming a community service role has developed a strong sense self-responsibility and self-respect.

Mo, without a leash, and I exit the building and walk down Main Street. I have a renewed feeling of the future. We drive a few yards, down Main Street and onto East Broadway Street to the school district office for my appointment with Mary Jo, the superintendent of Stafford schools and a former doctoral student at Wichita State University. As usual, I am not on time, but Mary Jo understands. She greets me at her office door with a big smile. I explain that I spent longer in the Center than I expected. I smile and say, "Actually, I was having too much fun to leave." She responds, "I knew you would enjoy the students."

We spend some time renewing our friendship and catching up on each other's lives. She has a summer home on Table Rock Lake, about three hours south of my home. We, of course, compare fishing stories. As usual, I lose.

As I ask Mary Jo, or "MJ," as she is often called, the three standard questions about her town and community, she smiles and comments about my focus on the broad-question design that allows participants to tell their stories in their own words. She adds, "Some things never change."

Mary Jo begins our conversation by providing an overview of Stafford, including the main industry, a new facility, and a lost business. She says, "Agriculture is the big industry in the Stafford area. We depend a lot on farming and ranching." She smiles and states, "The new county hospital is located in Stafford. Stafford County Hospital is a twenty-five-bed facility with a twenty-four-hour emergency medical service." Her pride in the hospital and Stafford being chosen as its location is obvious.

She pauses before continuing. "Stafford used to be a self-sustaining community. We have restaurants, mechanics, a grocery store, and banks. In December, Duckwall's closed their variety store." MJ reflects, "Now we are no longer self-sustaining. Duckwall's closed forty stores in Kansas and Nebraska. Our nearest shopping towns are Pratt, twenty-five miles; Great Bend, thirty-five miles; and Hutchinson, thirty-five miles." Mary Jo is upset about losing the store and local shopping, as well as Duckwall's abandoning so many small, rural towns.

She immediately changes to a positive attitude about Stafford and its future. MJ says, "I have lived in many small towns in Kansas. They all have similar characteristics, but are distinctively different." Stafford residents are mostly middle-class citizens. Mary Jo states, "People [of Stafford] have strong middle-class values. People help each other if there is a need." She provides a generic example by stating, "If a family is having a down time, they will find support. It may or may not be financial, but they will have support." She continues with a recent experience: "A teacher was going through a crisis. I told him to hold his head up, and you will be surprised how many people love you. He did, and the situation became better." She pauses and adds, "Most [of the residents] would say they are Christian." She is referring to their religious persuasion of being Protestant or Catholic.

Mary Jo expresses concern that the values of people living in small towns, including Stafford, may change. Stafford, like many small towns, has experienced an influx of new residents. Mary Jo says, "I am afraid we are about to reach a 'tipping point' that could result in a change in values. So many of the new people have values that differ from the current values." A value that she certainly hopes continues is the strong relationship between the school and community.

The Stafford school district and the community have formed a partnership that benefits both entities. Mary Jo states, "Stafford school district is also a social-provider organization"— meaning they either provide partners for or are partners with the community to offer many social amenities. "Our school nurse has written over a half-million-dollars' worth of grants. We have new sidewalks, health programs, CPR [cardiopulmonary resuscitation] and AED [automated external defibrillator] training, and dietary programs. We also have a marriage counselor who comes to the school one day per week." The cost of $1,000 per month provides services for families and other members of the community.

The Dropout Recovery Center allows adults who do not have a high school diploma to complete their high school education. This free education not only helps individuals; it also helps the community, increasing the individuals' potential earning power. Recovery Center is usually not co-located with the school facilities. Separate locations enable Recovery Center students to avoid an environment that perhaps contributed to the high school dropout.

Community members strongly support school activities. "On Friday night, everyone is at the football game or basketball game," MJ states. Another example of community support is the rent-free building for the Entrepreneur Center.

Mary Jo cites a scheduling issue that exemplifies the community and school partnership. Stafford school board members have a notable presence in the state's school board association. The Kansas Association of School Boards (KASB) scheduled their "Stafford Grassroots Effort" meeting on a Wednesday night prior to Easter. The meeting conflicted with a church choir's rehearsal, which was critical because of the upcoming Easter service performance. Without being asked, the choir director rescheduled the practice for 8:30 p.m. Forty-five people attended the KASB meeting.

Board members of the Stafford school district are strong participants in KASB. Mary Jo proudly states:

> We do not miss meetings! Our members work with members from other districts and learn, and they feel good about their accomplishments. They see it as cutting edge. One of our board members was KASB president. This is a big deal for a small school. Locally, the school board is regarded more highly than [both the] city council and county commissioners.

My conversation with Mary Jo indicates her progressive actions to develop partnership that improve education and develop community.

I pose a final question: Would you please explain the thought process that allows you to be a creative thinker, a risk taker, and transformer of ideas into action?

"I do not consider myself a creative person. I listen to people, their recommendations."

Her words "I listen to people" is a definitive statement.

Our conversation has been informing and most of all, rewarding. The MJ's of the world visualize opportunities, dream the way it could be, and reward people by partnering with them to move ideas into actions. I express my gratitude, bid farewell to an old friend, and wish her well. She states in earnest her appreciation for including her school and town in the research.

As I drive south through town toward US 50, I reflect on my conversation with MJ. One person *can* make a difference. Her ability and confidence to include others is an essential element. But the key to unlocking the door to the room of change is being able to step back and allow others to enter in a leadership role. I feel very fortunate for my fifteen years as a "Shocker" [Wichita State University], as I had the good fortune while there to learn from MJ and many other students. Getting paid to learn—it cannot get much better than that.

Mo and I drive east on US Highway 50, tailed by the daily problem of *where do we stay tonight?* We head northeast toward Interstate 70, because tomorrow we will stop at the Starcraft trailer dealer in St. George, Kansas for a couple of minor repairs. It seems fitting to end our western journey at the same dealer where we began nine months before.

Our route on Kansas Highway 61 takes us through the northeast section of Hutchinson. As we drive along Kansas 61, I cannot avoid looking toward the east side of the highway, where a village of prairie dogs once called home. A relocation program moved them to western Kansas, and I miss seeing the little guys and gals peeking out of their holes in the ground. We call it "progress"; the prairie dogs probably call it "leaving our home

We drive two-and-a-half hours to a campground five miles east of Abilene. Following the routine, Mo and I are headed back to the historic cattle drive trailhead of the late 1800s. A historic town calls for a historic restaurant. After driving around town, I find Mr. K's Farmhouse Restaurant. The food, service, and atmosphere are all excellent. A server informs me that an original copy of the United States of America Constitution is on display at the Eisenhower Presidential Library. A one-and-a-half-hour wait at the library allows me to view (for about a minute) the fabulous document containing the signatures of George Washington, Thomas Jefferson, and Ben Franklin. Well worth the time.

I ask myself, "Where would we be without these three great men and their patriotic cohorts from our history?" I cannot fathom an answer.

The next day, after about thirty minutes with John and Stephanie at the Flint Hills RV Center, the trailer is ready for the next trip. As Mo and I travel our last leg of the trip, which is the reverse course of our first leg of the first trip, the mental process begins for planning the future trip or trips. It's a big question: trip or trip*s*. Should Mo and I make *two* trips, one northeast and one southeast, or should we *combine* the two trips into one?

After many miles and much thought, I decide on one trip in the fall. Mo and I will travel to Vermont and then down through the southeast to Georgia and west to Louisiana. The decision is made just in time to cross the Kansas-Missouri state line.

Two more hours of driving, and Mo recognizes Lincoln, Missouri. In her mind we are in the home stretch. Now I have to deal with a seventy-five-pound dawg pushing my arm with her nose, plus a continuous stare and intermittent whining. Soon, the trailer is parked unhooked, and one happy dawg is doing a property check.

Lincoln Fly-in

CHAPTER 24

Lincoln Fly-in

Saturday morning, and as usual, I am drinking coffee at the BB Restaurant and Bar with our version of the "World Problem Solvers." Someone says, "You-old aviator, are you going to the Lincoln Fly-in?" My response is, "I did not know about it, but yes, I am going."

It is another slow day at the lake, and the fish are not biting. In an hour, with pen and paper in hand, I am off to the fly-in. I arrive in Lincoln to a traffic jam; I have to wait for two oncoming cars to pass before I can make a left turn off the highway. Today, Lincoln is a busy.

Approaching the airfield, I see a large green field full of cars and of course dented pickups. I add with pride one more pickup with dents to the collection. People are everywhere; they are migrating from the greenfield parking lot toward the airfield; they are walking on both sides of the street and some down the middle. I eventually work my path through the maze of people to the airfield, only to see more people wandering around looking at parked airplanes, standing in groups talking, gathered around the food tent, and some kids in a line waiting for their orientation flight. Today, Lincoln's population has grown significantly. I still cannot believe that I had to wait for oncoming cars to pass prior to making a left turn.

I am excited to see so many people. But, my great excitement is to see some airplanes and talk aviation. My purpose for coming has suddenly taken a second priority.

The Lincoln Fly-in is as rural, small-town America as fried chicken, apple pie, and dented pickup trucks. Every year on a Saturday in September, Lincoln, Missouri (population 1,423) opens its aviation gates to small aircraft pilots, who land on the 2,940-foot north-south grass runway. Pilots donate their aircrafts, time, and fuel to give kids from ages seven to eighteen years old a free flight. Each child participant then receives a certificate. Glen, a past mayor, says, "It [orientation flight] makes the kids' day a success."

The story of the Lincoln Fly-in is about a small town that has doubled in size during the past thirty-five years and how becoming a bedroom community has changed the culture and Main Street. It is about Cody, who uses his airplane to check his herd of 200 Black Angus cattle, and how ranching has changed on his 600-acre ranch, located near Knob Noster, the home of Whiteman Air Force Base. The story also details how small-airplane aviation has changed due to increased federal regulations and will tell us why there are fewer private pilots and light aircraft slipping the surly bonds of earth and soaring into the clear blue sky.

It is a story about both rural America and a progressive small town that bears the name of our sixteenth president.

The Lincoln Airfield is a beehive of people, airplanes, and cars. There is a food tent, complete with non-alcoholic drinks and a lot of conversation. I greet a few people I know, but mostly listen and look at airplanes with memories and envy. There are a lot of airplanes there that are classified either as ultralight, sport, or experimental.

In the process of the day, I interview three people: two are aviators plus the past mayor of Lincoln. The aviators have vastly different backgrounds: one flies for a living, the other is a rancher. Art, who lives in Fair Grove about eighty miles south, flies professionally. Cody, the rancher, lives near Knob Noster, a town about sixty miles northwest of Lincoln. Glen, the past mayor, lives in Lincoln. All three men's ages appear to be in the early-to-middle sixties. The consistent theme among their stories is *change*.

We will begin with Art's story about change in aviation, with a focus on small airplanes and private pilots. Art has been flying for close to fifty years. He first flew in 1963, received his license in 1964, and started earning a living as an airmail pilot in 1973. He flew overnight airmail letters, which cost eight cents per letter. He next flew freight and later, people, on charter flights. He now delivers medical lab specimens out of Springfield, Missouri. He enjoys flying for a living. He says, "If it is business, you go, even if the weather is bad."

Flying is his passion, business, and pleasure. He keeps his sixty-five-mile-per-hour airplane at his home, where he has a 900' airstrip. He says, "Having my airplane at home is convenient. I can fly when I want, without driving to my plane." Art continues by stating that the fun of flying in some ways is offset by the increase in regulations and higher operating costs. "Greater expense has caused people to drift away from flying," he claims. He expands his thoughts by stating, "More flying regulations have increased costs of training and flying." He also mentions other issues related to increased costs: annual aircraft inspection, bi-annual airplane certification, and bi-annual pilot medical examinations.

The costs of required aircraft electronic equipment overshadow the increased expenditures required for aircraft maintenance and additional flight-training time. Art says that there are a lot more avionics required today than were necessary a few years ago. For instance, transponders are required around airfields. A transponder allows ground radar controllers to determine each aircraft's exact location. The recently required altitude encoder further allows the ground radar controller to determine aircraft altitude. Both of these requirements enhance flight safety.

Maintenance and the repair of aircraft electronics and avionics add to the costs. Radios have become more expensive, as well, with the increasing of operational frequencies from 100 to 720.

A possible change of flight navigational equipment may add to operational costs. Art says that the navigational system may change from ground-based to aircraft-based, which means GPS may replace ground-based navigation. I am vaguely aware of the changes . . . until he mentions GPS.

Other requirements have been safety-of-flight additions, but the absence of ground navigation sites boggles my mind. The GPS in my car has been a great aid during my travels. I depend on it. But I have difficulty imagining that a GPS will replace ground-based navigation systems. The concept should not be difficult to conceptualize, because we used airborne systems forty years ago, as a secondary navigational system. My look of astonishment causes Art to laugh and say, "Flying is changing."

Some pilots lessen the expense of flying by buying ultralight and sport planes, which are subject to fewer regulations. Art adds, "Sport planes cost a minimum $60,000."

He closes with, "It has been a great life, flying and having an airplane at home. Most kids will not have the opportunity." His final comment is accompanied by a shake of his head and a frown. I thank him and wish him luck, and he hurries back to his airplane to tend to some flying duties.

I meander, looking at airplanes, until I notice a man wearing a cowboy hat. I hurry over to meet the flying cowboy. He introduces himself, and in reply to my question referencing ranching, he says, "I raise cattle up by Knob Noster."

Cody and I very quickly engage in a conversation about cattle and airplanes. The conversation naturally becomes an interview. Cody tells me about his cattle, his Super Cub airplane, and the landing strip on his ranch. He adds, "My son keeps his Piper Colt, and my neighbor keeps his Piper J-3 at my airfield. Storing the airplanes gives me more contact with my son and neighbor."

I have personally always wanted to have a landing strip—and my own plane. I am big-time envious. I pose the question, "What is it like to keep your plane on your ranch?" Cody replies:

> It is a freedom thing. Late in the evening, I go for a flight up to the pasture to see my cattle. I keep a vehicle there so I can drive around and check the herd. I used to take feed so the cattle would come to me, but they got wise and stood on the landing strip so I could not land. They were waiting for their food, [so] I had to change the procedure. After checking the cattle, I hurry home to beat the darkness.

With his airplane housed on his farm, Cody creates an opportunity to serve his community. "I give the neighbors' kids rides. A couple of years ago, we had a bad windstorm. I flew the neighbors around to check their properties."

We pause and talk briefly about the flying neighbors. I then ask him, "How has life changed?" He immediately responds:

> Everything is faster: Internet [and] no letters. When I was growing up, people knew about animals. Today, the people do not understand farming. They do not understand fence lines. I cannot connect with the neighbors like I could when I was young. Neighbors are not farm-oriented. Kids have less interest in farming. Even though things have changed, I like our community.

His comments speak to the result that the influx of people with non-farming backgrounds has on the culture of a farming community.

He summarizes his experiences by saying that he has lived on a farm his entire life, except for the two years in the army and a brief stint working in California. He adds, "I flew for the United States Department of Agriculture in the San Joaquin Valley in California. The job prevented me from living on a farm."

He concludes with, "Farms have changed. They used to be 200–300 acres; now they are 3,000–4,000 acres. It takes this much land to make a living."

Cody and I shake hands. I tell him he is living the dream. He smiles and nods his head.

I roam around the aircraft parking lot, looking at a mixture of old planes and newer small planes. I watch a pilot open his aircraft's cowling and use a rope-pull to start his engine. I speculate with curiosity about how an engine with a rope-pull start can power an aircraft and break the bonds of earth to fly into the wild blue yonder. I watch as the aircraft and pilot depart the runway, flying off to the south. Apparently, it can happen.

I walk among the old USAF pilot-training aircrafts and take a short walk down memory lane, listening as my inner voice recounts stories that old pilots once told my peers and I during our early aviation careers. The stories of those pilots included several of the aircraft models now before me, and I realize that my peers and I are now the old storytellers.

Eventually, my aimless rambling leads me to the food tent. Donations for the food benefit a charitable cause. In the back of the eating tent lies a table surrounded with people who are laughing and talking. As expected, I see Wilbur, a friend, holding court with an audience. Wilbur is an icon in the community and famous for telling a story now and again. He is a typical small-town leader. A leader of *what*, we are all attempting to determine. But where there is Wilbur, there is always laughter and conversation.

After a burger and Coke, I walk around the area of the food tent, where I meet Glen. He is a longtime resident of Lincoln and its previous mayor. Our conversation is enlightening, as his comments about both Lincoln and the fly-in inform me that he possesses a wealth of knowledge about his transplanted hometown. An interview is born.

His initial focus is the Lincoln Airfield:

My dad helped build this hangar [the hangar we are leaning against]. The hangar was purchased from an airfield in Iowa. It [Lincoln Airfield] got started when the owner of the truck stop built a 2,000-foot grass strip. We received state funding to lengthen the runway. We have been upgrading and improving the airfield and runway since their inception.

He immediately shifts the conversation to Lincoln and its evolution over the past thirty-five years. He shares his thoughts about growth, saying, "Lincoln used to be a farm community, with farms of about 250 acres; now the farms are dramatically larger. There are about 10% [of] the number of farms as there used to be."

Even though the increased size of farms greatly reduced the number of farmers and their family members, the population has approximately doubled, from about 700 people thirty-five years ago. Glen comments, "We have become a bedroom community. Much of our growth has resulted from retired residents moving into the community."

Population transition from agriculture-based to a bedroom community, coupled with the introduction of corporate retail stores located less than ten miles south and twenty miles north, have distressed Main Street. Many of the storefronts there are vacant. Glen provides his observation of the transition by saying, "People go to Sedalia and Warsaw [to go] shopping. Everybody [in Lincoln] wants it to be like it was, [with local stores] with discount prices."

Even though downtown stores are sparse, several businesses adorn the outskirts of town. Restaurants, gas stations, a bank, and several service and repair businesses frame US Highway 65, which borders the east side of Lincoln.

The Lincoln Community Care Center and school district are two of the larger employers. They provide a focus for many community events. The Care Center hosts several events, including Halloween trick-or-treating for the Lincoln community, during which the Care Center residents give candy (provided by community members) to approximately 400 kids. The interaction between the residents, kids, and parents is an amazing event.

Local residents also participate in monthly community bingo, karaoke, local bands, and other events hosted at the Care Center, which all create a connection between residents and community.

The school and town leaders provide many community-uniting events. An array of school sporting events and other activities (such as music) provides a forum for the community to gather. Among other events, the town hosts its annual Lincoln Days: a well-organized celebration of local history.

The culture of Lincoln, even though it has changed, remains more consistent than many small-town bedroom communities. Values have remained fairly consistent. Both young and middle-aged adults provide a sense of stability. Their willingness to commute for work anywhere from thirty minutes to an hour has enabled them to remain in their hometown.

Glen finishes his remarks about Lincoln (or almost any small, rural town) by addressing the medical issue: "There is a shortage of doctors in rural communities." According to Glen, candidates ask about salary, work hours, and office appearance. It is very difficult to lure doctors and other medical professionals away from modern, well-equipped hospitals located in metro areas. The absence of sufficient local doctors results in residents traveling several miles for medical cares.

I thank Glen for his historical perspective of Lincoln. Even though a transplant to the community, he has invested much time and energy here. Community improvement, as opposed to culture change, has been the focus of his efforts.

I hope the readers enjoyed a day in Lincoln, Missouri—small-town America. I certainly enjoyed the day at the fly-in and talking about my adopted hometown. My final reflection of Lincoln is that it is a community focused on growth and unification.

Mo and I are preparing for our fourth and final trip through rural America. I am excitedly anticipating our travels to the northeast and southeast. My limited time in those two areas provides a glimmer of the coming venture.

I look forward to getting off the highways, following country roads, and visiting rural communities to meet and hear the stories of the people. The scenery—mountains and farmland—will be magnificent; the people and their stories will no doubt be intriguing. I can hardly wait!

Northeast and Southeast

CHAPTER 25

Pennsylvania, New York, and Vermont

Mo

I am excited and have been for a few days. Randy, the human I choose to hangout with, has been packing travel bags, a backpack, paper bags, boxes, and finally, the ice chests, which means leaving is eminent (another big word for dawgs—I have to admit that Golden Retrievers have a rather large vocabulary).

I was correct. The ice chests are in the truck. Randy opens the truck backdoor and says, "Let's go, Mo." Usually, I make a slow, lazy walk to the door and then stand and wait, like I am deciding whether or not it is a no-go. My delaying usually results in an up-tempo, "Get in, Mo!" But my slowness is just my way of showing that I am in control—and a way to raise Randy's blood pressure.

Not today, though! Even though I am definitely still in control, I do not want to chance missing a trip that required three days of packing.

The only mystery remaining is whether will we travel facing the sun or if the sun will be at our backs. My guess is that we will face the sun, because two of our previous three trips have started with our backs to the sun. Simple dawg logic tells that it is the sun's turn to be in front of us.

Wrong! Apparently, there is a third possibility: the sun at our *side*. I never thought this would be possible.

After two naps and a drive through a town with those irritating red, yellow, and green lights, we turn toward the sun. I was right! It is difficult to outsmart a dawg, especially a well-traveled Golden Retriever.

After several naps, begging for a dawg bone, and then more sleep, I awake to see the Big Arch. Soon, about lunch time, we cross the river Randy calls the "Big Muddy." I know it is lunchtime, because we have caught and then passed the sun. The sun is now the chaser, and we are being chased: the opposite of this morning.

While we are on the subject, it is time that I enlighten humans about my thoughts on the sun. I realize its power and necessity for the universe, but I question some of its behaviors. First, it disappears for its nightly sleep two or three hours before dawgs and most humans. We dawgs are required to remain on duty to ensure that the sun's sleep is not disturbed. This requires two or three hours of sleeping with one eye open. In the morning, we dawgs must get out of bed and check to make certain the world is safe for the sun to peek its head over the horizon. Roosters claim they awake the sun with their silly crowing—an inflated opinion of them, *by* them. Good dawgs are up eating, smelling, and marking danger spots well before any rooster's first crow. Then, and only then, does the sun show its face and brighten the world.

I am glad I could inform you about the real truth of the sun. Now, back to business.

More traveling, more boring driving, and more sleeping leads to—you guessed it—a boring afternoon. I am so bored that I do not even want to ask for a dawg bone. I would rather sleep. Finally, another city comes into view, the one with the racetrack. We are going to visit Randy's sisters and her family—and Skeeta, a big Husky-Akita dawg. Great! This is always fun.

We spend the night at Randy's sister's house, with a lot of petting, playing, and supper-table scraps.

The next morning, we continue our drive chasing the sun. A long nap, and I awake to an area of red, green, and yellow lights. Humans, as always, interrupt their chase (of whatever) and stop at red lights to blow their car horns. I will not stop for a red light, not if I am in hot pursuit of a squirrel or bunny. A chase is a chase, and nothing should impede or interfere.

With excitement, Randy blurts out, "There is a Tim Hortons coffee shop." A quick turn right, across a two lanes of traffic, and we pull into the paring lot. You guessed it; his quick turn resulted in many, many car horns sounding an alert: "Crazy driver in the area!"

Randy soon reappears with a big cup of coffee, big sweet roll, and big smile. Of course, I show my delight by being humble and polite. I am not stupid; I know what it takes to participate in the game called "sharing a sweet roll." It works! Sweet roll gone, crumbs cleaned up by the K-9 vacuum, I lay down for a long nap.

The long drive culminates at a KOA campground in Grove City, Pennsylvania. After dinner and a two-mile walk, I settle in for a good night's sleep. I jump up on the couch without any hassle, because Randy does not have papers spread in my sleeping spot. I dream about swimming in the lake, keeping the world safe by chasing big, dangerous animals, and doing dawg stuff, which does *not* include storytelling.

I awaken and decide Randy can do some work, including picking up the storytelling chore.

I am done! Let's have breakfast and a walk.

Randy

Mo and I travel east on Interstate 80, then northeast on Pennsylvania Highway 8, with the town of Franklin as our target for breakfast and (hopefully) an interview. Our travel takes us through a town that is not on my map and does not have a sign of identification, at least not one visible to me.

We travel onward, enjoying the beautiful mountain scenery. Finally, we arrive in our planned town of Franklin. A quick conversation with a man fueling his car at a gas station informs me that McNerney's Irish Tavern is *the* breakfast place.

We eventually find a parking spot that will accommodate a truck and camper. Mo guards the truck as I walk half a block toward a sign stating "McNerney's." As I approach the door, the volume of chatter lets me know I am at the right place.

From my first step through the door, the décor of McNerney's makes it obvious that I am in an Irish pub. A large Guinness beer sign makes me wish it was five o'clock. I walk past the crowd to the back of the room, where there is a large table and three unsuspecting coffee drinkers discussing the day's major events. They ask me to join them, which I do.

I enter the conversation by stating I like your town of Franklin, which Chuck immediately responds, "Good, but you are in Oil City." His response is followed by three hearty laughs and a chorus "Are you lost?" I respond, "Temporarily, but do not tell anybody." I join the laughter and receive a couple slaps on the back. Sometimes being an airhead is not all bad.

The three men agree to participate in the interview with a couple of caveats: Chuck says to first make sure I write "Oil City" and second, to spell their names "R-o-g-e-r," "J-o-h-n," and "C-h-u-c-k." I respond by verbally spelling "Oil City" and the three names as I wrote them in my notes. They all agree that I am getting on track, and it will be safe for them to begin telling me about their beautiful town and its history.

Roger and John are senior citizens, and Chuck, who still works, is around fifty years of age.

Now that I know where I am, it is a good time to describe and present a brief history of Oil City. The beautiful setting of Oil City amongst two bodies of water—the Allegheny River and Oil Creek—make for an interesting but complicated history of early settlement.

Oil City, surrounded by foothills, is situated in Venango County at the confluence of Oil Creek and the Allegheny River. Nature has defined Oil City, with its geographic wonders of mountains, foothills, and rivers. Beauty exudes from the natural environment and people and the diversity of both.

The Allegheny River, which flows from the northeast along the eastern side of Oil City, makes a lazy "S" around and through the town. The river bends at the south edge of town and progresses northwest, running through midtown and dividing Oil City into northeast and southwest sections. The indecisive river then forms a horseshoe turn and runs southwest, bordering the western section of town. The confluence of Oil Creek with the Allegheny River occurs at the north horseshoe bend. The patterns of the Allegheny River and Oil Creek, as well as the foothills and mountains, make for a majestic vision of water and scenery.

Older buildings add a pristine beauty to the setting, while the newer structures provide a sense of progress. The new and the old buildings complement each other, as do the young and old people and the ethnic diversity among residents.

A written description of Oil City beauty, however, can never adequately rival a photograph taken from above in a light aircraft. It is a setting I would love to circle in a Cessna aircraft until either a resident complained or I had a minimum level of fuel left.

The history of the area is as intriguing as the unique setting. The area of Oil City began during the early 1600s, when the Seneca Tribe settled on the land. In 1818, the Seneca Tribe lost the area in a land transaction made by Chief Cornplanter. The Holliday family purchased a nearby area in 1803. They later sold their property to Dr. John Nevins, who plotted the land. Development of the area was slow, with only three buildings, two of which were hotels built to accommodate men traversing in rafts. By mid-century, William Lay and James Bleakley purchased adjoining land south of the river. They named their towns Laytonia and Imperial City, respectively.

In 1871, the two towns were consolidated, with a charter decreed by the state legislature granting the name as Oil City. The town got its name from the discovery of oil. In 1859, Colonel Edwin Drake made Oil City famous when he drilled for oil. By 1871, more than a million barrels of oil were shipped annually from Oil City.

My conversation begins with Roger's historical perspective of Oil City and its community. Roger begins by stating:

> Oil City had about 25,000 people during the early 1950s. There were five train companies. We used to have a roundhouse [turntable that rotates a train car]. We did maintenance. There was a tunnel through the peak across the creek. We now have about 10,000 people.

John claims much of the decrease in population has been due to changes in the oil industry:

> The oil refineries are now gone. Pennzoil had two refineries, Quaker State had one, and CoreCo had one. There would be hundreds of train cars each week coming and going into Oil City. The reason the oil refineries relocated to coastal areas is ship transportation.

Long-time residents Roger and John team up to tell me about two unique Oil City buildings. Roger starts the story: "There were two structures beside the peak on the other side of the creek. One building was a hotel, which was only one-room deep. All rooms had a creek-side view." My look of wonderment creates smiles. John picks up the conversation by adding, "The other building was a five-story school, with a ground-level entrance to each story." I quizzically ask, "Is the ledge that narrow?" They nod their heads affirmatively, as Roger summarizes, "The ledge is *very* narrow."

The two longtime residents pause, allowing Chuck to add his thoughts from a more recent era. With Roger and John nodding their heads in agreement, Chuck states:

> Oil City is a good place to live. Our motto is "A special blend of people." People of Oil City live up to the town's motto. They are friendly and help each other when there is a need. We have Elks, Moose, Eagles, and Polish clubs, all of which bring people together.

After Roger and John verbally confirm Chuck's comments, he continues, "We do not have all the amenities, but they are close and can be easily reached. There is a shopping mall six miles south, in Cranberry Township. The land for the mall replaced several farms." Roger joins the conversation by adding, "Our Subway Restaurant is also a gathering place. We have a YMCA that provides programs and facilities for youth and adults of both genders. Oil City had a hospital until ten years ago." Chuck quickly adds, "We combined with Franklin to have a hospital in between the two towns."

Chuck changes topics, saying, "If you want to see your friends, go to Walmart or Home Depot. McDonalds is the young peoples' gathering place."

Chuck pauses and checks his watch, then says, "I must get back to work. *Somebody* at this table needs to work." He pauses and becomes serious, stating, "I am happy that my company moved me to Oil City. I like the people and town."

I thank Chuck as we shake hands and bid farewell. He thanks *me* for the conversation and humor. I reply, "I am happy to add humor, even though I was lost."

John and Roger continue to discuss the significance of the people living in Oil City. John says, "The Polish community is very close. The closeness of Oil City people transcends ethnicity."

They both agree that while ethnicity is valued and celebrated, it never overshadows the greater needs of the people of Oil City. John provides an example: "Neighbors help neighbors. There have been a lot of benefits [fundraisers] for a little girl who has a serious illness." Roger then mentions a little girl who was abducted twenty years ago on Halloween and killed. John states, "Every year there is a 'Halloween Memorial Walk.' "

They both agree that community significantly adds to their lives in Oil City.

John and Roger conclude our conversation with a few personal notes. Roger says that he graduated high school in 1945 and served one year in the navy: "The only ship I was aboard was the parade field."

John adds, "I was a manager of eleven Woolworth's five- and ten-cent stores [i.e., five-and-dime stores]. My last store was [in] Oil City. I stayed because I like the town and the people."

Roger concludes, "Oil City is a good place to retire, as long as you can get around the hills."

I thank Roger and John for their time and stories. They each say that they have enjoyed the conversation and hope I do not get lost again. I respond, "Me also, but there are no guarantees."

I return to the truck to find it has been well guarded by a soundly sleeping dawg. Mo and I take a short tour of Oil City to admire the town, its history, and its natural beauty. We eventually depart on US Highway 62, which follows the Allegheny River and skirts the Allegheny National Forest for several miles.

Our travel follows US 219 North to Interstate 86 in New York. Three hours of driving is enough, so we exit the interstate and travel a short distance to Hinsdale. Mo is ready to walk and smell, then smell some more. After a drink and a dawg bone, Mo waits in the truck as I get a sandwich at the gasoline-station deli.

Hinsdale, located in the eastern part of Cattaraugus County, has a population of about 2,100.

Founded in 1820, the town of Hinsdale was given the same name as a New Hampshire town. Native Americans inhabited the area during the eighteenth century. Today, in the approximated area of this small, quiet town, archeologists scour the land in search of Native American relics.

The food element of business is a line to a counter, where subway-type sandwiches are made to order. I join the line, and two things happen: First, I purchase a good sandwich, and second, I meet Robert, a person with an interesting past and positive outlook for the future. Robert, who is a senior citizen, consents to an interview.

He and I sit at a picnic table for our conversation, while Mo completes a search and investigation of the area. The first thing I observe is that every person who either enters or exits the gasoline station greets Robert. Some greet him with a "hello," while others have a brief conversation. The greetings are not disrupting; they are part of the story. Many people know and respect Robert as a valued member of the community.

When I mention to Robert that all the people passing by say "hi," he responds, "I am grateful to have a lot of friends." These few words clearly show that he is popular among the people of the community, and he is appreciative of other people. I write myself a brief note that states "listen carefully."

Robert immediately explains how the area has changed since he was growing up:

> When I was growing up, you could leave your doors unlocked, [and] people were friendlier. Now, [in] this day [and] age, you cannot leave your door unlocked. People are still friendly and help one another. New people moving in have different outlooks than town people [long-time residents].

His initial comments mirror those I have heard from several people. The words differ, but the message of a changed culture remains the same.

Prior to continuing his comments, Robert pauses for reflection. His thought process reveals a serious topic that he wants to ensure is clearly stated. He articulates these words:

The financial aspect of life is more difficult today than in the past. I am retired and live on a fixed income. Cost of living has increased more than the increase of my income. I worked for the same company for thirty years, but only have seventeen years toward retirement. The original owners sold to new owners, who went bankrupt after thirteen years. I lost my retirement for the last thirteen years of work.

He accepts the lost retirement as a fact of life and does speak negative about the second company. He maintains his positive attitude and does not dwell or show negative emotions.

Robert smiles and makes a quick transition to the positive aspects of the people living in Hinsdale:

Hinsdale has a lot of nice and helpful people. They rally around and help others. I am a member of the local fire department. I believe that it is important to help people and serve the community. Sometimes it is difficult being a firefighter, but it is important. I always help.

Robert once again pauses before he changes the subject to an amazing account of family and youthful years. I listen in awe as he continues:

My family is important and remains a focus of my life. I have a lot of relatives here. Many of my family are dead. I was brought up in a home with seventeen kids, 15 of which were foster children. I was one of the fifteen foster children. My foster parents treated me like I was one of their [own] kids.

His expression changes to a smile as he continues, telling a story about his foster mother: "My foster mother lived to be 106 years old. My family took care of her until she had to go into the nursing home. Family means everything." He pauses and reflects before continuing his thoughts: "After my foster mom experienced mental dementia, she would tell me to go and milk the cows. Family remains important. I live with my thirty-eight-year-old son, who has a condition that prohibits him from living alone."

Robert reflects for a short time before changing the conversation to the present day. He transitions the discussion by relaying, "I lived most of my life in Ischua, a few miles north of here. Ischua is now a rural delivery [mail] of Hinsdale." Decreasing size and loss of his school leads him to thoughts about the longevity of Hinsdale schools. "We have a school, but we may not have it much longer. We are losing kids." Robert relates loss of his hometown and the possibility of losing Hinsdale's school as issues of social turbulence for kids. He explains that it is important to have a good, stable place to grow up.

He summarizes his thoughts with a final impactful statement: "Rural America is changing."

I thank Robert for his time and memorable stories. After Robert and I say farewell, Mo and I head toward the truck. The brief walk and drive provide time for me to reflect on Robert's account of his life, especially his childhood years. His childhood influenced his life, positive attitude, and commitment to community and family. He is grateful for his support as a child and as an adult. He values other people. He seizes the best of each opportunity. Robert chose the high road.

Mo

Randy and I are heading down Interstate 86 with our backs to the afternoon sun. We drive and then drive some more. Every time I awaken, we are still driving. Boring! Finally, we arrive in a city. I know because cars are racing on multiple-lane roads. I am thankful there are no red, yellow, and green lights. People are just driving fast and doing the single-finger wave, which I do not understand. Sometime, somewhere, we change to a highway with signs that depict "88" instead of "86." Randy played a trick on me.

Things become more confusing as we drive on roads with trucks that meet us side by side. I wonder if he knows where he is going? I soon realize he does not. He pulls out the map, then the telephone, into which he asks the question, "Do you have any camping spots?" It is a little late for this question, because the sun is rapidly fading to its sleep position.

The answer must have been "yes," because Randy's response is, "We will be there soon."

Not true. Not even *close*.

I'm hungry. We are driving on narrow roads, which always leads to *lost*. We are now going on the same road we had been—in the opposite direction. Lost, we are.

Finally, we arrive. It is dark. Set-up will be fun tonight. My goal is to eat: to heck with setting up. Randy comes out of the office building with a flashlight. Why? He has two in the camper. Oh, "in the camper" means we cannot get to them. Good planning!

He says that he will start keeping a flashlight in the truck for dark set-ups. I bet that never happens.

Set-up takes a long, long time. I wait for dinner. I hear words I should not be hearing. Finally, lights come on in the trailer, and I eat supper. I go directly from food dish to couch. I have had all the fun I can stand for one day. As I drift off to sleep, I remember there is a lantern in the back of the truck. I wish I could talk. Too late to worry about what could have been.

The next morning, we are up early. I eat and guide Randy on the morning walk. After a productive walk of smelling and sightseeing, Randy heads to the shower, while I assume the "rest position" in the backseat of the truck. Soon I hear Randy walk by the truck on his way around the lake. Strange behavior: He is walking from one shower building to another shower building. Oh well, not my problem.

After what seems a long time, he opens the truck door to get ready for tear-down. He mumbles, "Bleep, bleeping restroom closed," and something about the other side of the lake. This is a good time to pretend that I am sleeping.

Eventually, with trailer in tow, we drive out of the campground to the tune of, "We are never coming back here!" Now I am *really* going to sleep. Randy can take it from here.

Randy

We stop for a late breakfast at Friendly's Restaurant in Oneonta, a town of about 14,000 people. Seat selection is difficult because most of the tables are vacant, and there are too many choices. I am one of four customers. Soon, the couple three tables away leaves, and I am one of *two* customers left. It is not a surprise; it is very late for breakfast. The workers are at work; the retirees are doing retired stuff. Or it might be my hat? Interview prospects look dim. The good news is that the food is great, and the server and entire staff make me feel like I am an old friend. In fact, Toni, the server, starts a conversation, which leads, in about fifteen minutes, to an interview during her break. Am I good at getting interviews or what?

While waiting for Toni, I will give you a brief insight into the early days of Oneonta. Henry Scrambling first settled in the area around 1783. He left during the Revolutionary War, only to return with his brothers after the United States gained its independence. A settlement named "Millford" was formed in 1800 and became a town in 1830.

Millford changed its name to Oneonta in 1832. A popular, but unsubstantiated, belief is that Oneonta in Iroquois means "place of open rocks."

After the railroad reached the area, the village grew rapidly, and in 1908, it was incorporated as a city. At one time, Oneonta was the home of the largest locomotive roundhouse in the world.

Our history lesson comes to an end when I hear a human voice. A mail carrier, having breakfast during his day off, tells me a little about Oneonta. He says that he likes working here because the people are so friendly. He continues by informing me that delivering mail is difficult because of the numerous hills. The hilly city is located in the northern foothills of the Catskill Mountains, between Binghamton and Albany, with the westward-flowing Susquehanna River bordering the south part of town.

With a cup of coffee in hand, Toni, the server, scurries to my table just as the postal worker finishes his story. She immediately begins by telling me about her childhood. "Oneonta was a great place to grow up. There were not many drugs and not much crime. We had drive-ins [restaurants], swimming pools, outdoor ice-skating rinks, and indoor roller-skating rinks." She explains that there were several bars in town, but they were mostly on Broadway, River, and Market Streets. She again smiles and reflects on her happy childhood and her town by saying, "I very much enjoyed school, growing up in Oneonta, and my neighborhood."

Her neighborhood consisted of family and friends:

I lived on a dead-end street, Liberty Street. Everyone called us "the dead-end street kids." When I walked up Liberty Street, everyone asked where I was going. My grandparents, aunts and uncles, and cousins lived on Liberty Street. My grandparents were Italians. They had an arranged marriage in America. It was great seeing my family everyday.

Toni pauses to reflect momentarily before concluding, "Liberty Street is gone. It was taken out to build Interstate 88. It was a very good way to grow up."

The demise of Liberty Street is one aspect of how Oneonta has significantly changed over the years. Toni explains, "Oneonta is a college town; it used to be a railroad town with a locomotive roundhouse. The main industries now are colleges and hospitals. Some people work at Corning. The school district is a big employer." She adds, "The community is hurting for jobs. My mother worked for Homer Folks, a tuberculosis hospital. Homer Folks closed, and the building is now used for job corps. It brought in a lot of troubled kids."

Even though her hometown has changed and Liberty Street is gone, Tony remains positive about Oneonta and life.

Toni looks at her watch and states that her break is about over. She adds, "The boss does not care if I am a little late returning, but I would feel guilty." She then says, "I want to add a few things. Oneonta is a great place. It has remained the same in some ways, such as population and people helping each other. The people are great!" With this last comment, she jumps up and says, "I should get back to work."

I thank her and add that I really appreciate that she gave up her break to tell me about Oneonta. She responds, "I am happy that I could tell you about our beautiful town and people." As she gets up to go, the mail carrier states, "Toni, you are the face of Oneonta." She blushes and hurries back to work.

I really lucked out gaining an interview with Toni. Family and community are very important to her. Her story about Liberty, the dead-end street, and closeness of family are one of a kind. My only regret is that we did not have more time.

Thank you, Toni, for working through your break.

I start the truck and tell Mo, who is stretching, that we are going to Vermont. We head east on Interstate 88 until we pick up Interstate 90 at Albany. Two-and-a-half hours and 115 miles later, we arrive in a beautiful, quaint town with a welcoming sign that states "Bennington, Vermont."

Nestled between the Taconic and Green Mountains, the historic town of Bennington offers a peaceful scenic beauty not only to the approximately 15,000 residents but also to the many tourists. Colonel Governor Bennington Wentworth chartered Bennington on January 3, 1749. Four families from New Hampshire first settled it in 1761.

Bennington is located in Bennington County, which was created on March 17, 1778, and is the oldest and one of the first two counties of Vermont. Unity County consumed eastern Vermont, and Bennington the western portion.

Bennington is one of two shire towns (county seats) of Bennington County. It is the largest town in southeastern Vermont with a population of 9,074) and the sixth-largest municipality (after Burlington, Essex, Rutland, Colchester, and South Burlington). Vermont is indeed a rural state.

Bennington is known for the 1777 Revolutionary War Battle of Bennington, which was actually fought a few miles west, in New York. A 306-foot tower that commemorates the battle is made of stone and was erected in 1891.

After parking the truck and camper on a side street, Mo and I are off to tour the downtown. The first thing I notice is the serenity of the environment.

Downtown presents character with inviting well maintained area downtown. Streets are adorned with welcoming storefronts and other friendly embellishments. People walk about with the deliberate pace of the relaxing setting.

Eventually, I enter the Full Bellies Restaurant. The late lunchtime finds the restaurant occupied by more employees than customers. Just as I finish eating, a man in his late sixties enters and talks with the employees. He stops at my table for a brief chat, which soon becomes an interview. Only after a statement about the restaurant do I realize that Gary is half-owner of Full Bellies.

Gary begins by telling me that he has lived in this city for all of his sixty-eight years. "I never wanted to move. Bennington, years ago, was a small, laid-back town. Most everybody knew everybody."

During the 1950s, weekend-night shopping was very typical of small-town America. Gary adds:

> On Friday nights, the downtown was packed with people. Stores stayed open until nine o'clock. There were popcorn and peanut wagons. You could smell peanuts the length of Main Street. Since then, shopping centers have been built on the edge of town. They killed off 90% of downtown. On Friday nights, you can count the number of people on Main Street with one hand. Downtown reinvented itself with offices and a few tattoo shops.

Many stories and my own memories speak clearly to the fact that Friday nights in downtown rural America were special for rural kids growing up during the 1950s.

Population in Bennington has increased vastly since the 1950s. Gary states, "In the 1950s, the population was around 5,000 people; the town has grown considerably to [anywhere from] 20,000 to 25,000 people. Growth is due mostly to people moving in to Bennington." Gary's population estimate includes the area surrounding the town of Bennington.

The influx of people and the lack of industry have resulted in unemployment. "There is a lot of unemployment. Pay scale is not the best. Cost of living is about average."

Gary believes that there has been a significant change in the social values in Bennington and the southeast community of Vermont. Criminal activity, drug abuse, and people needing financial assistance are ever-present in today's Bennington. Gary believes that many people do not want to work:

> Life and values were much different during the 1950s. When I was young, parents could not buy much, so if you wanted something, you had to

work. As a sixth grader, I worked with a guy before and after school, mowing lawns and the cemetery. I shoveled grain out of boxcars. As far as I can see, work never hurt me. Back in the 1950s, I would have been embarrassed to ask for help.

Gary succinctly captures the feelings of many adults who lived their teenage years during the 1950s: "Work in rural areas was available, and our community was small to enough to allow teenagers to be known and trusted to do labor. Teenagers worked because we needed income, as well as to gain respect among the adults."

Some of the 1950s work ethic is prevalent today, but perhaps not as widespread or as noticeable. As a 1950s teenager, work for me, personally, was plentiful; it took place on our farm and on our neighbors' farms. I could plow the fields of our farm until 9 p.m. and still be prepared for school the next day, which probably is not possible in today's world. Gary is correct about the shift in work ethic, but in part, societal issues may have influenced the change. Nonetheless, there has been a transformation in work ethic. Gary sadly states, "I can honestly say that I am glad I am not a teenager now. Today, they [teenagers] have so many hurdles to cross to get things right." His statement not only reflects work ethic but social pressures on today's youth. He gives an example: "A young girl had a bad experience. She got into trouble, but her parents stuck with her. She is going to college next year." Gary's statement captures two meaningful issues for today's youth and parents: complexity of life and family support.

The issue of unemployment causes me to ask, "What is the main industry in Bennington?" Gary responds, "There is not a main industry. We have a company that makes armored plating for the [US] Department of Defense. Another company makes steering columns for automobiles." Many of the town residents must travel for employment. Gary cites examples: "Quite a few people drive to Albany to work. [A] few work at the Albany Medical Center. Some drive to Green Island, close to Albany, to work in the arsenal."

Gary expands on the issues of unemployment and society, moving beyond Bennington and into another southeast Vermont rural community: "My wife is from Woodstock, Vermont, where a company bought all of the farmland and built houses. There is no industry, including agriculture, remaining in Woodstock. A lot of the residents are retired."

In essences, Woodstock has become a retirement community, partially at the expense of the demise of farming.

Our conversation transitions to values and support of people. Gary illustrates the values of his generation with a story: "A guy from a group home comes into the Full Bellies Restaurant. We give him two pancakes and coffee—everyday." It is part of the young man's routine. It is also a part of Gary's routine. It is one way of giving back, giving to others.

Gary's final statement summarizes both his story and his feelings: "Overall, Bennington is a great place to live." I think, *It* must *be, to keep a man with Gary's qualities.*

It certainly is beautiful. My previous travels through Vermont have revealed to me the state's natural beauty and hospitality of its people, both of which exist in abundance. Red barns dot the countryside, as do old, white churches with steeples. The roads are not wide, but winding. They create the wonder of what beautiful scene might lie just over the next hill or around the curve. I could get lost in Vermont and never feel lonely.

I thank Gary for his time, candid remarks, and sharing of stories about Bennington, Vermont. Mo and I spend time walking around downtown, soaking up the ambiance before continuing our trip.

We depart Bennington on US Highway 7 to start our trek toward Staunton, Virginia: our stop for the following day and the weekend. Staunton is on our agenda; I want to visit an old friend and past neighbor there.

I stop at a roadside market to purchase some Vermont sugar-maple syrup. The friendliness of the people is not disappointing. Shopping in the store is a fun experience.

Prior to leaving, I do a quick map-check for our route to Staunton. The route we have chosen will take us too close to New York City, hardly rural and less than inviting, especially when pulling a trailer and trying to find a campground.

With a troubled mind, I start the drive south. At Pittsfield, Massachusetts, I make the decision to head west on US Highway 20, which will eventually lead to Albany and Interstate 88. As we drive and check for campgrounds, Oneonta seems to be our best choice. The drive on rural highways is very scenic, but slow. In fact, the travel is testing my driving skills. To intensify the issue, I am asking myself, "Why did I not make this decision prior to leaving Oneonta for Bennington?" Foresight would have eliminated tearing, pulling, and setting up the trailer, probably in the dark—again!

Mo

There is some stress in the front seat, so I am taking over the story to lessen the excitement and increase our odds of finding a campground. I am aware of the stress level because there is a whole bunch of soft talking, which I call "mumbling," even though I have been told it is just "thinking out loud."

Uncertainty of location is a common phenomenon in this truck. There are maps, continual checks of the GPS, and some serious head scratching. The sun is heading rapidly for its nightly sleep, which exacerbates the issue. Miles of winding, narrow roads lead us to the campground.

A quick check-in at the office, and Randy returns to the truck with a big smile. "I like this campground! The people are friendly, the campsites are nice, and the facilities are good. I just wish we did not have to set up in the dark," Randy exclaims. He omits "setting up *again* in the *same* campsite" from his conversation. But he is a happy camper, which is good.

I give 2-to-1 odds, however, that there is not a flashlight in the truck.

As we drive toward the same campsite we occupied the night before, I shake my head in amazement and ask myself, "Why?" As we back into the spot, Randy says with a great pride, "We do not need a flashlight. There is a lantern in the truck bed right beside the cooler." Duh! I knew that! Did I *tell* you there would be no flashlight in the truck? Did I *tell* you there was a lantern in the bed of the truck? People are only smarter than dawgs because they can talk, which is sometimes a curse.

I observe the camper set up from my favorite spot beside the picnic table. Finally, I eat. Three steps and a jump, and I am curled up on the couch sound asleep. Some other dawg will guard the sun tonight. To say I had a tough day is an understatement.

CHAPTER 26

Virginias

Today, Saturday, is a planned travel day with the destination of Stanton, Virginia. I intend to visit a town in northeast West Virginia. I have spent very little time in this area and hope to interview someone about life in this part of the country. Our chosen route is Interstate 88 to Binghamton, then Interstate 81 to Stanton, Virginia. A beautiful fall day with breathtaking scenery of mountains, farmland, and small villages, sprinkled with a few metro areas, all mark our route.

The six-hour drive of beautiful scenery rapidly transitions into metropolitan area, which today is synonymous with being lost. The routine of narrow streets and passing the same buildings several times ends as quickly as it began. A short interstate drive leads us to a small town beautifully situated in tree covered mountains. The sign appropriately states *Inwood*. My immediate thought is a town in the woods, how appropriately named. The best is yet to come, stories by two people, who are well informed and care deeply about their town and people, make my day a success.

It is early afternoon as we arrive into the small town of Inwood, which I soon learn is located in the Eastern Panhandle of West Virginia. Until today, I am unaware that West Virginia has *two* panhandles. Most of my West Virginia travels have been limited to the northern portion of the state and the narrow Northern Panhandle, a sixty-four-mile north-south strip of land between Ohio and Pennsylvania. When people speak of the panhandle, I always assume it is in reference to the Northern Panhandle. I now am acutely aware of the Eastern Panhandle because I am walking the streets of Inwood, one of its towns.

The Eastern Panhandle, which contains the three counties of Berkley, Morgan, and Jefferson, is nestled between Maryland to the west, north, and east and Virginia to the south and southeast. The panhandle, attached to West Virginia by a narrow strip of land to the southwest, is slightly less than a two-hour drive from Washington D.C., the nation's capitol, and Baltimore, Maryland. Its attachment, physically and culturally, more approximates its neighbors to the east than to the parent state of West Virginia.

A great commonality of West Virginia and the Northeast Panhandle is natural beauty. Its beauty attracts visitors and residents from the metropolitan areas to the east. The Eastern Panhandle webpage asserts that its sense of rich ethnic and cultural diversity make it "typical West Virginia."

Development of the Inwood area began with the coming of the Cumberland Valley Railroad. The CVRR and beautiful mountainous landscape lured people to come to the area and develop a recreational area named "Inwood Park" ("park in the woods"). The CVRR, the park, and nature's rich, bountiful resources all attracted more people. The number of residents created the need for a town and a post office. A town named "Gerrard" was born, but short-lived.

Jonathan Newton applied for a post office, but the name "Gerrard" was rejected because of its similarity to Gerrardsville, a neighboring town. Gerrard was renamed "Inwood," and the post office became a reality in 1890.

There are two competing axioms on why the town name was changed to Inwood. The most compelling is that the town was named for the park. The second story claims that a cousin of Jonathan Newton influenced the name: Newton's cousin, who was visiting from California, showed Newton a postmarked letter with his hometown of Inwood, California. Regardless of why, Inwood became the name of choice.

Perhaps both stories have some truth. I choose to believe Inwood gained its name from the park; you are free to choose what you believe.

Inwood continued to grow, with the addition of a grain elevator and an apple-processing plant. Stored crops, along with wood products like bark and railroad ties, were shipped from the Inwood station, making it one of the most profitable on the CVRR line. The town's growth was further stimulated when C. H. Musselman opened an apple-processing plant: the first to exclusively produce applesauce. Locally grown-and-processed agriculture products were major factors for the growth of Inwood and its surrounding area.

Inwood today, as it was a century ago, is a very appealing community for people who desire to escape city life for rural living. The appeal for new residents is substantiated by Inwood's growth of forty-two percent during the first decade of the twentieth-first Century, when the number of residents increased from 2,084 to 2,954.

A century of improvements in transportation and communication has made it possible for the once-beautiful vacation spot to become a rural, slower-paced residency. Improved transportation, proximity to larger cities and employment, coupled with lower taxes and lower cost of living, create enticing incentives that attracts new residents to Inwood.

The once-small, quiet town has outgrown its infrastructure. Rapid growth, cultural change, and stretched infrastructure make an interesting story told by two longtime residents.

The story of Inwood is described through the eyes of Faye and Kenny. Faye, who is the attendant of a state-owned produce market, has worked for both the federal and state departments of agriculture for thirty-six years. Kenny, a volunteer firefighter, does not mention his vocation. I estimate Faye's age to be about sixty and Kenny's to be around forty years. Their individual stories, captured by separate interviews, complement each other and meld into a very clear, informative story about Inwood and its recent changes.

Faye and Kenny begin their discussion by addressing the attractiveness of Inwwod and how that attractiveness has created troubling physical changes to their town and life style. Faye states, "Taxes are cheaper in West Virginia than [in] Maryland and Virginia." Kenny later adds, "We are close to D.C. [Washington], which allows for daily commutes to work."

Faye and Kenny quickly transition their remarks to the physical changes of Inwood. They describe physical effects differently with similar end results. Referring to the road adjacent to the market, Faye claims, "This busy blacktop road used to be gravel." Kenny [referring to the same road] later tells me, "There is about a forty-five-minute wait on Main Street during the hours from 3:15 to 6:15 p.m." In some respects, the timing of their comments was parallel, as they addressed cultural changes using the example of the visible inconvenience of traffic.

The issues foremost on the minds of both Faye and Kenny are rapid growth and the ensuing cultural change of their once-small-town environment. "Inwood used to be mainly a farming and orchard community," Kenny comments. Faye supports his statement by saying, "Inwood used to be very small, a little part of West Virginia. People were nice and friendly for the most part. Now it is not so friendly. People are busy and do not want to be bothered." Kenny shares similar feelings with a slightly differing view: "Everybody used to look out for everybody; now that has changed. We have a lot of people moving here because they do not want to live in a city. It has caused chaos."

Kenny and Faye elaborate about cultural changes. Faye states, "People who have moved in [to town] changed the culture. We lost some businesses, such as gas stations [and] mom-and-pop grocery stores. We now have a Food Lion grocery store, five banks, and one restaurant." Kenny speaks more pointedly, "People come here for the quality of life and culture, and then they try to change it.

An example is [that] we were traditionally a hunting town; now some people oppose owning any kind of guns."

Another issue that makes Inwood susceptible to culture change is the Eastern Panhandle's remoteness to the remainder of the state. Kenny claims:

> The culture of the Panhandle has always been different from the rest of West Virginia. Our location separates us from the remainder of the state. The rest of the state's residents do not associate the Eastern Panhandle with having the same values, problems, and demographics of other West Virginia areas.

Isolation from the other parts of West Virginia and changes of rapid growth both result in Inwood residents feeling stressed about their day-to-day lives. According to Kenny, the long-time residents feel a sense of being disconnected from the remainder of their state.

The rapid increase of people has affected Inwood in ways beyond traffic congestion and culture. In most instances, salaries and wages for jobs held by original residents have not maintained pace with income earned by new residents, who mostly work in large metro areas. Farm and orchard land has been turned into housing developments, thereby reducing agriculture-related jobs normally held by original residents. Some farms were sold because they were no longer profitable to operate. Farm product prices have remained fairly constant, while material and equipment prices, as well as labor costs, have increased. These monetary disparities have resulted in reduced or negative farm profits and sale of farmland.

Faye believes that the reduction of agricultural business has further contributed to the loss of jobs:

> Many people are struggling. We lost a lot of jobs in agriculture. The social cultural has changed, as many new residents desire to cling to the values of their previous community and lifestyle. In some instances, the values of the past, mainly [of the] farm and orchard community, collide with values people have brought from their [own] urban setting.

Faye and Kenny's remarks claim that agriculture, which was a main reason for the settlement of Inwood, is becoming extinct.

Closure of two large employers has exacerbated the financial woes of Inwood. Kenny and Faye mention that General Motors and Corning have both closed their plants during the past few years. The closing of the two plants eliminated good-paying jobs for the residents. To illustrate the impact of the two closures, Kenny states, "Now the IRS [Internal Revenue Service] and [US] National Guard are our major employers." These two entities, however, employ fewer workers.

Financial issues of Inwood have affected community volunteer functions and family values. Kenny states, "As the financial issues and the economy worsen, people need second jobs. This makes it difficult for fire departments and other programs, which are staffed by volunteers." Kenny states, "80% of the local fire departments are volunteer." He then pauses before making a profound statement that relates financial issues to family:

> When I was in high school, life was 50% slower. Stores closed at 10 [p.m.]. Sunday was a day to go to church and spend with your family; now we get up and go to work on Sunday. The reason people have changed is [that] the country has changed.

His final statement strongly asserts that personal values in America have shifted from family-centered to work-centered. He expands causes of social change beyond the issues in his small town.

Increased criminal activity has accompanied the population growth of Inwood. Kenny is careful, however, not to blame the new residents: "There is an increase of criminal activity. Many of the crimes are violent, such as robberies, shootings, and car hijackings. New and old residents alike commit the crimes. I believe the increase of criminal activity can be related to income issues." In other words, he strongly believes that most crimes are driven by financial need.

Through all the changes and difficult times, Faye and Kenny remain positive about their hometown and community. They strongly believe that their hometown is a great place to live. Faye and Kenny still like calling Inwood home. Faye enthusiastically says, "We have a pretty view." She pauses, waves her arm to show the produce, and says, "All of the products in our farmer's market are grown in West Virginia." Her comments and actions exude pride.

Kenny shows his pride by stating, "Inwood is a good community. We are 'West Virginia Tough.' We will make the best of the situation and remain a strong community." Kenny holds a strong link to West Virginia and considers himself a West Virginian, even though he believes the Eastern Panhandle is considered remote from the remainder of the state.

Faye and Kenny provide me with an entirely new perspective on West Virginia and the Eastern Panhandle, as well as on the perils of a rapidly growing small town. I am very thankful for their time and insight. I thank both Faye and Kenny for their interviews.

My interview with Kenny occurred while sitting on chairs in front of a fire truck. As I depart the fire station with Mo, who has been on a continuous exploration, I feel proud to be part of a country with strong people like Faye and Kenny: people who are dedicated to community and country.

To Mo, a fire station is a fire station. Her behavior emulates her time at the Osage Valley Fire Protection District station: checking all wastebaskets, ensuring everyone pets her, and taking a nap in the center of the action.

As we depart Inwood, I pull off the road and stop for one last look at the town. I imagine the original days, when tourists from the large metro areas visited this virgin land. Subsequently, I attempt to visualize ten years in the past—before the growth. Then, and only then, do Mo and I start our two-hour travel southwest on Interstate 81, heading to the KOA campground in Stanton, Virginia.

While we trek along, I reflect on our trip through Pennsylvania, New York, Vermont, Massachusetts, and the Eastern Panhandle of West Virginia, including all the stories I've heard from all the people I've interviewed. Rural Americans have many commonalities, as well as several differences. The people share many ideas, values, and difficulties. Two pronounced common traits are love of community and strong resolve to build a life in the town or community that they love. They are loyal to their town and community. As I ponder the stories of the past few days, I look forward to the next week of our journey.

Our southeasterly travel on Interstate 81 welcomes us to the beautiful, scenic Shenandoah Valley. Native American legend tells us that the valley's beauty was created when the heavens gave their "celestial benediction" from the "brightest jewel" of each star to the limpid waters of Shenandoah Valley. The valley gained its name from "Shenandoah," the "clear-eyed daughter of the stars."

United States Highway 11, which mirrors Interstate 81, traverses the center of the valley. These highways derived their route from a well-worn Native American path that eventually became known by the settlers as the "Great Wagon Road." German and Scotch-Irish immigrants used the path to travel and establish early settlements. One of those settlements is Staunton, our goal for the weekend.

Welcome to Staunton, Virginia: home of Woodrow Wilson (the twenty-eighth president of the United States) and also home of the famed country quartet, the Statler Brothers. Both Staunton and Augusta County have rich histories, dating back to the early days of the colonial period. They are located in proximity to early Virginia politics, which vied with Boston leaders for creation of the Declaration of Independence and the writing and early interpretation of the Constitution.

The courthouse was constructed in 1745 to administer the vast land embodied as Augusta County. Land entrusted to Augusta County stretched from as far west as the Mississippi River to most of the area that is known today as Indiana, Kentucky, Ohio, Illinois, western Pennsylvania, and most of West Virginia.

Staunton also is the home of my old Colorado neighbor and close friend, Buck. To our family, he was known as "Uncle Buck." My daughter, Kerri, was on the James Madison University faculty at Harrisonburg, just thirty miles north of Staunton. Visits to Kerri were accompanied by visits to Buck and his family. The visits offered me an opportunity to rekindle friendships and become familiar with the beautiful Shenandoah Valley. *This* visit, which was designed to visit with Buck, unfolds into a much greater opportunity.

Staunton with the population of approximately 24,000, is the seat of Augusta County and the principle city of the Staunton-Waynesboro metropolitan area. Waynesboro, population approximately 21,000, is located about ten miles east of Staunton. Much of the 118,000 population of the Staunton-Waynesboro metropolitan area lives in Augusta County, beyond the limits of the two cities.

In 1732, John Lewis and family were the first to settle in the area, followed closely in 1736 by William Beverley, who received a 118,491-acre land grant from the British Crown. The town, developed at Beverly's Mill Place, was platted in 1747. It is named in honor of Lady Rebecca Staunton, the wife of Royal Lieutenant Governor Sir William Gooch.

During its early years, the town of Staunton was connected to government, power, wealth, culture, and sophistication: traditions that all remain today.

Geographically, Staunton sits in the midst of the beautiful Shenandoah Valley, which is bracketed by the Appalachian Mountains to the west and the Blue Ridge Mountains to the east. The picturesque valley runs northeast and southwest, from Winchester to the north and Roanoke to the south, approximately. The lush vegetation of trees and grass provides what appears to be a soft, peaceful landscape that exudes its calming beauty over the towns along the route. The Shenandoah Valley's natural setting seems to demand beauty and quality of life from the towns, communities, and people.

By the middle of the nineteenth century, Staunton began laying a foundation of services that remain an integral aspect of today's culture. Location attracted early transportation amenities, such as improved roads north and south, as well as east and west. By mid-century, the railroad that reached the area further improved access for people and marketing of agriculture products: an endeavor that remains today. The Staunton/Augusta Farmers Market, which opened in 1993, is currently one of Virginia's most successful markets.

In 1828, the establishment of one of the first institutions to serve mentally handicapped persons continues today as Western State Hospital. During the first half of the nineteenth century, Staunton perceived the need to educate all people, with a focus on underserved populations. Leaders of Staunton pursued and gained a state-level "special needs" school.

In 1838, the Virginia State Legislature selected Staunton as the site for the educational facility to serve children with sight and hearing handicaps. The school, now called the Virginian School for the Deaf and Blind, continues innovative services to persons with special needs, offering an outreach program that enables students to attend VSBD part-time, while maintaining attendance and academic progress at their community school.

The decade of the 1840s saw three female academies open in Staunton. The most famous began in 1842: the Augusta Female Seminary, a Presbyterian school founded by Rufus W. Bailey. The institution continues today as Mary Baldwin College, named for the school alumnus who led them through the troubled times of the Civil War.

The 1870s saw three more educational areas open up in the Staunton community. The first was schools for the African-American community; the second was the public school system of Staunton; and the third was Staunton Military Academy. Today, the Staunton Military Academy, Virginian School for the Deaf and Blind, and Western State Hospital all remain—even after 150 years of service.

Staunton also has an equally strong commitment to the theatre and arts. Among the many attractions are the Woodrow Wilson Presidential Library and the Museum of American Frontier Culture. An example of theatres and theatrical companies is the American Shakespeare Company of the Blackfriars Playhouse, a replica of Shakespeare's playhouse of the same name. The locally renowned Stonewall Brigade Band was originally formed as the Staunton Mountain Sax Horn Band. Five of the band members became members of General Stonewall Jackson's Brigade during the Civil War and thus changed their name. Last but not least, for country-western fans, the Statler Brothers have maintained their residence and community presence in their hometown of Staunton. They purchased their old elementary school, which was then renovated into their museum. As we will soon learn from Buck, the arts transcend traditional settings and include the accessibility of free park performances.

Our tour of several parts of Staunton, a beautiful campground, and friendly people all have me excited about a peaceful evening and eagerly anticipating tomorrow.

Saturday night around the campfire is relaxing. Mo visits our neighbors on both sides of our camper. She has been a good dawg, and I trust that she will behave herself. She behaves . . . until temptation overrides common sense, and my back is turned to her. When I am not looking, she does a smell-check of one of our neighbor's charcoal grills, which belongs to two women from Quebec, Canada. They speak French and minimal English. My English with nil French creates a language barrier. Needless to say, I apologize and try to make an uncaring dawg show humility. They understand very little of what I say, though I do recognize one lady gruffly using the word "chien," French for "dawg." My apology and Mo's uncaring attitude has minimal affect on creating a harmonious neighborhood. Two ladies, who were not dawg lovers before today, are less dawg lovers tonight. Thank you, Mo.

One Golden Retriever stays close to our campfire for the remainder of the short evening. But on the bright side, for protection, every time our neighbors see Mo outside, they "circle their wagons" for prevention or protection. They are prepared to defend themselves. Some people are quick learners, while some dawgs never learn. One human and one dawg retire early to a safe haven in the camper.

On Sunday morning, a five-mile walk and working around the camper are somewhat awkward, while having one hand occupied with a leashed dawg. Mo has forgotten, or does not care, why she is confined to a leash. But I remember. This afternoon, we are going to visit Buck and reminisce about old times from our Colorado days. I am sure that a dawg story, horse story, and kid story will add humor to the conversation.

Mo's and my tour of Staunton reveals an old, well-maintained downtown, many parks filled with people, Woodrow Wilson's home, the Statler Brothers' Museum, and many other sights. Eventually, our tour leads us to Buck's townhouse. Buck and I visit, watch the NASCAR race, and catch up on old times. Thirty plus years ago I was fascinated with Buck's knowledge of the history of

Central Virginia, Augusta County, and Staunton. Our conversation today resurfaces my awareness of his knowledge. I decide to break two rules: no Sunday interviews and no interviews of close friends or family. Buck's stories make my decision a good one.

True to form, Buck begins with an impact statement, one I do not suspect. Instead of leading with a story about Staunton, he makes a historical statement about America's founding fathers. He says, "The United States basically started out of Boston and Virginia." There is some Virginia pride in his remark, but I certainly cannot argue with his statement. He continues by stating, "Several very active members of the Constitutional Convention were from Virginia and Boston. They laid the foundation of the two primary political parties we know today."

George Washington, first president and commander of the Revolutionary Army, was a Virginian. Thomas Jefferson, the third president and a Virginian, was the author of the Declaration of Independence. James Madison, the fourth president and also a Virginian, argued many points that were instrumental in the formulation of the Constitution. The historical dialogue and disagreement between John Adams (the second president) and Thomas Jefferson about implementation of the Constitution accent the great thinkers and leaders and their contributions to the founding of America. Ironically, two of these great Americans—John Adams and Thomas Jefferson—passed away on the same day: July 4, 1826, fifty years to the day after approving the Articles of Confederation.

In moments Buck is telling me the story of the early years of Staunton and Augusta County. He is on a historical roll. He chronicles:

> The county of Augusta was formed in 1737, when it broke away from Orange County. At one time [i.e., originally], Augusta County extended as far north as Pittsburgh [Pennsylvania] and as far west as the Mississippi River. At that time, West Virginia was part of Augusta County and Virginia. West Virginia broke away [from Virginia] during the Civil War and fought with the North. They became a state in 1866.

I am continually amazed at not only his historical knowledge but also his attention to detail.

Staunton established its prestige early by being named the capitol of the Northwest Territory. Two railroads running through town provided early transportation and the means to attract wealth. Buck says:

The town is full of money. There is no industry, because it is not wanted within the city limits. It has always been that way. There has been little change since 1950, due to no industry. Downtown is healthy. We have very little crime. The strip mall is deteriorating because of corporate retail stores. Many little stores have closed.

There is an irony that corporate stores in Staunton are leading to the deterioration of strip malls. This phenomenon is directly counter to the accounts of many previous statements by participants of small towns. The people have predominantly claimed that corporate stores *created* the development of strip malls.

Buck changes from material to social issues, which I recall as always having been important to him. During our time together in Colorado, when he would discuss Staunton, Buck would always focus on the people. His stories were often personal.

Buck states with pride, "County and town people have a lot of interaction." He embellishes his remarks by adding that the interaction occurs not only at the governing level but also at the individual level of communication. As always, he believes that historic events and people set the stage for today. One such issue is the integration process of his southern town.

He expounds on the healthy social and cultural environment today and the contribution to successful integration over forty years ago. He explains, "There are no racial problems. Integration was smooth thanks to one man, Thomas McSwain, the superintendent of schools. His leadership of integrating the school system was a model for the remainder of society." A detailed history of McSwain's life contained in an obituary depicts him as a leader who could build community. He passed away on April 24, 2010, at the age of ninety-five years.

Staunton has always been a center for education. "Mary Baldwin College, until recently, was an all-women's school. Male students may now attend Mary Baldwin, but they cannot reside on campus," Buck states. His previous home was about one block from the campus. A few years ago I, myself, would walk on their track.

At one time, there were two military schools for boys. Buck explains, "Staunton Military School was located in the town, and Augusta Military School was located ten miles from Staunton. Both were schools for male students. Currently, there is a private school, Stuart Hall High School, open to students outside of Staunton."

Staunton is very supportive of the arts and public amenities, such as parks, sports, and golf courses. Buck proudly states, "There is a lot of culture [arts], such as theater. Shakespeare is one of the very popular theater attractions." With a big smile, he tells me, "Stonewall Jackson Brigade plays in Gypsy Park on Monday nights, Tuesday is jazz night, and Wednesday night is country and western. These events occur from Memorial Day through Labor Day."

When we lived in Colorado during the 1970s, Buck would tell me about the free Statler Brothers concert on the Fourth of July in the park. He would explain that on the day before the concert, people would place lawn chairs in the park to reserve their spots for the concert. I recall thinking, *What a public-spirited town and community!*

He further explains now that Staunton has three public golf courses, Little League baseball, and summer college baseball.

We could not conclude our conversation without discussing a Saturday-morning farmers market. Buck and Barb, his wife, enjoyed picking vegetables. Buck tells me with pride, "On Saturday morning, there is a farmers' market at Warf City [a parking lot]. I go about every Saturday." It is good to know some things never change.

Buck is very proud of the town he always called home, whether he lived in Alaska, Greenland, Colorado, or Staunton. Our conversation today, my many visits to the area, and hearing stories as a neighbor all validate Buck's statements: "Staunton is a good place to live. It is a good place to raise kids."

Buck walks me to the truck and says "hi" to Mo. We recall the years when Buck's Irish Setter, Darcy, and my Golden Retriever, Boomer, terrorized the neighborhood. Actually, I remember four kids who also did pretty well keeping things stirred up. After a few memories and laughs, Buck looks at Mo and asks, "Is Mo as mischievous as Boomer?" Without hesitation I reply, "Worse." Then I give Mo a big hug, thank Buck, and say farewell. I walk away with a tear in my eye.

It is really good to visit with Buck. Catching up on our lives and reminiscing was very meaningful. Buck's participation in an interview, sharing his knowledge of Staunton, and most importantly, his pride all result in an unexpected pleasure. Staunton is not a small town in population, but it is in characteristics: community, neighbors, and sharing good and difficult times. The characteristics exemplify my idea of a small town and the concepts spoken by many of the people I have met during my four trips through rural American.

No matter how many miles away from the Shenandoah Valley he is, Buck never forgets his hometown or his roots. He is a man of strong character and a contagious laugh. It was difficult, however, visiting him without having Barb there to add her thoughts and give us guidance. Losing her a few years ago left a void in our visit today, not to mention a much larger hole in the lives of her family. Thank you, Buck!

Back at the campground, I do some necessary housekeeping in preparation for a busy week of traveling and talking with rural Americans. During our walk and outside camper work, Mo stays close: not by her own choice, but for the sake of goodwill in the neighborhood. She has fun, meets new people, and does her thing. One event cannot break her spirit. Her attitude of "moving on" is contagious. I am not and was not upset with her. Her lust for life and fun sometimes take on human values. I do not care. It is part of hanging out with a dawg. She is a dawg and will do dawg things. She is not easily dissuaded, especially when she thinks she is right. The best I can hope for is not to change her mind, but rather to alter the course of her actions.

With the arrival of darkness, I start transcribing notes while Mo catches a one-eyed nap on what has become her couch. I wonder what she is thinking?

Mo

This couch is getting to be one of my favorite places. Notice I said "my." The use of "my" was spoken with intent and purpose. Early evening, while the lights are shining, is not a good time for a sound, two-eyed sleep. It *is*, however, a good time to reflect and make sense of my experiences. As I ponder the occurrences of the last two days, I think about meeting Randy's long-time friend and learning about what my human's life was like before I came along. I enjoy making new friends and seeing new sights.

A problem that lingers on my mind, however, is how some dawgs' actions are misleading. I bet you think you know where this going? Many people consider dawgs as "man's best friend [gender neutral]." But. (And there is always a "but" when things are not totally as smooth as a Golden's coat of hair.) Our mission in life is to protect our human, not always an easy task. A knock on our house door means that I race to the door and get between Randy and the visitor. Meeting a new person or dawg on the street or road requires me to grant approval, again, being first on the scene. Some people think we bark just to hear ourselves bark—not true. Each bark actually provides a message or sounds a warning.

In conjunction with all of our duties, one that is little known is our mission to ensure that food is safe for human consumption. (See? You just *thought* you knew where this was going.) In many instances, particularly those involving green beans or carrots, a smell is usually sufficient. Other times, especially involving meat, more caution is necessary, such as tasting or eating a sample. Tasting is always an option but is not always applied. Again, it is situational. Sometimes a smell is enough to ascertain (another dawg big word) that the meat is safe, and under no circumstances will it require a taste. This frequently occurs with an over-abundance of garlic, onions, or other spicy seasoning on meat.

A good learning point for humans, especially those not well versed in dawgology, is dawgs' responsibility to guard and protect your food. If you don't need a dawg's assistance in determining fitness of food to eat, tell us. Of course, some over-protective, assertive dawgs, which I am not, may override your decision. But if you only *think* the food is good, rather than knowing for sure, then you probably need assistance. In that situation, you should secure the expertise of your friendly dawg. Many dawgs, including me, are available to help neighbors, friends, or anyone who is not fortunate enough to share his or her life with a happy tail-wagger.

Randy

Interstate 81 is the door, and the mountains framing the highway are the windows for a new week of adventure. Our path is the same one taken by settlers almost three centuries prior, when they headed toward an unchartered life in an unknown country. The great American spirit of seeing over the next mountain or around the curve is what drove them. The surrounding beauty and the belief of the beauty over the horizon both undoubtedly provided encouragement for them to continue their exploration.

Meeting people and viewing the beauty beyond the view through my windshield are exciting thoughts that compel us to search for towns and communities. What was once an old Native American path has been transformed into a highway and serves us well as we continue our exciting, but less adventurous modern-day exploration. Breakfast and an interview are foremost on my mind. Lexington, which is about a thirty-minute drive from Staunton, appears to be the likely spot.

Lexington, the seat of Rockbridge County, is the home of Washington and Lee University, and Virginia Military Institute. Many homes and other structures are older buildings, but well maintained. Their beauty and style commemorate the South as it appeared prior to the Civil War. Stonewall Jackson's home is one of those buildings. History and historical buildings support tourism, one of the community's largest industries. Stonewall Jackson, Robert E. Lee, and Traveller, Lee's big grey horse, are all buried in the beautiful small, historic town. It is interesting to note that two well-known men of history were born in Rockbridge County: Cyrus McCormick, the inventor of the reaper (for harvesting small grain), and Sam Houston, a senator from two states who was active in the settlement of Texas.

Like Augusta County, the area that is now Rockbridge County began with a royal grant. Benjamin Border, recipient of the grant, made portions of the land available to farmers wishing to settle in the area. The county received its name from the rock bridge, which later became known as the Natural Bridge of Virginia. It is believed that the rock bridge, which is considered by some to be one of the seven natural wonders of the world, was formed when a cavern collapsed. Native American legend states that the bridge appeared just in time to provide an escape path for the Monacan tribe to escape from an enemy. The phenomenal bridge, regardless of origin, stands today.

The Virginia Legislature established Lexington as a town and county seat of Rockbridge County in 1778. They chose "Lexington" as the name to commemorate the first great battle of the Revolutionary War. In 1790 Lexington established its future educational industry with the Liberty Hall Academy. Today, secondary education is their primary industry, employing over 30% of the population.

Lexington has a population of approximately 7,000, while Rockbridge County a little over 22,000.

The crowded parking lot of a fast-food restaurant entices me for breakfast, and it is here I meet Ray. We begin a conversation that becomes an interview. He talks with me about growing up in Lexington and how it has changed. He begins by saying, "It [Lexington] is a different community than when I grew up during the 1950s and early 1960s. Most of my kin [relatives] lived on the same street. We borrowed from each other. My grandfather and his brother had twenty-six kids." He smiles and says, "There were a lot of relatives."

Ray reflects for a moment and continues by adding:

> The culture has changed since I was a kid. People helped each other while I was growing up. People seemed to be more honest when I was a kid. Television created a big change. We used to get one channel. Some peo-

ple on the hill got two channels. There is so much knowledge now. Today, we get state, country, and world news on several channels. Media make it a lot different.

Ray concisely summarizes how media has made the world seem smaller in comparison to fifty years ago, when we both had children.

There are a few moments of silence as Ray and I reflect. It seems as if we are suspended in time while we ponder his statement. I think of my teenage years and what it was like listening to the radio. Big news back then would have been a murder in Indianapolis, our state capitol fifty miles away. Today, murder seems more common and is hardly news, but it still always brings the same reflective question: "Why?" Why does someone take another person's life? I did not understand fifty years ago, and I do not understand today. A question that lingers for me is, is murder more prevalent today, or does the media provide better, timely news?

I continue my reflection concerning two issues that I previously heard from interview participants. The first is the similarity of Ray's and Toni's statements about family living on the same street. Families, including mine, seemed to coalesce during the middle of the Twentieth Century and prior times.

My second thought involves comments by Don of Calvert City and Ray about mass media. Don viewed media of today as detriment for local news and knowing about community. Ray, on the other hand, believed mass media and world news was a positive characteristic. A plausible answer may be that Ray lives in a town with television stations at nearby Roanoke-Lynchburg, where as Don's community had access to one channel within 80 miles. Lexington's proximity to TV stations plus location of being in the same region and state makes local news reporting more likely.

Ray pulls me from my trance when he tells me, "I was in the navy twenty-five years. I got out after four years, then went back into the navy. I enjoyed my military career, but I also enjoy being back in Lexington." Ray pauses briefly and continues: "I enjoy talking about Lexington, but my knowledge about the area has limitations. It would be good if we could find someone who can address recent years." After a visual search, he smiles, looks across the room, and says, "There is Frankie. He knows a lot about Lexington and Rockbridge County. He will talk with you." Before I can say, "That would be great," Ray quickly crosses the room and speaks with Frankie. He returns and tells me Frankie will join us in a couple of minutes after he, Frankie, finishes breakfast.

Did someone say that people do not help each other today? Not Ray, and as it turns out, not Frankie, either. They both are "old school." I thank Ray for his time and his help. He introduces me to Frankie and listens to our conversation a short time before leaving for another engagement. As I say thanks to Ray, I think, *Life is good in rural America. People still help each other, especially the senior generation. Perhaps the younger generation does, too, and we do not recognize it.*

My thoughts abruptly transfer to Frankie as he begins explaining that he lives in Buena Vista, located about six miles east of Lexington, in Rockbridge County. He grew up in the small industrial town during the 1950s. Frankie says, "The population has remained about the same since I was a kid. A picture of a 1971 sign states 'Buena Vista: 6,002 Happy Citizens and 3 Old Grouches.'"

Buena Vista, a town with a rich *Old South* culture, has a population of 6,650 Frankie tells me.

The village, originally named "Green Forest," was granted a town charter in 1890. The growth and ensuing charter can be attributed mostly to the efforts of Benjamin C. Moomaw and the arrival of the railroad in 1880, which enticed several businesses.

Frankie is very active in the community. He tells me, "I was a disc jockey, and for twelve years, I did the play-by-play for football and basketball games." He continues, "On Friday nights the whole town turns out for football games. We have between 5,000 and 6,000 people at each game." Frankie adds, "I serve on the Buena Vista City Council."

He tells me that his mother was a schoolteacher, his dad was an industrial electrician, and his son served in the United States Air Force. Frankie feels honored by his mother's dedication to the youth of her community and his son's service to the country. He has followed the family tradition as a committed public servant.

Following the brief introduction of himself and his family, Frankie transitions to a cherished time of his life: his youth and teenage years. He describes:

> When I was young, the people of my small town helped each other. Sense of community and helping each other is still present today, but [is] not as strong. Friday nights, Saturdays, and Saturday nights were big in Lexington and Buena Vista. They were both big business towns. We used to hang out at Seay's Drug Store and the Main Street Drug Store. They had soda fountains. There were no drive-ins. The American Legion had dances for teenagers on Friday nights, usually sock hops. Once in a while, they would have live music. Those things are now gone.

Two things appear to be prevalent when people tell me about their teenage years: first, a smile always accompanies the explanation, and second, the hangouts usually no longer exist.

Frankie explains the four greatest changes of Buena Vista: "The loss of retail stores, industry leaving the area, school consolidation, and new people moving into our community." He momentarily reflects before continuing, "The loss of retail stores has changed downtown."

I expect him to discuss these issues in the order he mentioned. Instead, he pauses and reestablishes the order by grouping the loss of retail stores and the influx of new people together at the *end* of his thoughts, accentuating their affects on culture.

He *begins* with an embellishment of how the loss of industry has affected the area:

> Flooding was a great issue in losing some industries. The Maury River, which bisects Buena Vista, has a history of flooding. We had a lot of industry until the floods of 1969 and 1985. Hurricane Camille hit in 1969. There was another flood in 1985. Several industries left following the floods. Some of the lost industries include Reeves' Brothers, a magnet wire company. There also was a large silk mill. Today, Mohawk Carpet, which is located in Glasgow about seventeen miles away, employs around 15,000 people. Our people have to go somewhere else to work.

Closure of the silk mill may be attributed to the national trend of the late 1900s and early 2000s of moving fabric operations to overseas locations. Most of those moves were due to labor costs. Whatever the issues, loss of industry impacted Buena Vista, Virginia. Residents must choose between traveling to work and moving.

Rockbridge County school consolidation created considerable changes to the community, especially socially and economically. The school districts of Rockbridge County, as in many rural communities, have experienced major consolidation. Frankie reflects, "At one time, there were five school districts in Rockbridge County. Now there are only two: Lexington and Rockbridge County['s] consolidated schools. The consolidation included schools located in Buena Vista, Natural Bridge, and Fairfield." School closings create an array of feelings about the affect on education and community. Regardless of the feelings, there is always a period of adjustment after school consolidations. Frankie ends his remarks about school closures by stating, "Lexington and Buena Vista were always big rivals."

The cultural and social behaviors of Buena Vista have changed during the past few years. Some of these changes can be attributed to new residents. Another issue, the loss of old businesses that represented the "Old South" culture, has pronouncedly affected culture and tourism. Frankie expounds:

> Many of the new people do not share the importance of our local heritage of being an old Southern town. Many of our new people did not come from an old Southern culture. Another issue is the loss of older, established retail businesses. The loss of established retail businesses, which exuded Southern culture, changed the character of the town. Some of losses of businesses and other changes have made it difficult to promote our legacy as an old town of the South. It has negatively affected our tourism industry.

As he speaks, the emphasis of Frankie's voice and mannerisms accent his strength of belief concerning these issues as being instrumental to both the change of culture and the loss of tourism. He does not allow, however, the loss of Southern culture to impede his positive beliefs about the future.

He quickly transitions to a positive amenity in Buena Vista: that is, an institution of higher learning. Frankie explains, "Southern Virginia University has a little over 800 students. The university is not church-affiliated; however, students are required to adhere to an honor code that includes dress and moral standards." The small university obviously contributes to the social and cultural aspect of Buena Vista and its community. It also provides educational opportunities for local and out-of-area residents, as well as enhancing the economy.

Frankie demonstrates his positive attitude and faith in Buena Vista with other positive thoughts. He proudly claims, "One constant is a very, very low crime rate—and no gangs. Continuing public relations about criminal activities and gangs by our police personnel are factors in the success." He momentarily pauses and says, "Young folks have to go somewhere else to find employment." He concludes with a smile and a positive remark, "Buena Vista is a bustling little town."

His pride and commitment to Buena Visit and Rockbridge County is etched in his smile. He states his appreciation to me for the opportunity to talk about his town. I thank him and say, "With your contagious positive attitude, Buena Visit will remain a bustling town."

Mo and I head west on Interstate 64. It takes us about two hours to travel seventy-five miles on the winding, hilly road. Our slow speed can be attributed, in part, to gazing at the beautiful mountain scenery, seasonal fall colors, and babbling streams. In late morning we officially exit the Appalachian Mountains and enter the Allegheny Mountains. In my mind, crossing the state line into West Virginia coincides with the demarcation of mountain ranges. This is my lucky day; I love the mountains. We travel on until a sign identifies our next stop, stating in bold letters "Lewisburg: Coolest Little Town in America."

My curiosity to learn about the "Coolest Little Town in America" gets the best of me. Whether it is time to stop or not, we are going to stop. My passion of the hour is to learn the story of why and how Lewisburg became one of the "coolest" towns in America. Our short drive to town allows me to set the stage of the "Coolest Town" and neighboring communities.

The rural area surrounding Lewisburg, known as Greenbrier County, is a focal point of beauty and activities that make it a highly desirable tourist destination. Lewisburg, the seat of Greenbrier County, has about 4,000 residents. The county is home to about 35,000 people and eight towns (seven incorporated and one unincorporated).

Greenbrier County was formed in 1778. Its history, as is true of many small towns and communities, is not only interesting but also the foundation of the future, if for no other reason than the rich culture and tradition, passed down through the generations.

According to Native American myth, the area of Greenbrier County hosts the bones and ghosts of European settlers, known by Shawnee as "Azgens." The legend continues that Shawnee ancestors annihilated the Azgens. The identified spiritual area could only be hunted with the adherence to very strict rules. Folklore prohibited settlements and homesteads. Shawnee belief was that violation of the rules would result in ghosts rising from the caves and slaying the people. The Native Americans, of course, fought to preserve their ancestral beliefs and the hunting grounds.

Lewisburg is named for Andrew Lewis, a surveyor of the area in 1751 and later, an army colonel. As an army colonel, Lewis and his over-1,000 men defeated the famous Shawnee Chief Cornstalk in 1774, during the Battle of Point Pleasant. The victory ceased the Native American raids of 1763 termed "Pontiac's Rebellion," which destroyed two European settlements in Green County due to the fact that during the raids, men were killed and women and children were captured, virtually eliminating the earliest settlers of Greenbrier County.

Greenbrier citizens withstood many battles of early day settlements, as well as those of the Civil War. Their generational resolve gave citizens the strength to build a thriving town, community, and county. Today, Lewisburg has many industries, one of which is tourism—without motels.

Lewisburg is the home of the West Virginia School of Osteopathic Medicine, one of twenty-nine in the United States. In 1902, Andrew Carnegie donated money to build a Carnegie Hall to house the Lewisburg Female Institute, which later became the Greenbrier College for Women. Currently, the hall is the home of an incorporated cultural center that annually serves over 75,000 patrons.

The nearby town Fairlea, population approximately 1,700, is the home of the West Virginia State Fair and the Green Brier Classic Concert Series, featuring such performers as West Virginia native Brad Paisley, Keith Urban, Reba McEntire, Rod Stewart, Lionel Richie, and other great performers. White Sulphur Springs, nine miles away, also hosts a Professional Golf Association tournament. Lewistown, Fairlea, and White Sulphur Springs all attract many visitors with their activities, beauty, and hospitality. The golf classic and music concert, held during the same dates, allow for long days of fun-packed entertainment. Tourism transcends Lewisburg to include Green Brier County.

A sign indicating a left turn brings me back to the reality of driving. A short drive on US Highway 219 leads to downtown Lewisburg. Mo and I immediately engage in a scenic walk of downtown streets. We walk Jefferson Street, passing Greenbrier Valley Baking Company. We turn and walk down Washington Street, transiting the Stardust Café, The Wild Bean, and Julian's Restaurant. The few people walking the streets are tourists, enjoying the same sights as Mo and I. Being interrupted for an interview would surely rate just below a flat tire on their list of fun events.

Interview possibilities look bleak, as most residents have abandoned the streets for work. When all else fails, I find a bench and develop a plan.

I sit, lost in thought, on a bench in a small park on Jefferson Street. When a local resident stops to pet Mo, the sun brightens. Eventually, she realizes there is a human on the other end of the leash. You know the routine. She asks me "Mo questions": "What's her name?" and "What breed is she?"

I am tempted to say, "Her name is 'Rowdy,'" but I realize that humility is the best course. I reply, "[Her name is] 'Mo,' and she is a Golden Retriever."

The woman continues to pet and talk with Mo. Of course, Mo, who has received no attention all day, is basking in the limelight. Finally, the lady and I begin a conversation, which leads to me explaining my research and asking if there is someone I can talk with about the beautiful town. She ponders briefly and states, "I'm on my way to the bank–" Stopping in mid-sentence, she then says, "Come back to the art gallery; I can go to the bank later."

I murmur under my breath, "Thanks, Mo! You bailed me out again."

The woman, whose name is Ellen, leads the way as we walk about half a block to the Tuckwiller Art Gallery. As we walk, she tells me that she is employed as a nursing-home activities director and also works one day a week for her cousin at the art gallery. Ellen explains that her cousin is the owner of Tuckwiller, and her brother, Robert Tuckwiller, is the artist. He lives in Newport, Virginia, about a one-and-a-half-hour drive from Lewisburg.

When I take my first steps through the door of Tuckwiller Art Gallery on Washington Street, I know that a painting will leave with me, no matter how hard I resist. An hour and a half later, and my concern becomes reality. As I write this, a painting of a man and dawg riding on a horse-drawn sled while crossing a shallow stream adorns my living room wall.

Ellen begins her story by telling me that she lived much of her life away from Lewisburg:

> I grew up here [and] married a navy man. When he passed away, I came back home. My sister told me that I would not like it because it had changed. It has changed, but I like living in Lewisburg. The increased number of people is a big issue. Growing up in the 1950s and 1960s, it was much smaller. You knew practically everyone on the streets. If I skipped school or went to the drug store for lunch, my parents knew before I got home from school.

Her last statement depicts the same adage I have heard from many rural people: namely, that adults took shared responsibility for the well-being of all the kids in their community.

The comments about parenting lead Ellen to transition her thoughts to family. As she begins to talk about her childhood home, her cousin (the owner of Tuckwiller Gallery) enters the gallery. Her cousin's timeliness is perfect, as if she planned her arrival to add to the discussion about family.

Following introductions, she busies herself with paperwork, but occasionally takes time to add an insightful comment. Ellen continues:

The farm where we lived was the farm my great-great-great grandfather bought for one of his daughters. He bought houses for all his daughters when they got married. A lot of kinfolk live around here. A lot of kinfolk are buried here. My dad was also the sheriff. He and my grandfather owned a Ford automobile dealership. My grandfather sold Model T's [Ford cars].

Ellen pauses as if to collect her thoughts and decide how the story should continue. Her pause allows time for me to reflect that farms frequently remain in the family for several generations. It seems a farm creates an emotional tie between generations.

Ellen then shifts her story to her childhood education experiences. "I went to a two- or three-room school, with grades first to eighth. For high school, we were bussed into town." Her school pride becomes evident as she states, "When we were in high school, kids from our school could conjugate verbs and do math that town students could not do. There were sixty-eight students in our grade school and sixty-nine in our graduating class." These statements clearly depict her pride in having been a country kid who attended a small elementary school.

A short pause, and she transfers to the social aspect of her teenage years:
Friday and Saturday nights were not special in Lewisburg when I was a kid. We had a drive-in restaurant, Spud's, which is still open. Neely, who was a dairy farmer, owned a shop on the corner. They sold ice cream and milkshakes. The neon cow in front of his building marked our hangout.

She briefly pauses, then jumps to another aspect of her youth that was obviously both very meaningful and joyous:
Neighbors used to help each other. Nobody could afford all the equipment needed for farming, so neighbors shared work. Women fixed big lunches. We had community events in churches, such as chicken and fish dinners. We had bear-meat dinners [social gatherings with bear meat served as the main dish]. They also served "wraps," which were like wild onions.

Her comments about bear meat and "wraps" reflect her pride in the uniqueness of West Virginia. Her description of events clearly explains the closeness of people and the power of the community. Together, the statements accent

West Virginia's mountain heritage and pride of living outside the mainstream. If I lived in West Virginia, I would feel the same.

Our conversation halts for a few moments as Ellen considers the next words to express her thoughts. She begins by stating:

Lewisburg has lost several businesses during last several years. We had two grocery stores, a shoe store, [a] clothing store, and a jewelry store that [all] have now closed. Now we have a mall at Fairlea, about two miles away. [In] the other direction, we have two large retail stores.

Changes in her hometown go beyond businesses, extending to people and culture:

Lewisburg has grown over the years since I grew up on a farm. A lot of new people have moved into Lewisburg. Many of them have moved here to retire. The new people affect the culture. They like the life [here], but when they get here, they want things to be the way they were before they [the people] moved.

Ellen continues by providing an example of a simple but notable change in culture: "If you are trying to make a left turn, native residents will allow you to make the turn as they wait. New people do not wait." In Ellen's view, this small gesture speaks volumes about neighborly small-town attitudes.

Even though the people and culture have changed, Ellen still exudes pride about Lewisburg and it progress. She believes that the progression of three specific industries has been a factor in the recovery of her hometown. She claims, "Our main industries are farming, education, and tourism. She frequently uses the term "people industry" to include education and tourism. This is a purposeful terminology because she attaches great importance to serving people. She adds, "Farming consists mainly of beef and dairy cattle. There are some turkey farms." As we continue our conversation, she adds that all three industries combined are important and not discussed in their order of significance.

The conversation then changes to the growth of education. She explains, "Education is part of the people industry. Our educational profession has contributed to the economic structure and well-being of communities beyond Lewisburg. We educate people that serve well beyond Greenbrier County."

The growth can be illustrated by two previous educational facilities being converted to meet the present needs of the community and society beyond Green Brier County. Ellen says, "Greenbrier Military School has been converted into the West Virginia School of Osteopathic Medicine." This public university was founded in 1972 and annually serves approximately 800 students. Ellen continues, "A second educational facility, Greenbrier Community College, occupies the previous facilities of the Greenbrier Women's College, a seminary. Greenbrier is a branch of New River Community and Technical College." She summarizes the value of education by stating, "The educational profession has greatly contributed to the community economically, socially, and professionally. Our education programs affect [places] beyond Greenbrier County...."

The thriving tourism industry has been a great boost to the Lewisburg community. This industry requires planning, effort, perseverance, and strong community. Ellen states, "Thirty years ago, some people thought we needed to have an industry. Most people agreed that tourism should be that industry. They [the local people] developed a plan to assume the historical perspective. The plan was meticulously developed and implemented."

An example of planning and action involved negotiation with the state government of West Virginia. An issue deemed small and insignificant at the state level was of huge importance to the people of Lewisburg. Ellen expounds, "The tourism committee petitioned the state government to change the interstate signs to a historical look. When the state refused, the people of Lewisburg formed a phone tree [arranged for several people] to call state officials. State officials changed the signs."

Signage was important but only one element of changing the town's image. Ellen adds, "The electrical lights [in town] look like gaslights." The emphasis of her statement speaks clearly to the importance that she attaches to the new lighting. As our conversation continues it becomes more obvious that each element of their plan, although one aspect, combines to create the historical image and enhance tourism of Lewisburg. She concludes her comments on this topic by saying, "The amenities are worth the effort; they add to the historical ambiance of the town."

Ellen proudly transitions to a historical event that is a fixture in the community. Ellen relates the story:

> We have one annual parade that commemorates Lewisburg's history. The New Year's Day Shanghai Parade is open to everyone and is conducted no matter the weather. The last person in the parade, usually the sheriff, carries a "pooper scooper" to pick up horse droppings. The pooper-scooper person is considered a position of honor. The parade is based on the log-

gers' traditional New Year's Day exit from town. The somewhat-inebriated loggers would grab bystanders to walk with them as they strolled down the street. Thus, the tradition of the Shanghai Parade was born and has become embedded as part of our culture.

Some minor good humored practices, such as loggers a century ago, enticing citizens to walk with them as they departed town on New Yea's Day created an annual parade. It is amazing to me how some small acts by people can create traditions that endure and become end posts that anchor the fence of life.

Ellen shifts in her chair and looks me directly in the eye: "We have a lot of cultural events for a small town. The Trillium Theater has dance productions, gives dance classes, and also shows old and new movies." She thinks for a few seconds, then says, "A theater group, Green Valley Theater, has plays and musical concerts. Every month there is a new play. Sometimes we have two or three [plays] running at a time. We also have a Carnegie Hall built by Andrew Carnegie."

Lewisburg is in a good location. Ellen says, "Charleston is one-and-one-half hours away. The state fair is in Fairlea, two miles away. Greenbrier Hotel at White Sulphur Springs [is] nine miles away. White Sulphur Springs hosts an annual professional golf tournament, with live concerts at night during the competition." The area, through planning or non-planning, has established a tourism industry that provides an economic base for the small towns to flourish—while maintaining their culture of mountain life.

With a smile, Ellen ends, "Lewisburg is a nice place to live." I add, "If your choice in lifestyle is a small, friendly town with a purpose [that is] surrounded by beautiful, scenic mountains, [then] Lewisburg, West Virginia would be a great choice. It certainly meets my criteria of a nice place to live." She smiles and states, "You summed it up well."

I thank Ellen and her cousin for sharing their vast knowledge of Lewisburg and Greenbrier County, as well as for helping me select a meaningful painting that tells a story. With a painting in my right hand and a leash with a dawg in my left, I have a feeling of utopia . . . until my world suddenly transitions from peaceful tranquility to chaos.

Mo

Randy wakes me from a one-eyed sleep with the jingle of my leash and collar. I have been a good dawg. Bored, but a good dawg. As he fastens the collar, I grab the leash and growl, my signal that a tug-of-war is on. I get serious quickly, with a deeper growl and a harder yank on the leash. I notice Ellen and her cousin's astonished looks and big eyes. They believe that this is a serious fight. This is great! I met my first objective of creating a sense of reality. I then notice that Randy's face shows concern. Maybe my timing is bad, but a tough dawg cannot back down and lose face. So I escalate the battle with a more vicious growl and a stronger, heartier jerk on the leash.

Just then, Randy ruins the whole match by saying, "Mo, heel!" Good Golden Retrievers—and I am a good Golden—always follow two commands: "heel" and "sit." I am not sure why, but my mother engrained this into my behavior before she turned me loose on the world.

Randy and I walk toward the door; I have my head held high, and Randy is smiling. Everyone bids their farewells, and Ellen and her cousin show relief that their gallery is still in one piece. Randy's expression shows delight of not having to buy several damaged paintings.

All is well. We take the long walk to the truck. Randy looks at me, smiles, and states, "Well, Mo, you added excitement to the day." He smiles, gives me a big hug, and says, "You are a great dawg, Mo. You heeled when I asked you." I wag my tail and give him a well-deserved lick on his jaw.

Soon we are headed toward the sun on a wide road, with a field between us and the trucks and cars going where we have been. An hour passes before the sun moves to our right. The next two hours, we stay on the same wide road. Then, suddenly, the cars and trucks are passing close to us as they speed on their way. This kind of road requires me to be on full alert; naptime is over.

We travel forever on winding roads and up and down hills. The forests and mountains are beautiful, as are the fields of domestic-grown evergreen trees. My concern of where we will stay tonight does not seem to be shared by anyone else in the truck. It is obvious that the sun is moving toward its sleep time, and we are aimlessly heading down the road.

Randy

Our drive south on our route to North Carolina is as beautiful as our morning drive. I am in awe of West Virginia's beauty to the extent that my slow speed and frequent stops to take pictures is resulting in very slow progress. A big brown nose and two wide eyes are my constant companions. Mo seems to be enjoying the drive and scenery. Eventually, as we cross the West Virginia and North Carolina state lines, I notice the sun staring to peek over the mountaintops. Time to start searching for a campground.

CHAPTER 27

Carolinas

The sun setting heightens my concern for finding a campground. We stop in a restaurant parking lot and begin the Internet search for a campground. A quick telephone call and the sound of a reassuring voice terminate my worries. The good news is that there are vacant pull-through spots; the bad news is the campground is about a one-hour drive.

The hour passes quickly as I follow my Garmin's guidance. We finally turn off the curvy, hilly road to what I assume will be a short, final leg of our daily excursion.

Mo

We depart the highway for a gravel road that is a really narrow, steep, winding climb. Just as we turn onto the rough road, the sun goes to sleep. When we need his light the most, he says goodnight. I escalate my alert status to wide-eyed and ears up. We cannot make the first turn, so we back up and pull up, accompanied by language that hurts my sensitive ears. Finally, and I mean *finally*, we pull into the campground, set up the camper, have dinner, and walk. Then it's couch time.

Next morning, we are off for a short drive to Boone, North Carolina. When we get to the campground entrance, Randy makes a good choice: If we turn right, we will go back to the famous gravel road, and if we turn left, we will be on blacktop. He chooses a left turn . . . because I am pushing him with my nose.

Fifteen minutes later, we are in Boone. Why did we not use the blacktop road *last night*? Randy heads off to the Mountain House Restaurant. I guard the truck and take a one-eyed nap.

Randy

The beauty of the Blue Ridge Mountains comes to life in Western North Carolina in a county christened for a Native American word meaning "beautiful river" and a city named for early American explorer Daniel Boone. Boone was much more than explorer, however: He served in the Virginia Legislature and in both the French & Indian and Revolutionary Wars. He was also a father of ten and a businessman. He is most noted in history, however, for his willingness to explore and build a new life: a new life that afforded opportunities for others who followed, such as in Boone, North Carolina. The county is Watauga; the town is Boone.

In 1849, a legislative act established Watauga County with land taken from surrounding counties. Boone became a town and approximately twenty years later, the county seat. The marriage of Watauga County and Boone created a home for future generations: inhabitants who relished the same rivers and natural beauty that brought Daniel Boone back annually to hunt game. Each summer since 1952, the town celebrates its heritage by hosting an outdoor amphitheater production called *Horn in the West*. The play celebrates the life of the town's namesake and famed explorer, as well as the lives of other early settlers. The celebration and natural beauty combine to make a great tourist attraction.

The area is blessed with such natural wonders as the Watauga River, State Line Ridge, Hanging Rock Bridge, South Fork of the New River, Dugger Mountain, Egg Knob, and Blowing Rock. Many of the activities and constructed tourist attractions, such as the Appalachian Heritage and Cultural Museums, are esthetically attached to the beauty of the area. Residents of Boone and Watauga County aggressively preserve the nature that Daniel Boone so aggressively pursued during his lifetime and the beauty of a river defined by the Native American word "Watauga."

Boone had a 2010 population of 17,122: nearly double the 1970 population of 8,754. Situated at an elevation of 3,333 feet, Boone and its surrounding community have beauty and a year-round moderate climate that fuel tourism—one of the many employment prospects of the area. The other large employer is education. Appalachian State University provides excellent educational opportunities for local, state, and regional students. Friendly people add to the inviting attractiveness of the area.

Sitting and scanning the Mountain View Restaurant menu, I ask myself, "How do I keep finding such beautiful towns with knowledgeable people and great stories?" The only possible answers are 1.) luck or 2.) that the United States is blessed with numerous adoring towns and exceptional people. I choose the latter explanation because it seems more reasonable.

I also wonder how I could possibly have taken such a difficult path to the campground when an easier route was available. I like to think it was the fault of the GPS, but as the driver, it is difficult to fix responsibility on technology.

Mo is correct; the final short miles of driving last night overshadowed the entire afternoon. The memory of the difficult drive will soon be replaced, however, by my experiences of beautiful scenery and good people.

It is good to sit back, drink hot coffee, and take a deep breath. As I continue to peruse the Mountain View menu, my server refills my coffee cup. I briefly explain my project to her and ask whom I might interview. She immediately responds, "Betty, the previous owner and current cook. You really need to talk with Betty. I will ask her." A recommendation that decisive demands action; Betty, hopefully, will be my next conversation partner.

Within a few minutes, Betty appears at my table and introduces herself. She smiles, speaking with enthusiasm and excitement about sharing her story and life in Boone and Watauga County. I immediately know this is going to be a fun and informative conversation.

She begins by telling me, "I have lived here [in Boone] my whole life and grew up during the 50s. I was one of ten children living on a farm with cows, horses, and a garden. We moved to town when I was nine." Her positive demeanor clearly speaks to a happy childhood, even though she was forced to make a major adjustment to her lifestyle. She adds, "My dad was a shoe cobbler. Now there is not a shoe-repair shop in town." Her final remark is not an optimistic remark about progress.

Betty, although not in a hurry, speaks quickly and with a purpose, as she transitions our conversation to her professional life: "I have been involved in restaurants since I was eighteen years old. I have owned my business for forty years. Work is my hobby." As she continues to talk, it becomes obvious that owning a restaurant is about serving the public—more pointedly, her customers. She clearly states that greeting regular customers by name is essential in her world of food service. Betty deems that customer relationships are the responsibility of the employees. "Many customers become regulars, and a relationship is developed between them and the employees. When one of our customers die[s], it is like losing a member of the family."

Some of the employee and customer relationships may soon be jeopardized, however. Mountain View's location for the past eight years will soon change. "We lost our lease. Moving may cause loss of some customers," Betty comments. Longevity in one location develops a community of customers. "We will lose some customer-employee relationships that have developed over the past few years." Her comments and mannerisms clearly reflect that customers are friends, not sources of revenue.

As she speaks, I reflect on when I, myself, entered the Mountain View Restaurant. I received a personal greeting from the maître d', and she offered a choice of tables before informing me of my server's name. My server appeared immediately, with choices of coffee. She gave me a menu and a brief explanation of favorite choices. She then asked if I needed anything while I made my choice.

The personal friendliness creates a feeling of having eaten here many times, even though it is only my first visit. The employees treat me with TLC, as if they know about last night's troublesome drive and flashlight camper set up and today's issues of driving a truck-camper through downtown while trying to find a parking spot. But it isn't that they know; it's that all guests are honored with friendly, helpful service. Employees reflect Betty's vision of customer service.

Betty exudes the principals of servant leadership: a leader committed to meeting the needs of both customers and employees. Employees who emulate Betty's work standards are difficult to locate and maintain. She says, "[The] work ethic of some people is pitiful." Employees who do not meet her standards are let go, resulting in a high rate of employee turnover. Betty continues, adding, "Last year we had 242 W-2 forms: a big turnover of employees. People coming to America are willing to work, whereas US people are not willing to do some jobs." She believes government handouts affect work ethic among people.

Betty pauses and looks me in the eye. It is obvious that she is finding the words to discuss a serious issue. She says, "The restaurant business in Boone is going to change. Boone's recent passage of a law to sell liquor by the drink will change the restaurant business in Boone. Sale of liquor at restaurants increases profits and entices corporate-owned restaurants." Betty believes that losing locally owned restaurants will detract from the concept of neighborhood relationships between employees and customers. Local business owners know the people because they are members of the same community.

During our travels, many people have expressed that locally owned businesses possess strong employee-customer relationships.

Betty has high hopes for her hometown. She believes the future will be a reflection of the past. "Boone has always been friendly. There is little crime and not much drugs." She pauses to consider her remarks. "Things have drastically changed in business," she adds. "It is more difficult to find good people to work. This is not good for employers, workers, and the public. It is harder to find caring people."

Betty changes her focus to development: "Downtown has been built up with shops for tourism. We need to develop kid attractions, because kids have a large input into tourist destinations. With minimal industry, it is hard to survive without tourism."

Betty ends our conversation on a positive note with impact statements: "It is a great place to raise kids. We are a town with friendly people." I thank Betty and she responds that she very much enjoyed talking about Boone. I ask her one more question: "What do you recommend for breakfast?" She immediately replies, "Eggs, grits, country ham, and biscuits."

I take her advice. Breakfast is great, but much larger in size than my appetite will permit. If you are ever in Boone, North Carolina, make sure to find the new location of the Mountain View Restaurant. The atmosphere and food will be quite memorable. Perhaps you will have the opportunity to meet a great cook and an even better hostess.

Mo and I drive around Boone to see more of the town before departing for a southerly drive on US Highway 321. The state road provides good company until we pass Hickory, North Carolina. An inviting county road grabs us for a relaxing drive through beautiful country scenery of fields, grassland, and crops. We stop in some small towns to buy gas and visit with the locals. As we enter Interstate 85 toward Spartanburg and Greenville, the state and county roads end all too soon. We stay in a campground between the two towns. I had been in the area years ago, when I flew an F-101 US Air Force aircraft to the major maintenance facility located in the area. Revisiting the area forty years later causes me to think about old times and friends.

The next morning, we travel south on Interstate 185 for about forty-five minutes. The first thing I notice is that everything has changed during the years. The second thing I realize, or admit, is that I am lost. A large set of "golden arches" and a sign stating "Pelzer" do not cure my continuous impairment of being lost, but they do give me hope for an interview, breakfast, and a dose of reorientation. After minimal investigation, without the help of Mo, I realize that we are on the outskirts of Pelzer.

I eventually learn that the area we are approaching encompasses the three towns of Pelzer, West Pelzer, and Williamston. The year 2013 population review reveals that Pelzer is the smallest of the three, with ninety-one residents; West Pelzer is in the middle, with 886; and Williamston is the largest, with 4,039. All together, they have a total of slightly over 5,000 people.

Pelzer and West Pelzer, which are separated by South Carolina Highway 20, are individually incorporated, but share a post office and telephone exchange. Williamston, the remote neighbor two-and-a-half miles south, shares the Saluda River with Pelzer. As the Saluda River approaches the northern edge of Pelzer, it interrupts its southerly flow to form a horseshoe around the northern, eastern, and southern boundaries of the town, prior to assuming its southerly direction. It gives the appearance of protecting Pelzer from the world, without intruding on its relationship with West Pelzer.

The three towns share amenities, such as Anderson School District One and proximity to the large employment and market center of Greenville. Similar travel time of twenty-five to thirty-five minutes to work and parallel unemployment rates indicate that Greenville is the employment center for the towns. The three towns maintained a similar unemployment rate from the year 2000 to 2010, further supporting the fact that residents share a single employment area. The towns have maintained a stable population from 1970 to 2010.

Williamston appears to have been the first settlement. While riding horseback through his property in the year 1842, a man named West Allen Williams stopped one lazy afternoon for a nap. The product of his nap was a dream of a healing mineral spring. He awoke to a trickling sound that, of course, aroused his curiosity—to the extent that he searched the area until he found the spring. In 1851, the railroad arrived, and news of the healing water spread fast. People came from as far away as New York and other northeastern states. Williamston soon became known as the "Saratoga of the South," referencing to a similar spring in New York.

The town grew, with hotels and other amenities, until the Civil War, at which time the tourists from the North no longer visited the mineral water spring. Williamston lost its attraction and impetus to grow. After the Civil War, the towns of Pelzer and West Pelzer were formed to support the cotton industry. These two towns, along with Williamston, form one population center.

Back to reality and an attempt to answer the question, where exactly are we? The familiar setting of McDonald's, with food in hand amidst a few friendly people, makes being lost less threatening. As I approach a table occupied by two friendly senior citizens, I explain my research and tell them that I would like to talk to someone about Pelzer. Then, with a small hesitation, I add, "I am lost." My admission is followed by an immediate response: "We know. We were laughing at you."

Sara and Phil introduce themselves and ask if I would like to join them. A conversation leads to an interview and an interesting perspective of life in a "mill town" during the middle of the twentieth century. Sara was born in 1942 and raised in Pelzer. Phil has lived in the area less than fifteen years, a fact of which Sara reminds him when he becomes overzealous with facts about *her* hometown. The fun couple provides an interesting perspective about life and change in Pelzer.

Pelzer, the once energetic mill town, is not only small in population but also in landmass. The total area of the town is less than two-tenths of a square mile. Pelzer began around 1896 as a cotton mill town and was not incorporated until 1952. "Cotton mill town" means that the corporation owned the houses, stores, and most, if not all, of any other amenities.

Sara's story describes a small town, owned by a mill company. Her story weaves through the decades of the Depression and World War II to a time of social and financial employee independence. Sara's narrative continues beyond the depression and war era to a time when kids no longer assumed that mill employment was their only option. The students completed high school and sought other employment. The account parallels the transition of a town's change from a shopping-market area to a Main Street with few businesses. For me, the scenario is a blend of joy and sadness.

Sara's story begins with these words:

Three of the four local mills were physically located in town. The people who worked in the local mills lived in Pelzer, mostly in mill housing. My grandmother and grandfather lived in mill housing and worked in the mill. The next generation, my mother and dad, worked in the mill and lived in mill housing. Most people of my parent's generation did not finish high school; they went to work in the mills. The next generation, my generation, finished high school, and many moved away. My children's generation went to college and did not return.

Her comments clearly state that from the early twentieth century and through both the Great Depression and World War II, there was a close bond between the mill owners and workers: a bond that lessened with Sara's generation in the years after World War II.

During the generations of both Sara's grandparents and her parents, the people of Pelzer possessed a very strong physical sense of community that centered on public activities. Sara describes community in these words:

During the 1930s and 40s, we had a ball [baseball] team. We played a lot [of] ball. We had a mill baseball team, [and] most of the towns had their own baseball teams. In the 1940s, there was a bowling alley and motorcycle races. On the Fourth of July, we had all kinds of games and big celebrations.

She hesitates and sighs, adding, "Mom and Dad's generation looked out for each other. People would help others. After them, it all went away." Sarah paints a verbal picture that during the 1930s and 1940s, the people of Pelzer were very community oriented. Their life was focused around mill-sponsored activities, friends, and family. Those years encompassed the very difficult times of the Depression and World War II. The mill helped the workers and families through the two difficult decades.

At mid-century, the town was a lively community with many stores. Sara explains, "During the 1950s, we had a row of stores in Pelzer. There were clothing stores, a drug store, a grocery store, and a general hardware store that also sold lumber and nails." The lively marketplace was tied to the employment of the mill workers. Sara says, "All of the mills are now closed. Mill Number 4 was located on a hill. It was purchased around the year 2000 and has since been torn down." The sadness of the passing of a memorable time is obvious in her voice.

The 1950s were a time when people had money and were relieved from the pain and threat of the Depression and a world at war. It was also the decade when rural America experienced transformation, as many farmers traded their tractors and plows for jobs in cities. Mill-town residents emulated the same social constructs as farmers and families. Downtown Pelzer deteriorated, as did Main Street in most small farm towns.

Mill closure resulted in loss of jobs and more residents, especially young people, moving away from Pelzer. "A lot of people now travel to work and to do their shopping," Sara says about today. The community is changing with the advent of a few new residents. The number of new residents, however, has not replaced the number of departing residents. Sara states, "Some people have moved into our community. We are more diverse. New people changed the culture. A lot of houses have been vacated, and [then they] deteriorated." Her emotions of sadness about the loss of friends and population in general and the addition of new members of the town are very obvious as she speaks with me.

Sara quickly bounces back and shows excitement and the spirit prevalent in her life experiences and strong sense of community. Her remarks and emotions are similar to a rollercoaster ride; she knows the downward ride will reach bottom, but she also has the energy to rise to a new peak. "One Saturday a year we have a reunion called 'Blast from the Past.' People who attended high school in Pelzer come back. Last year was the first annual reunion. We had 3,000 people. This year it is on October 15th." The excitement in her voice clearly projects that Pelzer's third Saturday in October this year will be filled with people from the past, the renewal of old relationships, conversation, and a shared love of community. Pelzer of the 2000s will become Pelzer of the 1940s, 50s, and 60s.

Sarah's excitement is contagious. I suddenly have a need to paint in my mind a mental picture of her town. My low-key approach of being a listener transitions to being a questioner. I blurt out the question, "What would I see if I drove down Main Street?" Sarah begins her description of town with only a moment of hesitation by stating, "It is Highway 8. You would see Bi-LO grocery, a Methodist Church, the old house still stands where the mill superintendent lived, another Methodist Church, school, and auditorium."

The words of school initiate a change of her thoughts. As quickly as she begins her narrative of the town, she changes course to describe the school system with these words, "The high school serves Williamston, Pelzer, and West Pelzer. It is called Palmetto High School. The elementary and junior high schools are located between the towns. There is a vocational school in Williamston."

She then rapidly transitions back to her verbal picture of Pelzer by adding, "As you continue to drive, you would see old two-story houses and the post office. Next is the old high school, which houses a program for people who have not finished high school. The oldest church in town is Presbyterian."

As I hear the words of her description, I picture a drive down Highway 8, blanketed by homes and other buildings that mark a period when life was not a period of hustle and bustle like today's era. If the buildings could only talk, we would hear laughter and the conversations of dedicated workers with a strong sense of community.

Phil, the "new" person in the community, senses that Sara needs a break. A good listener throughout Sarah's and my conversation, he picks up the conversation with his unbiased comments: "Pelzer has nice people. They are very friendly, but not nosey. There is very little crime and drugs in our town." Sara, having experienced enough quiet time, smiles and says, "Pelzer is a great place to live. I am the only one of my family who lives in Pelzer."

I sit back, take a deep breath, and realize I have walked through a totally new experience: the positive attributes of a mill town.

As I am thanking Sara and Phil, one of their many friends who briefly spoke with them during our conversation—a man called Tony—joins us. Sara introduces Tony and states, "You should talk with him; he grew up in Pelzer." Thus, a second interview is born. As Sara, Phil, and I bid farewell, I think how lucky I am to hear about an old mill town. Tony will undoubtedly enhance an already informative morning.

Tony provides a different perspective than Sara about their hometown. He focuses on a period of time slightly later than Sara's. The two stories are complimentary and reveal a greater perspective about growing up and living in a mill town. His story focuses more on community life, employees and their families, and changes since the mill closures.

Tony immediately begins our conversation by saying, "I live in Piedmont. We have the best of both worlds: [the] advantages of a small town and living fifteen miles from Greenville, a town with a population of about 60,000." He continues, "My father-in-law was in the [US] Air Force and worked at Donaldson Air Force Base."

Donaldson AFB is the Logistic Center where I flew the previously mentioned F-101 aircraft for maintenance. As Tony excuses himself to refill his coffee cup, I think about how the world is actually a pretty small place.

Tony tells his story as a walk down memory lane. He openly reaches into his past through personal stories that illustrate the value of community. His story depicts a unique way of life that will never return. It is about the cohesiveness of a community that is bound by more than the commonality of a single vocation, such as farming. It also describes the relationship of company owners, managers, and employees. Tony adds to his story the stigma of living and working in a mill town. It is about a time that deserves our understanding.

Would this way of life be appropriate in today's culture? is not the question to ponder. Rather, instead of dwelling on the comparison of today and yesterday, consider a time in our nation when we were experiencing an economic depression and an era between two world wars. The threat of Hitler in Europe and Japan in Asia was ever present on peoples' minds. The risk of war coupled with high unemployment and financial hardships were ever present on peoples' minds. Survival was a goal for many people. Perhaps the support for and commitment to working-class laborers provided by company-owned towns provide security and survival for many people.

Following World War II, when a sense of normalcy returned to the citizens of our nation, mill towns transitioned from company ownership to incorporated public towns. Transition to private ownership of homes soon followed incorporated towns.

Tony's story changes my perspective of company-owned towns, such as mining and milling towns. His story helps me gain a clearer perspective of the way people—not only in company-owned towns but also other cultures—provided aid to people in need. Our conversation causes me to more deeply examine my beliefs about company and mining owned towns.

Tony begins his own story by stating, "I grew up during the 1960s in Pelzer, a mill town. My dad, like most people, worked in the mills." The mill owners were very supportive of their employees. "I played baseball as a youth in a mill-sponsored program. All we [players] had to do was show up. Mills took care of us; they furnished the equipment." The mills were also supportive of the greater community. Tony says, "The mills paid part of the policemen's salaries; the county paid the remainder." Mill owners in Pelzer, and many other locations, provided support for their workers to create a better life for those workers and their families. The owners' efforts were a large factor in creating a strong sense of community among employees and families.

Members of the community embellished the concept of support and had a strong attitude of caring and helping each other. In essence, citizens possessed a strong sense of community. In addition to helping other adults and families, kids received the benefits of the community. Tony says, "Anything I did, my father and mother knew about it. I knew everybody. If the police caught us doing anything wrong, they would say, 'We are going to call your dad.'"

Everyone, including the police, assumed responsibility, through a caring attitude, for other people. Tony adds, "We never had to lock our doors."

The sense of community extended to helping with financial assistance for meeting basic needs. "I was in a car wreck when I was fifteen years old. The accident, which occurred when we were coming back from a basketball game, killed two boys." He pauses, then continues, explaining, "Medical expenses while my dad was temporarily out of work placed a strain on our money. If it had not been for mill workers, we would have starved." The strength of the loving act and community spirit lingers in his mind after a period of over forty years.

Community spirit and being responsible for your neighbors, even though prevalent among the mill-worker community, did not extend between communities of mill workers and non-mill workers. There was a lack of understanding and appreciation between mill employees and other rural, non-mill workers living in the area. Tony states, "They [non-mill worker residents] called us 'lint heads.' Everyone thought we were stupid. Other people thought mill people had money; mill people thought other rural people had money. In reality, mill people had as much money in the bank as anyone." The two cultures did not clash but lacked understanding of each other.

Tony quickly drops the subject of misunderstanding between communities and transitions to his adult life.

Life in Pelzer began to change during the early 1950s. Mill companies began selling homes to their employees, creating opportunities for private ownership. Tony proudly states, "When I got married, I bought a mill house." He appreciated the mill company providing him, as a young adult, the opportunity to become a homeowner. He valued the opportunity to own a home.

Mill companies made other changes during the later years, which Tony believes to be detrimental to factory operations. He states, "Management always came up through the ranks. Later, they [company owners] started bringing in college-educated managers. It did not work." Tony summarizes that the new breed of managers did not know the operation of the mills from the worker perspective, but more importantly, they did not understand the culture. Tony says it was harmful to the operation. He continues, "They [mill owners] started sending plants overseas, which eventually resulted in plant closure, loss of jobs, and a change in the culture."

People who lost their mill jobs either drove out of the community to work or relocated to areas that offered employment. People who had lived in town and worked their entire lives for one employer were forced to seek employment in another area. Tony states, "The culture changed when the mills closed, and everyone had to go somewhere else to work. I retired when the mills closed." In some respects, mill workers lost their strong community. Tony pauses for time to reflect, then concludes, "People who have been here their whole life are the same."

His final statement concerning unchanging character summarizes the strength of mill worker values and their sense of community. The question that goes unanswered—the question I would not pose to Tony because it might have created supposition or forced him to make a judgment that was uncomfortable—was, did the people who moved away from Pelzer change? Tony did not address the issue of his own volition, perhaps for a reason: a reason he did not wish to address with me. And perhaps the question is best left unanswered.

I thank Tony for his insight, candidness, and sharing his personal story. We bid farewell. I return to the truck after a rather lengthy absence. Needless to say, getting out of the truck is high on Mo's agenda, second only to an extended run. As I watch her run and hunt the open area outside the rural McDonalds, I think about the concept of company towns and their value. This has been a great morning. I have spent time in mining towns before, but have never heard stories and perspectives from residents about their lives.

This has been a very enlightening morning. I would like to say that I planned this morning, but I did not. I just showed up. John Hoyle, my doctoral advisor at Texas A&M University, told me more than once (*a lot* more than once), "Randy, 90% of success is showing up!" He may well have been correct.

Time to go. I ask Mo to get in the truck. She has developed a case of poor hearing. When I call her, she completely ignores me! Extreme challenges require extreme actions. I coerce her with a dawg bone. Suddenly, her hearing has returned to normal. Eventually, one Golden Retriever jumps into the truck, and we continue our journey.

First on my agenda is, you guessed it, a trip down Highway 8. The short drive brings life to Sara's description. The live scenery adds reality to her verbal picture. Churches and schools are in place. I try to create an image of Pelzer fifty years ago, when Sara was in high school, and Tony was a child roaming the neighborhood. The clarity of that time focuses on people talking, friends greeting each other, and the bustle of a small town.

My short drive down Main Street ends all too soon, but since we are on Highway 8, Highway 8 seems to be a good route to travel. We soon turn onto US Highway 25. Mo and I head in the general direction of *south*, enjoying rural South Carolina scenery. As we meander along state and county highways, forty-five minutes of sightseeing leads us to a small highway café at the intersection of two roads in the vicinity of High Shoals. One o'clock in the afternoon, and the scarcity of restaurants along our route makes this little café the spot of choice for a late lunch. While enjoying a sandwich, I meet Jimmy, who is delivering a dealer trade car. Our conversation about his previously small hometown leads to an interview.

Our conversation also leads to enlightenment about a small town located amidst a large metropolitan statistical area (MSA). The portrayal of this small town is unique, rivaling any stories I have heard during my travels through rural America. The town is Dallas; the MSA is Charlotte, North Carolina. Dallas had an overall thirty-year population decline, from 1970 to to 2000, when the trend reversed and increased 28% from 2000 to 2013.

Dallas, located about twenty-five miles northwest of Charlotte, is part of Gaston County. Dallas was named in honor of the eleventh vice president of the

United States, George Miffin Dallas. The area encompassing Gaston County received its first European visitors during the 1750s, but was not established as a county until 1846. At the time of Gaston's recognition as a county, it did not contain a settlement. Dallas became the planned community meant to satisfy the requirement that the county seat be located no more than two miles from the Long Creek Baptist Church.

Gaston County experienced a wave of population growth during the late nineteenth century, due to the rapid development of textile mills and the coming of the railroad. Population growth was focused in the area of a railroad intersection known as "Gaston Station." The area in proximity to the station became the town of Gaston. On January 1, 1911, after three referendum votes, Gaston became the seat of Gaston County. Even though a chapter in the life of Dallas had ended, the community has today restored the historic courthouse.

Jimmy's story is about the plight of a small town located in a large metropolitan area. The growth of the metropolitan area has changed several small towns and communities, such as Dallas, North Carolina—Jimmy's hometown. He tells me, "I have lived most of my life in Dallas, except for living twenty-five miles away in Lincoln, North Carolina from 1961 to 1971." He pauses with a smile and says, "Later in life, I moved to Florida for two years. I made this move to get my retirement from my long-term employer, who relocated from North Carolina."

Dallas incorporated in 1863. In 1872, town commissioners refused to allocate money to build railroad bridges over several creeks. Failure to appropriate funds for the bridges resulted in the rerouting of the railroad and an ensuing decline of Dallas that eventually resulted in the county seat being moved to Gastonia. Today, Gastonia, located about five miles south of Dallas, is the thirteenth largest city in North Carolina, with a population of approximately 72,000.

Jimmy begins his story with a lifelike verbal picture of the growth of Dallas and surrounding area:

> Dallas has maybe 4,500 people, but the surrounding area is much larger. The town has not kept pace with the surrounding community and Gastonia. Population of Dallas has increased about 40% during the past twenty years. We are the victims of urban sprawl.

He pauses, then continues, "Many of our farms have been sold to build houses. In 1972, when I built my house in the country outside Dallas, I could walk across the road; now [the traffic is so heavy] I cannot get out of my driveway." He concludes with a sigh, "The neighboring Gastonia area is about five times larger than when I was growing up." Growth of the area surrounding Dallas is much greater than the growth that Dallas, itself, has experienced during the past twenty years.

In many instances, rapid growth of areas surrounding small towns has adverse affects on local businesses. Numerous small-town stores are replaced by corporate retail businesses. For the convenience of new residents, the new businesses are usually located outside the town perimeter. The trend of locating businesses beyond small-town limits occurs in rural *and* metropolitan areas. The result is usually the start of a decaying process on Main Street. Jimmy places reality to this phenomenon by relating it to his small town. He embellishes:

> Dallas is a small town. Its businesses are drying up, but the surrounding area is becoming larger. We did have many businesses; now we have none. Some of the lost stores are due to corporate stores locating in the Dallas area. People who live in small communities tend to shop in large market areas—if the driving distance is not too far. The larger shopping area has more choices and larger stores. We then lose our stores.

His verbalization of the plight of downtown Dallas is descriptive of small-town America overall. I once considered the problem to be a rural one, but Jimmy refutes my belief, and I have been awakened from thinking "small, rural town" to "small towns *everywhere*."

His story takes a turn from lost businesses to lost industries. Jimmy describes how loss of industry in the surrounding areas has changed considerably during his lifetime. He explains:

> Cherryville, approximately twenty-five miles northwest of Dallas, once had [anywhere from] eight to ten cotton mills and a furniture factory; now they have all closed. Plants have closed, and everyone has to go out of town to work. People used to walk to work; now they have to drive a good distance. Traffic on the Cherryville-Dallas Road [Highway 270] has tripled during the last three years. Corporate retail stores also hurt Cherryville's businesses. Some [people] work locally at McDonalds or other service-related jobs.

His words clearly explain that local employment options are either to travel or accept lower pay. He also reminds me that our society has become mobile, with the need to commute to work. As I listen to Jimmy address life today in comparison to when we both were younger, I guess where he will lead the discussion. He does not surprise me, and I have been looking forward to this part of his story.

After a brief reflection, Jimmy speaks about his youth and school experience. He tells me that he was born in 1939 and left school prior to graduation to go to work. His fond memories of his education and the era of his youth are evident as he describes his school: "When I was a kid, there were 300 students in our [entire] school [grades 1–12]; now there are 300 in junior high [alone]." After a pause and a sigh, he continues, "There are more teachers now than there were students in the little school where I went. They even built a new building." His remarks describe more than his school experience: They portray the change of his town, community, and his life.

His concluding thoughts summarize our conversation and his love for his hometown: "The culture has changed. There is more hustle [and] bustle today. It is not as friendly today as when I was growing up. I used to know everybody; now I don't even know my neighbor."

I thank Jimmy for the insightful conversation, his candor, and his time. Jimmy departs the restaurant and drives north; Mo and I drive south. I think, *Our paths will probably never cross again, but we share a commonality about rural life.* I mentally thank Jimmy for his time, his words, and his spirit of community and commitment to hometown. My spirit sags as I reflect on his all-too-familiar comment: "I used to know everybody; now I don't even know my neighbor."

Jimmy, like many rural folks, has pride and ownership in the community of his youthful years. For many, pride and ownership is grounded in their roots, their time and place for development of lifetime values, their happy time. They cherished their community—as it was while they were growing up—and it's painful for them when that community no longer reflects their memories. Perhaps the 1970s television series "Happy Days" was more than a name; perhaps it reflected the happy days of our teenage years.

Mo and I travel in a southwesterly direction, with a goal of finding a campground. Our route takes us from one country road to the next. The calm trip with minimal traffic, coupled with a sleeping dawg, provide the peacefulness for me to reflect on Tony's story about the support that his family received while living in a mill town.

The concept of helping people cope with the depression causes me to think about a personal story of how one man with the financial means assisted a young married couple realize their dream of becoming a farm family. The years was 1938, the midst of the depression. Bill Winship, the John Deere dealer in my hometown of Rushville, helped this couple. The story goes like this:

Mr. Winship, without collateral or down payment, gave this young couple a loan on equipment to begin farming. He also told agriculture vendors that he was financially backing this couple to purchase seed, fertilizer, and other necessities. What did Mr. Winship receive in return? A lifelong friend and the satisfaction of watching my dad and mom become successful farmers and eventually landowners. I still remember Mr. Winship's smile, warm greeting, and patting me on my head every time we met. Mr. Winship, without knowing, became my lifelong model of stewardship.

A sign stating Athens, Georgia ahead snaps me back to reality. The distance to Athens, the weariness, the time of day all inform me it is time to seek a campground. Foremost, it becomes clear that the Athens, Georgia area is our best (maybe only) possibility of finding a campground. The state line on this segment of our trip provides a demarcation of areas. The Deep South, which in my mind begins in Georgia, is an area unto itself. So as we approach the Savannah River—and also the South Carolina-Georgia state line—we say farewell to this segment of our trip. Thanks for joining us on our visits to Virginia, West Virginia, North Carolina, and South Carolina. Nature's scenery is phenomenal; warm and friendly people with commitment to their lifestyle and community are abundant. These last few days have been fun and enlightening. I love my work, if you consider talking with great people work.

CHAPTER 28

Georgia and Alabama

"Greetings" from south of the Georgia–South Carolina line. After crossing the Savannah River, Mo and I continue our meandering on back roads. What a luxury to completely ignore time! A "Campground Ahead" sign gets my attention. It will be a new experience and fun to set up camp during daylight hours, take a walk to enjoy the nature's beauty, and burn the energy of a Golden Retriever. It also will allow me to clear my head prior to accomplishing my nightly task of transcribing field notes into records of interviews.

Mo

Finally, we find a campground. While Randy sets up camp, I will enlighten you on how our drive from High Shoals really went. Most of the afternoon, we sort of faced the sun on roads with mainly pickup trucks meeting us. I think, although no one will admit it, that we spent a lot of the afternoon lost. We stopped for some short walks around towns and talked with people. During our walks, I frequently heard the question, "Can you tell me the location of a campground?" The responses were always, "There are none around here." This interaction, which was about the sum of Randy's conversation, was my first clue that we were lost. Most people talked to me. It is hard to resist talking to a good-looking Golden Retriever, which I most definitely am.

Eventually, we crossed a big river. After the river crossing, our trip was more in one direction: the first clue that we were no longer lost.

Finally! The trailer is set up, and we are off for a walk—and all before dark! I chase a few varmints, which should not be living in a campground. Many people stop and tell me how cool I am. Of course, I already know I am cool, but it never hurts to be reminded. People never mention that Randy is cool. It is difficult to recognize the coolness of a human when they are in the presence of a beautiful dawg.

After many what I term *no greetings* [people not speaking to Randy], Randy announces that it is time for him to type the field notes from today's conversations. That is what boring people do; they sit behind a computer and type. Social beings, such as a dawg with personality, do foot-to-hand shakes and receive pets and complements—and maybe a treat to eat. Humans get a head-nod and maybe a "hello" or "how are you?" Randy sometimes will respond, "I have a broken foot that really hurts when I walk." People do not listen. They respond, "That's good. Have a nice day." Humans are a weird species. It is good they have dawgs to balance their lives.

The next morning, after the normal routine, we are driving with the sun to our left. It is obvious that the driver has no idea where we are going. *I* might know, but I am not telling anyone. It is time for Randy to say something intelligent.

Randy

We are traveling and looking forward to a new day. Our driving plan is to not intermingle with Atlanta, Georgia traffic, which makes pulling a trailer a formidable task. The presence of large cities and their ensuing traffic make country driving far more appealing. Plus, the Atlanta Braves have a history of beating my beloved Cincinnati Reds in professional baseball. I do not have a grudge, however, because the Braves are good and deserve to win . . . but it still hurts.

We make a short drive and then turn south onto US Highway 129. We are once again traveling back roads. Our drive results in a brief tour of a couple of small towns. As we continue our drive on Highway 129, it becomes Main Street in Madison, Georgia. Main Street takes us through downtown, adjacent to the town square, which is accented by a historical courthouse. The courthouse, town square, and beautiful, historic homes substantiates that we are in the Deep South. The short drive into an obvious historical setting pulls me like a magnet. My goal becomes a conversation with someone who can bring the essence of Madison to life with the story of this historic town and community.

Morgan County was created in 1807 with land from Baldwin County. Madison, created and established as the seat of the county the same year, was incorporated in 1809. Morgan County remained part of Georgia's western frontier, with all land to the west belonging to the Creek Indian Territory, until the establishment of Walton County in 1818. The town and county flourished with the advent of three transportation systems: the stagecoach; the railroad in 1841; and the arrival of Interstate Highway 20 during the 1970s. Beauty and culture have been and remain still a primary focus of Madison citizens. They made their values known when they assured that the train station would be located at the edge of town to prevent compromising the beauty of Madison.

The primary entities of the beauty are the historic, well-preserved homes, mainly of antebellum architecture. The turn of the twentieth century saw Victorian-style homes and other buildings introduced to the area.

During General Sherman's Civil War campaign, termed the "March to the Sea," the beauty of Madison was situated in the path of intended destruction. Sherman's campaign was designed to break the will of the people on the side of the Confederacy by fighting and burning resisting towns within his army's path. There are two theories as to why Madison was preserved. One is simply that the town was too beautiful for destruction. The second theory includes General Sherman's relationship with Joshua Hill, a Madison resident and past Georgia senator. Mr. Hill, a senator and staunch Unionist, was granted permission to travel through Federal lines and meet with Sherman. The visit produced an agreement to preserve the town of Madison. Perhaps the preservation was a combination of the two theories, beauty and loyalty.

Today, Madison remains a thriving town that represents the pride of its ancestors. Madison has 4,000 of Morgan County's 18,000 residents.

Our drive continues south on Main Street until we are in the midst of beautiful, old homes, mostly in the antebellum style. Our drive around town reveals many beautiful homes that make an indescribable picture. My immediate thought is that I cannot leave Madison until I learn more about the unique historical mystique of this town.

Our drive back to the town square is deliberate and indirect, as I search and stop to gaze at each antebellum-style home. Surprisingly, I quickly find a three-spot parking place on a side street that will accommodate the truck and trailer. Mo and I are off on our walking journey of Madison and a mission to talk with someone. Exploration of the Southern-style courthouse square is enough to keep me occupied for an hour. The historic, beautiful courthouse I view today was constructed in 1905. Style and size of the courthouse demonstrate a commitment to serve the people and to the future of Madison and Morgan County.

As people stop to pet Mo, I explain my purpose to them and ask whom I should interview. The answers are unanimous: "Bruce, the mayor and hardware store owner." Mo and I wander a half-block off Main Street to the hardware store, which is adjacent the store where I parked the truck and trailer. A nosey dawg leads the way into an old-time, traditional hardware store. Bruce, the owner and mayor, is waiting on a customer, providing help in selecting the correct items and offering some thoughts on accomplishing the customer's task.

My first thought as I look around and listen to Bruce is that I have stepped back in a time. I feel that I am in Emery Jones' 1950s hardware store in my hometown of New Salem, Indiana.

Bruce entices me out of a trance of memories when he asks, "May I help you?" I stammer as I search for the words to ask him if he would participate in a conversation about his hometown. He responds, "Sure! I will talk with you about Madison." I am now really at a loss for words for the second question, and the subject of my intended question is wandering toward the back of the store with her nose to the floor, surveying the area. Finally, I clear my throat and ask if Mo can join us. Bruce smiles and responds, "Your dawg knows that she is welcome here."

He suggests that we talk in a section of the store that is surrounded with shelves and bins, where he has been sorting bolts and nuts. "I can work on my sorting as we talk," he suggests. A small stool becomes my chair. He asks if I am comfortable, to which I reply, "I have not been more comfortable in a long time." Bruce continues his chore of separating bolts and nuts as we talk. His cue to show me when he is making a critical point is to stop sorting and look me in the eye to deliver his response.

"Madison is the seat for Morgan County," Bruce explains. "The *Holiday Travel* magazine honored Madison nationally in 2001 as 'The Prettiest Small Town in America.'" I tell Bruce, "I am fortunate to have visited two nationally honored towns during the past week." He smiles and continues, "Most of the several antebellum-style homes have been restored." Bruce immediately explains that Madison was in General Sherman's direct path on the march from Atlanta to Savannah. Madison was spared the horrific destruction. Bruce explains, "The town, but not the countryside, was spared because of its beauty." I can verify firsthand the present-day exquisiteness of the restored homes. I can only imagine, however, the beauty of the houses during the 1860s. I am grateful for the sparing of Madison's beauty.

Bruce continues his story with a brief account of the history of Madison and adjacent areas. He begins by discussing agriculture's role in the Madison community. "Madison was never a textile community, like many surrounding towns; we were a pretty good-sized farming community. Our farms were diversified, but at one time we were the largest dairy county in Georgia." He thinks for a moment, then looks me in the eye and says, "Our population has historically been between 2,700 and 3,000. It is now around 3,900 people. Prior to the Depression, it was larger. It is a small town that has not grown much."

The current national economy has adversely affected the local job potential. "We are hurting for jobs. Industry has left and gone to other countries. We, however, have one new small industry." He continues to explain that the new industry has had a positive affect on the town and community in both population and financial growth.

Bruce pauses and stops sorting as he discusses the time when Tom Dupree had his business headquarters in Madison. Bruce's reflection clearly demonstrates a well-remembered, positive time for Madison and Morgan County. "Tom Dupree, who owned several restaurant franchises, located his business headquarters here. He paid for a lot of kids to go to Georgia Tech and the University of Georgia. While in Madison, he was the mayor for four years." Bruce then says that Tom Dupree sold his restaurant franchises and left town. Bruce concludes that the loss of Dupree's business adversely affected the economy.

A strip mall with corporate stores, as well as the loss of Dupree's corporate headquarters, has adversely affect downtown-area retail businesses. Bruce speaks about the downtown area as he stops sorting bolts, stating, "When the strip mall came to town in 1989, we lost several businesses. We often say that the corporate stores did more to hurt Madison than Sherman." The shopping mall is located south of town, on US Highways 129 and 441 and in proximity to Interstate 20. The location lures shoppers and travelers from the areas beyond Madison.

Bruce, true to his character, immediately redirects his thoughts to the positive. "A strong asset of Madison is a good school system. A lot of people move here because of the education system. A lot of people move in [Madison and Morgan County] and drive to work in Atlanta, which is about a one-hour drive." Madison's proximity to Interstate 20 makes the sixty-mile drive west to Atlanta a viable commute for employment. Bruce concludes, "Many residents must travel from Madison to work." The school system, convenient commute to employment, and the beautiful, rural setting all entice people to make Madison their residence.

The influx of new residents affected the culture, however. Bruce states:

We used to appoint a lot of new people to committees because they wanted to be involved. The new people wanted to change things. Changing the culture altered the way of life, resulting in Madison losing its Southern values and beliefs. It defeated the reason people moved to Madison.

Bruce's comments make it very clear that maintaining culture for existing and new residents is a priority. Preserving the culture of a small, Southern town preserves a lifestyle while continuing a safe environment.

An increase in crime, even though minimal, is of concern to the residents. Bruce makes a definite pause in his work to discuss this. He states with conviction, "We had our first murder last year. It was a domestic crime. There have been some robberies, mostly on the highway near the strip mall. We have some crime, but not to the extent of other towns and cities." Concern for limited criminal activity reflects the high safety standards of the mayor and community of Madison.

Bruce summarizes our discussion with his final comments: "Madison is a good place to live. Madison is a good place to raise kids." These capstone statements make a defining statement. The culture in Madison is as noteworthy as the beautiful decor. The human spirit is as strong and attractive as the stones of construction in Madison. The clean and attractive downtown area, even with a few vacant stores, clearly states that the vision of beauty and enticing culture has remained alive throughout the life of Madison.

I thank Bruce for his time, his story of Madison, and most of all, his hospitality, which allowed me to sit in his hardware store as he worked. The setting of our conversation is more meaningful than I am able to explain. So I walk in quietness with a Golden Retriever by my side. I silently thank Emory Jones and his wife for my childhood experience of their general store.

Mo

Oh boy, this is going to be fun. A female wearing a uniform is standing beside our truck writing in a book. Randy immediately asks if there is a problem. She responds, "You are illegally parked." The lady is a police officer, and it seems that she is writing a ticket. I nudge Randy with my nose, trying to tell him, "Now would be a good time for humility" (which is obviously not one of his strengths). He immediately pleads ignorance and asks, "How am I illegally parked?" His intentions might have been good, but his wording was not. The officer responds curtly, "You are taking three spots in front of this store." An obvious sign states "Store Parking." It is going to be difficult to plead ignorance.

The conversation becomes one of inquisition. The police officer asks, "What have you been doing?" The answer can be good or bad. Randy responds that he was interviewing the mayor, which is quickly followed by the police officer stating, "If you leave right now, I will not give you a ticket." I can hardly wait for Randy's response, as the officer is blocking the driver's door. Randy pauses—hopefully, he is thinking. I hope his response is not something like, "I would, but you are blocking the door."

Then something unbelievable happens. Read carefully, and do not miss this! Randy *humbly* says, "Yes ma'am, we are leaving right now."

The police officer steps aside, and Randy opens the door. I jump in at record-breaking speed and give the officer my best mournful look. Red Golden Retrievers can do that pretty well. Randy, Mr. "Never get in a Hurry," even gets in quick. He fastens his seat belt, starts the engine, and signals. We are off with a wave and Randy's best driving. From the front seat, I here a very non-contrite, "I wonder what her problem is?"

I nearly sigh. Some people never will learn.

This moment in history is the highlight of a rather uneventful remainder of the day. We camp, do the regular routine, and are off the next morning to no-one-knows-where. I need some rest to replenish my quick-thinking ability—in the event that I need to bail Randy out of another problem.

Randy

Our overnight stay at the campground is uneventful, with the exception of Mo's attitude. She displays an attitude of independence and being in control, like "you owe me." I stay in control by keeping the peace, allowing Mo to the lead way more than usual, which results in raised eyebrows of some campers. I enjoy a Southern-cooked catfish-and-hush-puppy dinner.

A short drive the next morning leads Mo and I to Interstate 85. With no planned destination, we turn onto the interstate to continue our drive in a southwesterly direction. Our trip from Madison to the campground and the drive this morning has both been mostly on back roads, interspersed with some interstates. Soon after we enter Alabama, a sign along the highway states that Tuskegee is a few miles ahead.

Tuskegee is the home of the World War II Army Air Corps pilots called "Red Tails." I have read and heard many stories, some firsthand, about the accomplishments of the Red Tail pilots, and our current proximity to Tuskegee clearly identifies our next stop. My excitement and impatience clearly demand close monitoring of the speedometer. Mo might not be able to get me out of another legal citation . . .

Today, Tuskegee, like many rural towns, is hampered with declining population and a high unemployment rate. The 2010 population was 95%

African-American, while the remaining 5% were classified as White, Hispanic, Asian, and Native American.

Tuskegee had an interesting beginning and a rich history. Tuskegee dates its beginning to 1833, when it was settled as the Macon County seat. The town received its name from a Creek Indian town with the same name. The Creek Indian Nation, along with France, England, and finally, the United States, owned the land where Tuskegee now sits. In 1819, the United States government changed Tuskegee's parent state from Mississippi to Alabama. Finally, Tuskegee became a settlement in 1833 when General Thomas Simpson Woodward, a Creek Indian War leader, built a home and named Tuskegee as the seat of Macon County.

Tuskegee maintained its prowess as a trading center, even though it was the only town in Macon County that did not have access to the railroad. Macon County's 608 square miles are home to about 21,400 people.

Tuskegee University; the training base for the famous World War II Red Tail African-American pilots; and notable citizens like Rosa Parks, Booker T. Washington, and George Washington Carver are all the foundation for the town's culture and recognition.

Lewis Adams, a literate former slave, had a dream for an African-American school. He approached W. F. Foster, a state senator running for reelection, and asked for his support. The state legislatures approved the educational institution, and Booker T. Washington made Adams' dream a reality on July 4, 1881, with the opening of Tuskegee Normal and Industrial Institute. The Education Center began as a one-room school serving thirty students. Washington served as the principal from 1881 until his death in 1915. One of his many accomplishments was appointing George Washington Carver as a member of the faculty. George Washington Carver, a renowned scientist, conducted agriculture research at Tuskegee Institute during the late nineteenth and early twentieth centuries. His globally recognized research created the path for Tuskegee Institute to later become a university with graduate programs and a school of veterinary medicine. Carver remained at Tuskegee from 1896 to 1946. The one-room school of 1881, a little over one-hundred years later in 1985, became nationally recognized as Tuskegee University.

The tradition of excellence continued in 1913, with the birth of Rosa Parks. Her family and neighbors in Tuskegee helped implant both a strong will and the need to make the world a better place. Even more, they helped embed the strength to stand up for the cause of equality among all humans. Parks served as secretary of the Montgomery Chapter of the NAACP. Her singular act of courage on a Montgomery bus in December 1955 spoke clearly to the inequality issues facing people of color. Her willingness to act with courage for the rights of herself and African-American people advanced recognition of issues that could no longer be ignored until equality for all had been reached. One person, one act of courage by Rosa Parks of Tuskegee, Alabama, kindled the fire for a movement that spread nationwide.

Tuskegee furthered its rich history as the training base for the African-American World War II pilots. World War II marked a time in our history of segregation, resulting in different training airfields based on race. The African-American pilots were termed "Red Tails" because of their aircraft's tail markings. United States military aircraft tail markings signify an aircraft's number (its identity), as well as the identity of the unit (i.e., squadron, wing, or group). Tail markings are a sign of status and pride among aviators.

The Red Tail pilots, who served with distinction and valor, earned a noteworthy status in our history: global, America, and the fighter pilot fraternity. I was honored to know and work with several Tuskegee Airmen and humbled to call two of those pilots "friends." They were Don Jackson and General Daniel "Chappie" James.

I knew Don during my life in Wichita, Kansas, where we both attended the same church. He is one of a kind. Don, at the age of eighty-plus years, never wears eyeglasses and rides his bicycle over fifty miles several days a month. He has a dry sense of humor that spreads joy and fun all around him. Don, even though proud, seldom speaks of his military days, World War II, or the past. He lives in the present and is a model for community building. I learned and laughed with Don on numerous occasions.

My association with General James, then a colonel, began during the spring of 1966 at Davis-Monthan Air Force Base in Tucson, Arizona. I got to know Colonel James, affectionately known as "Chappie," in 1966 and 1967, when he became the Deputy for Operations of the 8th Tactical Fighter Wing "Wolf Pack," located at Ubon Royal Thailand Air Base, where we flew together. In the middle 1970s, General James became the Commander-in-Chief of the North American Air Defense Command (NOARD) in Colorado Springs, Colorado, while I was serving as a command-level flight safety officer and aircraft accident investigator. Our relationship consisted of several "yes, sirs," along with some laughs and significant learning on my part.

During our Ubon days, Colonel James and Colonel Robin Olds, the wing commander, were visible at the club and joined in many fighter pilot games. Our tour of duty at NORAD permitted us to talk about old times and the future. Unfortunately, we lost Chappie not long after duty called him back to the Pentagon. He left many memories and a better world from the one he had entered years prior to his final flight into glory. General James' rank never changed his attitude about enjoying life and being "one of the guys." In many ways, he was a great role model. Above all, he was a friend.

Today, a visit to Tuskegee Air Field is a must. I have to see the aircraft hangars and runways, as well as walk the "grand," where many World War II heroes walked and trained. I decide that breakfast and some directions to the airfield are pertinent—especially directions. The number of cars and trucks adorning the McDonalds parking lot make the breakfast spot an easy choice. Breakfast in hand, I search for a table.

The very crowded restaurant poses a challenge to find an open table. Larry, an African-American man about forty-five years of age, solves my dilemma. He smiles and asks, "Would like to join me?" I gladly accept, and within moments, I am engaged in an interesting conversation, which becomes a two-way interview. I explain my research and ask if he would like to participate. A brief hesitation and a big smile accompany a firm, "Yes." Prior to my posing my three questions, Larry and I become acquainted via a conversation accompanied by several of his own questions. Larry's questions are not a test to establish my researcher credentials, but rather a friendly way of becoming acquainted with me. Our interesting conversation, which intertwines with the interview, lasts well over an hour. I am honored that he cares enough to get to know me. I love to travel and talk with rural Americans.

As we talk, several people stop at our table to greet Larry and me. Larry appears to be a magnet that draws people. Their conversations include a few jokes, as well as serious talk about the community. His friends make me, a stranger, feel welcome.

An eventual break from visitors permits us to begin the interview process, which merely adds structure to our conversation. Larry has an immediate response to my three questions. He begins by saying:

> We [Tuskegee] are an opportunity waiting to happen. We are a town with potential. Birmingham and Atlanta are only an hour and a half away. We are located near the state capitol and close to one of the state's two largest universities [Auburn]. Tuskegee University is here. We are unique by hav-

ing two veterinary schools within twenty-five miles [Tuskegee University and Auburn University]. We have great weather. The people are friendly and help each other. A lot of the people could live elsewhere but choose to live here. They may complain but will not leave.

Larry's words paint a picture of a town situated in an ideal location, landscaped with blue skies, great weather, and an abundance of friendly, helpful neighbors. His enthusiasm is contagious, but three minutes into the interview, I am two minutes behind in note-taking.

As I struggle to catch up, a voice interrupts my thoughts. Just in time, a grey-haired gentleman saves me by stopping to talk with Larry and greeting me. As our table guest talks with Larry, he intersperses positive comments about Tuskegee and its residents. Our visitor welcomes me to Tuskegee. He takes time to share his positive thoughts on his community and especially, the people. His pride of hometown is displayed in words, but more so in a gigantic smile. Smiles such as his are a true testament to sincerity.

Our friend excuses himself with a farewell and a hearty handshake, adding, "Come back again. You are always welcome." He drifts to another table to have coffee with friends. I, once again, am intrigued by how Larry is the focal point of so much activity at the restaurant.

Our conversation continues as if Larry had placed a bookmark in his thoughts. He says he believes that power of a community is rooted deeply in the nature of its people. He clarifies,
"Strength of a community is dependent on the strong character of its people. We believe in giving everyone a chance. We want to excel. We are happy when someone from Tuskegee succeeds." Larry accentuates his beliefs by providing examples of people and their achievements. His remarks clearly place the onus on the people: not leadership and not things such as amenities or businesses. The responsibility lies directly with the people.

Larry transitions to his internal beliefs and optimism: "I was raised by my grandparents. My grandmother always said, 'You can give out, but you can never give up.' I have always had high expectations. It is not over until it is over. Giving up is not an option." He continues his thoughts by stating that success may come after several attempts or may occur by changing the approach to goal achievement.

Larry's optimism reaches beyond a belief. He transforms that mindset into ideas:

This is a great place to locate businesses and industries. We have an abundance of labor. The cost of living is lower than many places. And we are located close to two large cities, as well as two universities. Potential workers range from college educated to hourly labor. People are anxious to work. We have good workers in Tuskegee.

In addition to the issues mentioned by Larry, the proximity of an interstate highway supports timely transportation. Also, Tuskegee and Auburn Universities provide research potential, as well as relationships that could enhance both the industries and educational institutions. Larry's belief is that Tuskegee is a good location for businesses and industries and could evolve into a win-win for all entities.

Our conversation moves to a time in the past and how change has moved that era into today. Larry begins by saying, "We have lost a lot of businesses." He cites hospitals as an example: "We used to have three hospitals. A lot of women came here to have their babies because other hospitals would not accept them. Now they can go somewhere else." Larry does not speak of the hospital losses as a negative issue, but merely as a fact of lost businesses.

Larry continues his thoughts about the loss of key people who have gained employment beyond the African-American communities:

We have always had obstacles. We lost many of our people from Tuskegee University and other professions because they could go elsewhere to work. This is a real problem because some of the best African-American leaders are not serving African-American communities. It is difficult to find replacements.

After a reflective pause, he says, "We do have strong Black leaders in our communities." He cites another need for improvement: "We do not have a vision; we need a vision. Everyone needs a vision."

He smiles and continues his comments about the leadership that Tuskegee University has offered in collaborating with the community. Larry speaks of a powerful, long-term relationship:

The Tuskegee University President, Doctor Rochon, has a vision to bring people and resources together. Tuskegee University and the community have always worked well together. The partnership has been in place for a long time, since when I was growing up. We had the "Jessup Wagon. It was a program with experts that goes out to work with the farmers on how to improve production.

The partnership was beneficial to both entities, providing expertise to the community, as well as research and learning experiences for faculty and students.

Larry has great hopes and believes that Tuskegee has a bright future, one that includes new businesses and industry, as well as many other aspects. I enjoy meeting Larry's friends and hearing supporting statements that substantiate his story. Everyone's positive attitudes reflect Larry's description of the people of Tuskegee. I benefit from Larry's beliefs that negative occurrences are opportunities for building positive elements.

My time with Larry was more than enjoyable and more than a time of gaining knowledge: It was a lesson in positive thinking. I thank Larry for his time, sharing about his hometown, and thoughts on the future.

Mo and I are in the truck, headed for Tuskegee Airfield. We wander around the area surrounding the airfield. I pause to think about a time seventy years before, when young Black airmen were learning to fly and preparing for combat. I look at the old buildings and think about the stories they could tell, if they could only talk. I see the sign marking "Chappie James Street" and think of the many laughs the general and I shared. Chappie served his country with humanity and then passed on, but will never be forgotten by many fighter pilots, especially me.

Today, I hold my head a little higher.

Mo

It is time for the dawg to pick up the story. Randy is one sad human. He asks me in a soft voice to come to the truck. He scratches my ears and gives me a big hug before I get into the backseat. I notice a tear in his eye. I need to help my human; this is what dawgs do.

Soon we are back on the highway with an 85 number and a lawn between the roads. The sun is at our backs. It is a beautiful day, with clouds coming toward us. All is well, except we do not have a clue where we are going. I hope Randy decides soon, because lunch is about an hour from now. If he is thinking about a destination, he usually forgets lunch: not good for a Golden! We enjoy our food.

As we approach Montgomery, a large city, Randy says, "Selma. We are going to Selma." There is only one thing wrong: I do not know how to get to

Selma, and I soon realize that I am not the only one in the truck with that lack of knowledge.

Things are never good all the time. It is beginning to rain. Actually, it is coming down in sheets. Cars and trucks—front, back, both sides, everywhere—surround us! I am on full alert when I hear Randy say, "Highway 80, Selma, right lane." This is not going to be pretty, not with a long line of trucks and cars in lanes between us and our turn-off.

Signal, slow-down, horns honking like a bunch of geese in my yard at home, then fists shaking, and people yelling behind closed vehicle windows. I am not sure if they are cheering us for our bravery or criticizing us for poor planning. Once again, we prevail and make our turn, but at a cost. We are now on the "bad driver list" of the people of this state, Alabama. I think, *This is state number twenty-nine: every state of our trip except Montana.*

As we travel a city street, I learn about about the meaning of traffic lights. Green is now my favorite because it allows humans to perform at their best – go and yell. As always, the excitement and the city both pass, and we are on a road bracketed by fields and cattle. After a forever-drive, we stop at a combination gas station and restaurant. I get out and run, eat a dawg bone, run some more, then assume guard duty in the backseat of the truck. Randy is off to lunch with the idea of gaining an interview. For me, it is one-eyed sleep with ears on full alert.

Love my human, even though it is sometimes difficult to know why.

Randy

Selma, the seat of Dallas County, is located in the rich, black-dirt area that is well-suited to growing cotton. The population of Selma is slightly greater than 20,000.

Dallas County gained recognition in February 1818, when it was created on land gained from the Creek Nation's cession in 1814. The county received its name in honor of Alexander J. Dallas, the United States Treasury secretary from Pennsylvania. William R. King, future vice president of the United States, planned a town on the banks of the Alabama River. In 1820, the town became incorporated with the name of "Selma."

At the time of inception, no one dreamed that this new town would be the center of so many historical events that would be instrumental in shaping the future. Selma was the center of many Confederate war events.

Selma's connection to the railroad and Alabama River enabled it to be a center for manufacturing of war materials and the building of the C.S.S. Tennessee, an ironclad navy ship. On March 31, 1865, the Federal Army defeated the Confederate Army at the Battle of Ebenezer Church. The next day, April 1, 1865, the Federal Army once again prevailed during the Battle of Selma. Within days, General Lee honorably surrendered the Confederacy to General Grant at Appomattox, Virginia.

Slightly less than a century later, in 1940, Selma continued its patriotism by being the site for an airbase used to train United States pilots for World War II. The location and successful marriage of Selma and Craig Air Force Base resulted in the continuation of the training, until the base's closure in 1977.

One hundred years following the spring 1865 Civil War battles in Selma, a civil rights movement occurred that strongly influenced the changing of a nation. On March 7, 1965, Dr. Martin Luther King organized a peaceful march, beginning in Selma and terminating in Montgomery, the state capitol. The march was terminated after participants crossed the Pettus Bridge on the outskirts of Selma. State police and Dallas County Sheriff's Office personnel halted the march using physical force. The day turned violent. The march was termed "Bloody Sunday."

Two days later, on March 9, Martin Luther King led a second march to the Pettus Bridge. As planned, when halted by law enforcement personnel, Dr. King ceased the march, led a short prayer session, and turned the marchers around to return to Selma. Dr. King's actions were in compliance with Alabama Federal Court Judge Frank Minis Johnson's injunction to prohibit the march until he could hold hearings to act on the court order filed by Southern Christian Leadership Conference. A court order allowing the march from Selma to Montgomery was approved, opening the highway for the march to the state capitol.

On March 21st, two weeks after "Bloody Sunday," marchers numbering 3,200 departed Selma for Montgomery. According to the court order, no more than 300 marchers could proceed on US Highway 80 along the narrow two-lane route in Lowndes County. At the end of the first day, all but 300 marchers were transported back to Selma. When the march entered Montgomery County on March 24th, many of the original marchers returned and were joined by many new members. The "Stars of Freedom" rally was held that night and included many well-known entertainers, including Sammy Davis, Jr.; Peter, Paul and Mary; and Harry Belafonte, all of whom performed for the marchers. The freedom march and its cause, which both began in Selma, had gained momentum and recognition. The next day, on March 25, 1965, the march concluded—with 25,000 people reaching the state capitol.

Today, Mo and I arrive in the eastern part of Selma via US Highway 80. Numerous pickup trucks clearly mark Taylor's Restaurant as the spot for lunch. It is about 1 p.m., and the parking lot is still full of vehicles. I choose a table in the corner, mainly because it is the only one available. It becomes immediately obvious that the hearty group at the large, round table next to me is a mix of family and friends: all farmers or farm family. They are having way too much fun for me to miss, so I make a few well-chosen comments. They laugh and make a stranger feel welcome with some good humor. Ellis and I talk a little about farming. I explain that my purpose in life at this moment is to learn about Selma.

Ellis claims that he is the one to enlighten me.

The french-onion soup is so good that I forget about the few minute wait until his friends and family depart. Ellis moves to my table and begins to tell me about Selma. When he pauses, I state my usual three questions, which he is already on track to answer.

Ellis begins by stating, "We have friendly people. We help each other when needed. Farmers exchange work [and] help each other if a person does not have the equipment." He continues by relating that race and ethnicity are no longer an issue: "The people are usually pretty laid-back. Black and White people work together, play ball together, and go to school together." They also eat together, as confirmed by the diners at Taylor's Restaurant. Ellis continues by saying that a few people try to keep race an issue in order to make money.

He changes the topic to increased farm size and loss of population. He clearly outlines the relationship between larger farms, reduction of population, and loss of schools. Ellis states:

> I grew up during the 1960s and 70s. When I was a kid, we farmed about 150 acres. Today, our 1,700-acre farm operation consists of 500 acres that we own and 1,200 leased acres. When I was in school, we had two county high schools, [called] North and South. Our graduating class at South High had 150 students. Now there is only one county high school.

He pauses and reflects before explaining the human affects of declining population. He continues:

> Younger people are moving to larger towns. They go off to college and never come back. The average age of population is about ten to fifteen

years older than when I was a kid. About 80% of the folks I went to school with have left.

His words and passion clearly depict that the loss of the younger population is an emotional issue.

The loss of population can be demonstrated by comparing the sizes of Ellis' farm in 1960 to his farm in 2010. Using the change in size of his farm as typical to Dallas County, one farm today replaces approximately eleven farms from the 1960s and 1970s. Typically, each farm is the home of four or five people: two adults and two or three children. The eleven farms of the 1960s and 1970s were home to twenty-two adults and somewhere between twenty-two to thirty-three children. Replacement of one farm for the eleven reduced the Dallas County farm population by approximately 91%. The 91% reduction in farm population over a fifty-year period dictated a significant change in the local town, which serves the county.

Technology, as well as farm size, is a factor in the reduction of people living on farms. Improved technology—larger tractors and machinery, as well as automation—has contributed to the need for fewer farm employees. Agriculture has become a high-technology business, including the advent of experimental remotely operated tractors.

Demographics of Selma and Dallas County reveal the affects of young residents leaving the area to procure employment. In Selma, 27.3% of the total population is under the age of eighteen, while only 16.3% is over sixty-five. Dallas County, Alabama statistics are very similar, with 25.6% being under eighteen years of age and 15.3% being over sixty-five. Similarity of population loss in Selma and Dallas County reflect that the declining number of farmers and farm-family members reduces the need for agriculture businesses and other commercial infrastructure, which is commonly located in area towns. Last but not least, population loss means a decreasing need for schools. The neighborhood or community schools have become a thing of the past.

Ellis transitions to a brighter side by explaining the efficiency of larger farms. Larger farms, increased production, and higher market prices for cotton have all increased the profits. Increased profits allow farmers to invest in modern equipment, which enhances productivity and safety, also allowing farmers to invest in land and operate even larger farms. Ellis informs me that cotton prices have increased significantly. "We booked [contracted to sell] a lot of cotton at

$1.30 and $1.40 per bushel. I have never seen it that high. Our cottonseed, that plants 6 to 7 acres, costs $600."

Research of cotton yield over an eleven-year period reveals a range of pounds per acre in Alabama: from 583 during the 2006 drought to 952 in 2012. Weather, which is a large factor in cotton production (and any grain crop), is instrumental in determining profit or loss. Efficiency in farming contributes to larger farms.

After a pause, Ellis transitions to earlier times, when he was a child. He states:

> When I was really young, we came to town only on Saturday to do our shopping. I did come to town to play ball [baseball] when I got older. Now I come three or four times a day. I used to drive the school bus. The town is considerably smaller in population.

He pauses, then states with a grimace, "The area of the town is larger, even though our population has decreased."

Ellis then guides our conversation to the change in location for local retail businesses. He adds, "A lot of our businesses are gone or [have] moved to malls on the outskirts of town. The downtown area has changed with loss of businesses." He stops, smiles, and states, "I can show you better than I can explain. I will take you on a tour of town in my truck. You can see the downtown, and I would like to introduce you to Elton."

When I tell him that my dawg is in my truck, he says, "She can go with us."

I pay my bill, and we are out the door.

Mo is happy to be out of our truck and ready for a ride. She will not abandon her normal procedure of getting into a truck. She refuses to jump into the backseat of Ellis' truck on the passenger side, but instead walks around to the driver's side, because—in Mo's world "This is the way we do things in my world." To her, time is not important, and protocol is essential.

She takes one look at the folded-down seat and jumps up there, sitting down like it is an every-day occurrence—which it is not. So much for protocol! She usually rides on the floor with the seat up, both to allow her more space and for safety in the event of a sudden stop or worse. She understands, however, the *concept* of riding on the seat, because someone was once lucky enough to ride with her in the back of our truck. That person has never ridden in our truck again. I wonder why?

One look at Mo, and I know life will never be the same; she *likes* sitting on the seat.

Our tour begins with a drive by Pettus Bridge. Ellis explains that Pettus Bridge will be condemned in March and turned into a walking bridge. Passing a cemetery, Ellis explains that two tombstones—one marking birth and one marking death—are marked with dates prior to signing of the Declaration of Independence. As we continue our drive to Bloch Park Complex, Ellis tells me that when he was a kid, "Selma had two drive-in movie theaters, the Selman and Highway 81, plus the Glass House Drive-in Restaurant. We used to have four implement dealers; now we have none," he states as we pull into Bloch Stadium parking lot. As we walk across the parking lot, Ellis tells me that until two years ago, the city paid for youth sports. It now costs $10.

I recognize Elton immediately as an ex-athlete and coach. It turns out he is a retired high school teacher *and* coach, who remains dedicated to sports and youth athletics. Elton tells me with great pride, "The first baseball field [in Selma] was built in 1900. It was the first training site for the Chicago Cubs." After a pause, he continues by stating that the field burnt down in 1923. Then, in the early 1940s, a family said they would build a new stadium, if the city would name it after their grandfather. The stadium became Bloch Field. Elton then displays a big smile as he proudly states, "Lou Pinella and Doc Edwards played Class D ball [baseball] here." Pinella and Edwards went on to Major League careers: Edwards, a nine-year career as a catcher, and Pinella, a twenty-year career as an outfielder, with over twenty additional years as a Major League manager.

Both names and careers are familiar to me. Pinella gained recognition when he roamed the grass in right field of Yankee Stadium and as manager of the same club. He also managed the Cincinnati Reds and three other clubs.

Elton, Ellis, Mo, and I walk out to view a beautiful, well-groomed football field. As we stand and overlook the field, Elton tells me that Selma will host the state's Class 1, 2, and 3 high school track meet this year. I thank Elton for graciously accepting a no-notice visit from a stranger and for sharing the history of the stadium. As we walk to the truck, with Mo right beside me, I tell Ellis that his small-town pride and dedication to youth athletics and other activities is unequaled. He nods in agreement.

We leave the parking lot, driving toward downtown. Ellis tells me that the downtown has changed. He says, "On Main Street, we had a Sears, Penney's, Woolworth, and Cress [department store]. Sears and Penny's moved to the outskirts, and the other two closed. There were three walk-in movie theaters. The Walton Theater is now a performing arts center." Ellis points to the Washington Street Grocery and says, "My grandmother used to work there. The counter used to be full of chicken feet." We drive a little further, and Ellis says, "Two drug stores have been here 100 years." After a short reflection, he says that the YMCA used to furnish housing for men who needed a place to live.

A short drive later, we arrive back at Taylor's parking lot. I thank Ellis for his time, sharing of knowledge, and the tour. He says, "It is has been a pleasure to show and tell you about Selma, my hometown." His pride in Selma and Dallas County are obvious. His graciousness is rooted in downhome hospitality.

I have to coax Mo to get out of the backseat on the passenger's side, but she finally relents and is soon checking out the parking lot. I shake hands with Ellis and thank him again for his contribution to the story of rural America.

He drives off with a smile.

Mo and I make the short drive to Pettus Bridge. I have a need to walk the same ground that was walked by so many over forty years ago. Standing for a few moments of reflection with a bowed head, I reflect on Colin Powell's many statements about the progress of racially equality and a long way we have to go.

Mo and I head west toward Mississippi. For now, heading west is definitive enough to end such a great day and two meaningful interviews. This has been a memorable day.

A short drive, and we enter US Highway 80 on a westerly route. Our approximate two-hour drive brings us to the Alabama-Mississippi state line. As we leave Alabama, I reflect on the great day that Mo and I have experienced in Tuskegee and Selma. Larry's hospitality, along with his story and remarkably positive attitude made a deep impression on me. My time at Tuskegee Airfield and reflection on General James was special, and I remember him as a leader and friend. Our trip around historic Selma brought back memories from previous decades. This day has been packed with emotions and historical memories. I hope you enjoyed it a fraction as much as I did living it.

CHAPTER 29

Mississippi and Louisiana

Highway 80 marries with Interstate 20, just prior to the state line. A short drive, and our windshield is filled with a picture of Meridian, Mississippi and remnants of a not-so-bright sun. Just afterward, a large sign welcomes us to a KOA campground.

The bad news is that it is not early; the good news is that is not dark. A quick set up and a two-mile walk relaxes a weary traveler and burns some excess Golden Retriever energy. A catfish dinner, note transcription, short night's sleep, and we are ready for another day. I am a little sad because our traveling and interviews are close to ending.

Ironically, the end of our travels coincides with the end of the week. It is Friday morning, and we are headed southwest on Interstate 59 with no destination in mind. After an hour on the road, we stop at McDonalds in Laurel, Mississippi for breakfast, where I meet Jimmy and Bonnie. They are a retired African-American couple traveling from Bogue Chitto, Lincoln County, Mississippi to spend the weekend with one of their children and grandchildren. (Note: identifying Lincoln County with Bogue Chitto is necessary in order to distinguish the hamlet from a Native American reservation of the same name in Kemper and Neshoba Counties.)

The unincorporated town of Bogue Chitto was named from the Choctaw term describing a river. "Bogue" means "swift-flowing river," as opposed to "hatchie," which means "sluggish, deep, and broad river." The pronunciation is "bow guh chit-uh." Bogue Chitto is located in the southwest area of Mississippi, south of the state capitol, Jackson.

The town, which originated prior to 1856, was settled when Joseph Hart, a local landowner, constructed a water-powered sawmill. He gave land to the railroad to build a depot. Bogue Chitto became a municipal territory in 1871, was chartered as a village in 1892, and was granted town status in 1904. In 1944, the town of Bogue Chitto, as by proclamation of the governor, lost its municipal status as a town. Over fifty years later, in 2009, the citizens of Bogue Chitto applied for hamlet status. A decree by the state legislature and approval from the Lincoln County Board of Supervisors in 2009 granted Bogue Chitto hamlet status. Today, the hamlet has a post office, school district, several churches, a truck stop, several stores, and a volunteer fire department.

An 1891 document stated that the "current population of 225" had "nearly doubled during the last few years." The document went on to claim that Bogue Chitto was one of the oldest towns in the area because it had been present since the railroad.

The early economy was focused on the two sawmills owned by Brister and Company, plus J.M. Taylor's fine watermill and gin, located a half-mile from town. Local lumber businesses resulted in the town's buildings being totally of wood construction, making them vulnerable to fires. The all-wooden construction of the town's buildings was totally destroyed by fire twice.

After introductions, I explain my research of rural America. Jimmie and Bonnie are both happy to participate. I have met some really great people during breakfast, and these two definitely make the list. Even though they are anxious to be on their way, each exudes a sense of calm with their polite, mild, well-spoken mannerisms. I truly enjoy our conversation and realize that my self-improvement will be enhanced with internalization of their calmness.

Jimmy begins our conversation by saying, "Bogue Chitto is a nice place to live. The population is little over 500. We have friendly people that help each other." Bonnie adds, "People and things have changed over time, such as loss of businesses and people. Lack of available work is a factor for the loss of people." Jimmy enhances Bonnie's statement by saying:

> Bogue Chitto is becoming smaller. We used to have a bank, but it moved to the headquarters about ten miles away. Other businesses, such as an auto repair shop, a clothing store, and some grocery stores, have been lost. A lot of young people move away. They go where the jobs are. Very few people move in. The people are not as friendly as they used to be.

Bonnie nods her head in agreement with Jimmie's statements.

She then embellishes his comments by adding, "We used to have four grocery stores; now we have one. There are only a couple blocks of Main Street." Jimmie contributes:

> The Medical Center left [closed]. Now we go must go twelve to eighteen miles for medical service, depending on where we go. There used to be a doctor in a nearby community that made house calls. He passed away. Now no one makes house calls.

After some thought Jimmy concludes, "We even lost our sawmill." This means the main purpose for the settlement of Bogue Chitto no longer exists as a business.

Human behavior and work standards have changed in conjunction with the transformation of community. Jimmy states, "I was raised on a farm. We grew corn, sugar cane, peanuts, potatoes, watermelon, and ran a sawmill." He then explains his adult work life, stating, "I retired from the railroad as a maintenance engineer. After I retired, I hauled trees and farmed a little. Now I don't do anything." Jimmy developed work habits as a youngster on the farm, habits that have followed him through life. His next statement very clearly defines that work ethic: "Work is a part of life."

Jimmy is not certain that a strong work ethic is as prevalent today as it was years ago. He says some young people are not willing to work. He also views farming as a less labor-intensive profession than it was in the past. He cites the simplicity of a single-crop tree farm: "Farmers [today] raise plantation [pine] trees that are cut down when they reach six to eight inches in diameter. The tree is taken to the sawmill in one piece. They are used to make plywood, toilet paper, and paper towels." His comparison of tree farming today to his experience seems less labor-intensive. "Modern farm machinery is more efficient and has certainly changed the way we work," he adds.

Jimmy and Bonnie emulate the culture of hard-working people. They have worked hard, and the hard work has rewarded them with a comfortable, satisfying life. I particularly appreciate and enjoy how they support and enhance each other's thoughts. Jimmie and Bonnie truly treat and respect each other in the same way they, themselves, hope to be treated: a great characteristic to practice.

They could easily be the poster couple for the retired generation. They approach our conversation with the same effort and commitment as they obviously do to their work. I tell Jimmy and Bonnie farewell, wish them a safe and fun weekend, and express my gratitude. They wish me well on my journey and say good-bye. I have a feeling that they honor and respect everyone as they do each other.

Mo and I continue our drive on Interstate 59 to US Highway 98, where we turn southwest. A drive of a little less than two hours finds Mo and I walking around the streets of a small town. In reply to my question, "What is the name of your town?", a resident gives me a strange look and responds, "You are in Tylertown." I thank her and continue my walk.

A short distance later, I smell the unmistakable scent of barbeque baby-back ribs. One look at Mo tells me that she also is tuned-in to the scent. We round the corner to see smoke and smell an even stronger, inviting aroma. Investigation tells me that the meat section of the grocery store is barbequing baby-back ribs to sell. I want to meet the person who organized this Friday-morning event. The man and woman cooking the ribs inform me that Charles, the meat-section manager, is responsible. The lady states, "If you can be patient and wait, he will soon be coming back outside." I think, but do not say, *I can be patient and wait; patience is one of my strongest attributes.*

Knowing in reality that patience is *not* one of my virtues, I think that in lieu of fidgeting, now would be a good time to tell you about Tylertown, the seat of Walthall County. Tylertown has an approximate population of 1,600 to 1,700 resident. An excess of 700,000 people lives within sixty miles of Tylertown, making it a daily commutable distance for employment. The southern Waltham County and Washington Parrish, Louisiana boundaries coincide with the Mississippi and Louisiana state lines.

Walthall County has only one town, Tylertown, and three unincorporated communities. Situated to the middle of a triangle, Tylertown is less than 100 miles from the state capitol of Jackson, Mississippi to the north; New Orleans, Louisiana to the south; and Hattiesburg, Mississippi to the east. Tylertown pride shows in their website statement, "We can't prove that [S]outhern hospitality was invented in Tylertown, but [we] suspect it was. Our folks are some of the finest that you will find anywhere."

The website of the Walthall School District states that Waltham has two high schools: Tylertown and Dexter. In addition to strong academic performance, each high school won a sate football championship between the years 2001 and 2009.

The couple who are barbequing ribs introduces me to Charles as he approaches the grill. He says "hi" and pets Mo, always a good sign. I explain my research and tell him that I want to learn about Tylertown. He responds, "I lived in Tylertown my whole life. I worked on the road [traveled] for a while, but lived here. I would be happy to help you."

We sit at the picnic table facing each other, me facing the grocery-store wall and Charles facing the parking lot and customers. Charles, who I estimate to be in his middle fifties, is African-American. He says, "I grew up in the 60s and early 70s. Some of the nicest people in the world grew up here. It is a good place to raise kids."

Tylertown exudes a slow pace of life. Charles states:

There is not a lot of social life in the county: not a lot of dances and other activities. We are a dry county and must go to another county for movies. [It is a] slow life. Walthall may be the only dry county in southern Mississippi. One of our biggest things is high school football. [At] home games, we have 800 to 1,000 people. We have about 800 students in high school [in Tylertown].

I ask, "What do you do in the spring?" He immediately responds, "Go to baseball games. In addition to high school baseball, we have Dixie Youth Baseball and youth softball." After a short pause, he continues, "We have Lake Walthall a few miles south. A lot of people fish." He does not tell me that fishing is really good on the fifty-five-acre lake, which means that Charles is a smart fisherman who does not tell strangers everything about the quality of local fishing.

As Charles and I begin our discussion about change, I hear a distinct, continuous slurping noise. Charles' huge, broad smile clearly states that I am missing something. I turn around to see Mo with her back toward me, chewing on a piece of meat so large, it extends well beyond each side of her mouth. I cannot see her expression, but the wide smile on the grey-haired, African-American man's face standing by her says it all. If possible, he is enjoying the moment more than Mo.

I feel like I am back in my childhood hometown with people I have known my entire life, people who welcome a stranger and his dawg. I cannot interrupt Mo and her new friend by going over and saying "thanks." The moment is theirs. Sometimes you must let your dawg talk for you.

After I collect my thoughts, I turn back to Charles, who realizes I need a moment. He displays a big smile in response to my own ear-to-ear grin. I am momentarily overcome by the friendliness and welcome of the people.

I stammer, so Charles picks up the conversation by explaining that Tylertown has experienced significant change during his life. "It has changed since I was a teenager. The changes are due mostly to loss of businesses and new people moving to Tylertown." He pauses and reflects on some difficult times:

Katrina affected us. People came from New Orleans and the Gulf Coast. We got hit hard. We had severe damage to buildings; we were without power for [anywhere from] fourteen to twenty-one days, depending on where you lived. Trees and power lines were the major damage. Some [previous residents] came home; some new people came and stayed.

Charles pauses for a brief reflection before he pursues another issue that is contributing to change, his statements similar to those I have heard all too frequently during my past year of travel. Charles says:

> Work has about dried up. We had lost a lot of businesses. A big loss was a paper-production company. Georgia-Pacific, which made paper products, shut down. They still have operations in neighboring towns. We have a factory and warehouses that manufacture costume jewelry. Each employs about forty to fifty people. Big source[s] of employment [are] chicken-processing plants in Pike County, about fifteen to twenty miles away. A lot of people drive to work. Hospital and education are the professional employment systems. We have a hospital in town.

Charles ends our discussion with a comment that is both unhappy and happy. He says, "A lot of our kids go to college, then live somewhere else to find a job." He realizes that unavailable employment is the issue, but he really dislikes losing the young people. He has strong feelings for the people of his town, as can be understood by his final comment: "Some retired people, who left during the 1960s and 70s to work 'up north' in the automotive industry in Michigan and Chicago, are moving back for retired life. They have not changed the culture. They like the slow life and comfort." He is happy to have *his people* coming home.

In my view, Charles is the ambassador for Tylertown, Mississippi. I have met a lot of people during my journeys the past fifteen months who were proud of their town, but none more than Charles. His feelings for Tylertown are deeper than the waters of Lake Walthall.

I thank Charles for his time and ask that he please thank Mo's new friend, who has left. He says, "I believe Mo's new friend received his thanks from her."

I ask Mo to come so I can put her leash on for the walk to the truck. She prefers to stay, but with some coaxing, she finally sits for her leash. As we cross the street, Mo turns and has one more look back.

Mo

The first thing I notice as we walk down the streets of Tylertown is that the people are friendly. The second thing I observe is that the people are very are polite and perceptive. I learn this when a lady responds to Randy's question, "What is the name of your town?" She replies—politely and with a smile—"Tylertown." She then looks at me and says, "You are a pretty dawg. You must be very smart," with a head nod toward Randy and a roll of her eyes. It does not take her long to realize who has the brains in this outfit.

Eight seam-cracks of sidewalk later I get a whiff of some good smells. I hasten my pace with a jerk on the leash. Not much hustle on the other end, so I pull again. I am headed for the smell of barbecue meat. Finally, Randy asks, "Mo, do you smell what I smell?" What a dumb question. Dawgs are famous for their ability to smell; humans are not so famous for their "whiffers."

Randy soon has his back toward the barbeque grill while talking with Charles. I have some freedom to roam. From over his shoulder, Randy says, "Mo, be smart. Stay out of trouble." Right! Now I am safe to *really* roam. Randy will forget about me for a few minutes. I am very careful not to hang around the grill, because that usually makes the cooks nervous and grouchy.

Finally, this cool man with a grey beard asks, "Mo, would you like to do a taste-test of ribs to see if they are okay for human consumption?" Okay, so maybe he does not include *all* those words, but he does say, "Taste?" I give him my best mournful look and walk beside him. He gets a piece of meat from the grill and carries it a short distance away from the cooking, directly behind Randy. I sit facing my new friend, with my back to Randy.

The piece of meat is so big that it sticks out both sides of my mouth. I try to be polite and quiet, but a big piece of great meat must be enjoyed, so politeness and quiet are off the platter . . . so to speak. My friend is smiling, as if he enjoys watching me relishing the meat. "Enjoy" is the big term in our endeavor.

I hear Charles laugh and then hear Randy say, "Wow! Mo, do you need some help?" I eat and eat some more. Randy and Charles talk. Finally, I finish eating. My friend gives me a pet on the head. We do a foot-to-hand shake, followed by a Golden hug—a big lean against his leg. He gives me one more pet and heads down the street to do some Friday-afternoon business. The third and fourth things I learn about this town are how friendly the people are and how great the baby-backs taste.

Randy

Once I could convince Mo that we should leave Tylertown, we drive southeast on Mississippi State Highway 48 to Interstate 55, where we head south. My goal for the afternoon is to have a conversation with a Cajun. My past experience clearly states that they have a unique view on life. I truly believe that writing a book about America without any Cajun input would make for an incomplete story.

A little over an hours' drive, and we are wondering around Amite, Louisiana, searching for a restaurant in which to have a late lunch and talk with someone. A sign stating "Cajun Food" and a parking lot full of vehicles both make the statement that *this* is the place. Cajun is great food, and to miss an opportunity to dine on the cuisine would be negligent. Most tables are taken, so I head to the back of the large dining room. A stranger sitting alone greets me with, "Are you new in town?" I respond, "Yes, I am." He asks if I would like to join him for lunch. The conversation, of course, leads to an interview.

Dominick's story is not about a town, but about his life, his ancestors, and their way of life. It is about what it means to be a Cajun. He lived his entire life in Louisiana and sixty-six of those seventy-one years on the "West Bank": the west side of the Mississippi River. A discussion of the chronology of the towns in which he lived, followed by a brief description of their histories create a foundation for his story.

Our lunch and interview occur in his current residency, Amite (pronounced ah-mit), the seat of Tangipahoa Parrish. The town rests at the intersection of Interstate 55 and Louisiana Highway 16, about one-hour north of New Orleans. Their webpage claims that the picturesque lawns and gardens of azaleas and dogwoods make Amite an attractive retreat for retirees escaping city life. Population has remained fairly stable around 4,000.

Dominick's life, intermingled with the intriguing towns, make the story unique from all the previous ones I have experienced during my touring of Rural America. Until he moved to Amite, Dominick had spent his entire life on what he calls the "West Bank": the native term that refers to the west bank of the Mississippi River. Dominick was born in Algiers, known today as Ward 15 of New Orleans. He lived there until his mid-teenage years. Ward 15 has the distinction of being the only ward west of the Mississippi River. Much of Dominick's story about his Cajun youth and ancestors comes from his early days in Algiers.

After its long, historic path from Minnesota, the path of Mississippi River becomes erratic as it approaches the Gulf of Mexico. The river, which we often call "Big Muddy," gives the appearance of extending its course in reluctance to end the journey. The path of the river uses several horseshoe bends to change directions and delay merging with the large body of salt water. One of those nooks forms a natural safe haven for a community: a community of a unique setting and culture while protecting a way of life.

Algiers Point, the area within the nook, was a small portion of the settlement along the twelve-mile stretch of land called "Algiers." The community and town of Algiers began in 1719 with French settlers, who were soon joined by Spanish immigrants. The Louisiana Purchase of 1803 brought many Europeans of various ancestries. The town, which housed the area's slaughterhouse and magazine-powder storage, received a growth spurt in 1827 with the beginning of the Algiers-Canal Street Ferry, a ferry still in operation today. Arrival of the railroad in 1852 kindled further growth of Algiers.

Through adverse affects of the War of 1812 and Civil War, as well as devastating fire, blight, and crime, Algiers maintained its Cajun culture for three centuries. The people of Algiers even made the New Orleans annexation of their community in 1870 a positive issue. Today, some people call the area "Ward 15." The people living within the nook of the big river, however, still call their community "Algiers."

During his teenage years, Dominick moved with his parents and siblings about nine miles west of Algiers, to Westwego, where he remained through the early years of his marriage. The suburb of New Orleans in Jefferson Parish had a 2010 population of 8,534. The approximate one-square-mile town has a very stable population. Westwego is located on the exterior bend of the Mississippi River, where the river turns from a southerly flow to a short easterly route.

The Texas and Pacific Railroad founded the town in 1870, when it constructed a railroad yard and docks on the Mississippi River. The state compensated the railroad to build a bridge over the Mississippi River. Although no one is certain how the town received its name, but folklore states that the railroad conductor yelled, "West we go!" as travelers departed the station heading west. A railroad engineer in 1873 publicized the name "Westwego" as the point where the railroad commenced its western route. The town was founded and incorporated as Westwego in 1919. It became a city in 1951.

A competing theory is that the railroad board of directors in New York established the name. Again, I choose the traveler's version, but you, too, are free to choose.

Dominick and his wife moved to Waggaman, where they lived for thirty-nine years. Waggaman, an unincorporated community in Jefferson Parish, is the home of Avondale Shipyards, one of Jefferson Parish's largest employers. African-Americans are 60% of the population, with Anglo-Americans accounting for 36% of the approximately 10,000 people recorded during the 2000 census. The town was named for US Senator George Augustus Waggaman, who lived from 1782 to 1843. He was a local resident and major landowner.

The three towns are in proximity to New Orleans on the western shore of the Mississippi River. Not until 2005 did Dominick, along with his wife, depart the West Bank and wander to Amite, which is over fifty miles east of the Big Muddy and about sixty miles north of New Orleans.

Dominick begins his story by telling me that he was born and lived in Algiers until his teenage years. He excitingly states:

> As a teen, we moved from Algiers to Westwego. We [Westwego] had drive-in theaters, walk-in theaters, and a drive-in where I could park and get hamburgers. We cruised Main Street. I had a ducktail [hairstyle], with curls on my forehead. We went to a lot of dances at the Firemen's Hall. I had a 1954 Ford, two-door, standard shift. It had Smitty [nick name for Smithy's] pipes [mufflers], skirts, and flippers on the front.

I immediately detect that we share a commonality which time has taken from us. It cannot, however, extinguish the memories. The phenomena of a forehead spit-curl and cool cars link many males who were teenagers in the 1950s.

Words can hardly express Dominick's emotions, which are particularly animated both in a smile and voice inflection, when he speaks of his ducktail, curls, and a 1954 Ford. He completes the 1950's description by looking me in the eye and saying, "I am seventy-one now."

His final statement reflects several emotions: "I lived through it. I still remember it. And I was part of a fun, historical time: the 1950s." A quiet moment follows while we reflect on a unique, happy phase of our lives.

Dominick's expression turns serious as he reflects on a more troubling time of his life. I briefly cannot understand why he makes such a quantum leap from the 1950s to the next topic, a time fifty years later. I soon realize that it is his *wife* who is the link from 1950 to the year 2000. The 1950s were the time period when he met, dated, and married his wife. She is an integral part of his story of moving from the West Bank to Amite.

He continues his account of his life by explaining, "We moved here [Amite] right after Katrina. The move was delayed because we could not sign papers until the emergency response was over." He pauses, then says, "My wife died from bone cancer after we moved here. She had been treated for fifteen years. We were married for fifty-two years."

Dominick changes the subject to talk about a fun and memorable time when he and his wife lived in Waggaman, where he worked for Avondale Shipyards:

> We lived in Waggaman for thirty-nine years. We moved into a new subdivision. It was just starting when we moved in. It took off and grew. The people were very friendly; most had kids. There were no fences from yard to yard. I worked forty-two years for Avondale, where I was a foreman for many years. I retired when I was sixty-four. Waggaman is on the West Bank.

Dominick proudly states that his ancestors and their customs constructed the foundation for his life and family orientation. As he moves the conversation to his lineage, it becomes obvious why he has a strong attachment to the West Bank: Most of his family lived on the west side of the Mississippi River. Dominick is very proud of his family, his heritage, and the early years of his life. He is especially proud of the Acadian legacy of his family, their struggle to survive, and their service to their country. His early years living with his Acadian ancestors created a large influence on his life and character. His story makes it very evident that his fun approach to life was inherited, both genetically and experientially, from his ancestors. It becomes equally clear that much of his strength is ancestrally based.

Dominick demonstrates his pride when he transitions the discussion to stories about relatives who served their country in time of war. He explains:

> My uncle Ernest Boudreaux fought in the Battle of Midway. When his ship sank, he spent forty-eight hours in the water. After salvage duty, they were taken to Australia, where he was ran over and killed by a train. My great-grandfather fought in the Spanish-American War. We were given a land grant, but never got the land.

History can sometimes be painful. To fight and survive forty-eight hours in the ocean, only to be run over by a train is unfathomable. To fight and be promised a land grant by your government, then not receive it is incomprehensible. War can be cruel for a person, but sometimes the aftermath presents an even greater unkindness.

Dominick continues our conversation by discussing his ancestors' relocation from Canada to the United States. His ancestors' relocation to the United

States occurred when the British expelled over 11,000 Acadians from the Maritime Provinces during the period of 1755 to 1763. Nova Scotia, New Brunswick, and Prince Edward Island, all located on the eastern seaboard of Canada, make up the Maritime Provinces. The Acadian people and families were relocated to several areas of the United States and some to France. Due to the loss of family, friends, and community, their new lives were disruptive and difficult. Today, the Acadians, now called "Cajuns," still ban together as a people and society. They recreated their community in the United States and hold on to it with great dedication. Their ancestral culture is their present way of life.

A distant great-grandfather named Boudreau came from Nova Scotia to America and settled on the West Bank of the Mississippi River. He lived off the land and taught his children to do the same. They, in turn, taught their children.

Dominick states, "His [my great-grandfather's] influence had an impact on the way I lived as a child." Dominick continues,

> When I was a kid, we raised chickens and hogs; we made lard. We ate the chickens, hogs, cracklings, hogshead cheese, blood sausage, and boudin cheese. When we butchered hogs, we used the entire hog—not a part was wasted. I hunted the swamps. I caught [anywhere from] 200 to 300 lizards a night and sold them for a nickel a piece. I ate oysters right out of the river. We hunted and ate nutria rats and raccoons.

Nutria rats, also known as "river rats," live in the southern wetlands. They can grow to weigh ten pounds. Dominick concludes with an exclamation point: "When I was a kid, we used outhouses. We never had a bathroom!"

Dominick moves our conversation to his family name, heritage, and language. His remarks concerning native language mirror many parental attitudes of today. Parents, who speak English as a second language, frequently avoid speaking the native tongue in the presence of their children. The parents are concerned it will affect their children's ability to learn English. He explains his immediate family heritage and the practice of adults speaking French in the presence of their children:

> On my dad's side of the family, my grandmother was a Hingel, and my grandfather was a Lala. They had seven kids. My grandparents all spoke French to each other, but never spoke it in front of their kids or grandkids. They did not want us to speak French in school.

Dominick continues his story about the power of heritage by telling me how he kept a promise to his dad: "I made a promise to my dad at the graveyard that I would never smoke again. I threw my cigarettes and lighter into a barrel. I have never smoked again in thirty-five years."

Dominick's conversation evolves to his children and granddaughter: "I have three sons. They hunt gators. I never did. I used to hunt, trap, and fish. Now I have horses." He then tells me that when he finishes lunch, he is going to go see his girlfriend, then pick up his granddaughter. He says, "My granddaughter and I are going to ride horses after school." His story clearly tells me that he is strongly attached to his wife, children, and now grandchildren. Family commitment extends back to childhood and his life with his lineage.

We just sit and talk for a short time. I then thank him and say farewell. He says that he was happy to tell me about his life and his family. He is proud of his ancestors: their culture and way of life. From our conversation about his family, it is obvious that Dominick is bringing the important elements of his past to the current generations.

Mo and I leave Amite to begin our long trek home to Missouri. The trip will be long—not because of mileage and time, but because it closes the chapter on having conversations with rural Americans, which is the discovery aspect of the project.

The three areas we visited during this trip made many statements and created equally as many questions. My experience of starting in Oil City in the midst of the Pennsylvania Mountains and concluding with an interview of a Cajun in Louisiana—not to mention all the places in between—marks the diversity of America. The variation in geography and uniqueness of history is immense. Cultural diversity is monumental. The differing cultures exemplifies the difference between peoples' behaviors and ancestral influence threaded through generations.

CHAPTER 30

The Trip Home and Reflections

Our final day on the road entails an eleven-hour drive through the beautiful country of northern Louisiana, the entire south to north miles of Arkansas, and finally southern and central Missouri. The flatlands and hills coupled with minimal weekend traffic provide an opportunity to reflect on our four trips during the past 15 months, about the scenery, and most importantly about the people who shared their stories. The mental pictures of the people, the settings where we talked, their communities, and the vast country along our path remain etched in my mind.

The experiences of the trips awaken in me the knowledge of the insurmountable strength of America and its people. The people and their culture accentuate the freedom demanded by James Madison, and others, as they framed the Constitution.

I truly enjoy being on the road in rural America, including the challenge of finding the next interview and the discovery included in each person's story—stories about their lives and their towns and communities. Perhaps the greatest attracter was meeting new people. As I look back, all four trips and my visits to the Missouri State Fair and Lincoln Fly-in provide a unique setting to meet new people and hear phenomenal stories.

As I planned the travel, I never considered the variance of each person's interpretation of the three questions and how it drove their responses. The broad interpretations were the same or similar, but how those applied to their experiences were unique. The question now becomes, what does it all mean?

Perhaps, the over arching questions that must be answered are: Can the population in rural America be stabilized to maintain viable communities, towns, and counties? Will the reduction of farm land due to urban and other development in conjunction with the trend of large farms result in the demise of the family farm? Will nature's water supply support population increase and dry land farming (areas where irrigation is necessary to produce crop)? Will rural America, as we know it, be recognizable to future generations? and Will my grandchildren's grandchildren recognize my story?

The rural culture is strong with uniqueness among areas of our travel. The distinctiveness allows individuality to meet the specific needs of the community.

There is however one unique experience for me and rural America. Whenever I travel the hundreds of miles to Rush County, Indiana, my life takes on a whole new meaning. I immediately feel a slower pace and calmness. Setting foot on the rich, black dirt of our family farm creates a sense of pride, an aura of accomplishment. We make a small input to feeding America, but we contribute. A stop at a local coffee gathering place entertains my soul with grassroots conversations that have changed little during the past several years. The well-being of people and community are paramount issues.

Morning conversations over coffee with the people I met during my travels, although unique, had a common thread with my Rush County friends. The names were different, but the people communicated the same sense of community, joys, and concerns as my lifelong friends do during their morning-coffee conversations. The uniqueness describes their culture, their history, and most importantly their people.

Thank you for joining Mo and I on the road. It has been an honor to meet and talk with the people representing rural America. Telling the story to you has been a mission of joy. As always in our family, Mo gets the last word.

Mo

This talk is way too serious, and anyway, we have an immediate problem: Where do we camp tonight? As usual, we have no plan. This time is different, however, because attendants at the campgrounds are not answering their phones—or the few who do, inform Randy that they are out of business or closed, which translates, in reality, to the same thing: no place to camp. Calling late (due to the traffic in the Baton Rouge area) exacerbates the problem. Actually, darkness is the problem. Well, darkness and no campground. In reality, it is poor planning, which is not a new characteristic. Why should I expect a change?

Experience never seems to qualify as a reason for a change of behavior in the front seat of this truck.

But as always, it works out well. We stay for the first time ever in a motel. I ride in a little room called an "elevator." The door closes, a bell rings, then rings again. The floor jerks, and the door opens. While we were in the elevator, someone magically moved the floors. I always believed rooms are not supposed to move: not true, apparently.

The people are different in an elevator. They bunch up in a corner away from me. They act like a bunch of sheep. The people act as if I might bite someone, or I smell bad—neither of which are true. I am still the same dawg I have been for the entire trip.

People and their behaviors change for no reason. We, the K-9 species, go with the flow. We adapt, but do not change.

The good news is that I have my own queen-size bed. Of course, I do not use it until Randy is asleep, and I get up before he awakes. No problem for anyone. At last it is morning, and we are on the road. We drive, then drive some more, stop briefly, and drive again until I recognize the scenery. We are going home to my lake, my yard, and my stuff. It has been fun, but it is time to see old friends and places. I hope you enjoyed our trip. I will talk with you later. Please excuse me while I smell the turf and visit my friends.

EPILOGUE

John Wilson Returns to His Farm after a Century

John Jefferson Wilson, my great-grandfather, would be mystified and challenged by the twentieth-century changes to rural America. The story that follows is a fictitious account of what it might be like for John Wilson if he returned to his farm 100 years after his death . . .

Mr. Wilson, who lived from 1844 to 1896, returns to life on his farm one century later, in 1996. He struggles to understand the twentieth-century changes to farming and the transformation of his hometown. He celebrates many positive attributes that have occurred in his community. Mr. Wilson attempts to make sense of the changes and use the positive attributes to revitalize his small corner of rural America.

John awakens this morning as he does every morning: with a cup of coffee. Except today is different; 100 years have passed, and it is 1996, not 1896. Cup of coffee in hand, he strolls out the kitchen door to check on his hogs, cattle, horses, and fields of grain. The first thing he notices is that a soybean field across the road from his home has replaced the one-room school. He further observes that there are no homesteads within sight.

A walk of his line fences causes him to realize that his 160-acre farm has expanded to 3,200 acres. Mr. Wilson is shocked! There are only corn and soybean crops, with an absence of cattle and hogs. A cold cup of coffee and strange surroundings cause him to depart from his easy-going, mild mannerism. He anxiously asks himself, "How can I farm all this land with a team of horses?" He then notices that his horse barn has been replaced by a large metal building. The open doors reveal three gigantic tractors, accompanied by big machinery and two semi-trucks.

The big attraction is a new version of the family car. The vehicle has a closed cab to shield the weather, as well as a big box behind the cab to haul tools. The seats are padded. A fifteen-minute exploration provides enough knowledge to drive slow. He culminates his first driving experience with backing the pickup out of the toolshed. He exits the truck with happiness and apprehension about his 100-year later experience.

He is filled with a sense of solace as he sees a large brick building standing adjacent to his property. The building is different, but it is unmistakably the

Little Flat Rock Christian Church, standing tall on its namesake riverbank. He reflects that at least one element of the community has stood the test of time.

A walk towards the building allows him to view the Little Flat Rock River. He is astonished to see that the water in the river bed is shallow and barely flowing. He states to himself, "My fishing stream has vanished with time."

In bewilderment, he makes the two-mile drive in his newly found truck to New Salem, where he hopes to talk with someone and capture a sense of this unfamiliar era. Instead, he is greeted by more overwhelming change. There is no restaurant in which to drink coffee, eat breakfast, or share the latest news. The stores are vacant; there are no retail businesses. The once-busy grain elevator sitting on the edge of town is vacant. The parking lot is empty.

He asks several reflective questions: "Why are there fewer inhabited houses and no stores or a grain mill?"; "Where are the bank and post office?"; "Where is New Salem High School, where my daughter graduated tenth grade?"; and "What happened to Main Street?"

Loss of New Salem's amenities clearly indicates that he must make the over one-hour horse-and-buggy trip to Rushville for shopping and necessities. He then realizes that his comfortable, heated, pickup truck will make the seven-mile trip to Rushville in half the time of the old horse-and-buggy ride to New Salem.

He sees change. John Wilson sees progress. He realizes that improved transportation and modern farm machinery have resulted in larger farms and less people.

His curiosity about Rushville overcomes his resistance. He decides to make the seven-mile drive up US Highway 52 to see how the past 100 years have affected Rushville. Well prior to crossing the Big Flat Rock River, he realizes that his county seat has grown. There are many new houses and businesses where there were farms. He notices that the Big Flat River is flowing with very little water. The same issue that burdens the Little Flat Rock River. He thinks aloud, "What has happened to our rivers."

Arrival in town brings more surprises. The first big change he notices is what appears to be a restaurant where people sit in their car, talk to a box, then drive forward to have their food handed to them through the building window. He concludes that coffee and conversation do not occur here.

As he continues his drive up Main Street, he sees the familiar courthouse. A big sigh of relief and a comment to himself, "One thing has not changed!" He immediately realizes that the three-color light means "go" on green, "accelerate" on yellow, "stop" on red. He then notices that the vacant store syndrome of New Salem is contagious and has spread to Rushville.

At the edge of town, he sees a restaurant with several pickup trucks. It takes him a moment to realize that pickup trucks have replaced horses and buggies. He concludes that this is the breakfast spot and a good place to find conversation. He ponders: "Should or should I not stop?" His answer is yes.

A walk through the front door enforces his realization about the significance of change during the past century. He first notices that morning coffee time includes women, not just men. Next, he notices that the conversation is not focused on farming but includes baseball, basketball, and movies, whatever these things mean. He listens in wonderment as he drinks coffee and eats bacon, eggs, and potatoes. The big surprise is that the cost of breakfast is as expensive as a weeks supply of groceries.

During his drive home he realizes the significant changes are to community. He thinks aloud, "I can learn and adapt to the new social behaviors of today. I can learn to use the equipment. The important issues concern how our community has changed during the past several generations." He finally arrives home to settle into his favorite rocking chair; the spot where he solves problems.

Mr. Wilson reflects with sadness about losses commensurate with change, but smiles with delight at the progress. He ponders necessary adjustments to his life. He reflects by asking himself two questions: "What issues beyond larger farms are causing loss of amenities and population?" and "How can 'we' recapture residents and community while maintaining progress?" His aim is not to recapture the rural America of the past, but to develop a future of employment and community that entices young adults to remain, as well as attracting new residents to be a part of our neighborly lifestyle. Rural America could then reinvent itself by creating employment opportunities and stimulating population growth.

Will John Wilson be successful? Will he create a model or models for other towns and communities?

Bibliography

Preface
1. Carolyn Dimitri, Anne Effland, and Nelson Conklin, "The Twentieth Century Transformation of US Agriculture and Farm Policy" (June 2005), (Unites States Department of Agriculture Economic Research Service)," accessed July 8, 2015, http://www.ers.usda.gov/media/259572/eib3_1_.
2. D. A. Erlandson, Edward Harris, Barbara Skipper, and Steve Allen, *Doing Naturalistic Inquiry: A Guide to Method*. (Newbury Park, CA: Penguin, 1993).

Chapter 2: Kansas and Colorado
1. Marian Franklin, "Battle of Morristown, Cass Co., MO 1861," *The Missouri in the Civil War Message Board – Archive*, accessed July 20, 2012, www.history-sites.com/cgi-bon/bbs62x/mocwmb/arch_config.pl?md
2. "Marysville's Early History," *Marysville Chamber of Commerce*, accessed July 27, 2012, www.visitmarysvilleks.org
3. Museums of Marysville KS Pony Express Barn. Marysville Chamber of Commerce, accessed May 30, 2015, www.marysvillemuseumsks.org#!about2/c17d6.
4. "Phillips County | - Colorado," accessed November 12, 2015, https://www/colorado.gov/phillipscounty.
5. "Smith Center, Kansas," accessed November 12, 2015, www.smithcenterks.com.

Chapter 3: Wyoming
1. "Diamondville—Wyoming Tales and Trails," accessed June 1, 2015, 222 www.wyomingtalesand trails.com/coal3a.html.
2. "Kemmerer, Wyoming," accessed June 1, 2015, www.kemmerer.org.
3. Lincoln County in Wyoming | accessed June 1, 2015, WyoHistoru.org, www.wyohistory.org/encyclopedia/Lincoln-county-wyoming.

Chapter 4: Southern Idaho
1. "Caribou County Idaho Home of Historic Soda Springs," accessed June 2, 2015, www.southeastida.com/cariboucounty/
2. "History | City of American Falls," accessed June 4, 2015, www.cityofamericanfalls.com/history,
3. Idaho state historical society reference, Oneida County, accessed June 3, 2015, history.idaho.gov/sites/default/files/updates/uploads/references…/0335
4. Largest Man-Tamed Geyser, Soda Springs, Idaho, accessed June 3, 2015, www.roadsideamerica.com/story/8509
5. Oneida County, Idaho: History and Information, accessed June 4, 2015, www.ereferencedesk.com/resources/counties/idaho.oneida.html

Chapter 5: Oregon
1. "Abraham Lincoln and Friends – Edward D. Baker (1811-1861)," accessed June 4, 2015, www.mrlincolnandfriends.org/inside.asp?pageID=73&subjectID=6
2. "Baker County Chamber …, History of Baker City, OR," accessed June 4, 2015, www.visitbaker.com/live_work/history.aspx
3. "The Battle Ball's Bluff Summary & Facts | Civil War.org," accessed June 4, 2015, www.civilwar.org/battlefields/ballsbluff.html

Chapters 6: Great Northwest and Family and Family Time
1. Kent History, accessed June 5, 2015, www.visitkent.com/culture/kent-history/

Chapter 7 Idaho Panhandle
1. "Bonners Ferry, Idaho," bonnerferry.com, accessed November 9, 2015, www.bonnersferry.com/AboutBonnersFerry,
2. "Boundary County, Idaho IDGenWeb Project," The GenWeb Team, accessed January 17, 2014, boundary.idgenweb.org,

Chapter 8: Montana
1. C. W. Guthrie, "All aboard for Glacier: The Great Northern Railroad and Glacier National Park," (Farcountry Press), accessed January 17, 2014, www.farcountrypress.com/details.php?id=110
2. Michael P. Malone, Richard B. Roeder, William A. Lang, "Montana: A History of Two Centuries," revised edition (Seattle and London: University of Washington Press, 1991)," accessed April 16, 2015, https://books.google.com/books?isbn=0295971290
3. "Welcome to the Tool County Heritage: Where the Cowboys Became Cowboys," Toole County Montana History & Heritage," Archway Self Publishing, accessed June 6, 2015, www.toolecounty.angelfire.com

Chapter 9: Dakotas
1. "Emmons County Courthouse," Brown County Courthouse, accessed April 4, 2015, www.emmonscounty.tripod.com
2. "Granary History | Brown County," accessed June 7, 2015, brown.sd.us/granary/history
3. "Groton, SD Community," City of Groton, accessed April 18, 2015, www.grotonsd.gov

Chapter 10: Minnesota
1. "City of Waseca," City of Waseca, accessed April 4, 2015, ci.waseca.mn.us
2. "Historic Waseca," Waseca Area Chamber of Commerce, accessed April4, 2015, www.discoverwaseca.com
3." Steele County Free Fair," Owatonna Press, accessed November 15, 2015, www.southernminn.com/owatonna.../article_8300fc84-f9ad-5892-89fe-2d
4. "Steele County QuickFacts," the US Census Bureau, accessed June 8, 2015, quickfacts.census.gov.qfd/states/.../27147.html

Chapter 11: Iowa
1. "History – First Lutheran Church," First Lutheran Church, accessed June 9, 2015, firstlutheranchurchstansgar.org/history.html
2. "Our History," St. Olaf Lutheran Church," accessed June 8, 2015, www.stolafchurch.org/our-history.html

Chapter 12: Missouri State Fair
1. "A Brief History of Downtown Sedalia," Historic Downtown Sedalia, accessed April 19, 2015, www.downtownsedalia.com/history.
2. "History Summary," Missouri State Fair, accessed November 9, 2015, www.mostatefair.com
3. "Mission and Vision," Missouri State Fair, accessed April 19, 2015, www.mostatefair.com/mission-vision/.

Chapter 13: Illinois
1. Dale Sanderson, *End of US highway 54* (Richmond, BC, Canada: Archway Publishing), accessed October 25, 2015, www.usends.com/50-59/054/054.html
2. "The History of Earlville, LaSalle County, Illinois," accessed April 20, 2015, genealogytrails.com/ill/lasalle/town/Earlville.html.

Chapter 14: Michigan and Ohio
1. James Battershell, Jr. "Short History of Hicksville, Ohio (1836-2009)," accessed July 18, 2015, www.villageofhicksville.com/hicksville-history.php

Chapter 15: Back Home Again in Indiana
1. "Indiana County-Level Census Counts 1900 to 2010," accessed July 18, 2015, www.stats.indiana.edu/.../historic_conts_county
2. "Indiana population counts – Census.gov," accessed April 21, 2015, https://www.census.gov/population/cencount
3. A. L. Gary and E. B. Thomas, eds. "History of Rushville, Indiana (Part 1) from Centennial History of Rush County, Indiana (Indianapolis: Historical Publishing Company, 1921), accessed April 21, 2015, history.rays-place.com/in/rushville-1.html

Chapter 16: Kentucky
1. "Calvert City," accessed April 21, 2015, www.calvertcity.com/
2. "Calvert City, Kentucky – City–Data.com," accessed April 21, 2015, www.city-data.com/city/Clavert-City-Kentucky.html
3." Land Between the Lakes – Kentucky Lakes Online," accessed April 22, 2015, www.kentuckylake.com.lbl.shtml
4. "Graves County Quick Facts from the US Census Bureau," accessed April 23, 2015, quickfacts.census.gov/qfd/states/.../21083.html
5." Mayfield Kentucky – Wikipedia," accessed April 23, 2015, en.wikipedia.org/wiki/Mayfield_Kentucky

Chapter 17: Tennessee
1." Dyersburg County Historical Society," accessed April 23, 2015, www.dyersburghistory.com
2. Dyersburg, Tennessee City - Data.com (2015), accessed April 23, 2015, www.city-data.com/city/Dyersburg-Tennessee.html

Chapter 18: Arkansas
1. "The Encyclopedia of Arkansas History & Culture," Walnut Ridge (Lawrence County), accessed April 23, 2015, www.encyclopediaofarkansas

Chapter 19: Oklahoma
1. "Minco OK Community Page," Minco, Oklahoma, accessed April 24, 2015, www.minco-ok.com/minco/

Chapter 20: Texas
1. "Childress, TX – Texas State Historical Association," Childress, TX, accessed April 27, 2015, https://tshaonline.org/handbook/.../hfc0
2. "Muleshoe, TX – Texas State Historical Association," accessed April 28, 2015, htpps://tshaonline.org/handbook/.../hgm

Chapter 21: New Mexico
1. "Las Vegas, New Mexico – More Wicked Than Dodge City," accessed November 9, 2015, www.legendsof america.com/nm-lasvegas.html
2. "Interesting history of Las Vegas, New Mexico and Santa ..." accessed November 9, 2015, takearoadtrip.com/las-vegas-history.html
3. "Santa Rosa New Mexico – City of Natural Lakes," accessed November 10, 2015, www.legendsofamerica.com/nm-santarosa.html

Chapter 22: Arkansas Valley, Colorado
1. "Holly, Colorado – Wikipedia," accessed April 29, 2015, wn.wikipedia.org/wiki/Holly,_Colorado
2. La Junta, Colorado – City-Data.com, accessed April 29, 2015, www.city-data.com.city/La-Junta-Colorado.html
3. "La Junta, Colorado – Wikipedia," accessed April 29, 2015, www.wikipedia.org/wiki/La_Junta,_Colorado
4. "Otera County QuickFacts from the US Census Bureau," accessed April 29, 2015, quickfacts.census.state.co.us/.../County/1...
7. Rocky Ford, Colorado – City-Data.com," accessed April 29, 2015, www.city.data.com/city/Rocky-Ford-Ccolorado.html

Chapter 23: West Kansas
1. "A Cowboy in Dodge City, 1882," EyeWitness to History," accessed April 30, 2015, www.eyewitnesstohistory.com (2000).
2. "Dodge City, Kansas – Wikipedia, accessed April 30, 2015, en.wikipedia.org/wiki/Dodge_City,_Kansas
3. "Stafford County, Kansas," accessed April 30, 2015, en.wikipedia.org/wik/Stafford_County_Kansas
4, "Stafford County, Kansas Official Website," accessed April 30, 2015, www.staffordcounty.org
5. "Stafford, Kansas – Wikipedia," accessed April 30, 2015, en.wikipedia.org/wiki/Stafford,_Kansas

Chapter 24: Lincoln Fly-in
1." Lincoln, Missouri – City-Data.com," accessed May 2, 2015, www.city-data.com/city/Lincoln-Missouri.html
2. "Lincoln, Missouri – Wikipedia," accessed May 2, 2015, en.wikipedia.org/wiki/Lincoln,_Missouri

Chapter 25: Pennsylvania, New York, and Vermont
1. "Bennington County Vermont GenWeb – RootsWeb," accessed May 6, 2015, www.rootsweb.ancestry.com/~vtgenweb/Bennington-Co-VT.html
2. "Oil City, PA History – Oil City, Pennsylvania," accessed May 4, 2015, www.oilcitypa.net/%20city/oil_city,_Pennsylvania.html
(Sources for written history include William H. Engle (1883), Derrick Souvenir Book (1896), Link - How Oil City Came to Be)
3. "Town of Bennington, Vermont – Serving People through," accessed May 6, 2015, www.townofbennington.org
4. "Welcome to the lively and historic city of Oneonta, New York," accessed May 5, 2015, www.oneonta.ny.us/
5. "1879 Everts History of Hinsdale – RootsWeb," accessed May 4, 2015, www.rootsweb.ancestry.com/~nycattar/1879history/hinsdale.html. Published in 1879 by Everts, edited by Franklin Ellis

Chapter 26: Virginias
1. "A Brief History of Staunton, Virginia," accessed May 7, 2015, www2.iath.virginia.edu/Staunton/history.html
2. "Buena Vista, Virginia: History – Web Feat, Inc," accessed May 11, 2015, www.webfeat-inc.com/buenavista/bvhistory.html
3. "Carnegie Hall West Virginian – Performing Arts- Lewisburg," accessed May 12, 2015, www.yelp.com

4. "Eastern Panhandle – West Virginia Division of Culture," accessed May 6, 2015, www.wvculture.org/.../eastern
5. "e-WV | Battle of Point Pleasant," accessed May 11, 2015, www.wvencyclopedeia.org/articles/1889
6. "Greenbrier County," accessed May 11, 2015, www.greenbriercounty.net
7. "Greenbrier County, West Virginia – State and County," accessed May 11, 2015, quickfacts.census.gov/qfd/states/.../54025.html
8. "History – City of Lewisburg," accessed May 11, 2015, www.lewisburg-wv.cpm/History.aspx
9. "History Section – City of Staunton, VA," accessed May 7, 2015, www.staunton.va.us/directory/departments-h-z/.../history
10. "Inwood, WV Population - Census 2000 and 2010," accessed November 9, 2015, censusviewer.com/city/WV/Inwood
11. "Inwood, West Virginia – Wikipedia," accessed May 6, 2015, en.wikipedia.org/wiki/Inwood,_West_Virginia
12. "Lexington, Virginia: History –LexVa.com," accessed May 6, 2015, www.lexva.com/leshistory.html
13. "Lewisburg, West Virginia – Wikipedia, accessed May 12, 2015, en.wikipedia.org/wiki/Lewisburg,_West_Virginia
14. "Lexington, Virginia: History – LexVa.com, accessed www.lexva.com/lexhistory.html
15. "Our History – Mary Baldwin College," accessed May 8, 2015, www.mbc.edc/about/history/
16. "Rockbridge County –Virginia Demographics," accessed May 10, 2015, www.virginiademographics.com/rockbridge-county-demographics
17. "The Greenbrier Classic –Welcome," accessed May 12, 2015, www.greenbrierclassic.com
18. "The History of Buena Vista – Buena Vista, Virginia," accessed May 11, 2015, www.buenabusiness.com
19. "The Natural Bridge –Natural Bridge of Virginia, accessed May 10, 2015, www.naturalbridgeva.com/recreation/the-natural-bridge
20. "Virginia School for the Deaf and Blind, accessed May 7, 2015, www.vsdb.k.12.va.us/
21. "Visit Lexington Virginia – lexingtonvirginia.com, accessed, www.lexingtonvirginia.com

Chapter 27: Carolinas
1. "Dallas, NC – Official Website – History," accessed May 17, 2015, www.dallasnc.net
2. "Dallas, North Carolina – City-Data.com," accessed May 17, 2015, www.city-data.com/city/Dallas-North-Carolina.html
3. "Daniel Boone – Daniel Boone Homestead," accessed May 12, 2015, www.danielboobehomestead.org/daniel-boone.html
4. "Historic Dallas – Gaston County Museum, accessed May 17, 2015, www.gastoncountymuseum.org/PDF/Brochure.pdf
5. "History – Town of Williamston, accessed May 15, 2015," www.williamstonsc.us/history/ Horn in the West, accessed May 12, 2015, www.horninwest.com
6. "North Carolina History Project: Watauga 1849, accessed May 12, 2015, www.northcarolinahistory.org/encyclopedia/593/entry/
7. "Pelzer, South Carolina – City-Data.com, accessed May 15, 2015, www.city-data.co/city/Pelzer-South-Carolina.html
8. "Town of Boone, NC, accessed May 12, 2015, www.townofboone.net
9. "West Pelzer, South Carolina – City-Data.com, accessed May 15, 2015, www.city-data.co/city/West-Pelzer-South-Carolina.html
10. "Williamston, South Carolina – City-Data.com, accessed May 15, 2015, www.city-data.co/city/Williamston-South-Carolina.html
11. "Town of Pelzer," accessed May 15, 2015, www.townofpelzer.com

Chapter 28: Georgia and Alabama

1. "Craig Air Force Base," Encyclopedia of Alabama, accessed May 21, 2015, http://www.encyclopediaofalabama.org/article/h-2592
2. "Dale Cox, "Selma, "Alabama: Historic Sites and Points of Interest," accessed May 21, 2015, http://www.exploresouthernhistory.com/selma.html
3. "Dallas County, Alabama history," Alabama Department of Archives and History, accessed May 22, 2015, http://www.archives.state.al.us/counties/dallas.html
4. "Editors, Encyclopedia Britannica, "Tuskegee University," Encyclopedia Britannica, accessed May 20, 2015, http://www.britannica.com/topic/Tuskegee-University
5. "History of Madison, Georgia," accessed May 18, 2015, www.historicgeorgiahomes.com/history.html
6. "Kindig, Jessie (contributor), "Selma, Alabama, (Bloody Sunday, March 7, 1965)," accessed May 21, 2015, http://www.blackpast.org/aah/bloody-sunday-selma-alabama-march-7-1965 www.citydata.com/city.Madison-Georgia.html
7. "Madison, Georgia – Official Website –Visitors History," accessed May 18, 2015, www.madisonga.com
8. "Melton, Brian (No 2, Summer 2002). The Georgia Historical Quarterly. "The town that Sherman wouldn't burn": Sherman's March and Madison, Georgia, in history, memory, and legend," accessed May 18, 2015, www.jstor.org/stable/40584537
9. "Morgan County, Georgia –State and County Quick Facts," accessed May 19, 2015, www.quickfacts.census.gov/qfd/…/13211.html
10. "Morgan County | New Georgia Encyclopedia," accessed May 19, 2015, www.georgiaencyplopedia.org…/morgan-co
11. "Selma," Encyclopedia of Alabama," accessed May 21, 2015, 13. http://www.encyclopediaofalabama.org/article/h-1635
12. "Selma-to-Montgomery March." *National Park Service*, accessed May 26, 2015, www.nps.gov/nr/travel/civilrights/a14.html
13. "Sherman's March – American Civil War –HISTORY.com," accessed May 19, 2015, www.history.com/topics/american-civil-war/shermans-march
14. Staff, History.com (2010), "Selma to Montgomery March, "accessed May 21, 2015, h4tp://www.history.com/topics/black-history/selma-montgomery-march
15. "Tuskegee, Alabama – City-Data.com," accessed May 19, 2015, www.city-data.com/city/Tuskegee-Alabama.html
16. Tuskegee University | Encyclopedia of Alabama," accessed May 20, 2015, www.encyclopediaofalabama.org/article/h-1583
17. "Tuskegee University Little Known Black History Fact | Book," accessed May 20, 2015, www.blackamericaweb.com/…/little-known-black-history-fact-tusk
18. "Tuskegee University Founded." African American Registry, accessed May 20, 2015, http://www.aaregistry.org/historic_events/view/tuskegee-university-founded
19. "United States Census Bureau (2015). "Macon County, Alabama State and County Quick-Facts." accessed June 20, 2015, http://quickfacts.census.gov/qfd/states/01/01087.html
20. Yerkey, Greg (2012). "Remembering the March to Montgomery," accessed May 26, 2015, http://www.christiancentury.org/blogs/archive/2012-09/remembering-march-montgomery

Chapter 29: Mississippi and Louisiana

1. Algiers Historical Society (ND). "The History of Algiers" (New Orleans, Louisiana), accessed May 29, 2015, www.algiershistoricalsociety.org/algiers-history.html
2. Algiers Point Association website," accessed May 30, 2015, http://www.algierspoint.org
"Bogue Chitto, Lincoln County, Mississippi," *Wikipedia*, accessed May 27, 2015, https://en.wikipedia.org/…Bogue_Chitto,_Lincoln_County,_..

3. "History (of Jefferson Parrish, Louisiana)," accessed May 29, 2015, https://www.visitjeffersonparish.com/about-us/history
4." Lincoln County Mississippi Genealogy & History Network website," accessed May 27, 2015, http://lincoln.msghn.org
5. S1 Civic Group (2015)."Waggaman, Louisiana 70094," accessed May 30, 2015, http://S1civicgroup.org/?page_id-109
6. Town of Amite City website, accessed May 29, 2015, http://www.townofamitecity.com
7. "Tylertown, Mississippi." *Wikipedia*, accessed May 27, 2015, https://en.wikipedia.org/wiki/Tylertown,_Mississippi
8. "Waggaman, Louisiana," accessed May 30, 2015, http://www.city-data.com/city/Waggaman-Louisiana.html
9. "Walthall County, Mississippi." *Wikipedia*, accessed May 27, 2015, http://en.wikipedia.org/wiki/Waltham_County,_Mississippi
10. Walthall County, Mississippi website," accessed May 27, 2015, http://www.co.waltham.ms.us/
11. "Westwego, Louisiana," accessed May 29, 2015, http://www.city-data.com/city/Westwego-Louisiana.html

Acknowledgements

Acknowledgements begin as appropriate with long term support from my son and daughter. Their encouragement, meaningful comments, and thought provoking questions caused me to rethink and improve my writing. In a way our challenging conversations seemed to be an extension of the dialogue we had around the nightly dinner table a few decades in the past.

Foremost, my thanks and appreciation goes to the the one-hundred and five new friends I made during Mo and my travels. Words can never express my heartfelt gratitude to the people who welcomed me into their town and told me the stories of their life and community. You are indeed rural Americans.

Sandy Gordon, my sister, and I have many discussions about rural America and life on the farm. Her insight filled many gaps, created by time, in my knowledge about the big picture and daily life in our home county, typical rural America. Her painting a verbal picture cleared my vision.

Every writer owes thanks to his or her editor. Angela Wade went well beyond providing insightful improvements to my writing by guiding me through a conceptual change. All the while she reminded me that this is my book. These words extended well beyond my having the final decisions to the issue of my responsibility to make the book the best it can be.

My appreciation to a childhood friend, Bill Fudge, and his wife Joan, of Fudge Photography, for their extraordinary picture of the *big read barn*. On a moments notice they answered a weekend call to bail me out with their photography skills.

My gratitude and deepest appreciation to Dog Ear staff, especially Megan, Adrienne, and Amber for their guidance and support during the process to transform my manuscript into a book beyond my expectations.

My final appreciation is for the special person in my life, Anita, who encouraged me, listened when I needed to talk, provided thoughtful support, and sacrificed *our time,* all without me realizing the magnitude of her kindness and guidance.

723-1723